THE BIBLE

God's Word
for the
Biblically-Inept™ SERIES

Larry Richards

CARTOONS BY
Reverend Fun
(Dennis "Max" Hengeveld)
Dennis is a graphic designer
for Gospel Films and the
author of *Has Anybody Seen
My Locust?* His cartoons can
be seen worldwide at
www.gospelcom.net/rev-fun/
and monthly in *Charisma*
magazine.

STARBURST PUBLISHERS®

P. O. Box 4123, Lancaster, Pennsylvania 17604

Larry Richards has written over 175 books, including theories of Christian Education, studies of the Bible and Theology, Devotional and Enrichment writings (e.g. *The 365-day Devotional Commentary*) and Study Bibles (e.g. *The Nelson NKJV Student Bible*). His *A Practical Theology of Spirituality* has been translated into 26 foreign languages and is used by schools in Europe, Asia, South America, Asia and the USA. Richards has served in the United States Navy and has a B.A. in Philosophy, a Th.M. in Christian Education, and a Ph.D in Social Psychology and Religious Education. He is General Editor of the *God's Word for the Biblically-Inept*™ *Series*. He resides in Hudson, Florida.

To schedule Author appearances write: Author Appearances, Starburst Promotions, P.O. Box 4123 Lancaster, Pennsylvania 17604 or call (717) 293-0939

www.starburstpublishers.com

CREDITS:
Cover design by David Marty Design
Text design and composition by John Reinhardt Book Design
Illustrations by Melissa A. Burkhart
Cartoons by Dennis "Max" Hengeveld

Unless otherwise noted, or paraphrased by the author, all Scripture quotations are from the New International Version of The Holy Bible.

To the best of its ability, Starburst Publishers® has strived to find the source of all material. If there has been an oversight, please contact us and we will make any correction deemed necessary in future printings. We also declare that to the best of our knowledge all material (quoted or not) contained herein is accurate, and we shall not be held liable for the same.

READ THIS PAGE BEFORE YOU READ THIS BOOK . . .

Welcome to the *God's Word for the Biblically-Inept*™ series. If you find reading the Bible overwhelming, baffling, and frustrating, then this Revolutionary Commentary™ is for you!

Each page of the series is organized for easy reading with icons, sidebars and bullets to make the Bible's message easy to understand. *God's Word for the Biblically-Inept*™ series includes opinions and insights from Bible experts of all kinds, so you get various opinions on Bible teachings—not just one!

There are more *God's Word for the Biblically-Inept*™ titles on the way. The following is a partial list of upcoming books. We have assigned each title an abbreviated **title code**. This code along with page numbers is incorporated in the text **throughout the series**, allowing easy reference from one title to another.

The Bible—God's Word for the Biblically-Inept™   TITLE CODE: GWBI
Larry Richards

> **The Bible—God's Word for the Biblically-Inept**™ is an overview of the Bible written by Larry Richards, one of today's leading Bible writers. Each chapter contains select verses from books of the Bible along with illustrations, definitions, and references to related Bible passages.
>
> (trade paper) ISBN 0914984551 $16.95   **AVAILABLE NOW**

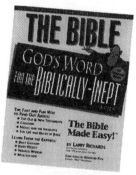

Revelation—God's Word for the Biblically-Inept™   TITLE CODE: GWRV
Daymond R. Duck

> **Revelation—God's Word for the Biblically-Inept**™ is the first in this new series designed to make understanding and learning the Bible as easy and fun as learning your ABC's. Reading the Bible is one thing, understanding it is another! Includes every verse of the Book of Revelation, icons, sidebars, and bullets along with comments from leading experts.
>
> (trade paper) ISBN 0914984985 $16.95   **AVAILABLE NOW**

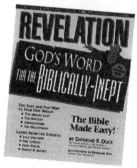

Daniel—God's Word for the Biblically-Inept™   TITLE CODE: GWDN
Daymond R. Duck

> **Daniel—God's Word for the Biblically-Inept**™ is a Revolutionary Commentary™ designed to make understand-ing and learning the Bible easy and fun. Includes every verse of the Book of Daniel, icons, sidebars, and bullets along with comments from leading experts.
>
> (trade paper) ISBN 0914984489 $16.95   **AVAILABLE NOW**

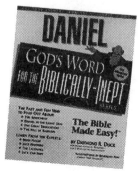

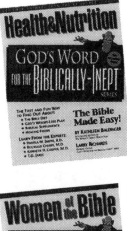

Health and Nutrition —God's Word for the Biblically-Inept™

Kathleen O'Bannon Baldinger   **TITLE CODE: GWHN**

Health and Nutrition—God's Word for the Biblically-Inept™ gives scientific evidence that proves that the diet and health principles outlined in the Bible are the best diet for total health. Experts include Pamela Smith, Julian Whitaker, Kenneth Cooper, and TD Jakes.

(trade paper) ISBN 0914984055 $16.95   **AVAILABLE FEBRUARY '99**

Women of the Bible —God's Word for the Biblically-Inept™

Kathy Collard Miller   **TITLE CODE: GWWB**

Women of the Bible—God's Word for the Biblically-Inept™ shows that although the Bible was written many years ago, it is still relevant for today. Gain valuable insight from the successes and struggles of women such as Eve, Esther, Mary, Sarah, and Rebekah. Comments from leading experts will make learning about God's Word easy to understand and incorporate into your daily life.

(trade paper) ISBN 0914984063 $16.95   **AVAILABLE MARCH '99**

Purchasing Information

www.starburstpublishers.com

Books are available from your favorite bookstore, either from current stock or special order. To assist your bookstore in locating your selection, be sure to give title, author, and ISBN #. If unable to purchase from a bookstore, you may order direct from **STARBURST PUBLISHERS®** by mail, phone, fax, or through our secure sebsite at:

www.starburstpublishers.com.

When ordering enclose full payment plus $3.00 for shipping and handling ($4.00 if Canada or Overseas). Payment in U.S. Funds only. Please allow two to three weeks minimum (longer overseas) for delivery.

Make checks payable to and mail to:

Starburst Publishers®
P.O. Box 4123
Lancaster, PA 17604

Credit card orders may also be placed by calling 1-800-441-1456 (credit card orders only), Mon–Fri, 8:30 A.M.–5:30 P.M. (Eastern Time). Prices subject to change without notice. Catalog available for a 9 x 12 self-addressed envelope with 4 first-class stamps.

INTRODUCTION

Welcome to *The Bible—God's Word for the Biblically-Inept.*™ This is a REVOLUTIONARY COMMENTARY™ designed to uncomplicate the Bible. It makes discovering what's in this amazing book easy and fun. You *will* Learn The Word.™

To Gain Your Confidence

The Bible—God's Word for the Biblically-Inept™ is for those who are not interested in all that heavy duty, tough-to-understand stuff. You can be sure that I have tried to take an educational and fun approach, but much effort has gone into keeping things simple. Most writers always end up making things so complicated when they try to explain them, so I make every effort to keep things as easy as 1, 2, 3. The Bible is God's Word, so why would you even think of going anywhere else?

What Is The Bible?

The Bible is a collection of 66 books written by many different authors. A list of these books is given in the front of most Bibles. There are two sections in the Bible: an "Old" Testament of 39 books, and a "New" Testament of 27 books. The Old Testament was written between 1400 B.C. (before Christ) and 400 B.C. The New Testament was written in about 70 years, between 40 A.D. (in the year of our Lord) and 100 A.D. The Old Testament deals with events before the birth of Jesus Christ. The New Testament tells about Jesus' birth, life, death and resurrection, and about the movement begun by people who believed that Jesus was the Son of God.

Centuries later, scholars divided the books of the Bible into chapters and verses. Thus Genesis 12:3 indicates the 12th chapter of the book of Genesis and the 3rd verse in that chapter. This helps readers locate specific Bible stories and teachings.

Why Study The Bible?

BECAUSE . . . For over two thousand years millions of people have viewed the Bible as a message from God. We can't see

---

CHAPTER HIGHLIGHTS

(Chapter Highlights)

Let's Get Started

(Let's Get Started)

THE BIG PICTURE 🔍

> **Genesis 1:1–2:3**
> The Bible begins,
> "In the beginning..."

(The Big Picture)

Just the FACTS

(Just the Facts)

☞ **Check It Out:**

II Kings 16-22

(Check it Out)

☞ **GO TO:**

Matthew 9:14-15 (fasting)

(Go To)

second death: *separation from God forever*

(What?)

What Others are Saying:

KEY POINT

When we acknowledge our guilt and trust Jesus as Savior, God forgives our sins freely and completely.

(Key Point)

What Others are Saying:

KEY Symbols:

Elijah's Ministry
the power of God

Elisha's Ministry
God's grace and willingness to support his people

(Key Symbols)

God. But what a special thing it would be if God would speak to us! And that's what the Bible claims to be: God speaking to human beings. Over 2,600 times the writers of the Bible claim to speak or write *God's words*—not their own.

Charles Swindoll: God's Word is for *you*, my friend, not just the theologian or the pastor; it's for you! There is no situation that you cannot face if you are really serious about spending time on a regular basis in the Book of books![1]

BECAUSE . . . Even people who do not believe that the Bible is God's Word need to know what's in the Bible. It's the best-selling book in history. Its stories and images have shaped Western civilization. Its moral code is the original source of most of our laws.

No person can claim to be "educated" without some knowledge of this book that has done so much to shape the world we live in.

BECAUSE . . . The Bible offers answers to questions we wonder about. Where did our universe come from? Are human beings really special? Where can I find meaning for my own life? How can I be a better person? How will the world end? What will happen to me after I die? If God is real, how can I know him? Whether you accept the answers the Bible gives or not, you owe it to yourself to know what the biblical answers are.

Billy Graham: God caused the Bible to be written for the express purpose of revealing to man God's plan for his redemption. Without the Bible, this world would be a dark and frightening place, without signpost or beacon.[2]

What's Amazing About The Bible?

1 The Bible is like no other book. It was written over a span of some 1,500 years. It is a collection of 66 different books by a number of different authors. Yet the Bible is one book, with a single story to tell!

2 The first book of the Bible was written in Hebrew some 3,400 years ago, and the last book was written in Greek about 1,900 years ago. Yet the Bible we read in English today is essentially the same as when its words were first written. Uncertainties about Greek words take up no more than a half page in the Greek New Testament—and not one uncertainty affects any basic Bible teaching.

Our English Bibles give a reliable and trustworthy account of what was originally written in Hebrew and Greek thousands of years ago!

3 The Bible contains predictions about the future *which have come true*! Hundreds of predictions have been fulfilled—centuries after they were written. There is only one way this was possible. God knew what would happen ahead of time, and he guided the Bible writers when they wrote their predictions down!

Why Have A Book On The Bible?

The only way to study the Bible is to read it. Yet just opening the Bible and starting to read may be confusing. While the Bible tells a single story, it's a story that has many parts. To understand any part, we need to know how that part fits into THE BIG PICTURE.

When you understand THE BIG PICTURE, you can open the Bible anywhere, and it will make sense to you. This book will help you master THE BIG PICTURE.

Billy Graham: It is better to have an understanding of the general structure of the Bible to get the most out of it.[3]

Why Use The New International Version (NIV)?

I have tried to look at the Bible as the experts would, but I have also tried to write it for the *Biblically-Inept*. I want it to be easy to read and understand. That's why I chose to use the New International Version (NIV) of the Bible. It is a scholarly translation that accurately expresses the original Bible in clear and contemporary English, while remaining faithful to the thoughts of biblical writers.

A Word About Dates

Many experts have differing opinions about dates in the Bible. Variations of one or two years in some cases are not uncommon. But archaeologists keep making new discoveries so that many of the dates are now known and thought to be accurate. Where discrepancies occur, the most commonly recognized date is given. Remember that in the Time Lines "c." indicates *circa* or *around* that date.

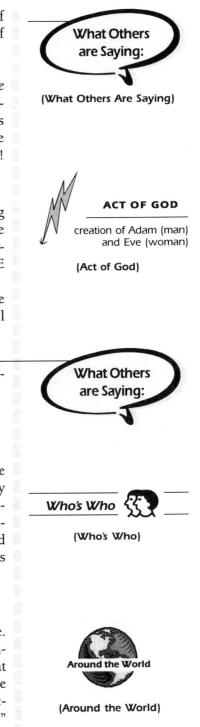

What Others are Saying:

(What Others Are Saying)

ACT OF GOD

creation of Adam (man) and Eve (woman)

(Act of God)

What Others are Saying:

Who's Who

(Who's Who)

Around the World

(Around the World)

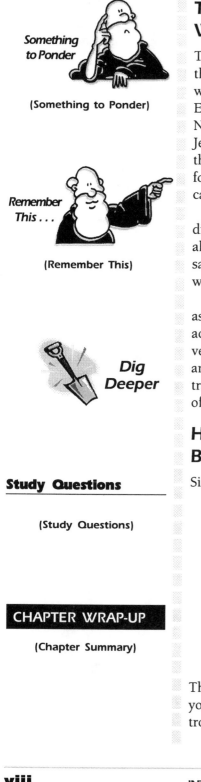

Something to Ponder

(Something to Ponder)

Remember This . . .

(Remember This)

Dig Deeper

Study Questions

(Study Questions)

CHAPTER WRAP-UP

(Chapter Summary)

The Language Of The Bible And When It Was Written

The first books of the Bible, written about 1400 B.C., and most of the Old Testament, which was completed about 400 B.C., were written in Hebrew. However, parts of the books of Daniel and Ezra were written in Aramaic, a related language spoken by most Near Eastern peoples from about 600 B.C. onward. The people of Jesus' day also spoke Aramaic in everyday situations, but studied the Bible in their ancient tongue, Hebrew. About 100 years before Christ, the Old Testament was translated into Greek, because most people throughout the Roman Empire spoke Greek.

The New Testament was written in the Greek spoken by ordinary people. This meant that the New Testament was easy for all people throughout the Empire to understand, so the message of Jesus spread quickly. All of the New Testament books were written between about 40 A.D. and 95 A.D.

Because the Old and New Testament books were recognized as holy, first by Jews and then by Christians, they were copied accurately and carefully preserved. Much later, chapters and verse divisions were added to the Bible to make it easier to find and remember the location of specific teachings. The many Bible translations we now have all try to express the original words of God in ways that people today can understand his message.

How To Use The Bible—God's Word for the Biblically-Inept™

Sit down with this book and your Bible.

- Start the book at Chapter 1.
- As you work through each chapter, read the **CHECK IT OUT** passages in your Bible.
- Use the sidebar loaded with icons and helpful information to give you a knowledge boost.
- Answer the Study Questions and review with the Chapter Wrap-Up.
- Then go on to the next chapter. It's simple!

This book contains a variety of special features that will help you learn. They're illustrated in the outside column of this introduction. Here they are again, with a brief explanation of each.

Sections and Icons	What's it for?
CHAPTER HIGHLIGHTS	the most prominent points of the chapter
Let's Get Started	a chapter warm-up
THE BIG PICTURE	summarizes passages and shows where they fit in the Bible
Just the FACTS	introduces books of the Bible
Commentary	my thoughts on what the verses mean
CHECK IT OUT:	Bible passages to follow along
GO TO:	other Bible verses to help you better understand (underlined in text)
What?	the meaning of a word (bold in text)
KEY POINT	a major point in the chapter
KEY Symbols:	mini-outlines to help you
What Others are Saying:	if you don't believe me, listen to the experts
Illustrations	a picture is worth a thousand words
Time Lines	shows how events fit into history
ACT OF GOD	indicates God's personal intervention in history or people's lives
Who's Who	identifies key people
Around the World	what's going on in the rest of the world
Something to Ponder	interesting points to get you thinking
Remember This . . .	don't forget this
Dig Deeper	find out more from the Bible
Study Questions	questions to get you discussing, studying, and digging deeper
CHAPTER WRAP-UP	the most prominent points revisited

There are several inerchangeable terms: Scripture, Scriptures, Word, Word of God, God's Word, Gospel, etc. All of these mean the same thing and come under the broad heading called the Bible. I will use each one at various times, but I will use "Bible" most of the time.

The word "Lord" in the Old Testament refers to Yahweh, the God of Israel. In the New Testament, it refers to Jesus Christ, God's Son.

One Final Tip

God, who gave us the Bible, is present whenever we read it, so it helps to read the Bible prayerfully. People who open their hearts to God and ask him to speak to them testify that he really does. Open your heart, ask God to speak to you as you read, and you'll be surprised how wonderfully the Bible will enrich your life!

CHAPTERS AT A GLANCE

PART I: The Old Testament

1: BEGINNINGS · 3

Genesis 1–11

Creation 4
Creation of Man and Woman 5
Satan and the Fall 6
The Flood 9

2: SETTING THE COURSE · 15

Genesis 12–50

Abraham 16
God's Promise 17
Abraham's Descendents 19

3: EXIT TO FREEDOM · 23

Exodus

Moses 25
Ten Plagues 26
Ten Commandments 28
Tabernacle 31

4: THE ADVENTURE CONTINUES · 33

Leviticus, Numbers, Deuteronomy

Laws for Holy Living 34
The Long Journey 39
The Law Reviewed 42

5: CONQUEST AND COLLAPSE · 47

Joshua, Judges, Ruth

Conquest of Canaan 47
When Judges Ruled 52
Simple Faith 55

6:   A NEW BEGINNING   **57**

I, II Samuel, I Chronicles

Samuel 58

Saul 59

Saul and David 60

David 62

7:   ISRAEL'S GOLDEN AGE   **69**

I Kings 1–11, II Chronicles 1–9, Job, Psalms, Proverbs, Ecclesiastes, Song of Songs

Solomon 70

Hebrew Poetry 71

Job 72

Psalms 74

Proverbs 76

Ecclesiastes 78

Song of Songs (Song of Solomon) ... 80

8:   THE NORTHERN KINGDOM   **83**

I Kings 12–22, II Kings, Jonah, Amos, Hosea

A Kingdom Divided 84

Elijah and Elisha 86

Jonah 88

Amos 90

Hosea 93

9:   THE SOUTHERN KINGDOM   **97**

I, II Kings, II Chronicles, Obadiah, Joel, Micah, Isaiah

Moral Leadership 98

Prophetic Voices 98

Obadiah 102

Joel 103

Micah 105

Isaiah 107

10: THE SURVIVING KINGDOM   **111**

II Kings 15–25, II Chronicles 29–36, Nahum, Zephaniah, Habakkuk, Jeremiah, Ezekiel

Judah Survives 112

Nahum 115

Zephaniah 116

Habakkuk 117

Jeremiah 120

Ezekiel 125

11: EXILE AND RETURN 129

Lamentations, Daniel, Esther, Ezra, Nehemiah, Haggai, Zechariah, Malachi

Lamentations 130
Daniel 131
Esther 134
Ezra, Nehemiah 135
Haggai 139
Zechariah 141
Malachi 143

PART TWO: The New Testament

12: JESUS, THE PROMISED SAVIOR 149

Who is Jesus 149
Jesus in the Old Testament 150
Jesus' Own Claims 153
Jesus in the New Testament 156
Why Jesus Came 159

13: THE LIFE OF CHRIST (1) 161

Matthew, Mark, Luke, John

The Four Gospels 161
Jesus' Miraculous Birth 165
John the Baptist 168
Jesus' Baptism 169
Jesus' Temptation 170

14: THE LIFE OF CHRIST (2) 173

Matthew, Mark, Luke, John

Jesus' Authority 174
Jesus' Teachings 179
Controversy 185

15: THE LIFE OF CHRIST (3) 187

Matthew, Mark, Luke, John

Jesus Faces Opposition 187
Jesus' Parables 191
Jesus Instructs His Disciples 192

16: THE LIFE OF CHRIST (4)   199

Matthew, Mark, Luke, John

Jesus' Last Week 199

Jesus' Last Day 204

Jesus' Crucifixion 207

Jesus' Resurrection 211

17: THE SPREADING FLAME   213

Acts

The Ascension of Jesus 213

The Jerusalem Church 216

Early Expansion of the Church 218

Missionary Journeys 220

Paul on Trial 223

18: EXPLAINING THE GOSPEL   227

Romans, Galatians

Understanding the Epistles 227

Romans 228

Galatians 238

19: THE PROBLEM-SOLVING EPISTLES   243

I, II Corinthians, I, II Thessalonians

I Corinthians 243

II Corinthians 249

I Thessalonians 252

II Thessalonians 255

20: THE PRISON EPISTLES   259

Ephesians, Philippians, Colossians

Ephesians 259

Philippians 263

Colossians 267

21: LETTERS TO INDIVIDUALS   273

I, II Timothy, Titus, Philemon

I Timothy 273

II Timothy 277

Titus 280

Philemon 283

22: THE SUPERIORITY OF CHRIST 287

Hebrews

Jesus, The Living Word 289
Jesus, Our High Priest 291
Jesus, The Perfect Sacrifice 295
Jesus' Continuing Ministry 296

23: THE GENERAL EPISTLES 301

James, I, II Peter, I, II, III John, Jude

James 301
I Peter 304
II Peter 306
I, II, III John 308
Jude 312

24: REVELATION 315

Revelation

Christ and the Church 317
From the Rapture to the Second Coming 318
The Millennium and Beyond 321

APPENDIX A — MAP OF PAUL'S MISSIONARY JOURNEYS 324

APPENDIX B — THE ANSWERS 326

ENDNOTES 329

INDEX 332

Part One

THE OLD TESTAMENT

REVEREND **F**UN

© Copyright Gospel Films, Inc. * www.gospelcom.net/rev-fun/

Where have you been Adam? And why are you on crutches? And who are all these women? And why is your chest all caved in and hollow-looking like that?

What Is The Old Testament?

The Old **Testament** is a collection of 39 books, which were written between 1450 **B.C.** and 400 **B.C.** They tell the story of God's special relationship with one human family, the family of Abraham, Isaac, and Jacob, which became the Jewish people. Through this people God revealed himself to all mankind. And through this people God set in motion a plan to save all who would believe in him from the terrible consequences of **sin**.

testament: covenant

B.C.: before Christ as opposed to A.D., which means "in the year of our Lord"

sin: "any" violation of God's will

Why Is It Called The "Old" Testament?

This collection of 39 books is called the Old Testament in contrast to the New Testament. The New Testament is a collection of 27 books, all of which were written in the first century. The New Testament continues and completes the story begun in the Old Testament.

Find Out About God—By Reading The Old Testament!

People have different ideas about what God is like. Anyone who wants to find out can begin by reading the Old Testament.

What's In The Old Testament?

The books of the Old Testament are divided into five different kinds of writings. Fascinating questions are raised and answered with these Old Testament writings.

THE PENTATEUCH

Genesis, Exodus, Leviticus, Numbers, Deuteronomy

Where did the universe come from?
What makes human beings special?
Why do people do wrong and evil things?
Does God care what happens to us?
How can I know what God expects of us?

HISTORY

Joshua, Judges, Ruth, I & II Samuel, I & II Kings, I & II Chronicles, Ezra, Nehemiah, Esther

What is God's plan for the world?
Does God control what happens in history?
Does it pay a nation to honor God?

POETRY

Job, Psalms, Proverbs, Ecclesiastes, Song of Songs (Song of Solomon)

Can I find meaning in life apart from God?
How do I communicate with God?
How can we survive suffering?
What guidelines help me make wise choices?

MAJOR PROPHETS

Isaiah, Jeremiah, Lamentations, Ezekiel, Daniel

Does God ever reveal the future?
What prophecies have already come true?
What sins is God sure to judge?
How will the world end?

MINOR PROPHETS

Hosea, Joel, Amos, Obadiah, Jonah, Micah, Nahum, Habakkuk, Zephaniah, Haggai, Zechariah, Malachi

How much does God love us?
Do people really "get away with" being wicked?
What kind of society will God bless?
What kind of society is he sure to punish?
Is our country in danger today?

1 BEGINNINGS

Genesis 1–11

- Creation
- Adam and Eve
- Satan and the Fall
- The Fall
- Sin
- Noah and the Flood

Let's Get Started

No one was present at the creation of the **universe**, so where did Moses, who wrote the first five books of the Old Testament, get his information? From the only person who was present when the world began: God. The Bible is a book of *revealed truth*, or **revelation**. These early chapters of **Genesis** don't argue that God exists. They assume that God exists, and they describe a beginning about which only God could know.

universe: *stars, space, and all that exists*

revelation: *what God has communicated to us*

Genesis: *the name means "beginnings"*

GENESIS

. . . the book of beginnings

WHO	Moses
WHAT	wrote Genesis
WHERE	while traveling in the wilderness
WHEN	about 1400 B.C.,
WHY	to reveal the truth about God and his relationship to human beings.

THE BIG PICTURE 🔍

Genesis 1:1-2:3 The Bible begins, "In the beginning **God created** the heavens and the earth." The rest of the passage tells how God shaped our universe, paying special attention to shaping the earth as a home for humanity.

Just the FACTS

☞ **Check It Out:**

Genesis 1:1–2:3

God created: *God made the universe from nothing*

God Made It!

What's Special About Genesis 1?

ACT OF GOD

creation of the universe

1 *The Genesis story of Creation was a truly NEW and DIF-FERENT account of origins.* Moses didn't get his ideas of Creation from earlier peoples. It was revealed to him by God.

2 *God is the focus of Genesis 1. ("God" appears 32 times.)* God designs and creates a stable, dependable universe that he says is "good," and he clearly cares about what he has created.

What Others are Saying:

R.C. Sproul: The whole realm of nature shouts of the design of the universe. This design must have a designer.[1]

Billy Graham: Intellectually, it is much more difficult not to believe in God than to believe in him.[2]

Ancient Ideas about Origins

	Mesopotamian	**Egyptian**	**Greek**	**Genesis**
View of the Gods	Many competing gods/goddesses	Many related gods/goddesses	Many warring gods/goddesses	One God
Nature of the Gods	Good and evil, petty, warring	Nature deities, manipulative	Adulterous, petty, limited	Good, all-powerful
Relation to Man	Mankind sprang from blood of slain **deity** (God)	No moral or personal relationship	Both subject to fate; no real interest in humanity	Humans created in God's image; loved by God
Material Universe	Corpse of the goddess Tiamat	Five myths give five explanations	The universe existed before the gods	One God is the Creator and Designer of all

Mesopotamian: *area now occupied by Iran and Irac (Iraq)*

deity: *a god*

image and likeness: *like God, people have intellect, emotions, will, etc.*

dominion: *responsibility to care for*

3 Human beings are special, since only they were created in the **image and likeness** of God. God gave human beings **dominion** over his creation, and from the very beginning they have been special to God.

What Difference Does It make?

Some believe that the universe is *impersonal* and "just happened." If this is true, one day our sun will burn out and the earth will become a dead, icy speck spinning through endless space. Long before that we will all die and be forgotten. But what if our universe is *personal*, created by a God who cares for human beings? Then we have hope. God may have a plan for our universe, and death may not be the end for those he loves! Whether or not God created makes all the difference in the world!

Ray C. Steadman: No matter how we may feel, or what may be our attitude toward God, we are bound, as creatures dependent on his love and and grace, at least to give thanks to him as our Creator.[3]

What Others are Saying:

THE BIG PICTURE

> **Genesis 2:4–25** This chapter gives details about the creation of human beings. God first created Adam and placed him in a beautiful garden, the Garden of Eden (see Illustration #1, page 6). Adam explored the garden and named the animals. When Adam realized something was missing, God formed Eve from Adam's rib. Adam realized that Eve was a person like himself, a partner he could love.

☞ **Check It Out:**

Genesis 2:8–23

Then He Made Man And Woman

What's Special About Genesis 2?

1 *Genesis 1 tells us how Creation happened. God said . . . and it was so (Genesis 1:3, 6, 9, 14, 24). God formed man from the dust of the ground and breathed into his nostrils the breath of life (Genesis 2:7).* The careful and unusual attention God gave to forming man reminds us that we are special, different from the animals.

KEY Symbols:

Breath of Life
never die

Ronald F. Youngblood: "Create" is a special verb in the Old Testament. It always has God as its subject; it is never used of human activity. You and I may make or form or fashion, but only God creates.[4]

2 *The breath of life.* The life God breathed into Adam was different from the life given to animals. An animal ceases to exist when it dies. When we die, our bodies return to dust, but we continue to exist as conscious, self-aware people forever.

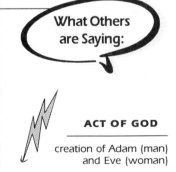

What Others are Saying:

ACT OF GOD

creation of Adam (man) and Eve (woman)

Illustration #1

Map of Eden—The first human civilizations developed in the Mesopotamian valley (modern Irac [Iraq] and Iran). Genesis places Eden in this area, listing four streams as Eden's boundaries. The only two known today are the <u>Tigris and the Euphrates</u> (see GWRV, page 133).

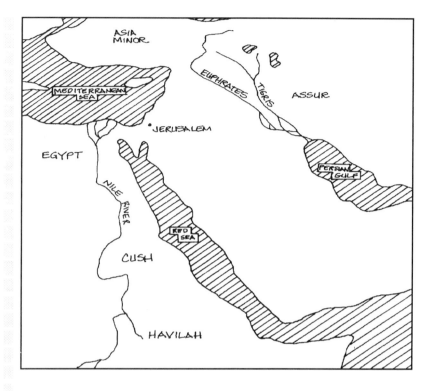

 **GO TO:**

Genesis 2:14 (Tigris and Euphrates)

 *KEY Symbols:*

Woman

> *a comparable companion*

 **GO TO:**

Isaiah 14:12–14;

Revelation 12:9 (Satan)

 *Who's Who*

 **GO TO:**

Matthew 25:41 (hell)

hell: *a place of fire and unending punishment for Satan and his followers*

3 *Woman created.* Woman was created as a *helper suitable* to Adam. The Hebrew phrase means a "comparable companion"—a person who was Adam's equal, not his servant. God intended man and woman to be partners in their life on earth.

THE BIG PICTURE

> **Genesis 3** <u>Satan</u>, in the form of a serpent, tricked Eve into disobeying God. Then Adam also disobeyed God. This sin had terrible consequences for the whole human race.

Satan Made Me Do It

SATAN: Also called the *evil one*, the *devil*, and the *great serpent*. Satan was once an angel named Lucifer and led other angels in a rebellion against God. Satan and his angels hate God and are intent on thwarting God's plans. Because God loves human beings, Satan hates humankind, and his success in the Garden of Eden introduced sin into the human race and corrupted human nature. Ultimately God will triumph and send Satan and his followers to what we call **hell**.

The Fall is the disobedience of Adam and Eve, and explains how two people created by a good God could produce a race marred by crime, injustice, hatred, and war. When Adam and Eve sinned, their very natures were warped and twisted. They passed on this twisted nature to all their offspring. The reason we choose to do things we know are wrong is because our human nature itself is twisted and sinful.

Why Did God Let It Happen?

Why put the **Tree of the Knowledge of Good and Evil** in Eden? God created human beings in *his* image. Since God distinguishes between right and wrong and makes **moral** choices, Adam and Eve too had to be given the opportunity to make a true moral choice. Otherwise they would have been puppets, not persons. God gave Adam and Eve the opportunity to make a true moral choice; he did not trick them into doing wrong.

What's Special In Genesis 3?

1 *Eve was vulnerable to* **temptation**. Because: 1) She didn't know what God had said (compare Genesis 3:4 with Genesis 2:16, 17), 2) She began to doubt God's motives (Genesis 3:4, 5), and 3) She relied on her own senses and judgment rather than on God's Word to determine what was truly "good" for her (Genesis 3:6). The result was disaster!

Ronald F. Youngblood: None of us is immune from the clever wiles of Satan, who *prowls around like a roaring lion looking for someone to devour* (II Corinthians 11:3).[5]

God's **commandments** aren't intended to deprive us. They protect us. The commandments show what will benefit rather than harm us!

2 *The Tree of the Knowledge of Good and Evil (see GWRV, page 323).* God had said *when you eat of it you will surely die* (Genesis 2:17). The day Adam and Eve ate, the processes leading to **physical death** was initiated. That day they also **died spiritually** and morally, and were alienated from God. People who remain alienated from God will be separated from God forever. The Bible calls this a "**second death**."

What Others are Saying:

Remember This . . .

☞ **GO TO:**

Deuteronomy 8:1 (commandments)

☞ **GO TO:**

Genesis 7:21 (physical death)

Ephesians 2:13 (spiritual death)

Revelation 20:12–14 (second death)

Something to Ponder

physical death: *the body dies*

spiritual death: *loss of relationship with God*

second death: *separation from God forever*

sacrifice for sins: *death of a substitute as a covering for sins*

☞ **GO TO:**

Leviticus 17:11 (sacrifice)

Ephesians 2:1–4 (sin)

Genesis 6:5 (evil)

☞ **Check It Out:**

Genesis 4–5

3 *The Fall dramatically affected Adam and Eve:* 1) They felt shame and tried to cover themselves (Genesis 3:7), 2) They became afraid of the God who loved them, and tried to hide from him (Genesis 3:8, 10), and 3) They felt guilty and began to blame God and each other (Genesis 3:12).

4 *Additional consequences of the Fall.* (Genesis 3:16) Women are driven to look to men for approval, and men try to rule over and subordinate women. Men who focus on work and who struggle to achieve at the expense of their families are acting out of sinful human nature.

It is a mistake to think of *sin* only as *crime*. Even actions that most people approve of can be expressions of sinful human nature. The workaholic and the woman obsessed with her appearance both miss out on God's best for human beings.

5 *God didn't turn against Adam and Eve.* He sought them out and then covered them with animal skins. This symbolic act was history's first **sacrifice for sins**.

THE BIG PICTURE

Genesis 4-5 These chapters show that Adam and Eve's offspring really did inherit their parents' **sin nature**. Their son Cain murdered his brother Abel. A few generations later Lamech broke the pattern of one husband/one wife by taking two wives, and justified murdering a man who *wounded* him. A lengthy **genealogy** brings us to the days of Noah, a time of wickedness when mankind's thoughts were *only evil all the time*.

What's Special In Genesis 4 And 5?

1 *Genesis 3 relates Adam's and Eve's Fall.* Genesis 4 shows that their sin nature was transmitted to their offspring. People are not sinners because they do wrong, but *choose wrong* because they are sinners. However many good deeds a person may do, one cannot change one's nature. The Bible teaches that we human beings need to be transformed from within by God.

2 *Genesis 5 lists men who were supposed to have lived hundreds of years.* Is this credible? Medical science has now linked most diseases that shorten human life, and aging itself, to gradual damage to our genes and chromosomes. People who lived shortly after God created Adam and Eve would have suffered very little genetic damage. We should expect them to have lived substantially longer lives than we do.

Inscriptions dating from 2250 B.C. to 2000 B.C. in Mesopotamia contain a list of kings who ruled **Sumer** before the Flood swept over the earth. The reigns ascribed to these kings range from 18,000 to 43,200 years! Clearly ancient peoples had a tradition of long lifespans before a great flood. Just as clearly, the Bible's report of lengthened lives is conservative.

3 *People speculate about the age of the universe and when human beings first appeared.* Genesis gives no hint of when the events it describes took place. The purpose of these early chapters of Genesis is to tell *where* the universe and human beings came from, not *when* God's creative work was done.

In the seventeenth century Bishop Usher used Bible genealogies to calculate the age of the earth. He computed 4004 B.C. as the date of Creation. Usher was wrong, because Hebrew genealogies normally do not list every person in a family line, just significant ancestors.

THE BIG PICTURE

> **Genesis 6–9** These chapters tell the story of a great Flood by which God wiped out most life on earth. The family of one man, Noah, survived the Flood. He obeyed God's command to build an Ark in which to preserve pairs of land animals that would then replenish the earth.

Lots And Lots Of Water

NOAH: Noah was a man who walked with God even though men <u>all around him were wicked</u> men. God told Noah he was about to wipe out the wicked with a great Flood. When he was told to build an Ark (see Illustration #2,

sin nature: the desire and tendency to choose to disobey God

genealogy: a list of family ancestors

KEY POINT

We sin because we *choose* to do wrong.

Something to Ponder

Sumer: the name of a Mesopotamian nation that preceded Assyria and Babylon

Something to Ponder

☞ **Check It Out:**

Genesis 6:9–22; 7:17–24

☞ **GO TO:**

Genesis 6:5 (wicked)

Hebrews 11:7 (faith)

Who's Who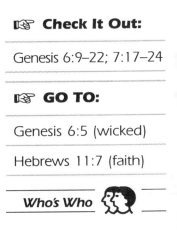

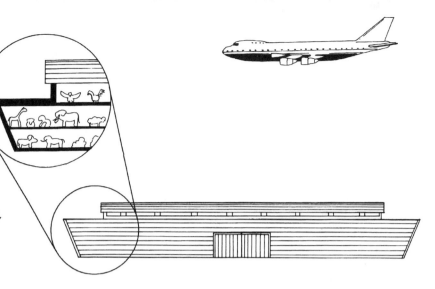

Illustration #2

The Ark—Noah's Ark was an unpowered wooden boat that was 450 feet long, 75 feet wide, and 45 feet high. It took Noah and his sons 120 years to build, but when finished, the Ark was roomy enough for Noah's family, all the animals, and food for everyone. This floating zoo would be home to Noah's family for over a year.

page 10), Noah trusted God and did as God said. <u>Noah's faith</u> is praised in the New Testament.

What's Special In Genesis 6-9?

1 *The cause of the Flood was human sin.* The New Testament points to the Flood as evidence that God is a **Moral Judge** who will punish the guilty. The story of the Flood is a warning to anyone who thinks God does not know or does not care about the wrongs he or she commits,.

2 *God's promise.* After the Flood God promised never again to destroy all life on earth by water. The rainbow that appears after storms is a visible reminder of that promise.

3 *An eye for an eye.* After the Flood God told Noah that from then on *whoever sheds the blood of man, by man shall his blood be shed* (Genesis 9:6). This is viewed as the institution of human government. Before the Flood each person was apparently responsible only for himself. Now God holds the community responsible for punishing wrong doing.

Was There Really A Great, Worldwide Flood?

The Flood was an *act of God* which revealed God as mankind's judge. It is a warning that there will come a time in the life of every person and every nation when God will no longer overlook wrong doing.

☞ **GO TO:**

II Peter 3:4–7 (judgment)

Moral Judge: God, in his commitment to punish sin

ACT OF GOD

the Flood

Peoples around the world, from the Middle East to China to the jungles of South America, tell tales of a flood that wiped out most human life. The best explanation is a tradition that goes back to a "real" event!

Scientists committed to evolution say "No." However, the recent eruption of Mount Saint Helens in Oregon has produced, in a few years, geologic formations that duplicate formations geologists have taught took millions of years to form.

How could mountain tops have been covered with water when there's not that much water in our oceans and our atmosphere? Some believe that before the Flood, the earth's surface was more level. But then the weight of the Flood waters formed ocean basins, and thrust up the mountains!

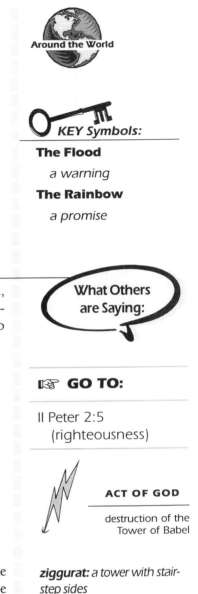

Around the World

KEY Symbols:

The Flood
a warning

The Rainbow
a promise

What Others are Saying:

☞ **GO TO:**

II Peter 2:5
(righteousness)

ACT OF GOD

destruction of the
Tower of Babel

ziggurat: a tower with stair-step sides

Ronald F. Youngblood: While the Ark was being built, Noah, a "preacher of righteousness," proclaimed a message of condemnation to the world of his day. Himself warned, he also warned others.[6]

THE BIG PICTURE 🔍

> **Genesis 10-11** Genesis 11 contains a *table of nations* which accurately identifies regions in which ancient ethnic groups lived. Genesis 12 relates that God caused ancient peoples to speak different languages when Noah's descendants failed to spread out and populate earth as God intended. The last verses of Genesis 12 set the scene for the introduction of Abram, a key figure in the Bible.

One Tall Tower

The Tower of Babel was a **ziggurat** (see Illustration #3, page 12), a pyramid-like construction common in the ancient Middle East and in South America. The ancients built temples on the tops of these towers. They were inventing their own religion, trying to reach God by their own efforts.

The Bible and other writings from the ancient Near East view Babel as the first city-based civilization. It's evil aspects are reflected in Scripture's portrayal of Babylon (GWDN, pages 16–17), which was founded on the site of ancient Babel.

Something to Ponder

Beginnings in Genesis

- universe (1:1)
- earth (1:3)
- life (1:20)
- human beings (1:27, 2:7)
- marriage (2:24)
- sin (3:6)
- consequences (3:14–19)

- promise (3:15)
- sacrifice (3:21)
- **procreation** (4:1)
- judgment (6:7)
- government (9:8)
- "religion" (9:8)
- language (11:1–9)

Illustration #3

Ziggurat—Towers like this were constructed by the people of Meopotamia over 5,000 years ago, and by the people of Central America 2,000 years ago.

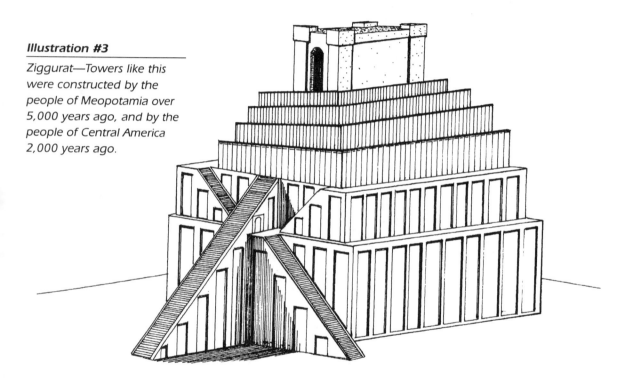

Study Questions

1. What difference does it make whether or not God "created"?
2. What makes human beings special?
3. How does the Bible explain the evils around us and our own tendency to do what we know is wrong?
4. What was the Fall and what were its consequences?
5. What does the Flood tell us about God?

- Genesis gives a unique account of the origin of the universe that has no parallels in the ancient world (Genesis 1).

- God created human beings in his own image and likeness, making human beings special (Genesis 1:27; 2).

- When Adam and Eve disobeyed God they died spiritually, and transmitted their sin nature to all their offspring (Genesis 3).

- The truth of the Bible's account of the Fall is seen in the big and little evils that mar society and each person's experience.

- The Genesis Flood revealed God as a *Moral Judge* who must and will punish sin (Genesis 6).

2 SETTING THE COURSE

Genesis 12–50

CHAPTER HIGHLIGHTS

- Abraham
- Abrahamic Covenant
- Abraham's Descendants
- Covenant Promises

Let's Get Started

The first 11 chapters of Genesis relate the early history of the human race. Beginning with Genesis 12, the Bible sets a very different course by reporting God's choice of one man. The man was Abraham, and his descendants were the Jewish people. The rest of the 905 chapters that make up the Old Testament trace the history of this one family, and what God has done through them.

Through Abraham's descendants God has revealed himself, dealt with sin, and reopened the way for a personal relationship with him.

Time Line #1

Important Persons and Events in Genesis 12–50

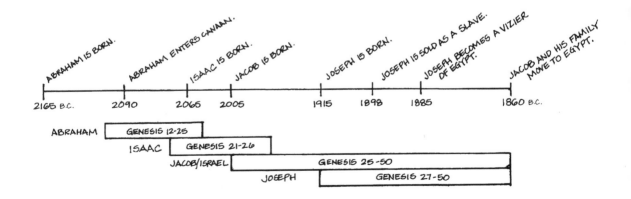

THE OLD TESTAMENT — SETTING THE COURSE

Illustration #4

The Fertile Crescent—The outlined area was called "the Fertile Crescent." Broad river valleys supported agriculture and served as trade routes in Abraham's time.

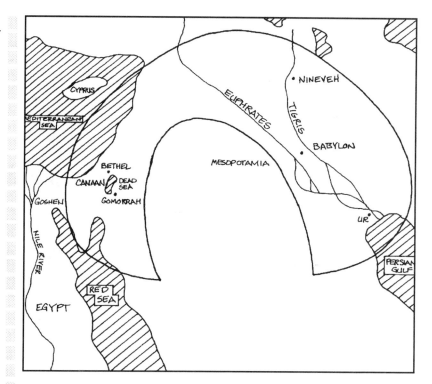

KEY Symbols:

Genesis 1–11
   the human race

Genesis 12 to the End of the Old Testament
   the Jewish people

Abraham: *"father of a multitude"*

covenant: *contract, oath, promise, or binding agreement*

Who's Who

salvation: *deliverance from sin*

faith: *not belief "about" God, but trust "in" him*

Lord: *in the Old Testament, Lord usually describes the essence of Yahweh; his power over his people, over the entire earth, and over all gods*

I Choose You!

ABRAHAM: When God spoke to Abram he lived in the wealthy but idolatrous city of Ur (see Illustration #4, this page). Abram chose to follow the Lord. Later his name was changed to **Abraham**.

Abraham's Relationship with God Sets the Course of the Bible in Two Vital Ways.

1) God made **covenant** promises to Abraham. These outline God's plan for **salvation**, which becomes more and more clear as the Old Testament unfolds.
2) Abraham's **faith** in God is shown to be the key to a personal relationship with the **Lord**. Stories about Abraham in Genesis 12–25 portray a man who was flawed, as we are, but who trusted God.

Genesis 12 God appeared to Abram and made a number of promises. These promises are known as the **Abrahamic Covenant**. Abraham responded by leaving his homeland as God commanded, and by going to a land that God showed him.

☞ **GO TO:**

Genesis 12:1–3, 7 (Abrahamic Covenant)

Genesis 15:9–18 (ceremony)

The Abrahamic Covenant

The covenant promises God made are commitments to Abraham. A special covenant-making <u>ceremony</u> was performed, which was done in ancient times to make agreements legally binding.

Some of God's covenant promises have already been fulfilled. Others have been partially fulfilled and will be completely fulfilled at history's end.

Abrahamic Covenant: *specific promises God made to Abraham*

The Covenant Promises God Made to Abraham

Something to Ponder

Genesis	God's promise . . .	. . . the promise kept
Genesis 12:2	*I will make you into a great nation.*	From Abraham sprang both the Jewish and Arab peoples.
Genesis 12:2	*I will bless you.*	God protected and enriched Abraham during his lifetime.
Genesis 12:2	*I will make your name great and you will be a blessing.*	Jews, Mohammedans, and Christians honor Abraham as founder of their faith.
Genesis 12:3	*I will bless those who bless you, and whoever curses you I will curse.*	Throughout history, peoples who have persecuted the Jews have experienced national disaster.
Genesis 12:3	*All peoples on earth will be blessed through you.*	Abraham's descendants gave the world the Bible and Jesus, the Savior.
Genesis 12:7	*To your offspring I will give this land.*	Israel remains the Promised Land of the Jewish people, to be occupied at history's end.

Abraham's Faith

Bible stories about Abraham do not hide his weaknesses or sins. Yet Abraham had great faith in God. When Abraham was 100 years old and his wife Sarah was 90, God promised them a son. Abraham believed God, and God counted Abraham's faith as **righteousness**. The New Testament says,

☞ **GO TO:**

Genesis 15:6; Romans 3:10, 20, 22 (righteousness)

righteous: *sinless in God's eyes*

Without weakening in his faith, he faced the fact that his body was as good as dead—since he was about a hundred years old—and that Sarah's womb was also dead. Yet he did not waver through unbelief regarding the promise of God, but was strengthened in his faith and gave **glory** *to God, being fully persuaded that God had power to do what he had promised. This is why "it was credited to him as righteousness." The words, it was credited to him were written not for him alone, but also for us, to whom God will credit righteousness—for us who believe in him who raised Jesus our Lord from the dead.* (Romans 4:19-24)

What Others are Saying:

Ronald F. Youngblood: Abraham's response to God's promise was one of faith. We are told that he *believed the Lord.* Genesis 15:6 gives us a concise definition of what faith is all about. "Faith" means "believing God, believing what God tells us."[1]

KEY POINT

Faith is simply taking God at his Word.

Max Lucado: You do not impress the officials of NASA with a paper airplane. You don't claim equality with Einstein because you can write H_2O. And you don't boast about your goodness in the presence of the Perfect [God].[2]

Kay Arthur: What does the Word of God mean when it speaks of faith? Faith is simply taking God at his Word.[3]

Both Old and New Testaments teach that only those who trust God and his promises have a personal relationship with him.

Remember This . . .

Getting To Know Abraham

Some Bible stories about Abraham display his human weaknesses. Some reveal his trust in God. Reading one or two of the following stories from each of the two categories will provide an understanding of both the weaknesses and the trust of Abraham.

Dig Deeper

Abraham's weaknesses revealed	Abraham's growing trust displayed
Genesis 12:10–20	Genesis 12:4–9
Genesis 16:1–16	Genesis 13:1–18
Genesis 20:1–17	Genesis 14:1–24
	Genesis 15:1–20
	Genesis 19:1–29
	Genesis 22:1–19

Robert C. Girard: An amazing revelation! Since becoming a follower of Jesus Christ there is a part of me that wants what God wants. Through the Spirit's operation a new creation, totally tuned to God and in full accord with his will, is rising from the rubble of the old life.[4]

God does not expect people to be "good" before he accepts them. God accepts people who trust him, and then he helps them become better.

Archaeology And Abraham

Some think that the stories about Abraham were made up. But **archaeology** makes it clear these stories contain authentic details. For instance, the raiding route that kings are said to have followed in Genesis 14 really was used 2,000 years before Christ. Laws and marriage contracts dating from Abraham's time indicate Sarah's offer of her slave Hagar to Abraham, so that Abraham could have a son a common practice at that time. A person making up these stories hundreds of years later would not have been able to include so many authentic details.

Four hundred years before Abraham lived, in . . .

England	Stonehenge was erected as a ritual center.
Egypt	Pyramids were constructed as tombs for kings.
America	Pottery was invented in what is now Georgia.
Babylon	Astronomers used a highly developed geometry system.
Asia	Bronze ornaments and tools were in use in Thailand.

And All Those After You

THE BIG PICTURE

> **Genesis 21–27** These chapters tell the story of Isaac, Abraham's son by his wife, Sarah. Isaac is important because he inherited the covenant which God made with Abraham, and passed it on to his son, Jacob.

ISAAC: The son of Abraham and Sarah, Isaac, inherited the covenant promises God gave to Abraham. Isaac married Rebekah, and their son Jacob also inherited God's promises.

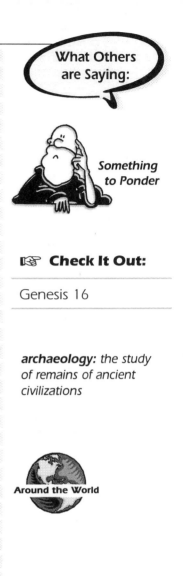

What Others are Saying:

Something to Ponder

☞ **Check It Out:**

Genesis 16

archaeology: the study of remains of ancient civilizations

Around the World

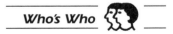

Who's Who

What About Women?

In the world of the Bible men were responsible to provide for their wives and daughters. Inheritance was passed on through the male line. As a result, most stories in the Bible are about men.

This does not mean that women are insignificant in God's eyes. Genesis 24 relates Abraham's concern to find the right wife for his son Isaac. That woman, Rebekah, made a courageous decision when she chose to wed Isaac. Rebekah showed a faith like Abraham's, for she too left her homeland in response to God's call.

Despite the **patriarchal** society in Old Testament times, evidence shines through that women also displayed faith in God.

THE BIG PICTURE 🔍

> **Genesis 25–50** These chapters tell the story of Jacob, who was next to inherit the covenant promises. Jacob's older twin, Esau, normally would have been his father's heir. But the materialistic Esau cared nothing for God or his promises, and traded his **birthright** to Jacob for a bowl of stew. Later, Jacob tricked his father into giving him Esau's **blessing**. When Esau threatened to kill Jacob, the latter fled to Haran. There Jacob married and had many children. Later, Jacob and his family moved to Egypt to escape a famine. The Israelites remained there 400 years.

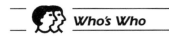 **Who's Who**

JACOB: Jacob was the son of Isaac and Rebekah; he was the next to inherit God's covenant promises. God spoke to Jacob several times during his life. On one of these occasions God changed Jacob's name to *Israel*. The old name meant "deceiver," while *Israel* means "God perseveres." The people who descended from Jacob/Israel, and the nation they established, are also called *Israel* (Israelites) in the Bible.

Getting To Know Jacob

Reading any two of the following stories will provide an introduction to the character of Jacob:

Jacob "steals" Esau's birthright.	Genesis 25:19–3
Jacob deceives his father.	Genesis 27:1–35
Jacob flees to his uncle, Laban.	Genesis 27:41–46
God speaks to Jacob for the first time.	Genesis 28:10–22

KEY Symbols:

Jacob
  deceiver

Israel
  God preserves

patriarchal: *ruled by males*

birthright: *the oldest son's right to inherit*

blessing: *here, an oral last will and testament*

 ***Dig Deeper***

Jacob marries two sisters.	Genesis 29:15–28
Jacob's wives compete.	Genesis 30:1–22
Jacob plans to return to Canaan.	Genesis 31:18–21
Jacob prays for protection.	Genesis 32:1–12
Jacob meets Esau again.	Genesis 33:11–20

Jacob's Four Wives

The Bible reports that Jacob had two wives and two **concubines**, who all together bore him 12 sons. Muslims deduce from this that a man is allowed four wives. Christians teach that marriage is a relationship between one man and one woman. *A man will leave his father and mother and be united to his wife, and they will become one flesh* (Genesis 2:24).

    The jealousy and unhappiness depicted in Genesis 29:31 to 30:24 show that **polygamy** is not a healthy state.

concubine: a secondary wife

polygamy: having several wives at the same time

By the time of Isaac and Jacob, in . . .

Europe	The first trumpets were played in Denmark.
America	American Indians worked large open-pit copper mines in Wisconsin.
China	Astronomers kept careful records of eclipses.
Europe	Horses began to be used as mounts.
Egypt	Wine jars identifying vintages and orchards were placed in tombs of the wealthy.

Around the World

When reading the Bible it's important to remember **narrative** passages describe what *did* happen, not what *should* happen.

narrative: story telling

A Coat Of Many Colors

THE BIG PICTURE

☞ **Check It Out:**

Genesis 37, 39–50

> **Genesis 36–50** Joseph was the favorite son of Jacob, but his jealous brothers sold him into Egyptian slavery. After many trials Jacob became **vizier** of Egypt, and God led Joseph to prepare Egypt to survive a great famine. Joseph was able to save the lives of his father and brothers during the famine by moving them from Canaan to Egypt, where their descendants lived for the next 400 years.

vizier: chief official

JOSEPH: The story of Joseph is one of the most encouraging stories in the Bible. Joseph held onto his faith despite suffering and unfair treatment. His words to the brothers who had betrayed him sum up the lesson we can learn from his life: *You intended to harm me, but God intended it for good to accomplish what is now being done, the saving of many lives* (Genesis 50:20). The story of Joseph reads like an exciting novel. Don't miss any of it!

What Others are Saying:

Mother Teresa: Make sure that you let God's grace work in your souls by accepting whatever he gives you, and giving him whatever he takes from you. True holiness consists in doing God's will with a smile.[5]

Study Questions

1. What is special about Abraham?
2. What is a covenant?
3. Why is it important to understand the Abrahamic Covenant?
4. Who inherited the covenant promises after Abraham died?
5. Why is faith important for a person seeking a personal relationship with God?

KEY Symbols:

Abraham
Isaac
Jacob (Israel)
Joseph

CHAPTER WRAP-UP

- God gave Abraham covenant promises for himself and his physical descendants (Genesis 12:1–3).
- The covenant promises outlined what God intended to do in the future.
- Abraham believed God's promise, and God credited Abraham's faith to him as righteousness (Genesis 15:6).
- All who trust God as Abraham did are the spiritual descendants of Abraham (Romans 4).
- The covenant promises given to Abraham were passed on to Isaac, Jacob, and to their descendants, the Jewish people.
- The rest of the Old Testament is the story of the Jewish people and how God worked out his covenant promises through history.

3 EXODUS

Exodus

Let's Get Started

As Exodus begins, the **Israelites** are slaves in Egypt. Then God calls a man named Moses to free his people. Exodus is the story of how God acted to break the power of Egypt and free the Israelites. God then led the freed slaves to Mount Sinai (see Illustration #5, page 24), where he gave them the Ten Commandments.

Israelites: God's covenant people; descendants of Abraham, Isaac, and Jacob

 **KEY Symbols:**

Mount Sinai
where God gave the Ten Commandments

Time Line #2

Important Persons and Events in Exodus

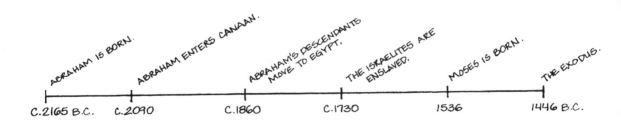

ABRAHAM IS BORN.

ABRAHAM ENTERS CANAAN.

ABRAHAM'S DESCENDANTS MOVE TO EGYPT.

THE ISRAELITES ARE ENSLAVED.

MOSES IS BORN.

THE EXODUS.

C.2165 B.C.   C.2090   C.1860   C.1730   1536   1446 B.C.

Illustration #5

Exodus map—Use this map
to locate where events in
Exodus took place.

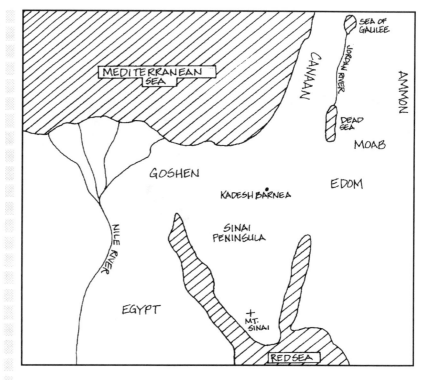

EXODUS

. . . *exit to freedom*

Just the FACTS

WHO	Moses wrote
WHAT	the story of the Israelites' deliverance from slavery
WHERE	in Egypt
WHEN	around 1440 B.C.,
WHY	to provide a record of God's power and his commitment to Abraham's descendants.

While the Israelites were in Egypt, in . . .

Africa	Horse-drawn chariots were added to the Egyptian army.
America	Sunflowers began to be cultivated and their seeds stored for winter food.
China	Human sacrifices were placed in the foundations of public buildings.
Syria	Glass began to be molded to form vessels and replace semi-precious stones.

Around the World

Not Me Lord

MOSES: Moses was an Israelite adopted into Egypt's royal family as an infant. When Moses was 80 years old, God called him to confront **Pharaoh** and free his people. God struck Egypt with 10 plagues to win Israel's freedom, and Moses led the two million freed slaves to Mount Sinai. There God gave the Ten Commandments and a code of law for the Israelites to follow. Moses led the Israelites for 40 years and died at age 120.

What's Special About Moses?

1 *Moses was God's choice to deliver the Israelites from slavery.*

2 *Moses was God's choice to give us the Ten Commandments.*

3 *Moses was God's choice to give Israel his Law and is honored in Judaism as the Law-giver.*

4 *Moses was God's choice to write the first five books of the Old Testament—Genesis, Exodus, Leviticus, Numbers, and Deuteronomy—and he was the first **prophet**.*

A High Priest

AARON: Aaron was Moses' brother and his companion during the Exodus period; he became the Israelites' first High **Priest** (see GWRV, pages 20–21).

THE BIG PICTURE

Exodus 1–6 Although adopted into Egypt's royal family, Moses hoped to free the Israelites. Upon killing an Egyptian slave driver, Moses fled to the Sinai desert. Forty years later God told Moses to return to Egypt and free his people. Moses, having been humbled, told God how inadequate he felt for the task. God promised to be with Moses, and God also promised that Moses would be successful.

What's Special In Exodus 1–6?

1 *The conditions under which the Israelites lived were truly brutal.* The plagues with which God later struck Egypt were a just punishment.

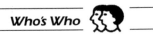

Who's Who

Pharaoh: *a title, king of Egypt*

prophet: *a person through whom God speaks and guides choices*

Who's Who

priest: *middleman between God and the Israelites*

KEY Symbols:

Moses
first prophet

Aaron
Moses' brother
first High Priest

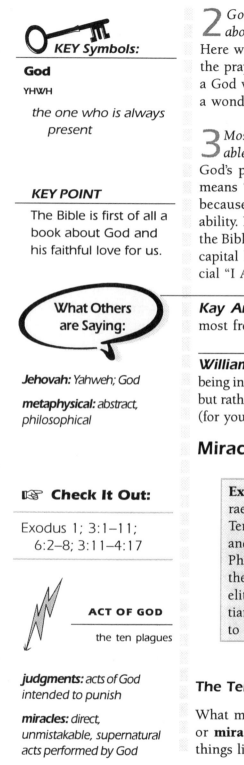

KEY Symbols:

God

YHWH

the one who is always present

KEY POINT

The Bible is first of all a book about God and his faithful love for us.

What Others are Saying:

Jehovah: Yahweh; God

metaphysical: abstract, philosophical

☞ **Check It Out:**

Exodus 1; 3:1–11; 6:2–8; 3:11–4:17

ACT OF GOD

the ten plagues

judgments: acts of God intended to punish

miracles: direct, unmistakable, supernatural acts performed by God

2 *God's words to Moses, when he announced that he was about to free Israel, help us to see what kind of person God is.* Here we see him as a God who keeps his promises, who hears the prayers of his people and responds to their suffering. He is a God who will act to deliver his people, and who has planned a wonderful future for them.

3 *Moses made excuse after excuse to explain why he was unable to accept God's commission.* God replied by telling Moses God's personal name. In Hebrew that name is *YHWH*, which means "the one who is always present." Moses would succeed because God was present with him, not because of his own ability. Here YHWH is translated "I AM." In English versions of the Bible, every time the word *LORD* appears with *ORD* in small capital letters, it means that the original Hebrew uses this special "I AM" name for God.

Kay Arthur: Of all the names of God, **Jehovah** is the name most frequently used in the Old Testament (6,823 times).[1]

William Sanford LaSor: [God's] existence is not a matter of being in the **metaphysical** sense—as if a philosophical statement—but rather in the relative or efficacious sense: "I am he who is there (for you)—really and truly present, ready to help and to act."[2]

Miracles!

THE BIG PICTURE 🔍

Exodus 7–19 When Pharaoh refused to free his Israelite slaves, Moses announced a series of plagues. Ten terrible **judgments** devastated the land of Egypt, and Pharaoh was forced to let the Israelites go. When Pharaoh changed his mind and pursued God's people, the Lord opened a path through the sea for the Israelites. But the pathway closed, and the entire Egyptian army drowned. God's people were free to travel to Mount Sinai!

The Ten Plagues

What marks the ten plagues that struck Egypt as acts of God, or **miracles**? Most involved natural phenomena and ordinary things like frogs, locusts, and hail. But:

1) These plagues were intense, far out of the ordinary.
2) They were announced ahead of time by Moses.
3) They began when Moses said they would begin.
4) They stopped when Moses asked God to stop them.
5) Many of them were selective, striking only the Egyptians and not the Israelites.
6) Both the Israelites and the Egyptians knew something **supernatural** was happening.

supernatural: *a direct exercise of God's power*

C. S. Lewis: A miracle is emphatically not an event without cause or without results. Its cause is the activity of God; its results follow according to natural law.[3]

What Others are Saying:

Ten Miraculous Plagues

1.	The Nile River is turned to blood.	Exodus 7:19–25
2.	Frogs cover the land.	Exodus 8:1–15
3.	Lice infest all of Egypt.	Exodus 8:16–19
4.	Flies swarm the Egyptians.	Exodus 8:20–32
5.	Egyptian herds die of disease.	Exodus 9:1–7
6.	Boils break out on the Egyptians.	Exodus 9:8–12
7.	Hail devastates Egyptian crops.	Exodus 9:13–35
8.	Locusts strip Egypt of vegetation.	Exodus 10:1–20
9.	Darkness blinds the Egyptians.	Exodus 10:21–29
10.	The firstborn sons of Egypt die, including Pharaoh's son.	Exodus 11:1–10; 12:9–36

Remember This . . .

More Miracles

Not only did God perform miracles to free Israel from Egypt, he performed miracles so that they could make it to Mount Sinai. After striking Egypt with the plagues, here's what else God did for the Israelites:

God shielded the Israelites.	Exodus 14:5–20
God made a path through the sea.	Exodus 14:21–25
God drowned an Egyptian army.	Exodus 14:26–31
God purified undrinkable water.	Exodus 15:22–27
God provided **manna** for food.	Exodus 16:1–5;13–35
God brought water from a rock.	Exodus 17:1–7
God assured a military victory.	Exodus 17:8–16
God displayed his power at Mount Sinai.	Exodus 19:16–22

Dig Deeper

manna: *miracle food that God supplied daily*

☞ **Check It Out:**

Exodus 7:3–5; 7:13;
   8:15

☞ **Check It Out:**

Exodus 12:1–14; 21–28

John 1:29–34

*Passover: a yearly
celebration reliving the
night God won Israel's
freedom from Egypt*

KEY POINT

God's revelation of
himself softens the
hearts of some and
hardens the hearts of
others.

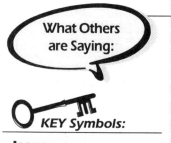

What Others
are Saying:

KEY Symbols:

Jesus
LAMB OF GOD

God
CREATOR

REDEEMER

What's Special In Exodus 7–15?

1 *God told Moses he would harden Pharaoh's heart and that Pharaoh would refuse to let the Israelites go.* Some ask, "Was it fair to punish Pharaoh if he couldn't help resisting God?" But all God did to harden Pharaoh's heart was to progressively reveal more and more of his power. As the same sun that melts wax will harden clay, so God's revelation of himself softens the hearts of some and hardens the hearts of others.

2 *On the first **Passover**, a lamb was killed and its blood was sprinkled on the doorways of Israelite homes.* When the angel who struck the firstborn sons of Egypt saw the blood, it "passed over" those homes. The New Testament recalls this event in Jesus' title, the "Lamb of God." It teaches that Jesus shed his blood in payment for our sins, that we might be saved from punishment for our sins.

3 *God told the Israelites to remember what he had done to free them by eating a Passover meal every year.* They were to serve the same food the people ate in Egypt on the night that God struck the firstborn sons of the Egyptians but spared his own people. Jewish families still celebrate Passover each spring.

4 *The miracles God performed in freeing the Israelites and bringing them to Mount Sinai are defining acts.* God is known throughout the Bible as the Creator who made the world, and the Redeemer whose mighty acts in history won the freedom of his people.

Norman L. Geisler: If God exists, then miracles are possible.[4]

Written In Stone

THE BIG PICTURE 🔍

> **Exodus 20–24** Moses led the Israelites into the wilderness to Mount Sinai. Clouds and lightning shrouded the mountain as God spoke to his people. God called Moses up to the mountain top and gave him the Ten Commandments. God also gave Moses additional laws for the Israelites to follow.

What Are The Ten Commandments?

The Ten Commandments teach basic morality. The first four reveal what it takes to have a good relationship with God. The next six show how to have good relationships with other people.

Check It Out

Exodus 20:1–17

Remember This . . .

The Commandments	How to keep them
A good relationship with God	
1. Exodus 20:3 Do not put any other gods before me.	Put God first in everything.
2. Exodus 20:4–6 Do not worship idols.	Reject ideas about God that he himself has not revealed.
3. Exodus 20:7 Do not take my name in vain.	Never speak or act as if God is not real and present.
4. Exodus 20:8–11 Keep the Sabbath holy.	Set aside a day to rest and remember God.
A good relationship with others	
5. Exodus 20:12 Honor your mother and father.	Show respect for your parents.
6. Exodus 20:13 Do not murder.	Do nothing with an intent to harm another.
7. Exodus 20:14 Do not commit adultery.	Be faithful in your commitment to your spouse.
8. Exodus 20:15 Do not steal.	Respect the rights of others.
9. Exodus 20:16 Do not testify falsely.	Respect others' reputation as well as their lives and property.
10. Exodus 20:17 Do not **covet**.	Care about others, not about their possessions.

KEY POINT

Only a God who is himself loving, faithful, and good would command his people to live this kind of life.

ACT OF GOD

God gave Moses the Ten Commandments

Robert Schuller: God gave us these ten laws to protect us from an alluring, tempting path which would ultimately lead only to sickness, sin, and sorrow. Following the Ten Commandments will result in spiritual health, mental health, and physical health. Killing, lying, stealing, and adultery are bad for the health! (Consider the current epidemic of venereal diseases!)[5]

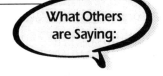

What Others are Saying:

covet: *a desire to possess what belongs to another*

What's Special In Exodus 20–24?

1 *God gave these commandments to his own people.* God did not give the commandments to strangers and say, "Keep them and you will become my people." A people who have been saved by God will *want* to live the kind of life the commandments describe.

☞ **Check It Out:**

Exodus 20:1

2 *God did not force the Israelites to accept his laws. He first ex* plained what he expected of them. He warned of punishment for disobedience, and promised blessings if the Israelites obeyed. The people promised, *Everything which the Lord has said we will do* (Exodus 24:3).

3 *The agreement God and Israel made at Mount Sinai is called the Law Covenant.* In ancient times a *covenant* might be an oath, a contract, a treaty, or even a national constitution. The Law Covenant is different from the covenant God made with Abraham. What are the differences?

	Abrahamic Covenant	Law Covenant
Who made commitments?	God only	God and the Israelites
Who must keep commitments?	God	God and the Israelites
What does the blessing depend on?	God's faithfulness	The Israelites' obedience
What happens if people sin?	God fulfills the covenant	God punishes the sinners
What happens if people obey?	God fulfills the covenant	God blesses the obedient
What kind of covenant is this?	Promise	Contract

4 *Two kinds of laws are given in these chapters,* **apodictic** *and* **casuistic**. Apodictic laws are universal and apply to all. The Ten Commandments are apodictic laws. Casuistic laws tell what a person should do in a specific situation. They apply only to people in the situation described. Exodus 22:5, 6 and 23:4, 5 are examples of casuistic or "case" law.

5 *After the Israelites had been given God's Law, they knew:*

1) what they were to do,
2) that *in their life on earth* God would bless them if they obeyed, and
3) that God would punish them if they disobeyed.

But the Law did not change the Abrahamic Covenant, nor the fact that God gives righteousness to those who have faith.

KEY POINT

In the Bible, only the Law Covenant is a contract between God and the Israelites. The Abrahamic and other covenants of the Bible are oaths or pledges, promises stating what God says he will do.

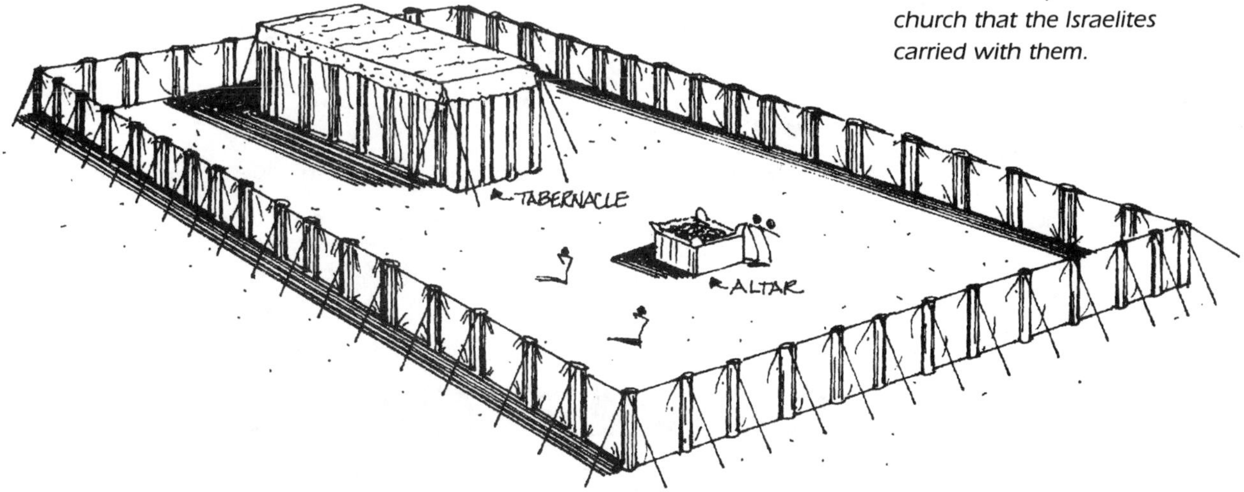

Illustration #6

The Wilderness Taber-
nacle—God designed each
feature of the portable tent
church that the Israelites
carried with them.

We'll Take It With Us

THE BIG PICTURE 🔍

Exodus 25–40 With the Law God gave Moses the blueprint for a **worship** center. What to do was explained in minute detail. Moses and the Israelites followed God's instruction and completed the worship center, which was called the **Tabernacle** (see Illustration #6, this page). When all was ready, Moses and the people assembled to **dedicate** the Tabernacle to the Lord.

What's Special About Exodus 25–40?

1 *The Tabernacle blueprint.* Why were God's directions so specific? Because each detail of the Tabernacle taught a spiritual truth. For instance, God instructed there to be only one door leading into the worship center to show that there is only one way to approach God—his way!

2 *The Golden Calf.* While Moses was on Mount Sinai, the Israelites urged Aaron to make an idol in the form of a calf. Many broke the first commandment and worshiped the idol, giving it credit for freeing God's people from Egypt. God pun-

☞ **Check It Out:**

Galatians 3:17–22

worship: honoring God
with our praise

Tabernacle: a tent, here the
"tent of meeting" where
God met with his people

dedicate: to set apart for
the service of God

☞ **Check It Out:**

Exodus 32:1–35;
40:34–38

Exodus 26:1–14

glory: in this case, a visible sign of God's presence

ished those who were guilty, as the Law Covenant specified that he should.

In spite of the fact that God's people broke his Law, God remained faithful to his promise to Abraham. When the Tabernacle was completed, God filled it with his **glory** to show he truly was present with his people

Study Questions

1. What makes Moses an important figure in the Old Testament?
2. What is a miracle?
3. What miracles did God perform to free the Israelite slaves?
4. What is the difference between a promise covenant and a contract covenant. Which kind is the Law Covenant?
5. What can we learn from the Ten Commandments?

CHAPTER WRAP-UP

- Exodus tells the story of the Israelites' deliverance from slavery in Egypt.
- Moses was God's choice to confront Egypt's Pharaoh and to announce the miraculous judgments that forced the Egyptians to free their slaves.
- After God freed the slaves, he gave them the Ten Commandments to teach his people how to maintain a healthy relationship with him and with one another.
- God promised to bless his people while they lived on earth, if they kept his commandments.
- God also gave Moses plans for a portable worship center, the Tabernacle, where they could worship and offer sacrifices.

4 THE ADVENTURE CONTINUES

Leviticus
Numbers
Deuteronomy

Let's Get Started

At the beginning of Leviticus, the Israelites have been delivered from slavery in Egypt and brought to Mount Sinai. Moses had given them God's Ten Commandments, various other laws, and the blueprint for a portable worship center, the Tabernacle.

While at Mount Sinai, God will also reveal laws for **holy living**. Then the Israelites will set out for the land God promised to give Abraham's descendants. But a tragic rebellion will lead to 38 years of wandering in the desert (see Illustration #7, page 34). Only after a new generation has replaced the men and women who left Egypt will the Israelites reach the borders of Canaan. There, just beyond the Jordan River, Moses will review the Law Covenant for the new generation.

holy: separated or set apart

holy living: a lifestyle fitting for people who are special to God

Time Line #3

Where the Action Takes Place

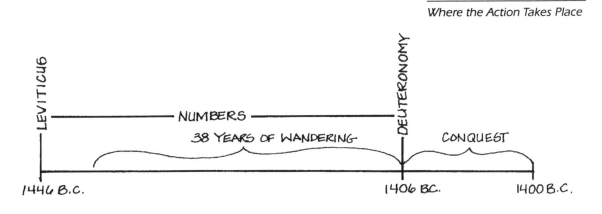

LEVITICUS

NUMBERS

38 YEARS OF WANDERING

DEUTERONOMY

CONQUEST

1446 B.C.   1406 BC.   1400 B.C.

Illustration #7

Map of Wilderness Wanderings—When the Israelites left Mount Sinai they traveled to Kadish Barnea, where they rebelled against God. After wandering in the desert for 38 years they traveled north to the plains of Moab. There, just across the Jordan River from the Promised Land, Moses reviewed God's Law.

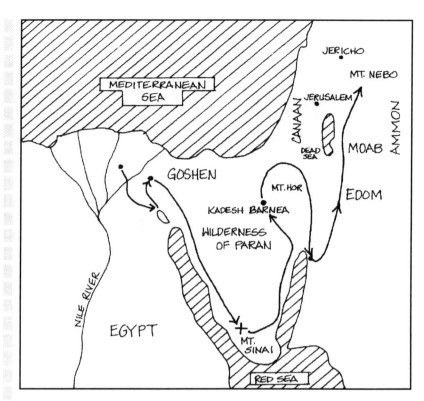

LEVITICUS

. . . laws for holy living

WHO   Moses wrote this
WHAT   book of laws
WHERE   at Mount Sinai,
WHEN   around 1446 B.C.,
WHY   to remind the Israelites they were God's special people.

Just the FACTS

Laws, Laws, Laws

THE BIG PICTURE

KEY Symbols:

Leviticus
about the Levites
  ▪ priests and worship leaders

Leviticus This word means "about the Levites." One topic in Leviticus is that of rules for the Levites, who were the priests and worship leaders. Leviticus contains many rules which apply to all Israelites. These laws are intended to remind God's people that they belong to him. The major subjects in Leviticus are:

- Offerings and sacrifices (Leviticus 1–7)
- Priests (Leviticus 8–10)
- Ritual law (Leviticus 11–15)
- The Day of Atonement (Leviticus 16)
- Practical holiness (Leviticus 17–22)
- Worshiping God (Leviticus 23–25)
- Conditions for blessing (Leviticus 26–27)

What's Special In Leviticus?

1 *Offerings and sacrifices (Leviticus 1–7).* When an Israelite wanted to approach God he or she brought an **offering** or a **sacrifice**. Sometimes a person wanted to approach God simply to express thanks. Sometimes a person needed to approach God because he or she had sinned. These chapters describe the offerings and sacrifices an Israelite would bring to a priest, who would then burn them, symbolically presenting the offering or sacrifice to the Lord. The offerings and sacrifices described in these chapters are explained on the chart below.

offering: a gift

sacrifice: death of a substitute in payment for sin

Dig Deeper

Name of Offering	Passages	Content	Significance
Burnt offering	Leviticus 1, 6:8–12	Animal or bird	Symbolizes complete commitment to God
Grain (meal) offering	Leviticus 2, 6:14–23	Grain or bread, with olive oil	Symbolizes devotion to God
Fellowship (peace)	Leviticus 3, 7:11–36	Unblemished herd of flock animal	Symbolizes thanksgiving
Sin offering	Leviticus 4:1–5:13; 6:24–30; 12:6–8; 14:12–14	The animal depends on what the offerer is able to provide	**Atones** for sin or **uncleanness**
Guilt offering	Leviticus 5:14–6:7; 7:1–6; 14:12–18	Valuable ram or lamb	Atones for sins violating others' rights, or uncleanness

Many important Bible terms are associated with sacrifices and offerings. It is important to know the meanings of these terms. As we will see, a misunderstanding of them can even lead to confusion about why Jesus Christ was born, and about the meaning of his death on the cross. Below is a list of terms and their definitions. After reading them, it would be a good idea to turn your Bible to Leviticus 5:1–10 and underline each term.

atone: reconcile with God

uncleanness: contamination by contact, which temporarily limits participation in community worship

Sin:	Any violation of God's will.
Guilt:	Not guilt feelings, but a consequence of sin which makes a sinner subject to punishment by God.
Confess:	To acknowledge personal responsibility for a sin.
Penalty:	A punishment due to a person who has sinned
Blood:	Representation of life (see Leviticus 7:11)—making an animal sacrifice acknowledged the fact that death is the appropriate penalty for sin against God.
Atonement:	When an Israelite offered the blood of an animal and acknowledged his or her sin, the blood covered that sin and restored the Israelite's relationship with God.
Forgiven:	A forgiven person no longer has to fear divine punishment.

☞ **Check It Out:**

Leviticus 5:1–10

The New Testament teaches that Jesus Christ, God's Son, gave his life on the cross as a sacrifice to pay the penalty for our sins. When we acknowledge our guilt and trust Jesus as Savior, God forgives our sins freely and completely. The repeated Old Testament sacrifices were object lessons, teaching this special language of sacrifice and salvation.

Something
to Ponder

2 *Priesthood (Leviticus 8–10).* Aaron and his sons were set apart as priests in a solemn ceremony, and the newly finished Tabernacle was dedicated. Only Aaron's descendants were allowed to present an Israelite's offerings or sacrifices to the Lord.

☞ **Check It Out:**

Leviticus 9

3 *Different kinds of laws (Leviticus 11–5).* There are two basic kinds of law in the Old Testament. One kind is *moral* law. Moral law is about what is right and wrong and about the way we treat God and other people. The other kind of law is **ritual** law, often called ceremonial law. Ritual laws were rules the Israelites were to live by simply because they were God's people, rather than because they represented what was right or wrong in and of themselves. Ritual laws were about worship, because a person who violated a ritual law became unclean and could not join others in worshiping God.

KEY Symbols:

Old Testament Laws
moral
- right and wrong
ritual
- ceremonial law

ritual: *having to do with worship practices*

Joni Eareckson Tada: God is telling his people what he expects of them in their worship. God wants his people to understand that all of life is spiritual; all of life's activities come under his domain. How we plow our fields or how we shop at the market. How we mate our animals or even how we talk to a gas station attendant. Everything we do can be a way of worshiping him.[1]

What Others are Saying:

Which of the five rules below do you think are examples of ritual law? Remember, ritual laws have nothing to do with moral right and wrong. (see Appendix B for Answers.)

1) Don't eat shrimp.
2) Offer a sacrifice after giving birth.
3) Don't commit adultery.
4) Help your enemy if his cattle get loose.
5) Wash your clothes after touching a dead body.

☞ **Check It Out:**

Leviticus 11–15

Something to Ponder

Terms Of Ritual Law

Uncleanness: A person who broke a ritual law became ritually unclean. That person could not take part in worship or eat sacrificed meat. In some cases the unclean person had to be isolated from others. This is an important concept in the Old Testament, where the Hebrew word for "unclean" occurs 279 times!

Cleansing: An Israelite who had broken a ritual law and become unclean could be made clean again. Usually this called for a period of waiting and then either a washing with water or a ritual of **purification**, which involved offering a blood sacrifice. After this the Israelite could rejoin others for worship.

Remember This . . .

☞ **Check It Out:**

Leviticus 13:45–45;
6:14–16; 16:29–34

purify: *to make ritually clean*

4 *Ritual laws (Leviticus 11–15).* The ritual laws in this section of Leviticus cover what the Israelites could and could not eat, what to do when a person was born, when a person contracted an infectious skin disease, had a bodily discharge, died, etc. Ritual laws reminded the Israelites that God was concerned with every aspect of their daily lives.

KEY Symbols:

Ritual Law
uncleanness
cleansing

☞ **GO TO:**

Leviticus 16:31 (blood
sacrifice)

☞ **Check It Out:**

Leviticus 18:6–18;
19:12–18; 20:22–26

worship: *praising God for
who he is and what he has
done*

leaven: *yeast*

fast: *go without eating*

5 *The Day of Atonement (Leviticus 16).* The sacrifices for sin described in Leviticus 1–7 could only atone for unintentional sins. What about the sins an Israelite committed knowingly, fully aware that he or she was doing wrong?

Once a year on the Day of Atonement the High Priest took a <u>blood sacrifice</u> into the inner room of the Tabernacle, the Holy of Holies (see GWRV, Illustration #5, page 153), to make an atonement *for all the sins of the Israelites.*

6 *Laws of practical holiness (Leviticus 17–22).* These chapters contain a variety of laws that the Israelites were to follow. Many of the laws were moral laws about relationships between people. Other laws were designed to strengthen the family, while still others were symbolic reminders that as God's people the Israelites were to be different from the peoples around them. *I, the LORD, am holy, and I have set you apart from the nations to be my own* (Leviticus 20:26)

7 *Worshiping God (Leviticus 23–25).* These chapters describe special festivals (see GWRV Time Line #4, page 335) during which the Israelites gathered to **worship** God. Some of these same festivals are celebrated as religious holidays by Jews today.

Jewish Festival	Date	Significance
Passover	14 Nisan (March/April)	Families share a meal and remember how God delivered the Israelites from slavery in Egypt.
Unleavened bread	15–21 Nisan (March/April)	Families offer sacrifices and eat bread without **leaven** as a reminder of the hurried departure from Egypt.
Firstfruits	6 Nisan (March/April)	A harvest-time, thanksgiving celebration.
Pentcost (Weeks)	5 Silvan (May/June	A thanksgiving celebration when newly ripened grain is offered and sacrifices are made.
Trumpets Rosh Hashanah	1 Tishri (Sept./Oct.)	This is a day of rest—the first day of Israel's civil year. The religious year begins with Passover.
Day of Atonement	10 Tishri (Sept./Oct.)	The High Priest enters the Tabernacle and makes the yearly sacrifice for *all the sins of the Israelites.* The people **fast** (see GWDN, pages 161–162) on this solemn day.
Tabernacles	15–21 Tishri (Sept./Oct.)	For a week the Israelites live in outdoor shelters, reliving the travels of the Exodus generation to the Promised Land.

8 *Conditions for blessing (Leviticus 26–27).* Leviticus closes with an important reminder. At Mount Sinai God made a *contract covenant* with Israel, promising blessings in this life to those who obey his Law, and warning of punishment in this life to those who disobey it. Leviticus 26 clearly states the rewards and punishments the Israelites can expect. But the chapter closes with a reminder that God's *promise covenant* with Abraham's descendants is still in force. One generation may fail, but God will not abandon his people. God says *I will remember my covenant with Jacob and my covenant with Isaac and my covenant with Abraham, and . . . I will not reject or **abhor** them so as to destroy them completely* (Leviticus 26:42, 44).

Numbers

. . . the long journey

WHO   Moses wrote this

WHAT   narrative history

WHERE   after reaching the borders of Canaan

WHEN   around 1406 B.C.,

WHY   to remind the Israelites of the consequences
of rebelling against God.

We Won't Be There Tomorrow

THE BIG PICTURE

Numbers The name is taken from two numberings of the Israelites, recorded in Chapters 1 and 26. After having camped for a year at Mount Sinai, the Israelites, led by Moses, set out for Canaan. Upon arriving, the Israelites refused to trust God and rebelled. For the next 38 years the Israelites wandered in the desert (see Time Line #3, page 33). During this time God provided for all their needs. When all the adults who had been freed from Egypt had died, Moses led a new generation that did trust him back to Canaan. Numbers has three main sections:

- Preparation for the Journey (Numbers 1–10)
- Journeying toward Canaan (Numbers 11–21)
- Waiting on the Plains of Moab (Numbers 22–36)

KEY Symbols:

Moses

contract (Law) covenant
- obey = blessing
- disobey = punishment

Abraham

promise covenant
- God will not abandon his people

abhor: detest; loathe

Just the FACTS

KEY POINT

It was because of their refusal to trust God and enter Canaan that they wandered for 38 years.

What's Special In Numbers?

1 *Preparation for the Journey (Numbers 1–10).* There were many things to do during the year that the Israelites camped at Mount Sinai. A census was taken and listed 603,550 men. With women and children, the people numbered over two million! The Tabernacle and its furnishings were constructed and dedicated (see Illustration #6, page 31). The descendants of Levi were set apart by God to care for the Tabernacle, and jobs were assigned to various Levite families. When all these tasks were completed, the Israelites were ready to leave for the **Promised Land**.

2 *Journeying toward Canaan (Numbers 11–21).* God was clearly present with the Israelites. His pillar of cloud and fire led them. His manna fed them daily. But instead of being grateful, the Israelites grumbled and complained.

When they reached the borders of Canaan, Moses sent out men to explore the land. The men reported that Canaan was fertile but that Canaan's inhabitants were powerful and their fortified cities frightening. Terrified by the report, the Israelites refused to obey God's command to attack and take the Promised Land. Under the Law Covenant, direct disobedience called for punishment. Moses prayed for the people, and the Lord pardoned their sin. But the Israelites could not avoid the consequences of their unwillingness to obey the Lord. Until the entire generation of those who were unwilling to obey God died out, the Israelites were forced to wander in the wilderness—waiting.

God's faithfulness underlined (Numbers 15–21). The first words of Numbers 15 remind us of God's faithfulness. The Israelites had rebelled. But God immediately told Moses, *Speak to the Israelites and say to them, "After you enter the land I am giving you . . ."* (Numbers 15). Despite the repeated failures to trust and obey God reported in these chapters, God intended to keep his promises and give the Israelties the Promised Land.

While the Israelites wandered in the wilderness, in . . .

Mesopotamia	The city of Nineveh, capital of Assyria, was founded.
America	Indians in Nevada used duck decoys in hunting.

Promised Land: the land God promised Abraham's descendents, modern Israel (Palestine)

☞ **Check It Out:**

Numbers 13:26–14:25

ACT OF GOD

God provided a pillar of cloud and fire to guide them, and manna for food

☞ **Check It Out:**

Numbers 15:1–21

Around the World

| America | Indians living near the Great Lakes wore shells from the Gulf of Mexico as ornaments. |
| China | An alphabet of 2,000 characters was in use. |

3 *Waiting on the Plains of Moab (Numbers 22–36)*. As the years of wandering drew toward an end, the Israelites followed a major trade route east of Mount Sinai. They avoided some of their enemies but fought others. The ruler of Moab was frightened, and sent for a man named <u>Balaam</u>. Balaam was reputed to have influence with supernatural powers. The ruler of Moab hoped Balaam would be able to curse the Israelites and so weaken them. Balaam tried to curse the Israelites, but God intervened and Balaam was forced to bless them instead.

Balaam was forced to confess *there is no sorcery against Jacob, no divination against Israel* (Numbers 23:23). God protects his people from evil spiritual powers.

Balaam's advice. Balaam wanted to earn the money the Moabites offered him, but Israel could not be cursed. So he suggested the Moabites try to turn God against his people! Following Balaam's advice the Midianite ruler sent young women to seduce Israelite men and invite them to sacrifice to idols. Balaam reasoned God would punish the Israelites himself, and they would be defeated by his Moabite clients.

God did punish, but only the guilty. God remained faithful to his promises to the people as a whole.

The second census. At this point in Numbers the adults who left Egypt have died and have been replaced by their grown children. A second census showed that despite these deaths, the Israelites were as numerous as before, with over 600,000 men. The new generation learned from their parents' failure. This generation obeyed the Lord their God.

The Moabites are defeated. Various laws are reviewed in Chapters 27–30. Chapters 31–33 relate the defeat of the Moabites and the request of several of Israel's tribes to be given the land the Moabites had lived on. These tribes agree to go with their brothers to help fight for Canaan.

☞ **Check It Out:**

Numbers 22–24

☞ **GO TO:**

Numbers 22:1–5 (Balaam)

Remember This . . .

☞ **Check It Out:**

Numbers 25; 31:1–16

☞ **Check It Out:**

Numbers 26

KEY POINT

God remains faithful to his promises.

Something to Ponder

Just the FACTS

KEY Symbols:

Deuteronomy
second law

Moses defines the boundaries of Canaan and makes plans. Moses explained to the Israelites how territory will be distributed to each tribe.

With God on Israel's side, the question is not *if* his people will take Canaan, but what is to happen *when* victory is achieved!

DEUTERONOMY
. . . the Law reviewed

WHO Moses preached

WHAT sermons reviewing God's Law

WHERE on the plains of Moab

WHEN about 1406 B.C.,

WHY to remind the new generation of Israelites what God expects.

I'll Say It Again

THE BIG PICTURE 🔍

Deuteronomy means "second law." The new generation of Israelites was about to enter the Promised Land when Moses reminded them of all that God had done for them. He summarized the way God's people were to live in order to enjoy his blessing. The book ends with an account of Moses' farewell blessing and his death. Major sections of Deuteronomy are:

- Remembering the journey
  (Deuteronomy 1:1–4:43)
- Reviewing God's Law (Deuteronomy 4:44–11)
- Rules to remember (Deuteronomy 12–26)
- Consequences to consider
  (Deuteronomy 27–28)
- Covenant commitment (Deuteronomy 29–30)
- Moses' farewell and death
  (Deuteronomy 31–34)

What's Special In Deuteronomy?

1 *Remembering the journey (Deuteronomy 1:1–4:43).* Moses retraced the 38–year journey from Mount Sinai to the border of the Promised Land. He urged the new generation to learn from history, and especially to develop a sense of wonder at the special relationship they had with the God of the universe.

2 *Reviewing God's Law (Deuteronomy 4:44–11:32).* Moses restated a number of laws given at Mount Sinai, including the Ten Commandments. Several themes in these chapters may raise questions.

> Q: **What does it mean to "fear the Lord?"**
> A: It doesn't mean "be afraid of." The phrase means "show respect for" by seeking to please him.
>
> Q: **What does "love" have to do with Law?**
> A: Love moved God to give Israel the Law, and love moves people to keep it. The Law showed how to express love for God.
>
> Q: **Why did God tell the Israelites to totally destroy the Canaanites?**
> A: God was punishing the immorality and idolatry of the Canaanites. If allowed to remain, their practices would have corrupted God's people.

Read the passages listed below and indicate which question it helps to answer. In the spaces provided, write *F* for fear, *L* for love, or *D* for drive out (destroy). (see Appendix B for Answers).

__ Deuteronomy 6:1–3   __ Deuteronomy 7:7–10

__ Deuteronomy 6:20–24   __ Deuteronomy 10:12–22

__ Deuteronomy 7:1–6   __ Deuteronomy 11:16–17

Lewis Goldberg: Deuteronomy describes how God blessed and showered his love on them because of his grace and mercy. What the Lord expected from Israel in return was an outpouring of love. While some people misappropriated God's intentions and developed a **legalistic** substitute, a **remnant** in every generation always deeply loved, honored, and served the Lord their God.[2]

☞ **Check It Out:**

Deuteronomy 4:32–40

KEY Symbols:

God
LORD

Fear the Lord
show respect for

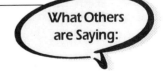

Dig Deeper

legalistic: *relying on good works rather than God*

What Others are Saying:

remnant: *the few within Israel who continued to trust God*

3 *Rules to remember (Deuteronomy 12–26).* These chapters take up many subjects discussed in Leviticus, such as clean and unclean foods, annual worship festivals, and various laws on marriage and relationships with neighbors. A few new themes are also introduced. Deuteronomy 17:14–20 limits the rights of any future king, while Deuteronomy 20 sets out humane rules for warfare. Deuteronomy 18 warns against seeking guidance through any **occult practice**, and promises that God will provide prophets to guide them in his way.

occult practice: any practice used to make choices with non-Christian, supernatural guidance

A Little Guidance

Old Testament Law gave rules to follow in daily life, but some situations simply were not covered in the Law. How could the Israelites know and follow God's will in such cases?

☞ **Check It Out:**

Deuteronomy 18:9–22

The Canaanites and other pagan peoples looked to the occult for guidance. They checked horoscopes, went to mediums or spiritists, practiced divination, and even engaged in witchcraft. God called these practices "detestable" and forbade them (see GWDN, pages 38–40; 101–102).

God then promised to send prophets to his people, like Moses, by whom God would give them special guidance when it was needed. Deuteronomy 18 gives three tests for distinguising a true prophet from a **false prophet**. The true prophet will:

false prophet: a person God did not send who claims to have a message from God

brothers: Jews

1) be "from among their **brothers**,"

2) speak in God's name, and

3) predict the future accurately.

As we go on in the Bible we will meet many prophets God sent to his people. We will also read many of their amazing predictions about the future!

4 *Consequences to consider (Deuteronomy 27, 28).* The Law Covenant is a contract covenant. When the Israelites kept the Law, God blessed them. When they disobeyed, God disciplined them. These chapters spell out both blessings for obedience and punishments for disobedience.

☞ **Check It Out:**

Deuteronomy
29:15–20

5 *Covenant commitment (Deuteronomy 29, 30).* Moses called on the Israelites to make a choice and to keep the covenant they had made with the Lord their God.

6 *Moses' farewell and death. (Deuteronomy 31–36)* God chose a successor for Moses to lead the Israelites. Moses blessed the people whom he had led for 40 years. Then Moses went to the top of Mount Nebo and looked over the Jordan River, where he was able to see the Promised Land. Moses died there, and God himself buried his faithful servant. The following, written some time after Moses' death, is a fitting **epitaph**.

epitaph: *eulogy; praise for the dead*

Since then, no prophet has risen in Israel like Moses, whom the Lord knew face to face, who did all these miraculous signs and wonders the Lord sent him to do in Egypt—to Pharaoh and to all his officials and to his whole land. For no one has ever shown the mighty power or performed the awesome deeds that Moses did in the sight of all Israel. (Deuteronomy 34:10–12)

Remember This . . .

Study Questions

1. What is the theme of Leviticus?
2. What Bible terms are linked with Leviticus' teaching on sacrifice? Why is it so important for us to understand these terms?
3. What is the difference between ritual law and moral law?
4. What made an Israelite unclean, and what could he or she do about it?
5. Why did the Israelites have to wander in the wilderness for 38 years after leaving Mount Sinai?
6. What roles does love play in the Law God gave to Israel?
7. What is a prophet, and how could the Israelites tell a true prophet from a false prophet?

KEY Symbols:

A True Prophet
a Jew
speaks in God's name
never is wrong

CHAPTER WRAP-UP

- At Mount Sinai God gave the Israelites laws for holy living, which are found in Leviticus.
- The offerings and sacrifices specified in Leviticus remind us that everyone sins and that the penalty of sin is death.
- The offerings and sacrifices specified in Leviticus teach us that blood atonement is required if we are to be forgiven.
- Moral laws were about right and wrong actions, while ritual laws governed actions that made an Israelite ritually unclean and temporarily disqualified to participate in worship.
- Numbers reports the rebellion of the Israelites. As a result, God

required them to wander in the desert for 38 years, and then an obedient generation replaced the rebellious one.

- Deuteronomy records Moses' last words to the Israelites as they were poised to enter the Promised Land.

- Deuteronomy makes it very clear that those who know God are to have nothing to do with occult practices.

- Deuteronomy emphasizes the fact that God was motivated by love to give the Israelites his Law, and that only love for God can motivate a believer to obey the Lord.

5 CONQUEST AND COLLAPSE

Joshua
Judges
Ruth

CHAPTER HIGHLIGHTS

- Canaan
- Obedience and Victory
- Judges
- Blessing by Trusting

Let's Get Started

God delivered the Israelites from slavery in Egypt and gave them his Law at Mount Sinai. A new generation of Israelites was ready to take the land God promised to Abraham hundreds of years before. The conquest to come would be successful, because this generation was willing to trust and obey the Lord. But the bright days of the conquest would soon fade, and idolatry and unbelief would doom the Israelites to centuries of oppression by foreign enemies.

JOSHUA

. . . the conquest of Canaan

WHO	An unnamed author wrote
WHAT	this history of
WHERE	the occupation of **Canaan**
WHEN	around 1400 B.C.,
WHY	to emphasize the importance of obedience to the Lord.

Canaan: the land God promised Abraham, from now on known as "Israel"

We're Finally There

JOSHUA: Joshua succeeded Moses as the leader of the Israelites. He was a man of faith who had been Moses' right-hand man and military commander during the years of wandering in the wilderness. (Some believe that Joshua was once an officer

Who's Who

Illustration #8

Map of Conquest—Canaan was not a united nation when the Israelites invaded. It had been settled by a number of ethnic groups, each of which lived in a small fortified city-state. When the Israelites arrived, the kings of these city-states united against them. Joshua's first thrust into Canaan cut the country in two, and the Israelites defeated first the southern and then the northern coalitions. The campaign against the Canaanites is still studied in U.S. and Israeli war colleges.

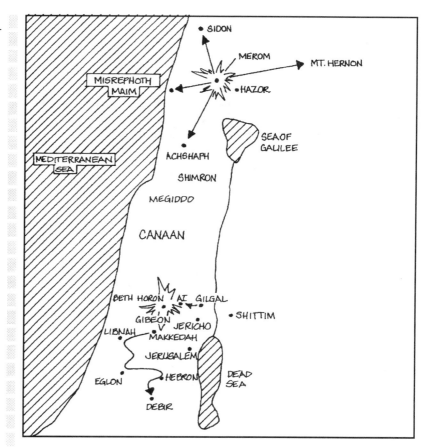

in the Egyptian army.) He was a spiritual as well as military leader and during his lifetime the Israelites were faithful to the Lord.

THE BIG PICTURE

Joshua Led by Joshua, the Israelites crossed the Jordan River and invaded Canaan (see Illustration #8, this page). In a series of military campaigns the Israelites defeated several coalition armies raised by the inhabitants of Canaan. With organized resistance put down, Joshua divided the land among the twelve Israelite tribes. The book of Joshua covers:

- Preparation for the invasion (Joshua 1–5)
- The conquest (Joshua 6–12)
- Division of the land (Joshua 13–21)
- Joshua's farewell challenge (Joshua 22–24)

What's Special In Joshua?

1 *Preparation for victory (Joshua 1–6).* The Israelites were about to attack a heavily populated land. These chapters of Joshua tell how God prepared them to meet the challenge. Four kinds of preparation are emphasized:

1) *Spiritual preparation of Joshua.* Like Joshua, anyone who wants to be a spiritual leader must be ready to submit to God and to claim God's promises.

2) *Secret preparation of the way by God.* Israelite spies, sent to the walled city of Jericho, discovered that the population was aware of God and his power. They were terrified. When God asks anyone to take a risk for him, he will prepare the way.

3) *Sensitive preparation of the Israelites.* God opened a path through the Jordan River to show that he was with Joshua as he had been with Moses. God was sensitive to the Israelites' need for evidence of his presence with Joshua.

4) *Heart preparation by the people.* The men of Israel were **circumcised,** and the whole community celebrated Passover. These acts expressed commitment to the Lord.

RAHAB: A woman who lived in Jericho and hid Israelite spies. Like others in the city she had heard that God performed miracles for his people. She shared their conviction that *your God is God in heaven above and on earth below* (Joshua 2:11). Rahab hid the spies, and when Jericho fell, only she and her family survived.

All the people of Jericho had the same information about God that Rahab did. But only Rahab chose to trust God rather than resist him. Faith is not just knowing the truth about God. Faith is responding to the truth we know.

2 *The conquest of Canaan (Joshua 6–12).*

Jericho. Joshua 6–8 is devoted to the fall of Jericho, followed by a defeat at Ai. Jericho was a walled city (see Illustration #9, page 50) that blocked access to the only pass which led into the heart of Canaan. God instructed Joshua to have the Israelites march in silence around the city for six days. On the seventh

☞ **Check It Out:**

Joshua 1:6–9: 2:8–11;
   4:1–14; 5:1–10

ACT OF GOD

God separated the waters of the Jordan River

circumcision: act of removing the foreskin of the male genitalia; signified faith in God's covenant promises

Who's Who

☞ **Check It Out:**

Joshua 3

Hebrews 11:31

Something to Ponder

☞ **Check It Out:**

Joshua 6:1–25

Illustration #9

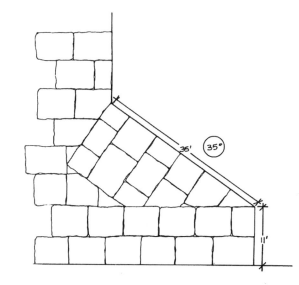

The Walls of Jericho—Above an 11-foot base wall, smooth stones sloped 35 feet at a 35-degree angle to join massive main walls. The city of Jericho was impregnable to direct assault by an army without siege engines.

ACT OF GOD

the walls of Jericho
fell down

☞ **Check It Out:**

Joshua 7, 8

booty: *spoils taken in battle*

☞ **Check It Out:**

Joshua 9

KEY POINT

Obedience to God means victory, and disobedience means defeat.

*Remember
This . . .*

day they circled the city seven times—shouted—and the walls fell down! Obedience to a seemingly foolish command of God led to a stunning victory.

Ai. At Jericho an Israelite named Achan disobeyed God's command not to take any **booty**. When a force of Israelites was sent to attack Ai, a small nearby city, the Israelites were defeated and 38 were killed. The two events placed side by side taught an important lesson. Obedience to God guaranteed victory. Disobedience guaranteed defeat.

Gibeon. The news of the victory at Jericho further terrified the Canaanites. One group, the Gibeonites, pretended to live outside Canaan and tricked the Israelites into making a treaty with them. When the deceit was discovered, Joshua insisted the treaty be honored because the Israelites had sworn in the name of the Lord their God.

Other victories. The southern and northern campaigns, which took several years, are briefly summarized in Chapters 10–12.

The major lessons taught in the book of Joshua are summarized in the first stages of the battle for Canaan. Below is a list of places and respective lessons.

Jericho	Obedience to God's will brings victory.
Ai	Disobedience to God's will brings defeat.
Gibeon	When uncertain about God's will, ask him for guidance.

3 *Division of the land (Joshua 13–21).*

Land for all (Joshua 12–19). The Old Testament presents Canaan as God's special possession, on which he settled the descendants of Abraham. Each tribe's holdings were given to it. Then the tribal territory was subdivided and distributed to **clans** and families by **lots**. Because God controlled the fall of the lots, each Israelite felt that God personally provided his or her home. Homesteads assigned at the conquest were to remain within the family, be passed from father to son, and never be sold.

Cities of refuge (Joshua 20). In Old Testament times the Israelites had no national or local police force. Violations of the Law were dealt with in the community. In the case of murder, a close relative to the victim was responsible for bringing the killer to justice. But the Law made a distinction between **premeditated** and accidental murder. Cities of refuge were established within one day's journey of any Israelite. A person who killed another could flee there and be safe until community elders determined whether the death was intentional or by accident. While murderers were put to death, those who killed accidentally were protected.

Cities for the Levites (Joshua 21). The tribe of Levi provided Israel's priests and worship leaders. The Levites were also to teach God's Law. Rather than being given a district of their own, the Levites were assigned towns and fields within the territory of the other tribes. Everyone needed access to those charged with communicating God's Word.

4 *Joshua's farewell (Joshua 22–24).* Many years after the victory over the Canaanites, Joshua summoned the Israelites and reminded them of all God had done. He challenged them to *fear the Lord and serve him with all faithfulness* (Joshua 24:14). Joshua's final exhortation is as relevant today as it was 3400 years ago: . . . *choose for yourselves this day whom you will serve. . . . but as for me and my household, we will serve the Lord* (Joshua 24:15).

☞ **Check It Out:**

Joshua 16

☞ **GO TO:**

Proverbs 16:33; John 19:24 (lots)

clan: a group of closely related families

lots: like dice

☞ **Check It Out:**

Numbers 35:6–25;

Joshua 20:1–9

premeditated: planned and intended

☞ **Check It Out:**

Joshua 21:1–3;

Leviticus 24:8

☞ **Check It Out:**

Joshua 24:1–27

KEY Symbols:

Tribe of Levi

LEVITES

responsible for communicating God's Word

JUDGES

. . . the long decline

WHO	An unnamed author wrote
WHAT	this brief history of
WHERE	events in Canaan
WHEN	from about 1375 B.C. to 1050 B.C.,
WHY	to underline the importance of national commitment to the Lord.

Just the FACTS

I'll Keep You In Line!

THE BIG PICTURE

> **Judges** After Joshua died, the Israelites again and again turned from God to the idolatry of **pagan** neighbors. This led to oppression by foreign enemies, until God's people returned to him and prayed for deliverance. God then provided leaders called **Judges** who threw out the oppressors. During the Judges' rule, the Israelites were at peace and remained faithful to God, but they quickly went astray, again, after the Judges died. The book of Judges has three main sections:
>
> * Causes of the decline (Judges 1:1–3:5)
> * Stories of the Judges (Judges 3:6–16:31)
> * Consequences of straying (Judges 17–21)

pagan: peoples who worshiped false gods

Judges: Israelite leaders; spiritual, political and military leaders

What's Important In Judges?

1 *Causes of the decline (Judges 1:1–3:5).* Not all the Canaanites were driven out during the conquest. Each Israelite tribe was told to **dispossess** those who remained, in order to protect God's people from spiritual and moral corruption. Some tribes failed to do so because of their lack of faith. Others directly disobeyed and *when Israel became strong, they pressed the Canaanites into forced labor* (Judges 1:28). Again and again their turning to worship the idols of Canaan's pagan peoples would bring disaster.

☞ **Check It Out:**

Deuteronomy 7:1–6

Judges 1:27–2:4

dispossess: put them out; cut off or separate from

What Others are Saying:

Howard Hendricks: Homes should be training grounds to develop habit patterns that serve Jesus Christ. And then we'll avoid the tragedy described in Judges 2:10—*another generation grew up, who knew neither the Lord nor what he had done.*[1]

2 *Stories of the Judges (Judges 3:6–13).* What was a Judge? A Judge was an individual whom God raised up to lead one or more Israelite tribes. The term *Judge* may give the wrong impression. These gifted individuals exercised all governmental powers during their time in office—executive, legislative, and judicial. Most were also military leaders. The office of Judge was not hereditary. God called individuals from different walks of life and empowered them to serve as Judges.

JUDGES: Who were the Judges? Twelve judges are named, and the chart below indicates the number of verses given to the story of each Judge. The stories given the most space have many lessons to teach believers today.

Judge	Number of Verses	Years of Peace Won
1. Othniel	4	40
2. Ehud	18	80
3. Shamgar	1	–
4. Deborah	53	40
5. Gideon	100	40
6. Tola	2	23
7. Jair	3	–
8. Jephthah	58	6
9. Izban	3	–
10. Elan	2	–
11. Adbon	3	–
12. Samson	97	20

DEBORAH: All ancient societies were patriarchal. Israel was no exception. Priests, town elders, political and military leaders, like the heads of households, were men. But at one time Deborah, a woman and a prophetess, emerged as the acknowledged leader, the Judge, of several of the northern Israelite tribes. What counted were the obvious gifts and the calling by God of this exceptional woman, not her gender. What still counts today is not how society limits us, but how God enables us.

GIDEON: The story of Gideon's victory with just 300 men against a much larger army is a favorite in every Sunday School curriculum. What's more fascinating is that even though Gideon was deeply aware of his weakness, and sought constant reassurance, he obeyed God *before* he was reassured. A weak person willing to obey God will be the strongest in the end.

KEY Symbols:

Judge
a leader
- executive
- legislative
- judicial

Who's Who

Something to Ponder

Who's Who

☞ **Check It Out:**

Judges 4:1–16

Who's Who

☞ **Check It Out:**

Judges 6, 7

Martin Luther: When God contemplates some great work, he begins it by the hand of some poor, weak human creature, to whom he afterward gives aid, so that the enemies who seek to obstruct it are overcome.[2]

JEPHTHAH: Jephthah (pronounced Jeff-thah) was the son of a prostitute. His father acknowledged Jeffthah and brought him up as one of his own. When the father died, however, Jephthah was thrown out of family, clan, and tribe. When war came, the tribal elders called Jephthah back to lead them. His letters to the invading Amorites show that Jephthah knew well the history of his nation's relationship with God. Early disadvantages need not limit the future of those who know God.

Jephthah's Daughter: Read Judges 11:29–40. Then vote. Did Jephthah kill his only daughter as a sacrifice to the Lord? YES___ NO___ (see Appendix B for the Answer)

SAMSON: Sunday School stories emphasize Samson's physical strength. The Bible emphasizes his moral and spiritual weaknesses. Although he was a Judge, Samson never delivered his people from oppression by the **Philistines**. Finally Samson's passion for a prostitute led him to betray the secret of his strength, which eventually brought about his death. No matter how great our natural gifts, only complete commitment to God will enable us to live up to our potential.

3 *Consequences of straying (Judges 17–21).* Judges closes with a description of three incidents which reveal what happens when a society loses its **moorings** by turning away from God's Word and his ways.

Straying from God Affects Us in Three Ways

	1. Spiritually	**2. Morally**	**3. Socially**
	Judges 17–18	*Judges 19*	*Judges 20–21*
The Act	Micah makes an idol and gets a Levite to serve as his priest.	A traveler threatened with homosexual rape turns his concubine over to the mob.	Civil war breaks out when the tribes attempt to punish the rapists.
The Result	Knowledge of God is lost or distorted.	Moral standards are abandoned or corrupted.	Social remedies for crime and injustice breakdown.

RUTH

... simple faith

WHO	An unnamed author wrote
WHAT	this beautiful story of
WHERE	a young woman who honored God
WHEN	during the days of the Judges,
WHY	to show that even when a society abandons God, individual commitment is honored.

Just the FACTS

A Pillar of Faith

THE BIG PICTURE

> **Ruth** This book of the Bible takes its name from the Moabitess daughter-in-law of Naomi. Naomi left Israel during a famine and returned years later after her husband and sons died. Ruth committed herself to Naomi and to Israel's God. Although in poverty, Ruth's virtue and character won the admiration of a relation of Naomi's husband, who married her. The union led to the birth of Obed, the grandfather of Israel's greatest king, David.

NAOMI: After her husband and sons died in Moab, Naomi, which means "pleasant," changed her name to Mara, which means "bitter." Yet through the loving support of her daughter-in-law Ruth, Naomi found comfort and a future.

RUTH: Ruth's famous words to Naomi express her commitment. *Where you go I will go, and where you stay I will stay. Your people will be my people and your God my God* (Ruth 1:16). Ruth's modesty and obvious commitment to her mother-in-law won the admiration of the community and the love of Boaz, whom she married.

BOAZ: An older man, Boaz was attracted to Ruth's character as well as her beauty. The story hinges on how Boaz played the role of the **Kinsman Redeemer** (see GWRV, pages 75–76), and how, by marrying Ruth, he gained back Naomi's lost lands for their child, Obed.

What's Special About Ruth?

1 *This gentle story, set during the days of the Judges, is in sharp contrast to the stories told in Judges 17–21.* It reminds us that even when a society breaks down, people of faith can live fulfilling and beautiful lives.

KEY POINT

Even when society breaks down, people of faith can live fulfilling and beautiful lives.

Who's Who _____

Who's Who _____

Who's Who _____

kinsman: *a close relative*

redeem: *to buy back*

---

2 *For thousands of years the relationship of Ruth and Naomi has served as a clear example of the costs and rewards of commitment.* It is no wonder that Ruth's words to Naomi (Ruth 1:16) have been woven into many marriage ceremonies.

3 *Boaz is a model of the Old Testament's Kinsman Redeemer.* When a man died childless, a *near kinsman* could marry the widow. Any son of the resulting union would gain the first husband's inheritance. But to rescue the lost estate, the redeemer had to be a *near kinsman*, and he had to be willing to accept the responsibility.

Many see Boaz as a **type** of Jesus Christ. To win back what we human beings lost through sin and spiritual death, Jesus had to become human (i.e. he had to become a true kinsman), and he had to be willing to pay the penalty for our sins. With his <u>death on the cross</u>, Jesus paid the penalty and won freedom and eternal life for us.

type: *a person or thing which is like another in an important respect*

☞ **GO TO:**

Colossians 1:21, 22 (cross)

KEY Symbols:

Jesus Christ
God's Son
won eternal life for us through his death

Study Questions

1. What time period do the books of Joshua, Judges, and Ruth cover?
2. What is the main message of the book of Joshua?
3. What is the main message of Judges?
4. What was a Judge, and what did the Judges do for the Israelites?
5. Name three of the four persons who are emphasized in Judges.
6. What is the main message of the book of Ruth?

CHAPTER WRAP-UP

- The book of Joshua tells the story of the Israelites' conquest of Canaan.

- The miracle at Jericho taught the Israelites that obedience to God's commands assures victory, and their failure at Ai taught Israel that disobeying God leads to defeat.

- Judges relates incidents that happened during a long period of time in which the Israelites often strayed from God.

- The Judges were political, military, and religious leaders that God provided when the Israelites looked to him for help.

- The Israelites suffered material, moral, and social decline during this era because of their failure to remain faithful to God.

- The book of Ruth reminds us that individuals can find blessing by trusting God even during times when their nations have turned away from him.

6 A NEW BEGINNING

I Samuel
II Samuel
I Chronicles

CHAPTER HIGHLIGHTS

- The Last Judge
- A Flawed King
- God's Anointed
- A Mighty Nation
- Davidic Covenant

Let's Get Started

During the age of the Judges Israel was a loose association of weak tribes, barely surviving in the Promised Land. In 1050 B.C. the last Judge, Samuel, **anointed** Saul, Israel's first king. The flawed King Saul was succeeded by David, who became Israel's greatest king. David united the Israelites into a single nation, defeated every foreign enemy, and established Jerusalem as Israel's political and religious capital. When David died in 970 B.C. the Israelites occupied ten times as much territory as when he became king.

__anoint:__ set apart for a task by pouring oil on a person's head

Stories Told And Retold

This pivotal period of Old Testament history is so important that its stories are told and retold in the Bible. The chart below shows how the Bible books that feature Samuel, Saul, and David overlap.

__Time Line #4__

Accounts of the New Beginning

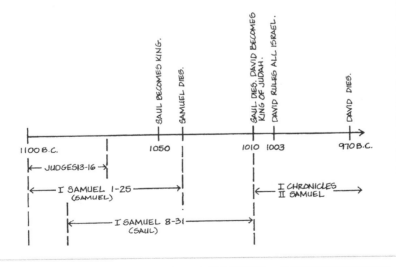

I SAMUEL

. . . origin of the monarchy

WHO	An unnamed author wrote
WHAT	this history of
WHERE	events in Canaan
WHEN	from 1050 B.C. to 1010 B.C.,
WHY	to record how Israel became a united nation ruled by kings.

Dedicated To The Lord

THE BIG PICTURE

KEY Symbols:

Israel's Leadership
God alone
Judges
kings

KEY POINT

Israel insisted on having a king, so God gave them one—a flawed one.

> **I Samuel** The book begins with the birth of Samuel and his dedication to the Lord. Early chapters highlight incidents from the ministry of Samuel, who was God's prophet and Israel's last Judge. Pressured by the people in his old age, Samuel anoints Saul as Israel's first king. The focus of I Samuel then shifts to Saul, whose flaws lead to God's rejection of him as king. Most of the book traces the relationship between Saul and a newcomer to his court, David, who will become king when Saul dies. I Samuel may be outlined as follows:
>
> - Samuel (Chapters 1–7)
> - Saul (Chapters 8–15)
> - Saul and David (Chapters 16–20)

 Who's Who

SAMUEL: As a child of three years, Samuel was dedicated by his mother to serve God at the Tabernacle. He later became Israel's last Judge and drove the Philistines from Israel's territory. When Samuel was old the Israelites demanded a king. On God's instructions Samuel anointed Saul, and later David, to become rulers of Israel.

What's Special In I Samuel 1–7?

☞ **Check It Out:**

I Samuel 1, 2

1 *Hannah's Prayer (I Samuel 1–2).* Hannah prayed desperately for a son and promised to dedicate him to the Lord. Her prayer answered, Hannah brought three-year-old Samuel to the Tabernacle, where he served God as priest, prophet, and Israel's last Judge. Hannah's prayer of praise expressed her joy, which came as a result of returning to God what he had given her.

2 *Israel's defeat (I Samuel 4–6)*. When a Philistine army invaded, two Israeli priests brought the **Ark of the Covenant** (see GWRV, page 166–167) to the battlefield at Aphek, counting on its magic powers to help them. The Philistines defeated Israel and captured the Ark. But the trophy, which symbolized God's presence, caused such terrible plagues that the Philistines quickly returned it to Israel. Though the movie *Raiders of the Lost Ark* is fiction, the Ark of the Covenant did exist, and the God of the Ark was and is real!

3 *Victory at Mizpah (I Samuel 7)*. Twenty years after the defeat at Aphek, Samuel purged idolatry from Israel and led the people back to God. When attacked by the Philistines again, Samuel prayed, and Israel won a great victory at Mizpah. It was such a decisive victory that it ended any immediate threat from the Philistines throughout Samuel's judgeship.

What, No Backbone?

SAUL: Saul, Israel's first king, was a tall young man whose early successes won him the allegiance of his people. Despite his impressive physique, Saul was morally weak. Under pressure, Saul failed to trust God and was unwilling to obey him. The result was that God eventually rejected his kingship.

What's Special In I Samuel 8–15?

1 *A matter of motive (I Samuel 8)*. Moses laid down laws under which Israel's kings were to rule. But when the Israelites demanded a king centuries later, it was because they wanted to be *like all the nations*. Before, Israel had been different—responsible to and dependent on God rather than a human ruler. The demand for a king was an overt rejection of God's direct rule.

2 *Saul's flaws revealed (I Samuel 13, 15:1–26)*. Israel's kings were spiritual as well as political leaders. A king's commitment to God set the tone for the nation. Two incidents reveal why Saul was unfit to rule God's people.

The first incident. A massive Philistine army assembled to attack Israel. Samuel told Saul to wait, and that within seven days he would come and intercede with God. Saul waited, but more and more of his army left. Finally Saul offered a sacrifice himself. Samuel rebuked Saul by saying, *You acted **foolishly**. . . . You have not kept the commandment the Lord your God gave you . . .* (I Samuel

☞ **Check It Out:**

Exodus 25:10–22

I Samuel 6

Ark of the Covenant:
Israel's holiest object; the gold-covered box contained the Ten Commandments, and symbolized God's presence on earth

☞ **Check It Out:**

I Samuel 7:3–14

Who's Who

☞ **Check It Out:**

Deuteronomy 17:14–20; I Samuel 8:1–7; 12:6–25

KEY POINT

A king's commitment to God set the tone for the nation.

☞ **Check It Out:**

I Samuel 13:3–13

foolish: *not stupid but morally wrong*

13:13). Saul not only disobeyed God's prophet, he disobeyed God's Law. Only a descendant of Aaron was qualified to offer a sacrifice.

The second incident. God commissioned Saul to utterly destroy the Amalekites. When Saul failed, he made excuses: *I was afraid of the people* [his own army] *and so I gave into them* (I Samuel 15:24). This rejection of God's eternal authority resulted in God's rejection of Saul's earthly authority.

How often do we hesitate to do what we know is right, out of concern for what others might think or say?

No End To Jealousy

DAVID: A towering Old Testament figure. As the youngest son in a large family, David guarded the family sheep. Living outdoors David developed a great awe of God the Creator, and while protecting his sheep from wild animals, David learned to trust God's living presence and power. David came to Saul's attention when as a teenager he faced and killed the giant Philistine warrior, Goliath. Enlisted in Saul's army as a junior commander, David's exploits thrilled the nation but aroused Saul's jealousy. David married one of Saul's daughters, but eventually the paranoid and hostile Saul determined to kill his son-in-law, whom he saw as a rival. Chapters 16–31 feature many stories about David's adventures during the years that he first served, and then fled from, King Saul.

What's Special In I Samuel 16–31?

1 *David is God's Choice* (I Samuel 16). God sent Samuel to anoint Saul's successor. When Samuel assumed that one of David's impressive-looking brothers was God's choice, the Lord corrected him. *Do not consider his appearance or his height . . . man looks at the outward appearance, but the Lord looks at the heart* (I Samuel 16:7). David, who was physically unimpressive, was chosen because he had a heart for God.

2 *David vs. Goliath* (I Samuel 17). No story better illuminates David's utter confidence in God than the familiar tale of David's unequal battle with the armored and giant Philistine warrior. The defeat of Goliath (see Illustration #10, page 61) demoralized the Philistines and led to a great Israelite victory.

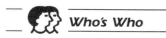
☞ **Check It Out:**

I Samuel 15:9–31

Something to Ponder

Who's Who

☞ **Check It Out:**

I Samuel 16–31

KEY Symbols:

Saul's Two Mistakes
  he made his own
    sacrifice
  he failed to destroy all
    the Amalekites

KEY Symbols:

David
  a heart for God

Illustration #10

How tall was Goliath?	What did a sling look like?	How heavy were sling stones?
At six cubits and a span, Goliath was over 9 feet tall!	It looked like a doubled rope with a leather pocket in the center.	Sling stones found on Isrealite battlefields were the size of tennis balls.

3 *Stories of David's Early Years (I Samuel 18–31).* The increasingly troubled relationship between King Saul and David is traced in the following stories. Reading two or three will provide a good amount of information about the respective characters of both David and Saul.

I Samuel	The Story
8:1–16	David's successes make Saul jealous and fearful.
18:17–30	Saul attempts to trick David into a fatal assault.
19:1–18	Saul hurls his own spear at David, then orders his death.
20:1–42	Saul's son Jonathan defends David's loyalty.
21:1–21	David is forced to flee the country.
22:6–23	Saul executes 85 priests who unwittingly helped David.
23:7–29	David assembles a small army, which Saul pursues.
24:1–22	David demonstrates his loyalty by sparing Saul's life.
26:1–25	David again spares Saul's life.
27:1–12	Discouraged, David leaves Israel and settles among the Philistines.
29:1–29	David avoids fighting Saul on the Philistine side.
31:1–11	Saul and Jonathan are killed in a battle with the Philistines.

☞ **Check It Out:**

I Samuel 17:20–54

Dig Deeper

II SAMUEL

. . . David's 40-year reign

Just the FACTS

WHO	An unnamed author
WHAT	wrote about the origin
WHERE	of Israel's royal line
WHEN	from 1010 B.C. to 970 B.C.,
WHY	to establish the right of David's descendants to the throne.

THE BIG PICTURE 🔍

II Samuel This book is a record of David's ascent to the throne and his many accomplishments during his 40-year reign. Both David's great strengths and personal failures are depicted for all to read. The book reviews:

- David's rule in Judah (II Samuel 1–4)
- David's uniting of Israel (II Samuel 5–24)

I CHRONICLES

. . . David's 40-year reign

Just the FACTS

WHO	An unnamed author
WHAT	reviewed David's reign
WHERE	over a united Israel
WHEN	from 1003 B.C. to 970 B.C.,
WHY	to encourage exiled Jews in the 500's B.C.

THE BIG PICTURE 🔍

I Chronicles This book emphasizes David's accomplishments that remind Jewish exiles in Babylon that God has promised to restore the monarchy ruled by a descendant of David, Israel's second king. The book contains:

- A record of David's acts (I Chronicles 11–29)
- Genealogies (I Chronicles 1–10)

A King After God's Own Heart

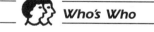
Who's Who

DAVID: I Samuel introduced David as a young, gifted, and perse-cuted officer in Saul's army and a member in his household. II Samuel and I Chronicles present a mature David who, under God, rules as King of Israel. David's great accomplishments are credited not just to his genius but to his commitment to the Lord. Truly, David's achievements were spectacular.

Larry Richards: The years of David complete Israel's transition from a loose tribal structure . . . to a **monarchy**. A number of important aspects of the transition are accomplished under David's leadership:

- Transition from government by Judges to an established monarchy.
- Transition from a loose **confederation** of tribes to a nation.
- Transition from **anarchy** to a strong central government.
- Transition from **bronze age** poverty to **iron age** economy and wealth.
- Transition from a subjected people to conquerors. David expanded Israel's territory some ten times!
- Transition from decentralized worship to centralized worship, with one city as both a political and religious capital.[1]

What's happening in the world while David is creating a nation? In . . .

Asia Minor	Ionian Greeks establish 12 cities.
China	An advanced mathematics textbook is published.
Europe	Gold is being used in jewelry.
India	The **caste system** is introduced, and the teaching of **transmigration** of souls originates.

monarchy: a government led by a king

confederation: closely associated but independent tribes

anarchy: living without laws

bronze age: a period of time when tools and weapons were made of bronze

Asia Minor: modern Turkey

Around the World

What's Special In The Books That Record The Events Of David's Reign?

1 *The Genealogy (I Chronicles 1–10).* The seemingly endless list of strange names puzzles people today. But to the Israelites the names were vital. Each name served to anchor in history the fact that, whatever might happen, the Hebrew people would remain God's chosen people. As descendants of Abraham, Isaac, and Jacob, the Jews are God's chosen inheritors of the covenant promises given to Abraham.

2 *David's seven-year reign in Judah (II Samuel 1–4).* After Saul's death the tribe of Judah recognized David as king. However, the Northern Hebrew tribes supported a son of Saul named Ishbosheth. Only after seven years, in 1003 B.C., was David named king of all the Israelites.

☞ **Check It Out:**

Genesis 12:1–3, 7

iron age: it began when people learned to make tools and weapons of iron

caste system: a way of classifying people by social groups they remain in for life

transmigration: the belief that after death a person may come back as a bug or animal

Illustration #11

Israelite Territory Before and After David's Reign—King David expanded Israel's borders to give his people ten times as much land as they occupied when Saul became King. The striped area of land indicates the extent of Israel's Kingdom before David's reign. The dashed line indicates the extent of Israel's Kingdom at the end of David's reign.

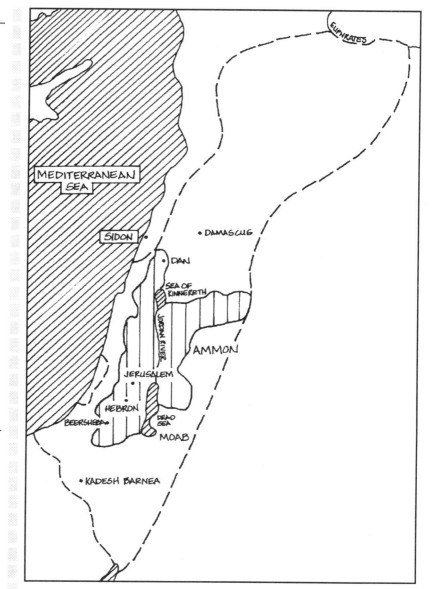

KEY Symbols:

Israel Under David
established monarchy
a nation
strong central
government
iron age economy
conquerors
centralized worship

3 *David's military victories.* Aided and guided by God, David's armies imposed crushing defeats on the nations that surrounded Israel. The victories expanded the territory controlled by Israel (see Illustration #11, this page) by ten times. The victories also gave David control of trade routes, which brought great wealth to Israel. The "war stories" illustrate David's conscious dependence on God; they are found in the following passages:

The War Stories of King David

The Enemy	The War Story
The Jebusites	II Samuel 5:6–16
The Philistines	II Samuel 5:17–25; I Chronicles 20:4–8
The Moabites	II Samuel 8:2
The Syrians	II Samuel 8:3–11; I Chronicles 18
The Edomites	II Samuel 8:13–14
The Ammonites and Arameans	II Samuel 10:1–19; I Chronicles 19

Dig Deeper

4 *The Davidic Covenant (II Samuel 7; I Chronicles 17).* God had promised Abraham, *all peoples on earth will be blessed through you* (Genesis 12:3), but God did not explain to Abraham how he would keep that promise. The Davidic Covenant revealed that God intended to keep his promise through a descendant of David.

King David longed to build a temple in honor of God, but God would not let him. Instead God promised to build David a **house**. God promised there would always be a descendant of David qualified to inherit Israel's throne. God's covenant promise to David concludes, *your house and your kingdom will endure forever before me; your throne will be established forever* (II Samuel 7:16).

This Davidic Covenant is the foundation of much Old Testament prophecy, which describes an era of world-wide peace under David's promised descendant. The New Testament gospels make it clear that the person the promises refer to is none other than Jesus Christ.

Jesus Christ, the only living descendant of David, will fulfill God's promise and rule an eternal kingdom. The enemy Jesus defeated in his resurrection was <u>death itself</u>. Truly *all peoples on earth are blessed by the forgiveness and eternal life Christ makes available to whoever will trust him.

5 *David's personal failures (II Samuel 11–18, 24).* The annals of other ancient rulers glorify their victories and ignore their defeats or personal flaws, but the Bible graphically describes David's sins and weaknesses. David is no mythical hero; he is a flesh-and-blood human being whose great strengths are matched by great weaknesses. Each story sketched below describes a sin or failure of Israel's greatest king.

☞ **Check It Out:**

Psalm 89:2–8; Jeremiah 33:20–22; II Samuel 7:1–17; Isaiah 9:6–7; Jeremiah 33:14–26

☞ **Check It Out:**

Matthew 1:1–16

I Corinthians 15:20–28

☞ **GO TO:**

I Corinthians 15:54–57 (death itself)

house: *here it is both a temple and a dynasty*

KEY Symbols:

Abrahamic Covenant
always bless descendents
- the Jews

Davidic Covenant
your kingdom will endure forever
- Jesus Christ

The Sins of King David

II Samuel 11	II Samuel 13	II Samuel 14	II Samuel 24
David seduces Bathsheba, and when she becomes pregnant, David arranges for her husband's death in battle.	When one of David's sons rapes a half–sister, David fails to act. The girl's full brother, Absolom, murders the rapist.	David neither punishes nor forgives his son Absolom. The alienated Absolom plans a rebellion in which many lose their lives.	David conducts a military census, which displays a lack of trust in God.

☞ **GO TO:**

Romans 5:9–11 (salvation)

Remember This . . .

Lessons from David's Flaws And Failures

1) Even the greatest saints have inherited Adam's sin nature. We all need the <u>salvation</u> God offers those who trust him.

2) David's sin with Bathsheba robbed him of *moral authority* in his own family and paralyzed his ability to correct his sons. There are consequences even to forgiven sins.

3) Although Saul and David both sinned, there was a significant difference between them. David took public responsibility for his sins, and openly sought God's forgiveness. Saul made excuses, and pretended all was right between him and the Lord. God can and will forgive our sins, but we must be honest with ourselves, with him, and with others.

What Others are Saying:

Blaise Pascal: It is equally dangerous to man to know God without knowing his own wretchedness, and to know his own wretchedness without knowing God.[2]

From David's Great Cry Of Confession:

Have mercy on me, O God, according to your unfailing love . . .
For I know my transgressions, and my sin is always before me.
Against you, you only, have I sinned and done what is evil in your sight . . .
Create in me a pure heart, O God, and renew a right spirit within me.
Save me from **bloodguilt***, O God, the God who saves me, and my tongue will sing of your righteousness.* (Psalm 51)

Something to Ponder

bloodguilt: a guilt incurred from bloodshed

St. Augustine: The confession of evil works is the first beginning to good works.[3]

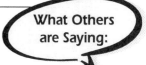

What Others are Saying:

6 *David's religious reforms (I Chronicles 22–26, 28–29).* Early in his reign David had brought the Ark of the Covenant to Jerusalem. When his military conquests were complete, David focused his attention on worship. He made detailed plans for the Temple his son Solomon would build. He contributed vast wealth to the project and collected only the best building materials. David also developed job descriptions for the priests and Levites who would serve at the Temple. He hired trained musicians and singers. One of David's greatest accomplishments was to personally write many of the songs and poems to be used in public worship. Many of these songs and poems are recorded for us in Psalms, the nineteenth book of the Old Testament.

When David died in 970 B.C. he left a powerful, wealthy and united Hebrew nation, eager to honor God and to celebrate him.

Study Questions

1. What three key figures marked the transition to monarchy?
2. What were conditions like in Israel when Samuel was born?
3. How had conditions changed by the time David died?
4. What were the most important differences between Saul and David? Why did one fail and the other succeed?
5. What were at least three of David's major accomplishments?
6. How did God's promise to David in II Samuel 7 relate to the covenant promises God made to Abraham?
7. What are some of the things that people today might learn from a study of David's life?

CHAPTER WRAP-UP

- I Samuel records the beginning of the Israelites' transition from a loose association of tribes to a nation ruled by kings.
- Samuel, Israel's last Judge, anointed Saul king about 1050 B.C.
- Saul failed to trust or obey God and was not allowed to found a dynasty.
- David, Saul's successor, succeeded in building Israel into a powerful and dominant nation of the Middle East.
- God gave a promise covenant to David, guaranteeing that a descendant of his would rule forever.

7 ISRAEL'S GOLDEN AGE

I Kings 1–11
II Chronicles 1–9
Job
Psalms
Proverbs
Ecclesiastes
Song of Songs (Song of Solomon)

CHAPTER HIGHLIGHTS

- Wisdom and Prosperity
- Solomon's Temple
- Books of Poetry
- Praise and Worship
- Seaching for a Meaning

Let's Get Started

David's kingdom dominated the Middle East through the reign of David's son, Solomon. The 80 years that David and Solomon ruled were Israel's golden age. The nation was prosperous and powerful. The two kings initiated great literary works, and a magnificent Temple was erected in Jerusalem. The golden age would soon pass, but its glories would be remembered.

Time Line #5

During these 80 years, the normally dominant powers, Egypt to the South, and the Hittites and Assyrians to the North, were weak and unable to threaten Israel.

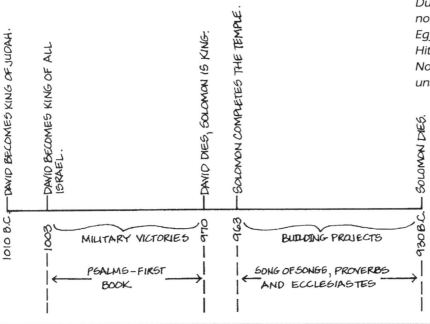

Even The Wisest May Fall

SOLOMON: Solomon succeeded David as king of Israel. Solomon was famous for his intellectual achievements. He wrote <u>thousands of proverbs and over a thousand songs</u>. He also became a botanist, cataloging plant life, and a zoologist, researching the habits of animals. Solomon found time to carry out many building projects, including construction of the magnificent Jerusalem Temple, which was one of the wonders of the ancient world. Solomon's wealth, like his wisdom, was legendary. Solomon's personal income, not including monies from taxes and trade, was <u>an annual 25 tons of gold!</u>

What's Special About Solomon's Reign?

1 *God appeared to Solomon (I Kings 3, 9; II Chronicles 1, 7).* God spoke to Solomon twice. At the beginning of Solomon's reign the young king asked for *a discerning heart to govern your people and to distinguish between right and wrong* (I Kings 3:9). This unselfish request pleased God, who promised Solomon wisdom, wealth, and a long life.

Later in Solomon's reign God spoke to Solomon again. The Lord encouraged Solomon to *walk before me in integrity of heart and uprightness. . . .* (I Kings 9:4) and warned Solomon about the danger of <u>disobedience</u>.

2 *Solomon constructed the Jerusalem Temple (I Kings 5–8; II Chronicles 2–7).* Ten of the 20 chapters that feature Solomon are devoted to the construction and dedication of the Jerusalem Temple (see Illustration #12, page 71). Clearly the Temple was important. But why? First, the Temple was the place where God met with his people. It was the only place where sacrifices could be offered, and prayers to God were to be made facing toward the Temple. Second, during the entire kingdom period the spiritual state of God's people was reflected in either their neglect of or their devotion to Temple worship.

Solomon's Temple was destroyed by the Babylonians in 586 B.C., but another Temple was later built on the same spot. That Temple was expanded and beautified in the time of Christ. It too was destroyed, by the Romans in 70 A.D.

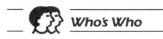

Who's Who

☞ **Check It Out:**

I Kings 1–11

II Chronicles 1–9

☞ **GO TO:**

I Kings 4:29–30 (songs)

II Chronicles 9:13 (gold)

☞ **Check It Out:**

I Kings 3:1–15; 9:1–9

☞ **GO TO:**

I Kings 9:6–30 (disobedience)

☞ **Check It Out:**

II Chronicles 3–6

KEY Symbols:

The Temple
where God met his people
a reflection of the nation's devotion to God

Illustration #12

Solomon's Temple—Solomon lavished tons of gold on the magnificent Temple he built to honor God. At today's prices, it would be worth five billion dollars!

3 *Solomon turned from God (I Kings 11).* Solomon's early promise was never fulfilled. Despite his youthful dedication to God, Solomon turned away from the Lord in his later years. In disobedience to God's Law, he cemented treaties with many nations by marrying women of foreign royal families. That choice led directly to tragedy.

☞ **Check It Out:**

Deuteronomy 20:7

Charles Swindoll: In Chapter 11, the hinge of I Kings, Solomon slips from fame to failure, from success to sensuality, from temple-builder to idol worshiper. His spiritual troubles, as with his father David, started at home. Solomon indulged his desire for foreign women—he had *seven hundred wives, princesses, and three hundred concubines.* And they *turned his heart away* from the Lord to worship their false gods.[1]

What Others are Saying:

Poetry—Who Reads That?

It's appropriate to pause here in our study of the Bible, and to explore the Old Testament's five fascinating books of poetry.

Israel's golden age was a time of great literary achievement. A collection of praise poems, the book of Psalms, was begun by David, who wrote many of them himself. His son Solomon recorded many of the brief sayings found in the book of Proverbs. Solomon also wrote a dark philosophical treatise (Ecclesiastes) and a **lyric poem** celebrating married love (**Song of Songs**).

These books with Job are poetry. But Hebrew poetry is unusual. Rather than depending on **rhyme and meter**, Hebrew poetry depends on setting ideas side by side, in a pattern called "parallelism."

lyric poem: having the form and general effect of a song

Song of Songs: also called the Song of Solomon

rhyme and meter: placing emphasis on syllables

The Basic Forms of Poetic Parallelism are:

Synonymous parallelism: the thought in the first and second lines is the same.

> *Our mouths were filled with laughter, our tongues with songs of joy* (Psalm 126:2).

• • •

Antithetical parallelism: the thought in the first line is emphasized by its opposite.

> *A kind man benefits himself, but a cruel man brings himself harm* (Proverbs 11:17).

• • •

Synthetic parallelism: the thought in the first line is developed or completed by thoughts in following lines.

> *I will lie down and sleep in peace, for you alone, O Lord, make me to dwell in safety* (Psalm 4:8).

Poetry that depends on rhyme or rhythm is difficult to translate. But Hebrew poetry can be rendered effectively in any language. The vivid power of Hebrew poetry was often used by the prophets to enhance their message. Such power is reflected in the five poetic books of the Old Testament: Job, Psalms, Proverbs, Ecclesiastes, and Song of Songs.

JOB

. . . the mystery of suffering

Just the FACTS

WHO	An unknown author
WHAT	related the story of Job
WHERE	in Mesopotamia
WHEN	some 2,000 years before Christ,
WHY	to explore faith's response to human suffering.

Oh, Woe Is Me

The Story of Job

☞ **Check It Out:**

Job 1, 2

1 *Job 1–2.* Job is a man singled out by God himself as *blameless and upright.* When Satan argues that this is only because God has blessed Job and protected him from harm, God permits Satan to attack Job. In a single day sudden tragedies strip Job of his wealth and family, but Job remains true to God. Even when Satan afflicts Job with agonizing open sores, Job remains faithful. Satan, proven wrong, is not heard from again. But Job's suffering continues.

2 *Job 3–31.* Three friends come to console Job and are stunned at his condition. Job, near despair, finally tells the three that he wishes he'd died at birth.

The three friends begin a dialogue with Job. Each of the three is convinced that God is just and righteous, and that God punishes sin. They conclude Job must have sinned. The friends urge Job to confess the hidden sin that God is punishing and to appeal for mercy. But Job's conscience is clear: there is no hidden sin. He can't explain why God is making him suffer, but he refuses to confess sins he is not aware of.

As the dialogue continues, Job's three friends press harder and harder. Job must have sinned, and sinned terribly. Job argues back that he has not sinned and that God isn't being fair.

3 *Job 32–37.* Job and his friends are at an impasse. Then a younger man named Elihu speaks up. He points out that suffering need not always be punishment. God may use suffering to teach and to get a person's attention. So Job's friends are wrong to attack him as a sinner, and Job is wrong to say God isn't being fair.

4 *Job 38–41.* Then God himself speaks to Job. God does not tell Job why he permitted the suffering. He simply reminds Job of two basic truths: God is great beyond human comprehension, and human beings are weak and limited.

5 *Job 42.* Job realizes it is not a creature's place to explain the Creator's doings. God rebukes the three friends, and then restores all Job has lost and more.

Thinking About Job

The book of Job does not tell us why God allows good people to suffer. It does remind us that people of faith respond to suffering differently than those without faith. Some, like the three friends, feel driven to ask "Why?" Others, like Job, learn to simply trust God no matter what comes.

The New Testament book of James notes *You have heard of Job's perserverance and have seen what the Lord finally brought about. The Lord is full of compassion and mercy* (James 5:11). Even when God permits suffering, his ultimate intent is to bless.

☞ **Check It Out:**

Job 8:1–7; 27:1–6; 31

☞ **Check It Out:**

Job 36:11–16

☞ **Check It Out:**

Job 38:4–18

☞ **Check It Out:**

Job 42

KEY POINT

God is great beyond human comprehension, and human beings are weak and limited.

Warren Wiersbe: God does not have to explain his ways to us. It is enough for us to know that he cares and that he never makes a mistake. We do not live by explanations: we live by promises.[2]

Max Lucado: God has given us peace in our pain. He covers us all the time. For when we are out of control, he is still there.[3]

PSALMS

. . . the book of praises

WHO	David and others
WHAT	penned these poems
WHERE	in ancient Israel
WHEN	over a span of centuries,
WHY	as an aid to private and congregational worship.

Let Us Praise The Lord

What's Special About Psalms?

1 *The five "books" within the book of Psalms.* Each *book* represents a collection of poems. The first book (Psalm 1–41) was collected in the time of David. The last book (Psalm 107–150) was collected around the time of <u>Ezra</u>, some 600 years later. Many of the psalms were used in worship before being included in one of the official collections.

2 *The very personal nature of the book of prayer and praise.* One of the most striking features of the psalms is the depth of emotion they display. The psalms remind us that whatever we may feel—anger or pain, thankfulness or joy—we can freely pour out our hearts to the Lord. As we share our innermost emotions with the Lord we can be confident that he hears and cares, and that God will work within our hearts as well as in our circumstances.

Psalms That Touch Our Hearts

How do we deal with strong emotions? What is the value of expressing our feelings freely in conversation with God? Below is a list of emotions along with a list of pairs of psalms. Reading at least two of the psalms will provide an introduction to how the psalms express emotion.

KEY POINT

Even when God permits suffering, his ultimate intent is to bless.

Just the FACTS

☞ **GO TO:**

Ezra 7:6–10 (Ezra)

KEY POINT

God hears our prayer and praise and in all things he is watching over us.

Expressions of Emotion

The Emotion	Scripture
Anger at others	Psalm 7, 36
Guilt over sins	Psalm 32, 51
Anxiety or fear	Psalm 23, 64
Discouragement	Psalm 42, 107
Joy	Psalm 33, 98
Loneliness	Psalm 25, 91
Stress	Psalm 31, 89
Troubled	Psalm 10, 126
Weakness	Psalm 62, 102
Envy	Psalm 16, 73

Dig Deeper

3 *Classification of psalms.* While we can describe the psalms by the emotions they express, these wonderful poems can also be classified by theme as shown below.

What's To Talk About?

Type of Psalm	Theme	Example (Psalm)
Penitential	Confess sins	6, 32, 51, 102, 130
Wisdom	Consider right choices	1, 37, 49, 73, 127
Messianic	Anticipate Christ	22, 89, 110
Imprecatory	Call on God to Judge	35, 58, 109, 137
Lament	Complain to God	4, 12, 26, 57, 88
Praise	Thanks for deliverance	18, 30, 34, 116, 138
Praise	Praise for God himself	103, 113, 117, 146

Remember This . . .

KEY Symbols:

The Book of Psalms
prayers
hymns
confessions
songs

4 *The book of Psalms' life-changing impact.* More than any other book of the Bible, the book of Psalms explores the personal nature of our relationship with God. Anyone who wants to grow to know God better will find the psalms an unmatched help and guide.

What Others are Saying:

Warren Wiersbe: The book of Psalms is a collection of very personal songs and poems. As the book grew over the centuries, its contents were adapted by the Jews for their corporate worship as well as for their personal devotions. In this collection you find prayers from sufferers, hymns of praise, confessions of sin, confessions of faith, nature hymns, and songs that teach Jewish history, and in each one the focal point for faith is the Lord. Whether the writer is looking back at history, looking up into the heavens, or looking around at his problems, he first of all looks by faith to the Lord. The psalms teach us to have a personal relationship with God as we tell him our hurts and our needs and as we meditate on his greatness and glory.[4]

Albert H. Baylis: Innumerable saints and sinners through centuries of time have been uplifted, consoled, inspired, and radically changed by reading and meditating on the Psalms.[5]

PROVERBS

. . . guidelines for daily life

Just the FACTS

WHO	Solomon and others
WHAT	contributed wise sayings
WHERE	in Israel
WHEN	some 900 years before Christ,
WHY	to help readers make good decisions.

Wisdom For Today

Charles Swindoll: What exactly is a proverb? The Hebrew root for proverb, *mashal*, gives us a clue. It means *to represent, be like*, conveying the idea of comparing the familiar with the unfamiliar to teach a guiding principle. Proverbs, by nature, are brief—the majority in this book are two lines. But these short, observant statements declare profound truths that give wisdom for life.[6]

The Book of Proverbs begins with a Statement of Purpose. The proverbs are:

Something to Ponder

> . . . *for attaining wisdom and discipline,*
> *for understanding words of insight;*
> *for acquiring a disciplined and prudent life,*
> *for doing what is right and just and fair* . . . (Proverbs 1:2, 3)

What's Special About Proverbs?

1 *The book of Proverbs states general principles.* These principles are applicable to all people everywhere, not just to believers. The proverbs are not promises given by God. They describe what will usually happen when a person makes a right choice, not what God guarantees will happen.

2 *The book of Proverbs is about choices.* The writers are not trying to convey information, but to guide decisions. The writers are concerned that we do the right thing, and avoid the harmful consequences of bad decisions.

3 *"Fear of the Lord" is critical.* The book of Proverbs clearly states that *fear of the Lord is the beginning of knowledge, but fools despise wisdom and discipline* (Proverbs 1:7). Fear of the Lord is not terror but a reverential acknowledgment of his power and his presence. Only a firm belief in God will keep human beings on the wise moral pathway described in Proverbs.

4 *Many topics are explored in the book of Proverbs.* The chart below lists Proverbs on a variety of topics.

KEY Symbols:

Fear of the Lord

a reverential acknowledgment of his power and presence

Dig Deeper

Topic	Selected Proverbs
Adultery	5:1–6 / 6:24–32 / 7:6–27 / 22:14 / 23:26–28 / 29:1 / 30:7
Alcohol	20;1 / 23:20, 21, 29–35 / 31:4–7
Crime	6:30–31 / 10:9–16 / 13:11 / 15:6, 27 / 16:8, 19 / 17:15, 23
Discipline	3:11–12 / 5:12–14 / 9:7–10 / 13:18, 24 / 19:18 / 22:15 / 27:5
Friendship	12:26 / 13:20 / 16:28 / 17:17 / 18:1, 24 / 19:17 / 22:10
Gossip	11:13 / 16:28 / 18:8 / 20:19 / 26:22
Government	8:15–16 / 14:28, 34–35 / 16:12–15 / 18:17 / 24:24–25 / 25:5
Laziness	6:9–11 / 12:24–27 / 13:4 / 15:19 / 19:15 / 20:4, 20 / 24:30–34
Lies	6:16, 17 / 12:17–19, 22 / 14:5, 24 / 17:4, 20 / 24:28–29 / 30:8
Love	10:12 / 15:17 / 16:6 / 17:9, 17 / 19:22 / 20:6
Neighbors	3:29, 30 / 6:16–19 / 11:9 / 14:20, 21 / 26:17–20 / 29:5
Parent/child	6:20–23 / 10:1 / 15:20 / 17:6, 21, 25 / 22:6 / 23:13–14, 22, 24
The Poor	13:8, 18, 23 / 14:20, 31 / 17:5 / 19:1, 4, 7, 17, 22 / 30:11–14
Pride	6:16–17 / 8:13 / 11:2 / 15:25 / 18:5, 18 / 18:12 / 25:6–7
Temper	14:17, 29 / 15:1, 18 / 16:32 / 19:19 / 22:24–25 / 29:11, 22
Wealth	10:2, 4, 15, 22 / 11:4, 28 / 13:8, 21–22 / 14:24 / 20:21 / 23:4–8
Work	12:11, 14, 24, 27 / 14:23 / 16:26 / 18:9 / 22:29 / 27:18, 23–27

Charles Swindoll: Common sense is good, but it's not enough. We need the love of and respect for the Lord to form the basis of our choices. So, take and read the Proverbs—and grow in the knowledge of God (Proverbs 2:5).[7]

What Others are Saying:

ECCLESIASTES

. . . *searching for life's meaning*

Just the FACTS

WHO   Solomon
WHAT   wrote this book
WHERE   as King in Jerusalem
WHEN   near the end of his life,
WHY   to ask whether human life has meaning apart
                from a personal relationship with God.

Searching For A Meaning Without God

The Story Behind Ecclesiastes

Near the end of his life Solomon lost his spiritual moorings and began to worship the gods of his foreign wives. During this time Solomon decided to search for life's meaning. He wrote, *I devoted myself to study and to explore by wisdom all that is done under heaven* (Ecclesiastes 1:13). Solomon would use his great intelligence to test and explore human experience. But he would limit himself to *all that is done under heaven.* Solomon would not consider truth revealed by God! He would search for meaning in the brief years human beings have to live here on earth.

And Solomon failed! Despite the fact that he had access to every pleasure, wealth beyond counting, and achievements which won the acclaim of all, Solomon summed up his findings in a few tragic words:

> *"Meaningless! Meaningless!"*
> *says the Teacher.*
> *"Utterly meaningless!*
> *Everything is meaningless"*
> (Ecclesiastes 1:2)

What's Special About Ecclesiastes?

1 *Ecclesiastes is a book of inspiration, but not of revelation.* Ecclesiastes is an accurate report of Solomon's reasoning. But not everything Solomon writes is true. This book is in the Bible to remind us of an important truth. Try as we will to find meaning apart from God, we will fail. For apart from God and his loving purpose for us, human life is meaningless.

KEY Symbols:

Inspiration
God makes sure that the message communicates what he wants it to

Revelation
God himself unveils truth we could not otherwise know

___

KEY POINT

Try as we will to find meaning apart from God, we will fail. For apart from God and his loving purpose for us, human life is meaningless.

Larry Richards: This book is not communication of truth from God, but an inspired report of Solomon's reasoning. What then is the value of this unique Old Testament book? It is not meant for us to use as a source of information. Instead it is meant to communicate in compelling and deeply moving tones a message needed by all mankind. Apart from the perspective on life God's Word provides, life truly is meaningless and empty.[8]

2 *Where did Solomon look for meaning? (Ecclesiastes 1:12–6:12).* The first half of Ecclesiastes, Chapters 1 through 6, contains a report of where Solomon searched for the elusive answer. Here are his conclusions:

Dig Deeper

Solomon's search for meaning	Scripture
Introduction	Ecclesiastes 1:1–11
Can knowledge provide meaning?	Ecclesiastes 1:12–18
Can pleasure provide meaning?	Ecclesiastes 2:1–11
Can accomplishments provide meaning?	Ecclesiastes 2:17–26
Can human beings make any real changes in the way things are?	Ecclesiastes 3:16–22
Man's fate suggests that life is meaningless.	Ecclesiastes 4:1–16
Man's inability to affect God's works suggests that life is meaningless.	Ecclesiastes 5:1–7
Can possessions give meaning to life?	Ecclesiastes 5:8–6:2
Man's inability to control his future suggests that life is meaningless.	Ecclesiastes 6:3–12

3 *How can we make the best of meaningless lives? (Ecclesiastes 7:1–12:8).* Solomon found that human life—if this life is all there is—can have no meaning. But he couldn't resist pointing out that even under the circumstances, some courses of action are better than others.

4 *Solomon's epilogue (Ecclesiastes 12:9–14).* As the book concludes, we can sense Solomon looking back over the years to the bright promise of his youth. Here are his recommendations:

> *Now all has been heard;*
>> *here is the conclusion of the matter:*
> *Fear God and keep his commandments,*
>> *for this is the whole duty of man.*
> *For God will bring every deed into judgment,*
>> *including every hidden thing,*
>> *whether it is good or evil. (Ecclesiastes 12:13, 14)*

KEY POINT

Fear God and keep his commandments, for this is the whole duty of man.

To Make the Best of a Meaningless Life	Scripture
Make the best choices you can	Ecclesiastes 7:1–12
Adopt a fatalistic attitude	Ecclesiastes 7:13, 14
Avoid extremes	Ecclesiastes 7:15–22
Be wise, avoid folly	Ecclesiastes 7:23–8:1
Submit to authorities	Ecclesiastes 8:2–10
Be God-fearing	Ecclesiastes 8:11–13
Enjoy the good things life offers	Ecclesiastes 8:14, 15
Enjoy life while you can: death awaits	Ecclesiastes 9:1–12
Follow wisdom	Ecclesiastes 9:13–10:20
Prepare for the future	Ecclesiastes 11:1–6
Enjoy your youth—old age is creeping up	Ecclesiastes 11:7–12:8

Dig Deeper

What Others are Saying:

Billy Graham: Youth is the time to decide for Christ and for Righteousness.[9]

SONG OF SONGS

. . . the celebration of love

Just the FACTS

WHO	A young Solomon
WHAT	wrote this love poem
WHERE	in Jerusalem
WHEN	during his early reign,
WHY	as a celebration of married love.

The Love Of A Lifetime

The Story Behind Song of Songs

Is this the story of Solomon's attempt to woo a young woman, the Shulamite, away from her rural lover? Or does the poem grow out of Solomon's one early experience of true love? Or is it simply an **allegory**, intended to depict the love of God for Israel, or of Christ for the believer? Charles Swindoll and many others think this poem is about true love, a love that was lost as Solomon abandoned **monogamous** marriage for politically motivated multiple marriages.

allegory: a story used to make a point

monogamous: a life-long commitment to a single spouse

Bruce Wilkinson: Solomon's relationship with the Shulamite was the only pure romance he ever experienced. The bulk of his marriages were political arrangements. It is significant that the Shulamite was a vineyard keeper of no great means. This book was also written before Solomon plunged into gross immorality and idolatry.[10]

What's Special About Song Of Songs?

1 *The poem is written in three voices.* The voice of the *Lover* is Solomon's. The voice of the *Beloved* is the Shulamite. The other voice is a *chorus* of the Shulamite's friends.

KEY Symbols:

Three Voices
Lover—Solomon
Beloved—Shulamite
chorus—Shulamite's
friends

2 *The poem is divided into three sections.*

   1) The Courtship (Song of Songs 1:2–3:5)

   2) The Wedding (Song of Songs 3:6–5:1)

   3) The Deepening Relationship (Song of Songs 5:2–8:14)

Charles Swindoll: What an ideal we have in Solomon's Song for Christian marriages! What freedom to be wildly in love, romantic, tender, and sensual. To be committed, secure, [and] happy.[11]

What Others are Saying:

☞ **Check It Out:**

Song of Songs 8:1–14

3 The Song of Songs, by its positive example, can disclose at least four things our marriages need.

  1) *Personal Attention.* Physical love is an art that cannot grow without being nurtured. It requires emotional intimacy, the enjoyment of being with one another.

  2) *Leisure.* Creativity, enjoyment, and playfulness only blossom in a relationship when they are cultivated in the soil of time.

  3) *Meaningful Getaways.* Special times away from the clutter and clamor of constant demands can refresh a relationship.

  4) *Security.* Reaching the deepest level of secure, peaceful love takes commitment.

KEY Symbols:

Marriages Need
personal attention
leisure
meaningful getaways
security

Study Questions

1. Who were the two kings who ruled during Israel's golden age?
2. What accomplishments marks Israel's golden age?
3. What four books of Bible poetry were written or begun during the golden age?
4. What characteristic of Hebrew poetry makes it possible to easily translate it into any language?
5. What is the theme of each of the following books of Bible poetry?

   Job _____

   Psalms _____

   Proverbs _____

   Ecclesiastes _____

   Song of Songs _____

CHAPTER WRAP-UP

- The years 1010 B.C. to 930 B.C. were Israel's golden years, marked by power, prosperity, and literary production.
- David and Solomon were the two kings who ruled during the golden years.
- The construction of the Jerusalem Temple was the most notable achievement of King Solomon.
- The period also witnessed the initiation of great poetic, literary productions.
- The book of Job, from an earlier era, explores how a person of faith can respond to suffering.
- Psalms, much of which was written by King David, is a guide to worship and a personal relationship with God.
- Proverbs, much of which was written by Solomon, gives practical advice on making wise and right choices.
- Ecclesiastes, written after Solomon was estranged from God, is a search for meaning in life apart from God.
- The Song of Songs is a poem exploring the joys of married lovers.

8 THE NORTHERN KINGDOM: ISRAEL

I Kings 12–22
II Kings
Jonah
Amos
Hosea

CHAPTER HIGHLIGHTS

- A Kingdom Divided
- Israel
- Speaking Prophets
- Writing Prophets

Let's Get Started

When Solomon died in 930 B.C. (see Time Line #6, page 112) the unified Hebrew Kingdom (see GWDN, pages 35–37) was torn apart. Two tribal groups to the south remained committed to rulers from David's family line. The Southern Kingdom was known as Judah. But the ten northern Hebrew tribes set up a rival kingdom, which kept the old name of Israel. From the beginning the kings of Israel abandoned God's Law in favor of a counterfeit religion. Despite the ministry of prophets sent to call Israel back to God, the Northern Kingdom continued on its fatal course. In 722 B.C. Israel fell to the Assyrians. Its citizens were taken captive and dispersed across the Assyrian empire.

I, II Kings

. . . a historical account

WHO	An unnamed author
WHAT	evaluated the reigns of kings
WHERE	from Israel and Judah
WHEN	between 970 B.C. and 586 B.C.,
WHY	to demonstrate the value of obeying and the danger of disobeying God.

KEY Symbols:

Northern Kingdom
ISRAEL (RETAINED NAME)

ten tribes
- Jeroboam
- Assyrian captivity

Southern Kingdom
JUDAH (JERUSALEM)

two tribes
- Rehoboam

Just the FACTS

☞ **Check It Out:**

I Kings 12

apostate: one who has
rebelled against what one
has believed

☞ **Check It Out:**

II Kings 16–22

KEY Symbols:

Prophets

speaking
- Elijah
- Elisha

writing
- Jonah
- Amos
- Hosea

We Don't Need Them

When Solomon died, the people appealed to his son Rehoboam for tax relief. The foolish young king refused. The ten northern tribes rebelled and crowned Jeroboam as their king. Jerusalem, the site of Solomon's Temple, lay in the South. That worried Jeroboam. If the people of the North went to Jerusalem to worship, as God's Law required, how long would they remain loyal to him? So Jeroboam created his own religion, one that mimicked the faith God had revealed to Moses. Jeroboam appointed his own priests, set up calf idols at worship centers in Bethel and Dan, and established his own religious holidays. While claiming that this religion was a vehicle for worship of the Lord, every act of "worship" was in direct violation of God's Law.

Every ruler of the Northern Kingdom supported this counterfeit religion and *did evil in God's sight.* There was no way that **apostate** Israel could survive or avoid God's judgment.

Overview

The chart on page 85 identifies the kings and prophets of the Northern Hebrew Kingdom. Not one of these kings sought to honor God. For fascinating insight into the lives of the evil rulers who governed Israel, read the stories told of King Ahab.

Prophetic Voices

God did not abandon Israel during the 200 years (930–722 B.C.) that the Northern Hebrew Kingdom existed. Again and again God sent prophets who warned the Israelites and urged them to return to him.

Two categories of prophets are found in the Bible. Some were *speaking prophets*, whose stories are woven into a historical narrative. Others were *writing prophets*, whose messages are recorded as books of the Bible. Elijah and Elisha were speaking prophets whom God sent to Israel. Jonah, Amos, and Hosea were writing prophets who preached in the North.

The books of the writing prophets are collected together at the end of the Old Testament. But to best understand the writing prophets, we need to understand the historical context in which their messages were given.

What was the message of the prophets God sent to the Northern Kingdom? And how are their messages important to us today?

Kings and Prophets of the Northern Kingdom

King	Prophets	Years Reigned	Scripture
Jeroboam I	–	22	I Kings 12–14
Nadab	–	2	I Kings 15
Baasha	–	24	I Kings 15–16
Elah	–	2	I Kings 16
Zimri	–	7 days	I Kings 16
Omri	–	12	I Kings 16
Ahab	Elijah	22	I Kings 16–22
Ahaziah	Elijah	2	I Kings 22; II Kings 1
Jehoram (Joram)	Elisha	12	I Kings 3–8
Jehu	Elisha	28	II Kings 9–10
Jehoahaz (Joahaz)	Elisha	17	II Kings 13
Jehoash (Joash)	Elisha	16	II Kings 13
Jeroboam II	Jonah and Amos	41	II Kings 14
Zechariah	Hosea	6 months	II Kings 15
Shallum	Hosea	1 month	II Kings 15
Menahem	Hosea	10	II Kings 15
Pekahiah	Hosea	2	II Kings 15
Pekah	Hosea	20	II Kings 15
Hoshea	Hosea	9	II Kings 17

What Others are Saying:

Charles Swindoll: The prophets did a lot more than proclaim, *The end is near.* They spoke to their times, rebuking kings, priests, and people for such issues as injustice, corruption, idolatry, empty ritualism, violence, divorce, pride, materialism, greed, and the oppression of the poor and helpless. If they would not heed to rebukes, the prophets warned of God's coming judgment against their faithlessness and sin. If they did repent, however, the prophets assured them of God's mercy, comfort, and blessings. . . . Though we don't have prophets today in the biblical sense, the voices of these Old Testament prophets resound with relevant truth.[1]

Preach It!

Most people know that the Bible contains miracle stories, but few are aware that hundreds of years of Bible history might pass without any miracles at all. In fact, most of the miracles recorded in Scripture took place in three relatively brief periods!

The *first age of miracles* spanned just 50 years. It included the cluster of miracles God performed through Moses to force Pharaoh to free his Israelite slaves, and additional miracles as Israel traveled to the Promised Land.

The *second age of miracles* also lasted about 50 years, during the time of Elijah and Elisha. The miracles performed by these two prophets served as a fresh revelation of God's power and grace at a critical moment when the Northern Hebrew Kingdom seemed about to adopt a pagan religion as its official faith.

The *third age of miracles* was inaugurated by Jesus, whose many miracles authenticated his claim to be God's Son. Christ's apostles also performed miracles in Jesus' name in the early days of the Christian church.

Remember This . . .

authenticate: provide proof

☞ **Check It Out:**

I Kings 17–19, 21

☞ **GO TO:**

Hosea 9:10 (Baal)

Baal: a Canaanite term for "god"

Three Ages of Miracles

First Age	Second Age	Third Age
• Moses	• Elijah, Elisha	• Christ, apostles
• 1446–1306 B.C.	• 860–810 B.C.	• 27–75 A.D.
• Revealed God as Lord	• Proved the Lord is the true God	• **Authenticated** Christ as God's Son
• Introduced the Old Testament	• Introduced the New Testament	

Elijah

Elijah was sent to Israel at a critical time. King Ahab had married Jezebel, the daughter of a pagan king. Together Jezebel and Ahab set out to replace worship of the Lord with the worship of **Baal** (see Illustration #3, page 12). The royal couple executed God's prophets and imported hundreds of false prophets from Jezebel's homeland. The effort seemed about to succeed when God sent Elijah to confront the king and demonstrate his power.

Fire From Heaven

Elijah called on God to stop the rains. For three terrible years no rain fell, and the land of Israel dried up. Ahab's powerful military was devastated as no fodder was available for his chariot horses. Then Elijah reappeared, and challenged Ahab to a duel between himself and 400 prophets of Baal. The contest took place on Mount Carmel, and was witnessed by thousands of Israelites. Baal's prophets cried out all day for their god to send fire and burn up a sacrifice they had laid out. But nothing happened. Then when Elijah called on the Lord to act, fire from heaven burned up the sacrifice and even the stone altar on which it lay. The people were convinced that *the Lord, he is God.* At Elijah's command, the people killed the prophets of Baal. The threat of Israel's paganization was turned back!

Stories of Elijah

Elijah is fed by ravens	I Kings 17:1–6
Elijah multiplies a widow's food.	I Kings 17:7–16
Elijah raises the widow's dead son.	I Kings 17:17–24
Elijah defeats the prophets of Baal.	I Kings 18:16–48
Elijah flees from Jezebel.	I Kings 19:1–18
Elijah announces Ahab's doom.	I Kings 21:1–28
Elijah is taken up alive into heaven.	II Kings 2:1–18

Elisha

Elisha was the apprentice and then the successor of Elijah. He ministered after the death of Ahab, through the reigns of Ahab's descendants Ahaz and Jehoram.

During the years Elisha prophesied, Israel was threatened by a powerful Syrian (or Aramean) kingdom led first by Ben-Hadad and then by Hazael. While Elijah had confronted Ahab and displayed the power of God, Elisha's ministry displayed God's grace and willingness to support his people. Despite the miracles Elisha performed on Israel's behalf, there was no great national return to God. Later Elisha anointed a military commander, Jehu, as the next king of Israel. Jehu wiped out Ahab's remaining family and purged Israel of the worship of Baal which Ahab and Jezebel had tried to establish. But Jehu continued to support the false worship system installed by Jeroboam decades before.

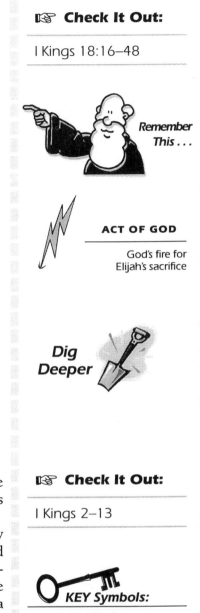

☞ **Check It Out:**

I Kings 18:16–48

Remember This . . .

ACT OF GOD

God's fire for Elijah's sacrifice

Dig Deeper

☞ **Check It Out:**

I Kings 2–13

KEY Symbols:

Elijah's Ministry
the power of God

Elisha's Ministry
God's grace and willingness to support his people

Stories of Elisha

Elisha divides the Jordan River.	II Kings 2:1–14
Elisha purifies bad waters.	II Kings 2:19–22
Elisha curses jeering young men.	II Kings 2:23–25
Elisha predicts a miracle victory.	II Kings 3:1–25
Elisha multiplies a widow's oil.	II Kings 4:1–7
Elisha promises a pregnancy.	II Kings 4:8–17
Elisha raises a dead son.	II Kings 4:18–37
Elisha makes poison stew harmless.	II Kings 4:38–41
Elisha multiplies loaves of bread.	II Kings 4:42–44
Elisha curses Gehazi with leprosy.	II Kings 5:1–27
Elisha makes an ax-head float.	II Kings 6:1–7
Elisha traps a Syrian army.	II Kings 6:8–23
Elisha shows his servant an angel army.	II Kings 6:13–17
Elisha predicts food for a besieged city.	II Kings 6:24–7:20

Dig Deeper

What Others are Saying:

Warren Wiersbe: During those days of political decay and national sin, God was using Elisha to call out a believing remnant of people to obey God. The whole nation was not going to be saved, even as the whole world today is not going to be saved.[2]

Write It Down!

JONAH

. . . God's reluctant messenger

Just the FACTS

WHO	Jonah
WHAT	announced judgment
WHERE	in Nineveh
WHEN	when Jeroboam II ruled Israel,
WHY	and he gave the city an opportunity to repent.

Swallowed Up

Jeroboam II was an evil but vigorous and successful ruler. During his 41-year reign the Northern Kingdom became a power in the Middle East. II Kings 14:25 tells us that he *restored the boundaries of Israel from Lebo Hamath to the Sea of the Arabah,* expanding Israel's borders almost to the extent achieved under David and Solomon. Jeroboam II's victories had been *in accordance with the Word of the Lord* given by a patriotic prophet, *Jonah the son of Amittai, the prophet from Gath Heper* (II Kings 14:25).

But when God called this same Jonah to go and preach against Nineveh (see Illustration #4, page 16), the capital of the Assyrian empire, Jonah hurriedly took a ship heading in the opposite direction—to Spain, not north to Assyria! In the book that bears his name, Jonah explains why he acted as he did.

> *I knew that you are a gracious and compassionate God, slow to anger and abounding in love, a God who relents from sending calamity.* (Jonah 4:2)

Assyria was the great enemy of Jonah's people. Jonah wanted God to destroy Nineveh, but he was afraid that if he warned the Assyrians they might repent, and God would not destroy them after all.

It is against this background that we read the adventures of Jonah, and ponder the significance of his familiar but misunderstood little book.

THE BIG PICTURE 🔍

Jonah This book contains four brief chapters.

- Jonah runs away and is swallowed by a great fish.
- Jonah thanks God for saving his life.
- Jonah goes to Nineveh, and the city repents!
- Jonah sulks, and is rebuked by God for his lack of compassion.

What's Special About Jonah?

1 *No whale tale (Jonah 1:17).* Early English versions translated a Hebrew word that means a 'great fish' as a 'whale.' The text makes it clear that God had to specially prepare the great fish that swallowed Jonah so that Jonah would not drown.

2 *Jonah's second chance (Jonah 3:1–3).* The Lord gave the disobedient Jonah a second chance to obey him. This time Jonah delivered God's message: *Forty more days and Nineveh will be destroyed.*

3 *The Ninevites "believed God" (Jonah 3:4–9).* The people of Nineveh believed God and displayed **repentance** by fasting and wearing **sackcloth**. The king himself demanded that all *give up their evil ways and their violence.*

ACT OF GOD

God delivers Jonah from the belly of the great fish

☞ **GO TO:**

Jeremiah 15:19; Isaiah 30:15 (repentance)

repentance: Not just sorrow for sin, but a commitment to change

sackcloth: a very coarse material similar to burlap

Warren Wiersbe: Jesus used Nineveh to illustrate an important point (Matthew 12:38–41). He had preached to that generation for three years and had reinforced his message with his miracles, yet they would not repent and believe. The Ninevites heard one sermon from one preacher, and that sermon emphasized wrath, not love—yet they repented and were forgiven.[3]

4 *Nineveh survived! (Jonah 3:10).* The book of Jonah introduces a vital principle. Most Bible prophecies of coming judgment are conditional. They describe what will surely happen—if the nation or individuals addressed fail to repent. But God is "gracious and compassionate." He will delay or withhold judgment if people only turn to him.

KEY POINT

God is "gracious and compassionate." He will delay or withhold judgment if people only turn to him.

5 *Jonah contained a powerful message for Israel (Jonah 4:2).* Jonah preached in Nineveh, but the message of the book of Jonah was for Israel, not the Assyrians. Prophets had long called on the people of Israel to repent and turn to God. Nineveh's survival was an object lesson for Israel. If God withheld judgment on repentant Nineveh, surely God would forgive his own people—if only they too would repent.

God's goodness to others reminds us that he yearns to be good to us too.

AMOS

. . . judgment coming

WHO	God sent a rancher from Judah
WHAT	to announce judgment
WHERE	on Israel
WHEN	during the reign of Jeroboam II,
WHY	because of the injustice and oppression that existed in the Northern Kingdom.

The Day Of The Lord

Amos was a rancher who lived in Judah when God called him to deliver his Word across the border in Israel during the reign of Jeroboam II. The Northern Kingdom was unusually prosperous at the time, but the very wealthy oppressed the very poor. Amos boldly took his message of coming judgment to the retreat of the rich at Bethel, one of the worship centers established long before by Jeroboam I. There the priest Amaziah threatened Amos' life and ordered him not to prophesy. But Amos boldly announced God's judgment on the priest, and finished his message of Israel's impending doom before returning to his ranch in Judah.

About forty years after Amos preached God's Word to an unrepentant Israel, the Assyrians under Sargon II crushed that nation and scattered its population throughout the Assyrian Empire.

THE BIG PICTURE 🔍

Amos The book of Amos contains a series of Amos' sermons to Israel. The topics of the sermons serve as an outline of the book.

- God will judge Israel's neighbors (Amos 1:1–2:5)
- God will judge Israel (Amos 2:6–16)
- Israel's sins identified (Amos 3:1–6:14)
- Five visions of doom related (Amos 7:1–9:10)
- Israel's ultimate restoration assured (Amos 9:11–15)

What's Special In Amos?

1 *God's complaints against Israel.* Amos powerfully describes the sins of Israel which cry out for judgment. Israel shows contempt for God by following the counterfeit religion instituted by Jeroboam I and by constantly violating God's moral Law. The wealthy in Israel show contempt for God by their sys-

☞ **Check It Out:**

Amos 2:6–8; 4:1–6;
   5:4–7,11–12, 21–24;
   6:4–7

False religion	Immorality	Injustice
I hate, I despise your religious feasts; I cannot stand your assemblies. Even though you bring me burnt offerings and grain offerings, I will not accept them.	Father and son use the same girl and so profane my holy name. They lie down beside every altar on garments taken in pledge. In the house of their god they drink wine taken as fines.	They sell the righteous for silver, and the needy for a pair of shoes. They trample on the heads of the poor as upon the dust of the ground and deny justice to the oppressed.
Amos 5:21, 22	Amos 2:7–8	Amos 2:6–7

tematic oppression of the poor. False religion, immorality, and raw material: all reveal how far the hearts of God's people are removed from him.

What Others are Saying:

Billy Graham: From the beginning of time until the present moment, man's ungodly quest for power, his determination to use his gift of free choice for his own selfish ends, has brought him to the brink of doom. The rubble and ruins of many civilizations lie scattered over the earth's surface—mute testimony to man's inability to build a lasting world without God.[4]

☞ **Check It Out:**

Amos 5:18–27

Day of the Lord: a time of terrible judgment; another name for the **Tribulation Period**

Tribulation Period: seven years of God's judgment at history's end

2 *The "Day of the Lord" (Amos 5:18–27).* The Old Testament prophets speak often of a *Day of the Lord* or refer to *that day*. These phrases have a special meaning. The **Day of the Lord** (see GWRV, pages 98–99) is a future moment in time when God will personally intervene in human history.

In most prophetic passages, as here in Amos, references to the Day of the Lord picture God acting to punish sin. As Amos warns, *Will not the day of the Lord be darkness, not light—pitch-dark, without a ray of brightness?* (Amos 5:20). For sinning Israel, the coming Day of the Lord would be dark indeed. For *"I will send you into exile beyond Damascus," says the Lord, whose name is God Almighty* (Amos 5:27).

☞ **Check It Out:**

Amos 8

3 *Five visions of doom (Amos 7:1–9:10).* Amos relates five visions which God showed him. The visions reveal that while God has withheld punishment in the past, he will do so no longer. *The time is ripe for my people Israel: I will spare them no longer* (Amos 8:2).

4 *A promise of future restoration (Amos 9:11–15).* The defeat of the Northern Kingdom by the Assyrians and the exile of the ten northern Hebrew tribes did not mean that God had voided the covenant promises given to Abraham over a thousand years before. While that generation of Israelites would be torn from the land, by history's end God would bring their descendants back to the Promised Land.

Something to Ponder

Each of the Old Testament prophets who predict divine judgment on God's sinful people include the same reassuring message. Whatever happens, ultimately God's promises to Abraham will be kept, and God's people will be blessed. Amos' last words, spoken in God's name, are:

"I will bring back my exiled people Israel;
*   they will rebuild the ruined cities and live in them.*
They will plant vineyards and drink their wine;
*   they will make gardens and eat their fruit.*
I will plant Israel in their own land,
*   never again to be uprooted*
*   from the land I have given them,"*
                    says the Lord your God.
                    (Amos 9:14–15)

HOSEA

. . . *covenant love*

WHO	The prophet Hosea
WHAT	contrasted Israel's ungratefulness with God's covenant love
WHERE	in Israel
WHEN	during the last 30 years of Israel's existence,
WHY	to explain the reason for Israel's immanent destruction by Assyria.

Just the FACTS

Keep On Loving

Hosea the prophet was married to an unfaithful wife. Yet he continued to love her deeply. Even though she abandoned him and her children for lovers, Hosea provided for her and ultimately brought her back home. Hosea's personal experience mirrored the experience of God with Israel. Although God loved Israel as a husband loves his wife, Israel had taken his many gifts and turned to idolatry.

KEY Symbols:

Hosea
unfaithful wife

God
unfaithful Israel

Hosea shares his personal story first. Then he recounts God's complaint against unrepentant Israel and expresses God's deep, continuing love for his unfaithful people.

THE BIG PICTURE 🔍

> **Hosea** The book has two stories to tell: the story of Hosea and his wife Gomer, and the story of the Lord and his people Israel.

I. The unfaithful wife .... Hosea 1–3

II. The unfaithful nation 4–14

A. Israel's sins denounced   4–8
B. Israel's doom announced   9–10
C. God's love affirmed   11
D. Discipline first   12–13
E. Then blessing   14

☞ **Check It Out:**

Hosea 3:1–4

What's Special In Hosea?

1 *Hosea's commitment to his wife (Hosea 3:1–4).* The commitment which Hosea displayed to his marriage is remarkable, especially in our day when divorce is so common. Hosea's willingness to keep on loving despite his deep hurt reminds us that marriage is a commitment that is not to be quickly set aside.

☞ **Check It Out:**

Hosea 4

2 *God's indictment of sinful Israel (Hosea 4:1–19).* Like the other prophets whom God sent to his people, Hosea spoke plainly about the sins which called for divine judgment. In unequivocal terms Hosea announced, *the Lord has a charge to bring against you who live in the land,* and he went on to spell that charge out:

There is no faithfulness, no love,
* no acknowledgment of God in the land.*
There is only cursing, lying and murder,
* stealing and adultery;*
they break all bounds,
* and bloodshed follows bloodshed.*
                    (Hosea 4:1–2)

☞ **Check It Out:**

Hosea 11

3 *God's love is unshakable (Hosea 11).* In one of Scripture's most eloquent passages God expresses his boundless love for Israel. From infancy God has cared for his people, like a parent teaching them to walk, protecting and caring for them. God's love is so deep that whatever the **provocation**, God simply will not let his people go.

What Others
are Saying:

provocation: *that which has aroused God's anger*

Warren Wiersbe: Hosea does not end on a gloomy note. He sees the future glory of the nation. Just as his wife was brought back from slavery and restored to his home and heart, so the nation would one day be restored to her land and to her Lord. These closing chapters magnify the faithful love of God in contrast to the unfaithfulness of his people.[5]

Study Questions

1. What sin fixed the destiny of Israel when the Northern King-dom was first established?
2. In what way were the kings of Israel alike?
3. What two speaking prophets are associated with the Bible's second age of miracles?
4. What two prophets ministered to Israel during the reign of Jeroboam II? What was the message of each to Israel?
5. What is the *Day of the Lord*?
6. What sins in Israel called for God's judgment? In what ways is our country today like ancient Israel?

CHAPTER WRAP-UP

- After the death of Solomon the united Hebrew Kingdom was divided, with the Southern Kingdom called Judah, and the Northern Kingdom Israel.

- The Northern Kingdom, Israel, was ruled by a succession of evil kings.

- Even though God sent prophets to warn Israel and turn the nation back to him, the people did not listen, and Israel fell to the Assyrians in 722 B.C.

- Among the prophets that God sent to Israel were the speaking prophets Elijah and Elisha.

- The ministry of Elijah and Elisha is notable because it occurred during one of three periods in which miracles were common.

- Jonah was an Israelite prophet whose mission to Nineveh provided proof that God would withhold judgment if a people repented of their sins.

- Amos was a writing prophet whose book contains sermons warning Israel that God would judge them for their idolatry and social injustice.

- Hosea was a writing prophet whose commitment to his unfaithful wife mirrored God's love for and commitment to unfaithful Israel.

9 THE SOUTHERN KINGDOM: JUDAH

I, II Kings
II Chronicles
Obadiah
Joel
Micah
Isaiah

CHAPTER HIGHLIGHTS

- Judah
- Godly and Ungodly
- Four Tests
- Army of Locusts
- A Messiah

Let's Get Started

Solomon died in 930 B.C. (see Time Line #6, page 112). When he died the ten northern Hebrew tribes broke away to establish an independent kingdom, Israel (see Chapter 8), whose capital would be Samaria. In the South, or Judah, descendants of David continued to rule from Jerusalem. Many in the North, unhappy with Jeroboam's decision to establish a counterfeit religion, moved south to continue to worship God at the Temple Solomon had constructed.

The two rival Hebrew kingdoms existed side by side for over 200 years, sometimes at war, sometimes cooperating against common enemies. When the Northern Hebrew Kingdom fell to Assyria in 722 B.C., Judah survived. Judah continued to be ruled by David's descendants until 586 B.C., when the nation fell to the Babylonians and its citizens were also sent into exile.

KEY Symbols:

Northern Kingdom

ISRAEL (SAMARIA)

ten tribes (Samaria)
- Jeroboam
- Assyrian Captivity 722 B.C.

Southern Kingdom

JUDAH (JERUSALEM)

two tribes (Jerusalem)
- Rehoboam
- Babylonian Captivity 586 B.C.

Just the FACTS

II KINGS

. . . a historical account

WHO	Unknown authors
WHAT	evaluated the kings
WHERE	of Israel and Judah
WHEN	from 970 B.C. to 586 B.C.,
WHY	to demonstrate the value of obeying God and the danger of disobeying him.

II Chronicles

. . . a commentary on history

Just the FACTS

Who	Unknown authors
What	highlighted godly kings
Where	of Judah
When	from 970 B.C. to 586 B.C.,
Why	to show that when God was honored and worshiped, Judah was blessed.

Now For The Southern Kingdom

While Israel and Judah struggled to survive, in . . .

Around the World

India	Medical schools used anatomical models.
Europe	Wheels with spokes began to be used.
Greece	The first recorded Olympic games took place.
England	Celtic peoples began to arrive.
Asia Minor	People began to use iron in utensils.

Overview

Dig Deeper

The chart below identifies the kings and the writing prophets of the Southern Hebrew Kingdom, Judah, from the division of the Hebrew Kingdom in 930 B.C. until the fall of Israel in 722 B.C. Note that most of II Chronicles is devoted to the rule of Judah's godly kings.

Kings and Prophets of the Southern Kingdom

Kings	Evaluation	Prophetic books	Years reigned	Scripture
Rehoboam	evil	–	17	I Kings 12–14; II Chronicles 11–12
Abijah	evil	–	–	I Kings 15; II Chronicles 13
Asa	godly	–	41	I Kings 15; II Chronicles14–16
Jehoshaphat	godly	–	25	I Kings 22; II Chronicles 17–20
Jehoram	evil	Obediah	8	II Kings 8; II Chronicles 21
Ahaziah	evil	–	1	II Kings 8; II Chronicles 22
Queen Athaliah	evil	–	6	II Kings 11; II Chronicles22–23
Joash	godly	Joel	40	II Kings 12; II Chronicles 24
Amaziah	godly	–	29	II Kings 14; II Chronicles 25
Uzziah	godly	–	52	II Kings 15; II Chronicles 26
Jotham	godly	Micah and Isaiah	16	II Kings 15; II Chronicles 27
Ahaz	evil	Micah and Isaiah	16	II Kings 16; II Chronicls 28
Hezekiah	godly	Micah and Isaiah	29	II Kings 18–20; II Chronicles 29–32

Moral Leadership

The kings of Judah were more than political leaders. They provided moral and spiritual leadership as well. The spiritual and political well-being of the nation was closely linked. In general the nation prospered under godly kings and suffered under ungodly kings.

A look at passages in II Chronicles, which describe the rule of two of Judah's godly kings (Asa and Jehoshaphat), provides a clear picture of what rulers did to encourage personal and national spiritual **revival**.

☞ **Check It Out:**

I Chronicles 14–15, 17

revival: heartfelt return and commitment to God

How Asa led . . . (II Chronicles)	How Jehoshphat led . . . (II Chronicles)
• did what was right and good (14:2)	• sought God personally (17:4)
• removed foreign altars and **high places** (14:3)	• followed God's commandments (17:4)
• commanded the people to seek the Lord (14:4)	• removed high places and **Asherah poles** (17:6)
• commanded the people to obey Gods laws and commandments (14:4)	• sent Levites throughout Judah to teach God's Law (17:9)
• relied on God when war came (14:11)	
• repaired the altar and offered sacrifices (15:8)	
• led a ceremony of covenant renewal (15:11)	
• deposed the Queen Mother for idolatry (15:6)	

Dig Deeper

King Solomon: Righteousness exalts a nation, but sin is a disgrace to any people.[1]

What Others are Saying:

Something to Ponder

Godly leaders can still influence nations for good. Ungodly leaders still erode the moral and spiritual fiber of a nation.

high places: hilltops where pagan deities were worshiped

Asherah poles: wooden symbols of a pagan goddess

Those Prophets Again

One of the most significant roles in the Old Testament was that of the prophet. A number of *speaking* prophets are mentioned in the Old Testament books of history. No less than 17 of the 39 Old Testament books are composed completely of the messages given by *writing* prophets.

What was the mission of the prophets, and why were they so important? The answer is found in the way ancient peoples sought supernatural guidance.

Stay Away From The Occult

oracle: *a prophet's utterance*

entrails: *internal organs*

medium: *one possessed by or consulting a ghost or spirit of the dead, especially for information about the future*

occult: *anything dealing with the mystic arts like Satanism, black magic, witchcraft, etc.*

divination: *trying to predict the future through omens*

sorcery: *black magic*

omens: *something that seems to be a sign of things to come*

Something to Ponder

horoscope: *a diagram of the heavens, showing the relative positions of planets and the signs of the zodiac, used to predict events in a person's life*

zodiac: *the 12 imaginary signs in heaven*

The Greeks went to Delphi to consult the **oracle** there. The Romans looked for signs in the **entrails** of a slaughtered pig, or in the direction taken by a flight of birds. The peoples of the Ancient Middle East consulted **mediums** or spiritists who claimed to contact the dead or some spirit. The religions of all ancient peoples involved some aspect of the **occult**, some search for supernatural guidance.

When the Israelites were about to enter Canaan, God warned them against all occult practices. The Bible forbids every kind of occult practice, labeling all of them *detestable to the Lord.*

*When you enter the land the Lord your God is giving you, do not learn to imitate the detestable ways of the nations there. Let no one be found among you who sacrifices his son or daughter in the fire, who practices **divination** or **sorcery**, interprets **omens**, engages in witchcraft, or casts spells, or who is a medium or spiritist or who consults the dead. Anyone who does these things is detestable to the Lord, and because of these detestable practices the Lord your God will drive out these nations before you.* (Deuteronomy 18:9–12)

Today people look for guidance in **horoscopes**, call the Psychic Network, and consult spiritists. These practices are still detestable to the Lord. God wants us to rely on him, not on the occult.

A Need For Special Guidance

God had given his people a written Law to guide them. But there were situations in which the nation or individuals faced uncertain choices and needed to know God's will. There were times when God's people strayed and needed to be warned and called back to his ways.

True Vs. False Prophets

But how could God's Old Testament people distinguish a true messenger of God from a pretender? Deuteronomy identifies four tests, and a true prophet could pass them all.

1) A true prophet will urge people to follow the Lord (Deuteronomy 13:1–4).

2) A true prophet will be an Israelite, not a foreigner (Deuteronomy 18:15).

3) A true prophet will speak God's Word in God's name (Deuteronomy 18:19).

4) A true prophet will make predictions that come true (Deuteronomy 18:21–22).

Today we can be sure that the prophets of the Bible truly were God's messengers, for we have hundreds of their predictions in Scripture which have been fulfilled. But when a prophet delivered a message in his own generation, all four of these tests were needed to authenticate him or her as God's messenger.

An Example From Scripture

God sent the prophet Jeremiah to urge the people of Jerusalem to submit to the Babylonians. One morning at the Jerusalem Temple, a prophet named Hananiah contradicted Jeremiah. Hananiah loudly announced in the name of the Lord that within two years the power of Babylon would be broken and Judah's captive king and nobles would be returned to Jerusalem. Hananiah passed some of the tests: he was a Jew, and he had spoken in the name of the Lord.

Jeremiah, a patriot, was delighted. But shortly after, God sent Jeremiah back to confront Hananiah. Hananiah had made up the message he delivered in God's name. Boldly Jeremiah said, *Listen, Hananiah! The Lord has not sent you, yet you have persuaded this nation to trust in lies* (Jeremiah 28:15). Then Jeremiah announced God's sentence. Before a year passed, Hananiah would die, *because you have preached rebellion against the Lord* (Jeremiah 28:16).

Two months later, Hananiah was dead. Jeremiah's words had come true. Jeremiah, not Hananiah, was God's prophet. The people of Judah were responsible for listening to and obeying God's words given through Jeremiah.

KEY Symbols:

A True Prophet

urges people to follow the Lord

an Israelite

speaks God's Word in God's name

all predictions come true

☞ **Check It Out:**

Jeremiah 28

KEY POINT

God's answer for his Old Testament people was the prophet: a person commissioned to speak in God's name and convey God's will to his own. God himself would provide all the guidance his people needed in order to know and to do his will.

When we read the writings of the prophets recorded in the Bible, we need to remember that each prophet had a message for his or her own generation. Yet that message will contain truths we can apply to our own lives today.

With this in mind, we can look at Bible books written by the prophets, who brought God's Word to the people of the Southern Hebrew Kingdom, Judah.

OBADIAH

. . . Edom's doom

WHO	The prophet Obadiah
WHAT	announced that
WHERE	because Jerusalem
WHEN	was plundered by the Edomites,
WHY	God would destroy Edom for attacking his people.

OK, That's Enough

At least four times in history the Edomites, a neighboring nation, attacked Judah and plundered Jerusalem. After one of these invasions, the prophet Obadiah announced that God would destroy Edom. In his covenant with Abraham God had promised, *I will bless those who bless you, and whoever curses you I will curse* (Genesis 12:3).

Obadiah's brief, one chapter book contains God's announcement that he will keep this pledge. The Edomites had marched through the gates of God's people, seized their wealth, and waited at the crossroads to cut down their fugitives (Obadiah 1:13, 14). Therefore God would see to it that the *house of Esau* (a synonym for Edom, which was founded by Esau) was consumed. *There will be no survivors from the house of Esau* (Obadiah 1:18).

☞ **GO TO:**

Genesis: 36:8, 9 (Esau)

chafe: become annoyed

William Sanford LaSor: People still **chafe** and groan under injustices in this world, and long for a day when things will be 'as they should be.' God promises that his day will come. And when it does, he will right the wrongs, restore the just possessions, and establish his rule on earth.[2]

JOEL
. . . final judgment coming

Who	The prophet Joel
What	shared his vision of near and final judgment
Where	in Judah,
When	possibly around 825 B.C.,
Why	as a warning and call to repentance.

Just the FACTS

Buzzzzzz . . .

Joel writes just after <u>a great swarm of locusts</u> (see GWRV, pages 128–131) had stripped Judah of all vegetation. He announced that God sent the locusts to call Judah to repentance. But as Joel contemplated the locusts, God gave him a vision of another invasion of the Promised Land at history's end. This hoard is a vast human army, which would also devastate the land and its people. At that time God himself would intervene. He would punish the nations and rescue his own.

How are the people of Judah to respond to this message from God? They are to return to the Lord with all their hearts, for *who knows? He may turn and have pity and leave behind a blessing* (Joel 2:14) for Joel's generation.

THE BIG PICTURE 🔍

> **Joel** This three-chapter book is divided into two sections. The first section (Joel 1:1–2:27) concerns the locusts that swarmed Judah from the North, which was unusual because most locust swarms were blown into the Holy Land from the South. The second section (Joel 2:28–3:21) is a vision of the coming Day of the Lord, a description of events that lie far in the future.

What's Special In Joel?

1 *The call to repentance (Joel 1:13–15).* Joel interprets the locust invasion as punishment for Judah's sins. He calls on God's people turn to the Lord quickly, lest something worse happen.

2 *True repentance (Joel 2:12–14).* In Bible times people openly displayed grief and sorrow. To show repentance they tore their clothing, smeared dirt on their faces, and wept loudly as they <u>sat in ashes</u>. Joel reminds Judah that God demands true repentance when he says **rend** *your heart, not your garments* (Joel 2:13).

☞ **Check It Out:**

Joel 1:1–12

☞ **GO TO:**

Revelation 9:3–11 (locusts)

KEY Symbols:

Swarm of Locusts
a vast human army

☞ **GO TO:**

Job 3:7, 8 (ashes)

☞ **Check It Out:**

Joel 1:12–14

rend: *tear or pull a garment apart*

☞ **Check It Out:**

Joel 2:25–27

3 *God's response to true repentance (Joel 2:18–27).* Through Joel, God promises to bless and protect his people when they repent and turn to him. *I will repay you for the years the locusts have eaten,* God says (Joel 2:26).

4 *History's end (Joel 2:28–3:21).* By seeing the locust plague Joel catches a glimpse of an overpowering human army that will invade the Holy Land in the distant future. God would use that occasion to bless his people, for he would judge the nations who invade it. In the end *Judah will be inhabited forever, and Jerusalem through all generations* (Joel 3:29).

The Message Of Joel

Joel had an important message for his generation. God is sovereign and speaks through events. The prophet rightly interpreted the locust plague as a call to Judah to repent.

Something to Ponder

Like Judah, we are to remember that God is in control of the events of our lives. How often are our troubles invitations to draw closer to God, that he might bless us.

What Others are Saying:

John Alexander: To deny sin is bad news, indeed. The only good news is sin itself. Sin is the best news there is, the best news there could be in our predicament. Because with sin, there's a way out. There's the possibility of repentance. You can't repent of confusion or psychological flaws inflicted by your parents—you're stuck with them. But you can repent of sin. Sin and repentance are the only grounds for hope and joy. The grounds for reconciled, joyful relationships. You can be born again.[3]

Something to Ponder

Both physical life and spiritual life have beginnings. One began when our mothers gave birth. The other begins when a person trusts Jesus Christ as Savior. God gives those people a spiritual life that lasts forever, guaranteeing that the believer will live eternally in heaven with God. This is what we call being *born again*—being born a second time, spiritually.

☞ **GO TO:**

John 3:16–18 (Jesus)

MICAH

. . . *judgment coming*

WHO   The prophet Micah, prophesying,

WHAT   warned of the destruction of both Samaria and Jerusalem,

WHERE   in Israel and Judah

WHEN   just before Assyria invaded,

WHY   because of the sins of both Hebrew kingdoms.

Just the FACTS

Repent Or You'll Regret It

Micah was a prophet who ministered in Judah during the reigns of Jotham, Ahaz, and Hezekiah. These were critical years for both Hebrew kingdoms, as an aggressive Assyria loomed just over the horizon, threatening their independence. Micah had a similar message for both Israel and Judah, which he delivered to their capital cities, Samaria and Jerusalem. That message was one of impending doom, for each society was corrupt. In clear and unmistakable words Micah presented God's **indictment**, spelling out the sins that called for judgment.

Micah's warnings to Israel fell on deaf ears. He lived to see Israel fall to Assyria, and to see its population taken away. But Micah also saw a godly king, Hezekiah, replace the evil Ahaz in the South. Through the influence of Hezekiah and the prophets Micah and Isaiah, Judah turned back to the Lord. While the Assyrians did invade Judah, Jerusalem and the Southern Kingdom survived.

THE BIG PICTURE 🔍

> **MICAH** God was about to step into history to judge his idolatrous people. Micah portrays the anguish his actions would cause. While God's sinful people lay awake plotting wickedness, God had set his own plan in motion. The present civilization would be destroyed, but a remnant of the people would be preserved. Leaders and prophets alike had led God's people astray; the nation must fall. But however devastating, this judgment would not be the end.
>
> One day God would bring back the exiles and raise a new Temple in Jerusalem. <u>A ruler would be born in Bethlehem</u> who would shepherd God's flock and bring peace to all the earth.

KEY Symbols:

Northern Kingdom
Israel
- capital—Samaria

Southern Kingdom
Judah
- capital—Jerusalem

indictment: *an official charge of wrongdoing*

☞ **GO TO:**

Micah 5:2 (ruler)

> For a time, however, Israel must lose its national identity because of the people's many sins. But at history's end God would restore Israel and would forgive his people's sins, as he had pledged to Abraham long ago.

What's Special In Micah?

☞ **Check It Out:**

Micah 3:1–7; 6:9–16

1 *Sins demand judgment (Micah 3:1–7; 6:7–16).* God is a Moral Judge, who is responsible for punishing sin. Micah draws a picture of political leaders who exploit citizens and of religious leaders who pretend that nothing is amiss. He goes on to describe a materialistic society in which the average person is dishonest and deceitful, practicing "religion" but unconcerned with justice.

Through Micah God makes it unmistakably clear that he will judge:

> *I will destroy your witchcraft and you will no longer cast spells. I will destroy your carved images and your sacred stones from among you; you will no longer bow down to the work of your hands. . . . I will take vengeance in anger and wrath upon the nations that have not obeyed me. (Micah 5:12–15)*

☞ **Check It Out:**

Micah 7:7–20

2 *Salvation depends on a Savior (Micah 5:2–5; 7:19–20).* Like other prophets who warned of coming judgment, Micah looked beyond the coming disaster to a day when God would save his people. In this book, written over 700 years before Christ, Micah identified the town where the promised Savior would be born!

In one of the clearest of the Old Testament's **Messianic prophecies**, Micah wrote:

Messianic prophecy: information about Christ revealed in the Old Testament

> *But you, Bethlehem Ephrathah, though you are small among the clans of Judah, out of you will come for me one who will be ruler over Israel, whose origins are of old, from ancient times. . . .*
> *He will stand and shepherd his flock in the strength of the Lord, in the majesty of the name of the Lord his God.*
> *And they will live securely, for then his greatness will reach to the ends of the earth. And he will be their peace. (Micah 5:2–5)*

Remember This . . .

Warren Wiersbe: It is this prophecy which led the wise men to Jesus. Of course, the Jews rejected their Prince of Peace, so there has been no peace in the world. But when Christ returns to earth, he will establish his kingdom of peace and there shall be no more war.[4]

What Others are Saying:

ISAIAH

. . . the Old Testament gospel

WHO	The prophet Isaiah
WHAT	warned of judgment
WHERE	to the people of Judah
WHEN	between 740 B.C. and 690 B.C.,
WHY	and conveyed hope, linked to the coming Messiah who will win salvation for individuals and the whole world.

Just the FACTS

A Coming Messiah

Isaiah also lived under the threat of Assyria and witnessed the fall of Israel. Like Micah, Isaiah urgently warned Judah to turn back to God. Isaiah supported godly King Hezekiah's efforts to bring about a spiritual revival. God honored the king's faith by turning back the invading Assyrians. Yet Isaiah's early ministry was devoted to continually exposing the sins of God's people, and to warning that God must and would judge them.

The theme of Isaiah's messages changed radically in the later part of his ministry, as reflected in Chapters 40–66. His visions carry him beyond the time of Judah's future defeat by another northern enemy, Babylon (see GWDN, pages 16–19), to portray a **Sovereign** God who is committed to deliver his people and to bless all mankind. Isaiah promises that in God's own time he will send his Messiah. Through this promised **Savior**, God will deliver individuals who trust in him, and purge the whole world of sin's corruption.

THE BIG PICTURE

KEY Symbols:

Jesus Christ
MESSIAH
SAVIOR

sovereign: God is in control of all that happens

Savior: one who delivers from danger and death

> **Isaiah** The prophet's name means *Yahweh is salvation.* No other Old Testament prophet pictures so clearly God's firm intention to save his people or describes more distinctly the coming Savior.
>
> The 66 chapters in Isaiah can be divided into three major sections, with subsections developing their themes.

KEY Symbols:

Isaiah
Yahweh is salvation

I. Words of Condemnation .... Isaiah 1–35
  A. God's case against Judah and Israel   1–12
  B. God's case against the surrounding nations   13–23
  C. God's case against all the nations   24–35

II. Agents of God's Wrath................................. Isaiah 36–39
  A. Looking back at the Assyrians   36–37
  B. Looking ahead to the Babylonians   3–39

III. Words of Comfort and Hope .... Isaiah 40–66
  A. The Sovereign God will deliver   40–48
  B. God's Servant-Savior will be the deliverer   49–57
  C. God's deliverer will save completely   58–66

KEY Symbols:

Assyria
the rod of God's wrath

☞ **Check It Out:t**

Isaiah 1; 5:1–7

☞ **Check It Out:**

Isaiah 10:1–12

KEY Symbols:

Jesus Christ
WONDERFUL COUNSELOR

MIGHTY GOD

EVERLASTING FATHER

PRINCE OF PEACE

Remember This . . .

What's Special In Isaiah?

1 *God's weariness with sin (Isaiah 1).* The Lord put up with the sinful behavior of Israel and Judah far too long. Even the revivals led by godly kings in the South had not touched the hearts of God's people. Any society which is satisfied with a "religion" but fails to produce a just society is doomed.

2 *God's use of human agents (Isaiah 10:1–12).* Isaiah identifies Assyria as the *rod of (God's) wrath.* The Assyrian invasion was not a random event, but something God allowed to punish the sins of Israel and Judah. God is in control of history, and the rise and fall of nations accomplished his purposes.

3 *Hope shines through the darkest of Isaiah's prophecies.* Although Isaiah 1–35 contains repeated images of judgment and coming doom, Isaiah frequently assures his hearers that God is committed to them, and he will keep his covenant promises to Abraham and David. Isaiah reveals that God's promises will be fulfilled through the gift of God's Son, who will be born as a human child.

> *For to us a child is born, to us a son is given, and the government will be on his shoulders.*
> *And he will be called Wonderful Counselor, Mighty God, Everlasting Father, Prince of Peace.*
> *Of the increase of his government and peace there will be no end.*
> *He will reign on David's throne and over his kingdom, establishing and upholding it with justice and righteousness from that time on and forever. (Isaiah 9:6, 7)*

This is just one of many prophecies in Isaiah about the coming Savior. As we will see later, these Old Testament prophecies unmistakably refer to Jesus Christ!

4 *Isaiah emphasizes God's sovereign power (Isaiah 40–48).* The comfort and hope that Isaiah offers to Judah is based on his understanding of the nature of God. The God of Israel and Judah is the Creator, who made and governs the universe. God is the one who has made covenant promises and who will surely keep them. He is the one who knows the future and who reveals it, for he controls the future. The idols men worship are nothing. The God of Israel and Judah is the All-Mighty, Sovereign Lord.

☞ **Check It Out:**

Isaiah 40:18–31; 42:5–9; 44:6–20

5 *There's a glorious future for the people of God (Isaiah 58–66).* The history of Israel and Judah had been marked by alternating periods of blessing and devastating tragedy. Isaiah looked beyond history and described a future of endless blessing after the Savior punished sin and established God's rule in the hearts of human beings.

☞ **Check It Out:**

Isaiah 60:15–22; 65:17–25

The Message Of Isaiah

Isaiah's message to the people of Judah was both timely, and timeless. He warned his contemporaries about coming judgment, yet reminded them that in the end God would rid the universe of sin and usher in a time of endless blessing for all who trust in him.

The timeless message of Isaiah is reflected in the prophet's emphasis on God's sovereign control of history and in his many predictions describing the ministry of the Savior that God would send to deliver his people. The Savior, Jesus Christ, described so powerfully by Isaiah has appeared with the offer of salvation for all. Ultimately Jesus will return to earth, and then all things truly will be set right.

KEY Symbols:

Jesus Christ
KING OF KINGS
LORD OF LORDS

Charles Swindoll: Isaiah may have been 'Prince among Prophets.' But even greater than the man was his message—news of new life, new hope, and a new world under the King of kings and Lord of lords.[5]

What Others are Saying:

Study Questions

1. What Bible books record the history of Judah after Solomon's kingdom was divided?
2. Why was it important that Judah be ruled by godly rather than evil kings?
3. Why did all pagan peoples adopt occult practices? What was God's alternative to the occult for his people?
4. What were the four tests of a true prophet?
5. Match each of these four prophets to one of the following:

Obadiah	The Savior to be born in Bethlehem
Joel	God's sovereign rule
Micah	Judgment on Edom
Isaiah	A plague of locusts

CHAPTER WRAP-UP

- When Solomon died in 930 B.C. his kingdom was divided, with the Southern Kingdom renamed Judah.

- Judah was ruled by descendants of David from its beginning to its fall to the Babylonians in 586 B.C.

- Many of the kings of Judah were godly and helped to begin religious revivals.

- God also sent both speaking and writing prophets to the kings and people of the South as his spokesmen.

- The prophet Obadiah predicted the doom of Edomites who had plundered God's people.

- The prophet Joel was given a vision of a terrible judgment to come at history's end before God fully restored his people to himself.

- The prophet Micah ministered during the years Israel fell. He not only warned Judah of coming judgment but also predicted the appearance of the promised Messianic King.

- The book of the prophet Isaiah contains both warnings and promises. Many passages predict the coming of a king who would also be the Savior.

10 THE SURVIVING KINGDOM

II Kings 15–25
II Chronicles 29–36
Nahum, Zephaniah
Habakkuk, Jeremiah
Ezekiel

CHAPTER HIGHLIGHTS

- A Godly King
- Nineveh
- Warnings, Warnings, Warnings
- Judah Falls
- Breath of Life

Let's Get Started

The Southern Hebrew Kingdom, Judah, survived the Assyrian invasion that destroyed Israel in 722 B.C. God answered the prayers of godly King Hezekiah and threw back the invaders. But the sins that led to Israel's defeat were deeply entrenched in Judah as well. Despite revivals under King Hezekiah and later under King Josiah, Judah experienced a spiritual and moral descent that demanded divine judgment.

II KINGS

. . . a historical account

WHO	Unknown authors
WHAT	evaluated the kings
WHERE	of Israel and Judah
WHEN	from 970 B.C. to 586 B.C.
WHY	to demonstrate the value of obeying God and the danger of disobeying him.

Just the FACTS

II CHRONICLES

. . . a commentary on history

WHO	Unknown authors
WHAT	highlighted godly kings
WHERE	of Judah
WHAT	from 970 B.C. to 586 B.C.,
WHY	to show that when God was honored and worshiped, Judah was blessed.

Just the FACTS

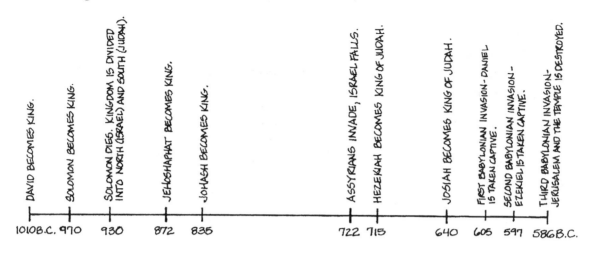

Timeline entries (left to right):

- DAVID BECOMES KING. — 1010 B.C.
- SOLOMON BECOMES KING. — 970
- SOLOMON DIES, KINGDOM IS DIVIDED INTO NORTH (ISRAEL) AND SOUTH (JUDAH). — 930
- JEHOSHAPHAT BECOMES KING. — 872
- JOHASH BECOMES KING. — 835
- ASSYRIANS INVADE, ISRAEL FALLS. — 722
- HEZEKIAH BECOMES KING OF JUDAH. — 715
- JOSIAH BECOMES KING OF JUDAH. — 640
- FIRST BABYLONIAN INVASION - DANIEL IS TAKEN CAPTIVE. — 605
- SECOND BABYLONIAN INVASION - EZEKIEL IS TAKEN CAPTIVE. — 597
- THIRD BABYLONIAN INVASION - JERUSALEM AND THE TEMPLE IS DESTROYED. — 586 B.C.

And One Kingdom Remains

When the Assyrian armies crushed Israel, Judah was ruled by Hezekiah. As soon as he became king, Hezekiah set out to revive Judah's faith in the Lord. That proved to be the key to Judah's survival. The Assyrian armies that crushed Israel also invaded Judah. They destroyed the fortified cities that guarded Judah's borders and threatened Jerusalem itself.

When an Assyrian envoy appeared outside the capital and ridiculed the idea of reliance on God, King Hezekiah and the prophet Isaiah appealed to the Lord. God answered their prayers with a sudden plague that killed thousands of Assyrian soldiers, forcing King Senecherib to return home. This pivotal event is recounted three times in the Old Testament, in II Kings 18–19, in II Chronicles 32, and in Isaiah 36–39. The lesson for future generations was clear. If God's people were fully dedicated to him, the Lord would protect and bless them.

But the lesson was not taken to heart. Seven kings succeeded Hezekiah of Judah. Only one of the seven, Josiah, was dedicated to the Lord. The nation drifted further into idolatry and its society became increasingly immoral and unjust. In 605 B.C. the first of a series of Babylonian invasions on Judah marked the beginning of Judah's end. Finally, in 586 B.C., Jerusalem was totally destroyed and its population was deported to Babylon (see GWDN, page 20).

☞ **Check It Out:**

II Chronicles 29–31

II Kings 18–19

ACT OF GOD

a sudden plague turns back the Assyrians

KEY POINT

If God's people are fully dedicated to him, the Lord will protect and bless them.

Overview

The chart below identifies the kings and the writing prophets of the surviving kingdom, from the fall of Israel in 722 B.C. to the fall of Judah in 586 B.C.

Dig Deeper

The Kings and Prophets of the Southern Kingdom

Kings	Evaluation	Years of Reign	Writing Prophets	Scripture
Hezekiah	godly	29	Isaiah Micah	II Kings 18–20 II Chronicles 20–32
Manasseh	evil	55	Nahum	II Kings 21 II Chronicles 33
Amon	evil	2	–	II Kings 21 II Chronicles 33
Josiah	godly	31	Zephaniah Habakkuk Jeremiah	II Kings 22–23 II Chronicles 34–35
Jehoahaz	evil	3 months	Jeremiah	II Kings 23 II Chronicles 36
Jehoiakim	evil	11	Jeremiah Ezekiel	II Kings 24 II Chronicles 36
Jehoiachim	evil	3 months	Jeremiah Ezekiel	II Kings 24 II Chronicles 36
Zedekiah	evil	11	Jeremiah Ezekiel	II Kings 24–25 II Chronicles36

Have It Your Way

When we read the accounts of godly kings like Hezekiah and Josiah, we cannot understand why Judah fell. But the revivals they led were superficial and brought about no permanent change of heart. Ezekiel, who was taken to Babylon as a captive in 597 B.C. and prophesied to the Jewish community there, was given a vision of Judah's sins. In his vision Ezekiel saw God's people worshiping pagan deities. As Ezekiel watched, God's *glory* (his visible presence) rose from the inner room (the Holy of Holies) of the Temple and withdrew from the Holy City. God's people had abandoned them. He would no longer protect them from their enemies.

☞ **Check It Out:**

Ezekiel 8–11

KEY Symbols:

The Holy City
Jerusalem

What Ezekiel Saw

- An idol by the altar of sacrifice.
  (Ezekiel 8:3–5)
- Judah's elders worshiping Egyptian deities.
  (Ezekiel 8:9–13)
- Women worshiping a nature goddess.
  (Ezekiel 8:14–15)
- Men praying to the sun, facing away from rather than toward God's Temple.
  (Ezekiel 8:16)

What God Said

> *. . . Is it a trivial matter for the house of Judah to do the detestable things they are doing here? Must they also fill the land with violence and continually provoke me to anger? Look at them putting the branch to their nose! Therefore I will deal with them in anger; I will not look on them with pity or spare them. Although they shout in my ears, I will not listen to them.* (Ezekiel 8:17–18)

What Others are Saying:

Warren Wiersbe: Everything that God had given the Jews was taken from them. They had no king on David's throne, nor do they have one today. They had no Temple, for it had been burned and its sacred vessels confiscated. Their Holy City was destroyed, and ever since that time has been the focal point for war and unrest in the Mideast. Their land was taken from them, and they were scattered among the nations. *Be sure your sins will find you out* (Numbers 32:23).[1]

Voices, Voices, Voices

God promised to send prophets to guide his people, and God kept his promise. At every critical point in the history of the surviving Southern Kingdom, prophets urged and warned God's people to turn to him. But their words fell on deaf ears. As we study the message of the prophets, we can only wonder at his patience and at what appears to be Judah's determined pursuit of God's judgment.

KEY POINT

Be sure your sins will find you out.

NAHUM

. . . consolation and warning

WHO	The prophet Nahum
WHAT	described the fall of Nineveh
WHERE	while in the Middle East
WHEN	while Assyria was still dominant,
WHY	to affirm God's intent to judge wickedness.

Just the FACTS

God Plays No Favorites

Nineveh, the capital of Assyria, had repented in the time of Jonah. But before long the success of the Assyrian armies replaced humility with an arrogant pride. The subsequent Assyrian assaults on Israel and Judah had been pitiless, marked by unusual brutality. The prophet Nahum, the exact time of whose life is uncertain, arose to announce that Nineveh was about to be judged by God. Bluntly Nahum proclaimed, *The Lord is a jealous and avenging God; the Lord takes vengeance and is filled with wrath. The Lord takes vengeance against his foes and maintains his wrath against his enemies* (Nahum 1:2).

KEY POINT

God plays no favorites. He will punish his own people if they choose to disobey him.

THE BIG PICTURE

> **Nahum** The prophet teaches that divine judgment of the wicked is certain. His brief book is divided into three parts:
>
> - God's anger against Nineveh is expressed (Nahum 1:1–15)
> - Nineveh's immanent fall is described (Nahum 2:1–13)
> - The carnage is graphically portrayed (Nahum 3:1–19)

ACT OF GOD

God destroys Nineveh with a flood

What's Special About Nahum?

1 *A basic principle is stated (Nahum 1:1–15).* Nahum states his thesis succinctly: *the Lord will not leave the guilty unpunished* (Nahum 1:3). In view of this reality Nahum urges the people of Judah to *celebrate your* [religious] *festivals, O Judah, and fulfill your vows* (Nahum 1:13). The God who is about to judge Nineveh will not hesitate to judge the guilty of Judah.

2 *Details of the fall of Nineveh are predicted (Nahum 2:6; 3:8–15).* The prophet describes a flood that would collapse palaces and open river gates to the enemy. Nahum foretells details about the fall of the city decades before the actual event.

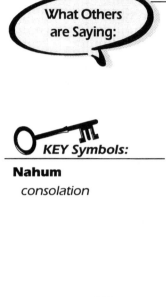
Ralph L. Smith: The city of Nineveh was built on the east bank of the Tigris River, and the river Husur ran through the city. According to a Greek story it was the rise of this river, causing a stretch of the wall to collapse, that brought disaster to the city.[2]

3 *Consolation.* The name Nahum means *consolation.* God wanted his people to know that he remained in charge of his universe, and that he would surely punish their oppressors. But the book of Nahum can also be read as a warning. God plays no favorites. He will punish his own people if they also prove to be wicked.

ZEPHANIAH

. . . judgment on Judah

WHO	Zephaniah
WHAT	prophesied judgment
WHERE	in Judah and Jerusalem
WHEN	during the reign of Josiah,
WHY	for the purpose of urging repentance.

Hear The Word!

Just the FACTS

☞ **Check It Out:**

2 Kings 22–23

☞ **GO TO:**

I Chronicles 34:29–31 (hear God's Word)

Josiah was Judah's last godly ruler. He became king when he was only eight, succeeding his grandfather Manasseh and his father Amon. These two kings whose combined rule extended over 57 years, had completely corrupted biblical religion, and Judah was filled with idolatry and injustice. In Josiah's eighteenth year a lost book of the Law, probably Deuteronomy, was recovered. When Josiah read it, he realized how far the nation had strayed from God's ways and set out to revive the true faith. Josiah restored worship in the Temple, tore down and burned the idols that infested the land, and got rid of practitioners of the occult. He called all the people together <u>to hear readings of God's Word</u> and urged them to follow it.

Despite the piety and zeal of the king, it was too late to reverse the national spiritual decline. While the nation would be preserved as long as Josiah lived, its sins called out for divine judgment, and judgment would surely come.

THE BIG PICTURE 🔍

> **Zephaniah** His mission was to warn Judah of a coming judgment that would sweep away Judah and her neighbors. Yet Zephaniah concluded with a word of hope. After judgment God would bring his people home. The book has three parts:
>
> - Announcement of judgment on Judah (Zephaniah 1:1–2:3)
> - Announcement of judgment on the nations (Zephaniah 2:4–15)
> - The promise of a future for Jerusalem (Zephaniah 3:1–20)

KEY Symbols:

Old Testament Prophets
God will judge
God will save

What's Special In Zephaniah?

1 *Judgment on Judah (1:1–2:3).* Zephaniah describes a coming great Day of the Lord that is fast approaching Judah. God will judge his own people as well as the nations that oppress them.

☞ **Check It Out:**

Zephaniah 1:14–18

2 *Hope for the future (Zephaniah 3:11–20).* While the Old Testament prophets bluntly warn their listeners to expect judgment, they also reaffirm God's lasting love for his own. Sins will be punished, but God is committed to save his people in the end. As God says through his prophet . . .

> *The Lord your God is with you, he is mighty to save.*
> *He will take great delight in you, he will quiet you with his love, he will rejoice over you with singing.*
> (Zephaniah 3:17)

HABAKKUK

. . . living by faith

WHO	Habakkuk dialogues with God
WHAT	about how God's justice can be understood
WHERE	in Jerusalem
WHEN	during the reign of Josiah,
WHY	in view of the coming Babylonian invasion.

Just the FACTS

Why God, Why?

Habakkuk was troubled. Despite Josiah's best efforts to stimulate revival, Judah's society is marked by violence and injustice. When Habakkuk asks God how he can permit this, the Lord reveals that he is about to send the Babylonians to punish his sinning people. But Habakkuk objects. The Babylonians are more wicked than the people of Judah! God reassures his prophet that the Babylonians aren't getting away with anything. Then God shares hidden principles of divine judgment with Habakkuk, making it clear that even when most successful, the wicked are still being punished. Satisfied, the prophet urges God to judge and purify his people quickly, even though he himself will suffer from the invasion.

THE BIG PICTURE

What's Special In Habakkuk?

1 *Judah's sinful society (Habakkuk 1:1–11).* Despite the outward appearance of a religious revival, Judah's society is marked by violence, conflict, and injustice. Habakkuk cannot believe a holy God can permit this to go on unpunished. When he prays, God tells him of the coming Babylonian invasion. God will punish sin.

2 *God's use of the "more wicked" (Habakkuk 1:12–17).* God's answer troubles Habakkuk. *Why are you silent while the wicked swallow up those more righteous than themselves?* The people of Judah are bad, but the godless Babylonians are worse! The success of the wicked makes it seem like God is uninvolved in human affairs.

KEY POINT

Even when most successful, the wicked are still being punished.

☞ **Check It Out:**

Habakkuk 1:2–4

KEY POINT

God is *not* silent!

3 *God is not silent* (Habakkuk 2:1–20). God reveals to Habakkuk that *while the wicked swallow up those more righteous,* God is not silent. In fact, God is judging even while the wicked seem to enjoy their greatest success! Here's how:

Habakkuk 2:2–4	Their success never brings the wicked satisfaction or peace.
Habakkuk 2:5–8	Their treatment of others creates enemies who will turn on them.
Habakkuk 2:9–11	Their guilt creates fear, however they struggle for security.
Habakkuk 2:12–14	Their future is empty, for God will rule on earth.
Habakkuk 2:15–17	Their disgrace is certain: violence leads to violence.
Habakkuk 2:18–20	They have no God to deliver them when their turn comes.

Don't envy the wicked. They may appear successful. But even while they appear successful outwardly, inwardly they are unsatisfied and insecure.

4 *In troubled times the believer will live by faith* (Habakkuk 3:1–19). God gives Habakkuk a series of visions of divine judgment in earlier times. Habakkuk realizes that when God judges his society he too will suffer. But then Habakkuk struggles through to faith.

> . . . *yet I will rejoice in the Lord, I will be joyful in God my Savior.*
>
> *The Sovereign Lord is my strength; he makes my feet like the feet of a deer; he enables me to go on the heights.* (Habakkuk 3:18, 19)

Norman L. Geisler: Although often neglected, Habakkuk's prophecy is one of the most influential in the Bible. Habakkuk 2:4 is quoted three times in the New Testament (Romans 1:17; Galatians 3:11; Hebrews 10:38), more than almost any other verse. It served as the basis for the **Protestant Reformation** and, through **Luther's** Commentary on Galatians, the conversion of **John Wesley**. Habakkuk is a book of faith.[3]

☞ **Check It Out:**

Habakkuk 2:4–20

Remember This . . .

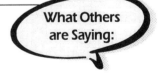

Something to Ponder

Protestant Reformation: a movement emphasizing salvation by faith that led to the founding of Protestant churches

Luther: Martin Luther; a German monk whose teaching launched the Protestant Reformation

What Others are Saying:

John Wesley: a British preacher who founded the Methodist church

JEREMIAH

. . . the weeping prophet

Just the FACTS

WHO   Jeremiah
WHAT   wrote this book
WHERE   urging Judah
WHEN   during the last 40 years of its existence,
WHY   to submit to Babylon.

Standing Alone

Jeremiah was a patriot who was commissioned by God to urge the people of Judah to submit to the Babylonians. This he faithfully did through the reigns of Judah's last five kings. But his unpopular message was rejected by his fellow countrymen, and Jeremiah himself was persecuted as a traitor. For 40 long years Jeremiah faithfully warned the nation that God was determined to punish his people's sins. He urged surrender as the only way to avoid national extinction. Jeremiah lived to see his prophecies fulfilled, to witness the destruction of Jerusalem and Solomon's Temple, and to see the people of Judah taken captive to Babylon.

THE BIG PICTURE

oracle: a message from God delivered by a prophet

> **Jeremiah** The book contains a number of **oracles**. These messages are organized by theme, though they were preached at different times during Jeremiah's 40-year ministry. An outline of the book reflects these themes.
>
> * Jeremiah's mission explained (Jeremiah 1–10)
> * The broken covenant (Jeremiah 11–20)
> * Judgment draws near (Jeremiah 21–29)
> * New Covenant promises (Jeremiah 30–39)
> * Jerusalem the fallen (Jeremiah 40–51)
> * History appendix (Jeremiah 52)

What's Special In Jeremiah?

Jeremiah's book is both long and powerful, filled with deep emotion and vivid images. Here are some of the many special features of this great Old Testament book.

Historical Context of Jeremiah's Oracles

Dig Deeper

Josiah's Reign

Jeremiah 2:1–3:4	Judah's sinful heart
Jeremiah 3:6–6:30	Jerusalem to be destroyed
Jeremiah 7:1–10:25	Ruin and exile
Jeremiah 11:1–13:27	The broken covenant
Jeremiah 18:1–20:18	The potter

Jehoiakim's Reign

Jeremiah 14–15	Prayers are fruitless
Jeremiah 16–17	Jeremiah's celebacy
Jeremiah 22	The king rejected
Jeremiah 23	False prophets charged
Jeremiah 25	Nebuchadnezzar
Jeremiah 26	Jeremiah threatened
Jeremiah 35	The recabites' example
Jeremiah 36	The burned scroll
Jeremiah 45	Promises to Baruch
Jeremiah 46–48	Against foreign nations

Zedekiah's Reign

Jeremiah 21	Advice for the king
Jeremiah 24	Zedekiah abandoned
Jeremiah 27	Judah must submit
Jeremiah 28	**God's iron yoke**
Jeremiah 29	To the exiles
Jeremiah 30–33	The New Covenant
Jeremiah 34	Judah's broken covenant
Jeremiah 37–39	Jerusalem's fall
Jeremiah 49	The nation warned

Under Governor Gedaliah

Jeremiah 40–43	The flight to Egypt
Jeremiah 44	In Egypt

Later

Jeremiah 50–51	Judgment on Babylon
Jeremiah 52	Jerusalem revisited

1 *Jeremiah's personal anguish (Jeremiah 15:12–18; 20:7–18).* It is almost impossible to imagine how isolated Jeremiah felt as a lone spokesman for God. He was a sensitive person, who was hurt deeply by the ridicule and hostility he constantly faced. Jeremiah's only recourse was to share his feelings with the Lord, which he records in several passages.

> *You understand, O Lord; remember me and care for me . . .*
> *I sat alone because your hand was on me and you filled me with* **indignation.**
> *Why is my pain unending and my wound grievous and incurable?* (Jeremiah 15:15, 17–18)

☞ **Check It Out:**

Jeremiah 20:7–18

God's iron yoke: his unchangeable purpose

indignation: frustration and anger

honed and buffeted: beaten into shape

Charles Swindoll: It is greatness of character and a life with depth that earns the respect of others. Those who have been **honed and buffeted**, bruised and melted in the furnace of af-

What Others are Saying:

*apologist: a person who
defends an idea, faith,
cause, or institution*

**Something
to Ponder**

**Remember
This . . .**

☞ **Check It Out:**

Deuteronomy 28:49–
68

fliction, and then emerge with emotional stability and inner strength—they are the ones who have a ministry in the lives of others. Their weakness is like a magnet, for when we are weak, he is strong.[4]

2 *The sins of Judah (Jeremiah 5:7–25; 10:1–16).* Jeremiah boldly confronted the people of his day about the sins that demanded judgment. But like men and women today who consider immorality a private matter, the people of Judah refused to repent. Compare what we read from a prophet like Jeremiah with stories featured in our newspapers and on television . . . and with the reaction of the guilty and their **apologists**.

Sins described . . .	Man's reaction . . .
"I supplied all their needs,	They have lied about the Lord;
yet they committed adultery	they said, "He will do nothing!
and thronged to the houses of prostitutes.	No harm will come to us,
They are well-fed, lusty stallions,	we will never see the sword or famine.
each neighing after another man's wife.	The prophets are but wind
Should I not punish them for this?"	and the word is not in them;
declared the Lord.	so let what they say be done to them."
—Jeremiah 5:7, 8	—Jeremiah 5:12, 13

But God did see, and he sees today. God will not leave the guilty unpunished.

3 *The punishment decreed (Jeremiah 25:1–14).* Moses had warned God's people of what must happen if they refused to honor and obey God. Now Jeremiah reminds them that again and again the prophets have urged, *turn now, each of you from his evil ways and your evil practices.* But Judah would not listen or pay attention. Through Jeremiah God says *I will summon . . . Nebuchadnezzar king of Babylon. . . . This whole country will become a desolate wasteland, and these nations will serve the king of Babylon seventy years* (Jeremiah 25:8, 11).

4 *The promise of a New Covenant (Jeremiah 30–31).* Genesis 12 records covenant promises God made to Abraham. These promises stated what God would do for and through Abraham's descendants. The key promise was that the whole world would be blessed through Abraham. Later God added a covenant promise to David—the one who would fulfill God's promise to Abraham would be from David's family line. Now Jeremiah reveals even more of God's plan for blessing humanity.

Jeremiah, whose mission was to announce the coming fall of his nation, was given the privilege of communicating the promise that one day God would make a New Covenant with his people. Jeremiah 31:31–34 describes this New Covenant.

KEY Symbols:

Abrahamic Covenant
a promise of blessing

Davidic Covenant
fulfillment through David's family line

New Covenant
a promise of forgiveness

"The time is coming," declares the Lord,
  "when I will make a new covenant
  with the house of Israel
    and with the house of Judah.
  It will not be like the covenant
    I made with their forefathers
  when I took them by the hand
    to lead them out of Egypt,
  because they broke my covenant,
    though I was a husband to them,
                    declares the Lord.

This is the covenant I will make with the house of
    Israel
    after that time," declares the Lord.
  I will put my Law in their minds
    and write it on their hearts.
  I will be their God
    and they will be my people.
  No longer will a man teach his neighbor,
    or a man his brother, saying 'Know the
    Lord,'
  because they will all know me,
    from the least of them to the greatest,"
                    declares the Lord.

"For I will forgive their wickedness
  and will remember their sins no more."
                  (Jeremiah 31:31–34)

Keys to Understanding the New Covenant

1.	2.	3.	4.
It replaces the Law Covenant.	It operates in the human heart.	It provides complete forgiveness.	The New Covenant was instituted when Jesus died on the cross.

We'll learn more about the New Covenant when we reach the New Testament. In fact, New Testament means New Covenant. But the important thing to note here is that in the darkest of times, through Jeremiah God gave his people what is surely the brightest, most wonderful promise in God's Word.

Madeleine L'Engle: It is a good thing that we are not God; we do not have to understand God's ways, or the suffering and brokenness and pain that sooner or later come to us all. But we do have to know in the very depths of our being that the ultimate end of the story, no matter how many aeons it takes, is going to be all right.[5]

Kay Arthur: You may relate to faithless Israel because you have not loved God as you should, or because you have not lived for him as you should have lived. My friend, know that God is still standing there in mercy, waiting for you to cry in faith, *Heal me, O Lord, and I will be healed; save me and I will be saved* (Jeremiah 17:14).[6]

☞ **Check It Out:**

Jeremiah 42–44

5 *The flight to Egypt (Jeremiah 40–44).* After Jerusalem was destroyed, most of the Jewish population was deported to Babylon. A few Jews remained under a governor appointed by Nebuchadnezzar. When that governor was assassinated, the remaining Jews were terrified and planned to flee to Egypt, but first they asked Jeremiah to ask the Lord what they should do. Jeremiah prayed, and reported God's Word. The remaining Jews should stay in their homeland. God would keep them safe. But if they refused to listen, and went to Egypt, Nebuchadnezzar would attack Egypt, and they would be wiped out.

Instead of listening to Jeremiah the people angrily rejected God's guidance. They told Jeremiah, *We will not listen to the message you have spoken to us in the name of the Lord. . . . We will burn incense to the* **Queen of Heaven** *and will pour out drink offerings to her just as we and our fathers, our kinds and officials*

Queen of Heaven: a
goddess worshiped by
pagan peoples

did in the towns of Judah and in the streets of Jerusalem (Jeremiah 44:16–17).

The last remaining Jews of Judah then left for Egypt . . . and disappeared from history.

Warren Wiersbe: A nation or an individual life can get to the 'point of no return.' If the clay becomes hard, it can no longer be molded. How important it is to yield to Christ early in life.[7]

EZEKIEL

. . . prophet to the exiles

WHO	Ezekiel
WHAT	warned the captives
WHERE	in Babylon
WHEN	six years before the fall of Jerusalem,
WHY	to prepare God's people for a lengthy captivity.

Not Wet, But Dry Bones

The Babylonians invaded Judah three times and on each occasion took a number of captives. In 597 B.C. Ezekiel was taken to Babylon after the second invasion. In 592 B.C., as a 30–year-old, he was called to be a prophet. His messages to the exiles in Babylon parallel the warning of certain defeat that Jeremiah was uttering at the same time in Judah. Through a series of visions Ezekiel was able to describe events for the captives that were taking place in Judah long before word from the homeland could reach them.

THE BIG PICTURE

Ezekiel The book contains a series of messages acted out and preached by the prophet. The bulk of the book dates from before the fall of Jerusalem and is about its coming doom. After Jerusalem was destroyed, Ezekiel spoke of a restored Jerusalem and of a new Temple to be built on the same site as the one that had been destroyed.

- Prophecies against Judah (Ezekiel 1–24)
- Prophecy against foreign nations (Ezekiel 25–32)
- Prophecies of restoration (Ezekiel 33–39)
- Prophecy of the rebuilt Temple (Ezekiel 40–48)

What's Special In Ezekiel?

1 *The emptied Temple (Ezekiel 8–11).* The people of Jerusalem based their belief that the city would not fall on the existence of God's Temple. Surely God would not permit his dwelling-place to be destroyed by pagans. But in a vision, Ezekiel saw God withdraw his presence from the Temple and the Holy City. Afterwards, the Temple was an empty shell. God would not remain with a people whose sins showed him total disrespect.

☞ **Check It Out:**

Ezekiel 18

soul: *here, the person himself or herself*

2 *Personal responsibility (Ezekiel 18).* Many in Jerusalem shrugged off the warnings of Ezekiel and Jeremiah. If their forefathers had displeased God, and he was intent on punishing them, there was nothing they could do about it. Ezekiel confronted this fatalistic attitude, announcing *the soul who sins is the one who will die* (Ezekiel 18:4).

Ezekiel's announcement is one of personal responsibility. In the coming invasion God would distinguish between the righteous and the wicked. The wicked would be killed while the righteous would survive to go into captivity. In Ezekiel 18, the prophet gives four examples to show that God deals with human beings individually.

What will happen . . .

1. If a righteous man has a violent son	the son will die.	Ezekiel 18:5–13
2. If the violent son has a righteous son	the righteous son will live.	Ezekiel 18:14–18
3. If a wicked man turns from his ways	he will live.	Ezekiel 18:19–23
4. If a righteous man turns to evil	he will die.	Ezekiel 18:24–29

☞ **Check It Out:**

Ezekiel 37

☞ **GO TO:**

Genesis 2:7
(breath of life)

I will judge each of you, each one according to his ways, declares the Sovereign Lord. Repent! Turn away from all your offenses. . . . and get a new heart and a new spirit. Why will you die, O house of Israel? For I take no pleasure in the death of anyone, declares the Sovereign Lord. Repent and live! (Ezekiel 18:30–31).

3 *The restoration of Israel described (Ezekiel 37).* Ezekiel is shown a valley filled with scattered and dried bones. He is told to prophesy, and the bones reassemble and are covered with flesh. But they do not live until they are given the breath of life (Ezekiel 37:1–10).

God explains the vision. The bones represented the Jewish people scattered throughout the nations. Their reassembling symbolized the Jews regathering to the Promised Land. But only when the people are filled with God's Spirit will they have life (Ezekiel 37:11–14).

Many believe this prophecy is being fulfilled in our time. For thousands of years the Jewish people were scattered throughout the world, with no homeland. Then, in 1948, Israel became a nation, but a secular state without spiritual life and vitality. When Jesus, the Messiah of the Old Testament returns to rule, God's Old Testament people will recognize him and be saved (Ezekiel 37:15–28).

4 *The rebuilt Temple (Ezekiel 40–48).* Like the other prophets, Ezekiel's message concluded on a strong note of hope. The prophet looks forward to a time of blessing at history's end, when God's people will live in their land and worship the Lord at a Temple that will be constructed at that time.

KEY Symbols:

Breath of Life
God's Spirit (Old Testament)
Jesus (New Testament)

KEY Symbols:

Ezekiel's Vision
dry bones
- scattered Jews
bones reassembling
- Jews returning to the Promised Land
God's Spirit
- gives them life

Study Questions

1. Revival under what godly king saved Judah when the Assyrians destroyed Israel?
2. What sins of Judah did the prophets point to as the cause of the Babylonian victory?
3. Name three of the four prophets who preached in Judah, the surviving kingdom.
4. Name the prophet who preached to the exiles in Babylon before the destruction of Jerusalem.

CHAPTER WRAP-UP

- Godly King Hezekiah's reliance on God saved Judah from the Assyrian forces that destroyed Israel (II Kings 18–19).

- The prophet Nahum described the coming fall of Nineveh as divine judgment on the Assyrians (Nahum).

- The prophet Zephaniah warned the people of Judah that God would judge them too (Zephaniah 1:1–2:3).

- The prophet Habakkuk predicted the Babylonian invasion as a punishment for Judah's sins (Habakkuk 1).

- The prophet Jeremiah struggled for 40 years to reach the people of Judah. His message was rejected, and he lived to see his predictions of disaster come true (Jeremiah 37–39).

- The prophet Ezekiel had visions in which he witnessed the sins of the people in his homeland and the withdrawal of God's presence from the Jerusalem Temple (Ezekiel 8–11).
- Despite the sins of Judah that called for judgment, God would deliver the righteous (Ezekiel 18) and would keep his promises to Abraham. He would save his people at history's end (Jeremiah 30–31).

11 EXILE AND RETURN

Lamentations
Daniel
Esther
Ezra
Nehemiah
Haggai
Zechariah
Malachi

CHAPTER HIGHLIGHTS

- In the Enemy's Land
- Going Home
- A New House
- Eyes on God
- What To Do?

Let's Get Started

In a series of three devastating invasions, the Babylonians under King Nebuchadnezzar stripped Judah of her wealth and population. In 586 B.C. the remaining Jews of Judah were re-settled in Babylon, many in the capital city itself. Some 70 years later the Babylonian Empire fell to the Medes and Persians. The new ruler, Cyrus (see GWDN, pages 126–127), reversed the Babylonian policy of resettlement, and permitted captive peoples to return to their homeland. But at first the captivity forced God's people to review their sins and ask a terrifying question. Has God totally rejected his people?

Three answers to that question are provided in the three books that reflect conditions during the captivity.

While the Jews were captives in Babylon, in . . .

Greece Solon the law-giver introduced a code of laws in Athens, and Aesop first told his fables.

Persia Zoroaster founded a new religion.

Assyria Water clocks were developed.

Lydia Coins made of gold and silver were introduced.

Africa Africa was circumnavigated by Phoenecian mariners.

Around the World

LAMENTATIONS

. . . the agony of defeat

WHO   Tradition says Jeremiah

WHAT   wrote these **dirge** poems

WHERE   in Babylon

WHEN   after Jerusalem fell,

WHY   to express the anguish felt by the Jewish captives.

dirge: a funeral song

Just the FACTS

Oh, Woe Is Me

acrostic: a poem in which each successvie line begins with the next letter of the 22-letter Hebrew alphabet

The people of Judah who had scorned the warnings of Jeremiah finally experienced the consequences of abandoning God. Their despair and anguish are captured in five **acrostic** poems that make up Lamentations.

THE BIG PICTURE

> **Lamentations.** Dirge poems which express anguish and sorrow were a common literary form in the ancient Near East. The poems of Lamentations express the sense of loss experienced by the captives in Babylon, who at last realize how foolish they were to have turned away from God. The five poems depict:
>
> • Jerusalem in mourning (Lamentations 1:1–22)
> • Jerusalem in ruins (Lamentations 2:1–22)
> • A call for renewal (Lamentations 3:1–66)
> • Restitution to come (Lamentations 3:1–22)
> • A cry for relief (Lamentations 4:1–22)

What's Special About Lamentations?

1 *Lamentations gives insight into the Jews' doubt and despair.* These poems express the suffering and regret felt by the exiles. It is their belated recognition that their own sins led to their present, pitiful state. Yet, even in darkest despair there was a glimmer of hope.

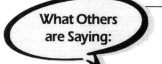

What Others are Saying:

Zion: a poetic name for Jerusalem

Samuel Schultz: The author vividly pictures the plight of God's people as exiles in foreign lands. Can the Lord have forgotten his people? **Zion** is in ruins and Israel seems to be abandoned. Out of a broken heart, crushed and overwhelmed with sorrow, the author makes his plaintive appeal to God who reigns for-

GOD'S WORD FOR THE BIBLICALLY-INEPT

Three Sentiments of Lamentations

Suffering	Confession	Hope
Is it nothing to you, all you who pass by?	Let us examine our ways and test them,	You, O Lord, reign forever;
Look around and see.	and let us return to the Lord.	your throne endures from generation to generation.
Is any suffering like my suffering that was inflicted on me, . . .	Let us lift up our hearts and our hands	Restore us to yourself, O Lord, that we may return;
that the Lord brought on me	to God in heaven, and say:	renew our days as of old
in the day of his fierce anger?	"We have sinned and rebelled	unless you have utterly rejected us
	and you have not forgiven. . . ."	and are angry with us beyond measure.
—Lamentations 1:12	—Lamentations 3:40–42	—Lamentations 5:19, 21, 22

ever, imploring him to restore his own. In confession of sin and an implicit faith in God rests the final appeal for restoration.[1]

2 *Lamentations reminds us to remain confident.* To the exiles, the Babylonian captivity seemed to be an unmixed tragedy. Yet God's people benefited from the captivity in many ways. After being sent to Babylon the Israelites were never again tempted by idolatry. There the **synagogue** was invented, as small groups of Jews began to gather to worship and study the Old Testament. In the end, the captivity proved to be a blessing, purifying God's people from many of the sins that had called for divine punishment.

synagogue: the local meeting place and assembly of the Jewish people during New Testament times

Only God is able to turn what we experience as a tragedy into a blessing in disguise.

Remember This . . .

DANIEL

. . . the influential captive

WHO	Daniel, a young captive,
WHAT	delivers prophecies
WHERE	as a student in the king's School in Babylon,
WHEN	around 605 B.C.,
WHY	to tell people about the future history of the world.

Just the FACTS

☞ **Check It Out:**

Jeremiah 29:4–7

Ezekial 8:1; 12:1–7

Dare To Be A Daniel

Most of the captives taken to Babylon settled in suburbs of the capital city, where they owned their own homes and raised garden crops. Records recovered by archaeologists indicate many Jews went into business and prospered. Daniel (see GWDN, Time Line #1, Appendix A), taken captive in the invasion of 605 B.C., was enrolled in a school that trained administrators for the Babylonian Empire. Daniel rose to become a high official in both the Babylonian and Persian Empires, showing God's continuing care of the faithful even in foreign lands. But Daniel was also a prophet, whose visions of the future told the captives that God remained in control of history, and that one day he would bring his people back to their land.

THE BIG PICTURE 🔍

> **Daniel** The Book of Daniel is divided into two parts. The first half of the book relates stories of Daniel and his relationships with world rulers. The second half of the book contains visions which God gave Daniel to reassure his people that, although gentile powers would rule the Holy Land for centuries, God was still in complete control of human history.
>
> • Daniel's life and work (Daniel 1–6)
> • Daniel's visions and prophecies (Daniel 7–12)

ACT OF GOD

delivered from the fiery furnace

handwriting on the wall

delivered from the lions' den

What's Special In Daniel?

1 *Daniel's personal experiences (Daniel 1–6).* Daniel developed a close relationship with Nebuchadnezzar and subsequent world rulers. Many believe that through Daniel's influence the Babylonian ruler became a believer. Several adventures of Daniel and his friends are recorded for us.

☞ **Check It Out:**

Daniel 8

Dig Deeper

Daniel's determination to follow God's Laws (see GWDN, pages 18–34)	Daniel 1:1–21
Daniel interprets Nebuchadnezzar's dream (see GWDN, pages 35–68)	Daniel 2:1–49
Daniel's companions in the fiery furnace (see GWDN, pages 69–94)	Daniel 3:1–30
Daniel and Nebuchadnezzar's conversion (see GWDN, pages 95–124)	Daniel 4:1–37
Daniel and the handwriting on the wall (see GWDN, pages 125–146)	Daniel 5:1–31
Daniel in the lions' den (see GWDN, pages 147–168)	Daniel 6:1–28

2 *Daniel's visions of future history (Daniel 7–12).* The book of Daniel reports visions of the future (see GWDN, pages 171–330). The visions showed that for centuries to come the Promised Land would be ruled by gentile world powers. Yet the visions were reassuring. A God who could predict the future was clearly in control of history! One day the promises given to Abraham and repeated by the prophets would surely be kept. The captivity definitely did not mean God had abandoned his people. He was still caring for his own!

The Visions of Daniel

Gentile Kingdom	God's Statue (Daniel 2)	Four Beasts (Daniel 7)	Two Beasts (Daniel 8)
Babylonian	Head of gold	Lion	
Medo-Persian	Chest/Arms of silver	Bear	Ram with two horns
Greek	Belly/Thighs of bronze	Leopard	Goat with one horn
Roman	Legs of iron/Feet of iron and clay	Strong beast	

These visions so accurately depict history that some have argued Daniel must have been written around 100 B.C., after the events, rather than in the 540's B.C., Daniel's actual date. Just as Daniel described beforehand, the Persian Empire was overcome by Alexander the Great (the goat with one **horn**), and on Alexander's death his empire was divided into four parts by his four generals (the four horns which replace the one)!

horn: in prophecy, symbolic of political power

3 *The prophecy of the seventy weeks (Daniel 9:20–27).* These verses contain the most spectacular prophecy in Daniel (see GWDN, pages 249–257). The prophecy gives a specific date for the appearance of Israel's **Messiah** in Jerusalem, counting from a future decree to rebuild Jerusalem. In a book called *The Coming Prince,* Sir Robert Anderson calculated that the Messiah, Christ, would enter Jerusalem and be acclaimed as king at the end of the 69th **week** on April 6, 32 A.D. But according to Daniel, the Messiah would then be cut off (killed)! And this is exactly what happened. Jesus made a triumphal entry into Jerusalem but then that same weekend he was crucified!

☞ **Check It Out:**

Daniel 9:20–27;
Matthew 21:1–11

week: seven years

literal: word for word

Lawrence O. Richards: To those who take prophecy in a **literal** way, the picture of Jesus crucified stands out in bold relief. So does a fact not known to Old Testament prophecy—that the

What Others are Saying:

Messiah would suffer and die, and that a great gap of time exists between the first coming of Jesus and his second coming. When this gap finally closes, the last week of Daniel, like the first 69, will see prophecy fulfilled as literally and strikingly as Daniel identifies the empires of Persia, Greece, and Rome.[2]

ESTHER

. . . born to be Queen

Just the FACTS

WHO	An unnamed author
WHAT	wrote this book
WHERE	in Persia
WHEN	between 460 B.C. and 350 B.C.,
WHY	to demonstrate through a series of unusual circumstances that God was taking care of his captive people.

God Watches Over All

Esther is one of the most unusual books in the Bible. It tells the story of a young Jewish woman who became Queen of Persia just in time to save God's people from extermination. While God is never mentioned in the book, coincidence after coincidence makes it clear that God is at work in what appears to be normal cause and effect to guarantee the security of his people. Even when exiled from their homeland, God has not forsaken his people. He guards and protects them.

THE BIG PICTURE

Esther When King Xerxes (see GWDN, page 275–276) divorced his queen he chose a young girl, Esther, as her successor. About the same time a high official in Xerxes court, Haman, felt he had been insulted by a lower official, a man named Mordecai who happened to be a Jew. Haman determined to wipe out the whole Jewish race as revenge, and was given permission to do so by Xerxes! But then through a series of amazing "coincidences," Xerxes decided to honor Mordecai, Esther revealed that she herself was a Jew, Haman angered the king and was executed, and the Jews were saved.

What's Special About Esther?

1 *The book illustrates the doctrine of divine* **providence**. God does not need to work miracles to protect his people. He is able to shape what appears to be the normal course of cause and effect so that his will is accomplished.

2 *The book delights readers of all ages.* Esther is best read through in one sitting, as a short story. Adults and children find the story fascinating, and are attracted to the brave young queen who risks her own life for her people.

providence: *God's shaping of events to accomplish his own purposes*

Warren Wiersbe: God's name is nowhere seen in this book, but God's hand is nowhere missing! He is "standing somewhere in the shadows" ruling and overruling.[3]

What Others are Saying:

The Return Home

In 538 B.C. (see Time Line #7, page 136) a pioneering group of 42,360 Jews set out for Judah, intent on reestablishing a Temple in Jerusalem. A second group, led by Ezra, returned 80 years later in 458 B.C., and a third group led by Nehemiah in 444 B.C. Once again there was a Jewish presence in the Promised Land. Yet throughout the last 500 years of the Old Testament era, far more Jews lived scattered throughout Persia and subsequent eastern empires than lived in the land God had promised to Abraham.

EZRA

. . .the exiles return

WHO	Ezra
WHAT	wrote much of this book
WHERE	in Judah
WHEN	around 430 B.C.,
WHY	to recount the Jews' return to Jerusalem.

Just the FACTS

NEHEMIAH

. . . Jerusalem's walls restored

Just the FACTS

WHO   Nehemiah
WHAT   wrote much of this book
WHERE   in Judah
WHEN   around 430 B.C.,
WHY   to recount the rebuilding of the city walls, which reestablished Jerusalem as a city worthy of respect.

Rebuild Those Walls

Ezra and Nehemiah recount the difficulties and challenges faced by the few Jews who chose to leave comfortable Babylon to return to the Jewish homeland. Those who did return were moved by religious fervor, first to rebuild the Temple, then to teach God's Law, and finally to restore Jerusalem's status as an important city by rebuilding the city's walls.

Who's Who

EZRA: Ezra was a scribe, a highly trained person who was well educated in the Scriptures. His commission from the Persian ruler was to administer God's Law in Judah. He led a second group of pilgrims from Babylon to Judah 80 years after the first group had returned.

Time Line #7

The Captivity and Return of the Jews

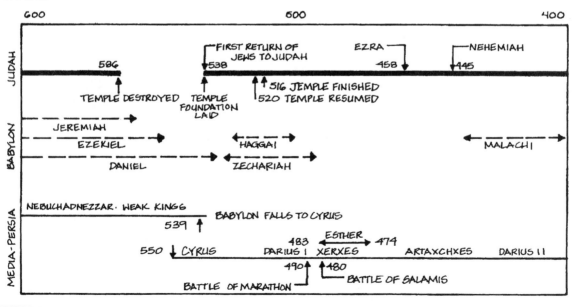

NEHEMIAH: Nehemiah was a high official in the court of the Persian ruler Artaxerxes in 444 B.C. When Nehemiah learned that Jerusalem's walls lay in ruins, he asked for and received a commission to be governor of Judah. There, despite opposition from neighboring peoples, Nehemiah succeeded in rebuilding the city walls and thus restoring Jerusalem's status as a significant city.

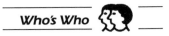
THE BIG PICTURE

Ezra The first Jewish return took place shortly after Cyrus the Persian conquered Babylon. Some 43,000 Jews returned, intent on rebuilding the Jerusalem Temple. While the temple foundation was laid immediately, opposition from the semi-pagan peoples then in the land delayed its completion for 18 years. Then, stimulated by the prophets Haggai and Zechariah, the Temple was completed in four years. Ezra himself led another group back to Judah, with authority to appoint **magistrates** and administer both Persian and God's Law.

The book is organized by the two returns it describes.

- The first return (Ezra 1–6)
- The second return (Ezra 7–10)

What's Special In Ezra?

1 *Cyrus' decree allowing the return (Ezra 1).* About 150 years before the Persians overcame Babylon, God through the prophet Isaiah had identified Cyrus by name as the ruler he would raise up to bring the Jewish exiles home. In the very first year of his reign, Cyrus the Persian fulfilled this prophecy. He issued a decree that permitted the Jews to return to the Holy Land, and to take with them the Temple treasures! At the same time, Cyrus permitted other displaced persons to return to their homelands also. Many believe that Daniel influenced this reversal of policy.

2 *Local opposition (Ezra 4–6).* When the Assyrians deported the people of Israel in 722 B.C. they had resettled the land with pagan peoples. The descendants of these people now offered to help rebuild God's Temple so they could worship there. The Jews refused. The locals were not members of the covenant community; they were pagans.

KEY Symbols:

Jews Returned
to practice their faith
- rebuild the Temple
- teach God's Law
to restore Jerusalem
- rebuild the wall

magistrate: *a government official with administrative and judicial responsibilities*

☞ **Check It Out:**

Isaiah 44:24–45:7

Ezra 1

☞ **Check It Out:**

Ezra 5

Angry, the locals began a campaign of lies, rumors and false accusations that halted work on the Temple for 18 years. The issue was finally settled when King Darius had his officials locate Cyrus' original decree in the archives. The victory of the Jews was complete, for Darius even diverted their opponents' taxes to pay for the Temple's construction!

☞ **Check It Out:**

Ezra 9, 10

3 *Ezra's reforms in Judah* (Ezra 7–10). Ezra arrived in Judah 58 years after the Temple was completed. He was shocked to discover that priests and people had married pagan wives in direct violation of God's Law. His prayer, confessing this sin, moved the people of Judah to repent. The foreign wives were divorced, and the people promised to faithfully observe God's Law.

THE BIG PICTURE 🔍

> **Nehemiah** Nehemiah gave up his position in the Persian court to become governor of Judah in 444 B.C. He rallied the Jews to rebuild the walls of Jerusalem and to repopulate the city. Nehemiah was also deeply concerned about the spiritual state of the Jews. He worked closely with Ezra to teach and enforce God's Law, always setting a personal example as a godly leader. The book can be divided into three parts.
>
> • The walls are rebuilt (Nehemiah 1–6)
> • The covenant is renewed (Neheniah 7–12)
> • Judah's sins are purged (Nehemiah 13)

KEY POINT

How important it is to have leaders we can admire, who set an example for society.

What's Special About Nehemiah?

1 *Nehemiah's moral courage* (Nehemiah 5, 6). Nehemiah himself was the key to the successful rebuilding of the city walls. He set an example in his selfless service, and with the courage he displayed when his own life was threatened by the enemies of the Jews. How important it is to have leaders we can admire, who set an example for society.

2 *Leaders influence the whole society* (Nehemiah 10). Nehemiah's example and Ezra's teaching moved the people of Judah to make a fresh commitment of themselves to the Lord.

3 *Nehemiah's final reforms (Nehemiah 13).* After a successful term as Judah's governor, Nehemiah returned to the Persian court for a time. When Nehemiah returned to Judah in 431 B.C., he found that the people had slipped back into their old sinful ways. Once again Nehemiah was successful in introducing reforms. But it was clear that without strong, godly leaders, the people would simply not remain faithful to the Lord.

William Sanford La Sor: Through the work of Ezra and Nehemiah, Israel's new identity became centered around the Law and [the] Temple. At this critical juncture, through the providence of God's redemptive acts, the identity of the people of God was created by the very religious forms and content that, prior to the Exile, never successfully became the center of their life.[4]

Prophetic Voices

Three prophets ministered to the little group of Jews who had come back to their homeland. Two of them were influential in moving the people to complete the Temple, which had been left unfinished for 18 years. The third prophet ministered after the time of Nehemiah, and provides a gloomy picture of a people who have again lost any interest in worshiping and obeying God.

HAGGAI

. . . rebuild the Temple!

WHO	The prophet Haggai
WHAT	preached four sermons
WHERE	to the people in Judah
WHEN	in 520 B.C.,
WHY	urging them to complete the rebuilding of the Temple.

Just the FACTS

God Has A New House

The Temple foundations had been laid but no work had been done on it for years. In part, this was because the Jews were struggling to **wrest** a living from a land that had been untended for decades. Then, on the 29th of August, 520 B.C., the prophet Haggai announced that material blessings had been withheld because God's people had failed to put him first. The little Jew-

wrest: *take in spite of great difficulties*

ish community took Haggai's words to heart, and, encouraged by additional messages from Haggai, set out to finish building the Temple.

THE BIG PICTURE

> **Haggai** Through a series of four dated messages the prophet moved the little Jewish community to complete rebuilding the Jerusalem Temple. The messages and their themes are:
>
> Put God first. Finish the Temple
> August 29, 520 B.C.
>
> God will provide needed finances
> October 17, 520 B.C.
>
> From this day I will bless you
> December 18, 520 B.C.
>
> David's throne will be established
> December 18, 520 B.C.

What's Special About Haggai?

1 *The glory of the new Temple (Haggai 2:1–15).* The little Jewish community was almost destitute. How could they rebuild the Temple or beautify it? Through Haggai God reminded the Jews that *the silver is mine and the gold is mine* (Haggai 2:8). So the Jews set out in faith to rebuild the Temple. Ezra tells us how God provided. The Persian ruler ordered the Jews' enemies to divert their tax money to pay for building the Temple!

By the time of Christ, the Temple constructed in the year 520 B.C. had been expanded and beautified to become one of the wonders of the ancient world.

2 *Blessing follows obedience (Haggai 2:10–19).* Haggai had made no promises when urging the Jews to finish the Temple. But after they obeyed, and the work was begun, God did give them a promise: *from this day on I will bless you.*

Martin Luther: Faith is a living, daring confidence in God's grace. It is so sure and certain that a man could stake his life on it a thousand times.[5]

☞ **Check It Out:**

Ezra 6:8–12

Haggai 2:1–15

KEY POINT

From this day on I will bless you.

What Others are Saying:

ZECHARIAH

. . . the future of Israel

WHO	Zechariah
WHAT	prophesied
WHERE	to the settlers in Judah
WHEN	at the same time as Haggai,
WHAT	to encourage them to rebuild the Temple and expect the appearance of the promised Messiah.

Just the FACTS

Riding On A Donkey

The prophet Zechariah preached his first sermon on the same day that Haggai preached his second message, October 17, 520 B.C. While Zechariah added his voice to Haggai's in urging the Jews to complete the Temple, the bulk of Zechariah is filled with visions. His visions incorporate powerful images that focus on history's end. Many of Zechariah's images are incorporated in the final book of the Bible, Revelation.

While Zechariah encouraged his own generation to rebuild the Temple, he wanted every generation of God's people to know that God will fulfill the visions of the future that were given to earlier prophets. God's Messiah will come, and his rule will be established on the earth.

THE BIG PICTURE

Zechariah This book is divided into two main parts. The first part of the book contains a series of visions about the future of the Jewish people and a response to questions about **fasting** by the returned exiles. The second part of the book describes God's intervention at history's end.

- *Part I*
  Eight visions   Zechariah 1:1–6:15
  Questions on fasting   Zechariah 7:1–8:23

- *Part II*
  God's shepherd rejected   Zechariah 9:1–11:17
  God's final intervention   Zechariah 12:1–14

fasting: not eating; in Bible times people fasted to show sorrow for sin or fervor in prayer

What's Special In Zechariah?

1 *The eight visions (Zechariah 1:1–8:19).* On February 15, 519 B.C., Zechariah was given a series of visions. Each vision has to do with the future of the Jewish people. Although gentile world powers would control the Holy Land, God would keep his ancient promises. Below is a list of what Zechariah's visions meant and where the visions can be found:

1) God is watching over Jerusalem. (Zechariah 1:7–17)

2) The nations that dominate Jerusalem will fall. (Zechariah 1:18–21).

3) God will protect and prosper Jerusalem. (Zechariah 2:1–13)

4) The Messiah will come and take away sins. (Zechariah 3:1–10)

5) God will provide the needed resources. (Zechariah 4:1–14)

6) God will punish evildoers. (Zechariah 5:1–4)

7) God will purify the land of wickedness. (Zechariah 5:5–11)

8) God's Messiah will be both priest and king. (Zechariah 6:1–15)

KEY Symbols:

God Will

watch over

eliminate enemies

protect and prosper

send a Messiah

provide for

punish evildoers

purify the land

send a priest and a king

Something to Ponder

Zechariah's prophecy	New Testament fulfillment
Rejoice greatly . . . Jerusalem. See, your king comes to you, righteous and having salvation, gentle and riding on a donkey, on a colt, the foal of a donkey. —Zechariah 9:9	They brought the donkey and the colt, placed their cloaks on them, and Jesus sat on them . . The crowds shouted "Blessed is he who comes in the name of the Lord." —Matthew 21:7-9
And the Lord said to me, "Throw it to the potter"—the handsome price at which they priced me! So I took the thirty pieces of silver and threw them into the house of the Lord to the potter. —Zechariah 11:13	When Judas, who had betrayed him, saw that Jesus was condemned, he . . . returned the thirty silver coins to the chief priests and the elders. . . . So Judas threw the money into the Temple and left. . . . they decided to use the money to buy the potter's field as a burial place for foreigners. —Matthew 27:3, 5, 7

2 *Questions about fasting (Zechariah 7–8).* During the captivity the Jews had observed two solemn holidays commemorating the fall of the city and the destruction of the Temple. Zechariah is asked whether, now that the Temple is almost completed, the people should continue to observe these holidays, during which they fasted. God's answer?

> *This is what the Lord Almighty says: Administer true justice, show mercy and compassion to one another. Do not oppress the widow or the fatherless, the aliens or the poor. In your hearts do not think evil of each other.* (Zechariah 7:9–10)

3 *God's intervention at history's end (Zechariah 9:1–14:20).* These chapters are remarkable because they contain a number of clear prophecies about the Messiah, which were fulfilled by Jesus Christ.

Compare just two of these prophecies and their fulfillments.

Warren Wiersbe: He predicts Christ's arrival in Jerusalem. This was fulfilled on 'Palm Sunday,' when Jesus rode into the city (Matthew 21:4–5; John 12:12–16) . . . Jesus came with peace. How did they treat him? Zechariah 13:7 tells us he was to be arrested (Matthew 26:31) and smitten. He was sold for the price of a slave (Zechariah 11:12; Matthew 27:3–10). The result: he was wounded in the house of his friends (Zechariah 13:6) and pierced on the cross (Zechariah 12:10). What a tragedy that the 'City of Peace' should reject her 'Prince of Peace' and crucify him.[6]

MALACHI

. . . *darkness falls*

WHO	The prophet Malachi
WHAT	wrote this last Old Testament book
WHERE	telling the people of Jerusalem
WHEN	around 400 B.C.,
WHY	to examine their actions and respond to God's continuing love.

☞ **GO TO:**

Matthew 9:14–15; Acts 13:3 (fasting)

Dig Deeper

What Others are Saying:

KEY Symbols:

Jerusalem
CITY OF PEACE

Jesus
PRINCE OF PEACE

Just the FACTS

We Haven't Done Anything Wrong

Nehemiah 13 gives details about the repeated sins of those who had resettled Jerusalem. Writing about 30 years later, the prophet Malachi makes it clear that within a few decades God's people were again indifferent to him. This last book of the Old Testament serves as a reminder that throughout history God had been gracious to his people, but again and again they had strayed from him. Surely God must do something dramatically different if he would keep his ancient promises, and redeem humankind.

The Old Testament closes on this somber note. Some 400 years would pass before new hope would burst into the world, as God sent his own Son to become a human being and bring lost men and women back to him.

THE BIG PICTURE 🔍

> **Malachi** The prophet challenges God's people to honor the Lord, but they insist that they are already on good terms with God. Malachi strips away their self-deceit, giving God's answers to objections they raised denying God's charges. Malachi makes it clear that God's chosen people:
>
> - Neglect God (Malachi 1:6–2:9)
> - Break commitments (Malachi 2:10–16)
> - Doubt God's presence (Malachi 2:17–3:5)
> - Deny God's significance (Malachi 3:4–4:2)

The book concludes with a promise and a challenge. God will send his people an Elijah to turn their hearts back to him . . . *or else I will come and strike the land with a curse.*

What's Special About Malachi?

1 *God affirms his continuing love for his people (Malachi 1:2–5).* In ancient times <u>God chose the descendants</u> of Abraham, Isaac, and Jacob, to be his own people, while rejecting any claim of the descendants of <u>Esau</u> to a special relationship with him. God has never wavered from that choice, and never will.

2 *God's people have become indifferent and unresponsive (Malachi 1:6–2:16).* Malachi points to actions which support God's charge. The people offer God broken-down animals as sacrifices, the priests view serving in the Temple as a burden, and

KEY POINT

Over and over again throughout history God has been gracious to his people, but over and over again they have turned their back on him. What is God to do?

☞ **GO TO:**

Romans 9:10–13 (descendents)

Genesis 36:1–9 (Esau)

the people are unfaithful to their spouses. If the people of Judah truly honored God in their hearts, their attitudes and actions would be very different indeed.

> People who care deeply about pleasing God are recognized by the lives they live, not by the words they speak.

3 *God marks and remembers individuals who love him (Malachi 3:14–18).* However corrupt the society we live in, people who love God are to meet together and honor him. Malachi contains these special words of promise concerning true believers.

> *Then those who feared the Lord talked with each other, and the Lord listened and heard. A scroll of remembrance was written in his presence concerning those who feared the Lord and honored his name.*
>
> *"They will be mine," says the Lord Almighty, "in the day when I make up my treasured possession. I will spare them, just as in compassion a man spares his son who serves him. And you will again see the distinction between the righteous and the wicked, between those who serve God and those who do not. (Malachi 3:17–18)*

Something to Ponder

KEY Symbols:

Israel

defective sacrifices
bored with worship
sexually unfaithful

People Today

minimal giving
abandon church-going
sexually unfaithful

Study Questions

1. What Old Testament book expresses the despair of the Jews who were taken captive to Babylon?
2. What book contains a specific prediction about the date on which the promised Messiah would enter Jerusalem as God's promised king?
3. Who were the two leaders whose books tell of the exiles' return to Judah?
4. What book of the Bible teaches by example that God is in control of the details of our lives?
5. What is the name of the ruler whom Isaiah predicted would permit the Jews to return to Jerusalem?
6. What two prophets encouraged the people who returned to finish building God's Temple?
7. Approximately when was the last book of the Old Testament written?

CHAPTER WRAP-UP

- The experiences of Daniel and Esther showed that God continued to care for his people even though they had been expelled from the Promised Land.

- Cyrus the Persian fulfilled Isaiah's prediction by permitting the Jews to return to their homeland and rebuild the Jerusalem Temple.

- The prophets Haggai and Zechariah moved the Jews to finish the Temple after construction had been halted for 18 years.

- Ezra was appointed by the Persian king to oversee the administration of Persian and God's Law in Judah.

- Nehemiah served as governor of Judah. He rebuilt the walls of Jerusalem and kept the people of Judah focused on keeping God's Laws.

- The last book of the Old Testament, Malachi, shows how difficult it was for God's Old Testament people to maintain their zeal for the Lord. To effectively deal with sin, God would have to do something truly new.

THE NEW TESTAMENT

REVEREND FUN

Yup, he's back up in heaven now with his father . . . but you know what they say, "what goes up, must come down."

What Is The New Testament?

The New Testament is a collection of 27 books, all written in the first century **A.D.** They tell the story of Jesus of Nazareth, the Savior promised in the Old Testament.

A.D.: "in the year of our Lord," as opposed to B.C., before Christ

Why Is It Called The "New" Testament?

This collection of 27 books is "New" in contrast to the "Old" Testament. It is also called the New Testament because when

KEY Symbols:

Old Testament
for understanding what God is like

New Testament
for understanding how we can have a personal relationship with Jesus

Jesus died on the cross and rose from the dead, he made possible a new relationship with God for everyone who believes in him.

Get To Know God Personally—By Reading The New Testament

The Old Testament helps us understand what God is like. The New Testament shows us how we can have a personal relationship with God right now. When we have a personal relationship with Jesus we can find fulfillment by loving God and loving other people.

What is in the New Testament?

The books of the New Testament are divided into four different kinds of writings. All of these books tell about Jesus Christ and what it means to be a follower of Jesus. The most important questions any person can raise are asked and answered in these New Testament writings.

THE GOSPELS

Matthew, Mark, Luke, John

Who is Jesus?
What did Jesus' miracles prove?
What did Jesus teach about God?
Why did Jesus have to die?
Did Jesus really rise from the dead?

ACTS

Acts

What happened to Jesus' followers after he rose from the dead?
How did the Christian movement spread?
Who did early Christians believe Jesus was?

LETTERS WRITTEN BY THE APOSTLE PAUL

Romans, I, II Corinthians, Galations, Ephesians, Philippians, Colossians, I, II Thessalonians, I, II Timothy, Titus, Philemon

What does it mean to be "saved"?
What special powers has God given to Christians?
What will happen when Jesus comes back?

LETTERS WRITTEN BY OTHER APOSTLES

Hebrews, James, I Peter, II Peter, 1, II, III John, Jude

How are followers of Jesus different?
Does God talk to believers today?
Where is Jesus and what is he doing right now?

REVELATION

Revelation

How will the world end?
What will happen to people who have not trusted Jesus as Savior?
What will heaven be like?

12 JESUS, THE PROMISED SAVIOR

CHAPTER HIGHLIGHTS

- God The Son
- I AM
- Jesus Said It
- The Word Became Flesh
- Everlasting Life

Let's Get Started

Everyone knows that the central figure of the New Testament is Jesus Christ. Most people have heard the story of his birth in Bethlehem, and know that we celebrate Christmas as his birthday. In fact, every time we look at a calendar or write the date, we acknowledge the fact that Jesus is the most important person who ever lived. The way we count time itself is by the days, months, and years before and after Jesus' birth! It makes sense then to find out just who this Jesus was as we begin to explore the second half of the Bible, the New Testament. The New Testament is about Jesus. But why? Who is Jesus, anyway?

Who Is This Jesus Anyway?

Everyone admits that Jesus was a real person. He wasn't just a myth or a fictional hero. He really lived. But people do have different ideas about him. Some say he was an ordinary but an especially good person. Some say he was an extraordinary person, who was close to God, much like other great religious leaders. Some people even argue that Jesus was a little bit mad, and pictured himself as some sort of Divine Messenger until he got himself killed by going too far.

Christians, though, have a very different idea about Jesus. For almost 2,000 years Christians have been sure that Jesus is actually God. Christians believe that God chose to become a human being and live among us. One of the earliest expressions

KEY Symbols:

Central Figures
Old Testament
- the Jews
New Testament
- Jesus

☞ **Check It Out:**

Acts 2:22–24

Hebrews 1:1–4

of this notion about Jesus is found in the **Apostles' Creed**—a statement that sums up the beliefs of early Christians.

The Apostles' Creed

*I believe in God the Father Almighty, and in Jesus Christ his only Son our Lord, who was born of the **Holy Spirit** and the Virgin Mary; crucified under Pontius Pilate, and buried; the third day he rose from the dead; he ascended into heaven and sits at the right hand of the Father, from thence he shall come to judge the quick and the dead. And in the Holy Spirit; the holy Church; the forgiveness of sins; the resurrection of the body; the life everlasting.*

So it's clear that to Christians, Jesus, who was a real person, is far from an "ordinary" or even an "extraordinary" man. Christians claim that Jesus was unique. Only Jesus can be called the Son of God, because Jesus was God the Son. Only Jesus rose from the dead and is in heaven today. Only Jesus will come back to judge the living and the dead at history's end.

But why do Christians look at Jesus in this way? The answer is that the whole Bible, not just the New Testament, teaches that Jesus is God.

He's In The Old Testament

There are hundreds of prophecies in the Old Testament that speak of an Anointed One whom God will send to deliver his people. In Hebrew *Anointed One* is *Messiah*. In Greek, *Anointed One* is *Christ*. So the name *Jesus Christ* really means *Jesus the Anointed One*, or *Jesus the Messiah*.

Many of the Old Testament prophecies describe what the coming Messiah will do. But some of the Old Testament prophecies state very clearly who the Anointed One will be. When we look at these prophecies, we find out that the Old Testament really does teach that the Christ is to be God himself! Here are some of these prophecies.

> *I will proclaim the decree of the Lord: He said to me, "You are my Son; today I have become your Father"* (Psalm 2:7).

KEY Symbols:

Jesus

GOD THE SON

ANOINTED ONE

MESSIAH

rose from the dead
will come back to judge

1 *Psalm 2 pictures the revolt of men against God (Psalm 2:1–3).
It describes God's response to the revolt (Psalm 2:4–6), and
tells of the future reign of Christ the Messiah (Psalm 2:7–9).*
These last verses express God's intention to install his Messiah
as the ruler of the whole world. In Psalm 2:7 God calls the
Messiah *my Son*. The phrase *today I have become your Father*
refers to a day when the Messiah is proven to be God's Son, not
to the day he was born. So we have to ask, what day was the
Messiah proven to be God the Son?

The New Testament says that when Jesus Christ was raised
from the dead he was *declared to be the Son of God with power*
(Romans 1:3). In Acts 13:32, 33 the Apostle Paul applies Psalm
2:7 to the resurrection, and so does Hebrews 1:5, where the
writer quotes Psalm 2:7 to show that as God, Jesus is greater
than angels. The prediction in Psalm 2 was right! God did provide proof that Jesus Christ is the Son of God.

> *Your throne, O God, will last for ever and ever; a scep-
> ter of justice will be the scepter of your kingdom. You
> love righteousness and hate wickedness, therefore God,
> your God, has set you above your companions (Psalm
> 45:5, 6).*

2 *This Psalm celebrates the final reunion of God with human
beings, using the metaphor of a marriage.* In this psalm the
bridegroom is the Messiah, who is not only addressed as God,
but who because he is God, will reign *for ever and ever*.

Dr. James Smith: Obviously, the only throne which could le-
gitimately be called everlasting would have to be occupied by
deity. Nathan's <u>oracle</u> which promised to David an everlasting
throne finds fulfillment in this Ruler. *He shall reign over the house
of Jacob forever, and of his kingdom there shall be no end* (Luke
1:33). For this reason Peter speaks of the *everlasting kingdom of
our Lord and Savior Jesus Christ* (II Peter 1:11).[1]

> *Therefore the Lord himself will give you a sign: The vir-
> gin will be with child and will give birth to a son, and
> will call him Immanuel (Isaiah 7:14).*

KEY POINT

Trinity—Christians use
this word to express
the Bible's teaching
that God is three-in-
one. An egg has yoke,
white, and shell, and
yet is one egg. God
has Father, Son, and
Holy Spirit, and yet is
one God.

☞ **Check It Out:**

Jeremiah 31:1, 2

Luke 1:29–35

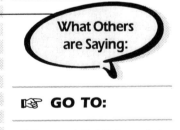
What Others
are Saying:

☞ **GO TO:**

II Samuel 7:12 (oracle)

3 *Three things are striking about this prophecy.* The first is that it speaks of the child of a virgin, born without a human father. The second is that the child is to be named Immanuel. The name in Hebrew means *God with us.* And the third is that Isaiah made this prophecy 700 years before Jesus was born!

What God promised through Isaiah was that God would come to be with us by being born as a baby to a virgin. And this is exactly what we celebrate at Christmas: the birth of the baby Jesus to the Virgin Mary!

KEY Symbols:

Immanuel
God with us

**What Others
are Saying:**

John F. MacArthur, Jr.: The virgin birth is an underlying assumption of everything the Bible says about Jesus. To throw out the virgin birth is to reject Christ's deity, the accuracy and authority of Scripture, and a host of other related doctrines that are the heart of the Christian faith. No issue is more important than the virgin birth to our understanding of who Jesus is. If we deny that Jesus is God, we have denied the very essence of Christianity.[2]

KEY POINT

No issue is more important than the virgin birth to our understanding of who Jesus is. If we deny that Jesus is God, we have denied the very essence of Christianity.

> *For to us a child is born, a son is given, and the government will be on his shoulders. And he will be called Wonderful Counselor, Mighty God, Everlasting Father, Prince of Peace. Of the increase of his government and peace there will be no end. He will reign on David's throne and over his kingdom, establishing and upholding it with justice and righteousness from that time on forever* (Isaiah 9: 6, 7).

4 *This prophecy of Isaiah makes it very clear that the Messiah is God as well as man.* Isaiah says that the *child* who is *born* is already a *son* when he is *given.* It was God the Son, not God the Father, who was born in Bethlehem. As far as his human family was concerned, he was a descendant of David, for his mother and step-father, Joseph, were both descendants of King David. But what does Isaiah say about him as the Son? Look at the names Isaiah assigns to him.

*Remember
This . . .*

- He is *Mighty God.*
- He is *Everlasting Father*, a phrase that in Hebrew means the father, or source, of Eternity!
- As the Messiah, he will reign on David's throne *forever.*

Clearly the Old Testament teaches that the child who is to be born is to be God himself!

Edward J. Young: With this revealed truth may our hearts delight, for he who is born the mighty God is therefore able to save all those who put their trust in him.[3]

What Others are Saying:

> But you, Bethlehem Ephrathah, though you are small among the clans of Judah, out of you will come for me one who will be ruler over Israel, whose origins are from of old, from days of **eternity** (Micah 5:2).

eternity: before time began or anything was created

5 This famous prophecy identifies Bethlehem (see Illustration #13, page 173) as the birthplace of the Messiah. Some 700 years after Micah made this prediction, Jesus was born—in Bethlehem. As the promised Messiah he is to be *ruler over Israel*. But this prophecy adds that although born as a baby, his *origins are from of old, from days of eternity*. And who has existed from eternity? Only God.

Once again we see that the Old Testament indicates that the promised Messiah or Christ is to be God as well as a human being.

☞ **Check It Out:**

Luke 1:34, 35

Matthew 1:20, 21

C. F. Keil: The announcement of the origin of this Ruler as being before all worlds unquestionably presupposes his divine nature; but this thought was not strange to the prophetic mind in Micah's time; it is expressed without ambiguity by Isaiah, when he gives the Messiah the name of *the Mighty God*.[4]

What Others are Saying:

> Then suddenly the Lord you are seeking will come to his Temple; the messenger of the covenant whom you desire will come, says the Lord Almighty (Malachi 3:1).

6 *The people in Malachi's day were asking "Where is the God of justice?"* God through the prophet warned them that *the Lord you are seeking* will come to *his Temple*. In this prophecy about the Messiah he is identified in the Hebrew as the Lord—God himself—who comes to his own Temple.

How Could He Claim That?

It's clear that the Old Testament did teach that the promised Christ was to be God as well as man. Some, though, have said that Jesus never claimed to be God. But when we read the gospels which describe Jesus' life on earth, we find that he really did say that he was God—and that his listeners understood his claims!

> *Jesus said to them, "My Father is always at his work to this very day, and I, too, am working." For this reason the **Jews** tried all the harder to kill him; not only was he breaking the **Sabbath**, but he was even calling God his own Father, making himself equal with God (John 5:17–18).*

Jews: not the Jewish people, but the religious leaders

Sabbath: Saturday, the seventh day of the week

1 Jesus' listeners understood what we might miss. In comparing what he was doing to God working in this world, and in calling God his Father, Jesus was actually claiming equality with God! The religious leaders either had to accept Jesus' claim and worship him as God, or reject Jesus' claim. They refused to believe that Jesus was God's Son, and instead tried to kill him!

What Others are Saying:

Lawrence O. Richards: It is foolish to argue that Jesus never claimed to be God. In this and many other words and actions he affirmed his deity, and was clearly understood by his contemporaries to do so![5]

> *"I tell you the truth," Jesus answered, "before Abraham was born, I am." At this they picked up stones to stone him, but Jesus hid himself, slipping away from the Temple grounds (John 8:58, 59).*

☞ **GO TO:**

Exodus 3: 14 (I AM)

2 When God revealed his personal name to Moses, he identified himself as *I AM*. John 8 records a debate Jesus had with some of the Jewish religious leaders. Christ not only claimed God as his Father but told them *Your father Abraham rejoiced at the thought of seeing my day; he saw it and was glad.* The leaders objected that Jesus, not even 50 years old, should claim to have known what Abraham had thought. Jesus' response was to claim that he existed long before Abraham was born—because Jesus was himself the *I AM*, the Jehovah, of the Old Testament!

Again Christ's contemporaries understood his claim of deity. They reacted by trying to stone him to death, because they did not believe he was who he said.

Craig S. Keener: I AM was a title for God. Jesus is claiming more than that he merely existed before Abraham.[6]

What Others are Saying:

> Simon Peter answered, "You are the Christ, the Son of the Living God." Jesus replied, "Blessed are you, Simon son of Jonah, for this was not revealed to you by man, but by my Father in heaven" (Matthew 16:16, 17).

3 Jesus had sent his disciples to circulate among the crowds, and listen to what they were saying about him. The disciples reported that everyone knew he was someone special, as great as the prophets of old. Jesus then asked the disciples who they said he was. Peter answered for them. Jesus was not merely a prophet but the Messiah, the Son of God.

Jesus' response to Peter makes it very clear that he confirmed the disciples' impression. Jesus was far greater than any prophet of old, for as the promised Christ, Jesus was God the Son.

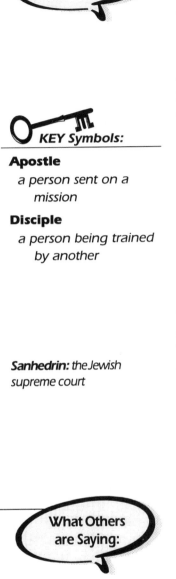

KEY Symbols:

Apostle
a person sent on a mission

Disciple
a person being trained by another

> The High Priest said to him, "I charge you under oath by the living God: tell us if you are the Christ, the Son of God." "Yes, it is as you say," Jesus replied (Matthew 26:63, 64).

4 Jesus had been arrested and dragged before the **Sanhedrin**. Finally the High Priest ordered Jesus to tell them whether he was the Christ. Note that the High Priest added *the Son of God*. The High Priest, who knew the Old Testament, was well aware that the Christ was to be God himself!

Jesus told them *Yes*. He was the Christ, and he was God the Son. Jesus knew who he was. The religious leaders simply refused to believe him.

Sanhedrin: the Jewish supreme court

C. S. Lewis: Christians believe that Jesus Christ is the Son of God because he said so. The other evidence about him has convinced them that he was neither a lunatic nor a quack.[7]

What Others are Saying:

Proof Positive

After Jesus was crucified and raised from the dead, the Apostle Peter preached a powerful sermon in Jerusalem. That sermon is recorded in Chapter 2 of the New Testament book of Acts. Peter talked about Jesus, whose miracles his listeners had wit-

☞ **Check It Out:**

Acts 2:14–36

nessed, and whose crucifixion, which had taken place just two months prior, they were well aware of.

Peter quoted Old Testament prophecies that foretold that the Messiah would die and be raised to life again, and that such proved the Messiah was God himself. Pointing to the resurrection of Jesus as the final proof, Peter announced,

> *Therefore let all Israel be assured of this: God has made this Jesus, whom you crucified, both Lord and Christ (Acts 2:36).*

The resurrection of Jesus was proof positive. Jesus was both Lord (God) and Christ (the promised Messiah). With the resurrection of Jesus all doubt about who Jesus is was put to rest.

He's In The New Testament Too?

After the resurrection of Jesus there was no room for doubt about who Jesus was and is. The New Testament makes a number of absolutely clear statements about him.

> *In the beginning was the Word, and the Word was with God, and the Word was God. He was with God in the beginning. Through him all things were made, without him nothing was made that has been made. . . . He was in the world, and though the world was made through him, the world did not recognize him. . . . The Word became flesh and made his dwelling among us. We have seen his glory, the glory of the One and Only, who came from the Father, full of grace and truth (John 1:1–3, 10, 14).*

1 John the Apostle was one of Jesus' followers. He wrote his gospel some 50 years after Jesus was crucified and raised from the dead. John's special name here for God the Son is *the Word*. What John is saying is that God the Son has always been associated with communicating God to human beings. As the Word he spoke to Abraham and to Moses. As the Word he spoke through the prophets. And now God the Son, the eternal Word, became flesh. He was born as a human being, and lived for a while among us. Jesus Christ is God and has always been God.

KEY Symbols:

Jesus (God the Son)
THE WORD

the Word he spoke to
    Abraham and to
    Moses
the Word he spoke
    through his prophets
the Word became flesh
    ▪ Jesus

. . . the gospel [God] promised beforehand through his prophets in the Holy Scriptures regarding his Son, who as to his human nature was a descendant of David, and through the Spirit of holiness was declared with power to be the Son of God by his resurrection from the dead (Romans 1:2–4).

2 The Apostle Paul reminds us that there were no real secrets about the coming Messiah. God had told his people about the Christ beforehand. All a person had to do was to read the Old Testament prophets to know that the Christ would be a descendant of David, and to know that the Christ would also be God! The resurrection of Jesus was the final proof that Jesus was the one about whom the prophets spoke.

Jesus was and is the Son of God. In Philippians the Apostle Paul urges Christians to follow Jesus' example of thinking of others. He then describes how much God the Son sacrificed in order to come to earth as a human being.

Your attitude should be the same as that of Jesus Christ: Who, being in very nature God, did not consider equality with God something to be grasped. Christ made himself nothing, taking on the very nature of a servant, being made in human likeness, and being found in appearance as a man, he humbled himself and became obedient to death—even the death of the cross. Therefore God exalted him to the highest place, and gave him the name that is above every name, that at the name of Jesus every knee should bow, in heaven and on earth and under the earth, and every tongue confess that Jesus Christ is Lord, to the glory of God the Father (Philippians 2:6–11).

3 While on earth Christ never stopped being God, but he gave up the prerogatives of deity. Jesus allowed himself to be treated as a slave and even put to death by creatures he himself had created!

Even though the Old Testament prophets said that the Christ would be God, some in the first century were confused. Was Jesus an angel rather than God himself? To make very clear just who Jesus was and is, the Apostle Paul wrote these words in a letter to the Colossians.

☞ **Check It Out:**

Luke 1:32

II Samuel 7:16

KEY Symbols:

Jesus
a descendent of David

KEY POINT

Remember the Davidic Covenant. God promised David that a descendent of his would rule forever.

He is the image of the invisible God, the firstborn over all creation. For by him all things were created: things in heaven and on earth, visible and invisible, whether thrones or powers or rulers or authorities, all things were created by him and for him. He is before all things, and in him all things hold together (Colossians 1:15-17).

KEY Symbols:

Jesus Is
the visible expression of the invisible God
the rightful heir to the universe
the Creator of all things

4 *Several phrases in this paragraph are important.*

. . . the image of the invisible God . . .

Jesus is the visible expression of the invisible God.

. . . the firstborn over creation . . .

In Bible times *firstborn* was a legal term which identified a person as the heir with the right to inherit an estate. Paul is not implying that the Son of God was created. Paul is saying that as God the Son, Jesus is the rightful heir to the universe.

. . . for by him all things were created . . .

KEY Symbols:

Angels
powers
rulers
authorities

To make sure that his reference to *firstborn* is not misunderstood, Paul goes on to declare that Jesus is the Creator of everything that exists. In the Bible *powers or rulers or authorities* are angels. Jesus can't be an angel, because he created every being that exists in the invisible as well as the visible realm.

Who is Jesus? He is the very one the Old Testament said the Christ would be: the promised Messiah, God himself! As God, Christ not only created the universe, but even now his power is all that holds the universe together.

In the past God spoke to our forefathers through the prophets at many times and in various ways, but in these last days he has spoken to us by his Son, whom he appointed heir of all things, and through whom he made the universe. The Son is the radiance of God's glory and the exact representation of his being, sustaining all things by his powerful word (Hebrews 1:1–3).

5 *The writer of Hebrews begins by reviewing how God has communicated with human beings in the past.* Those older ways of speaking to us have now been superseded.

These verses make a number of important points.

- God spoke to us by his Son.
- Jesus is the Son of God.
- The Son is the one who made the universe.
- The Son is *the radiance of God's glory.*
- The Son is *the exact representation of his being.*
- The Son even now *sustains* all things.

Remember This . . .

F. F. Bruce: He is the very image of the essence of God—the impress of his being. Just as the image and superscription on a coin exactly correspond to the device on the die, so the Son of God *bears the very stamp of his nature* (RSV, Revised Standard Version). . . . What God essentially is, is made **manifest** in Christ. To see Christ is to see what the Father is like.[8]

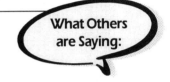

What Others are Saying:

manifest: *revealed, clearly seen*

So Why Did He Come?

When we look at the evidence, it's clear that the Old and New Testaments agree on who Jesus is. Jesus is God the Son. The Old Testament Messiah promised by the prophets was to be God himself. Jesus himself claimed to be the Son of God, and the resurrection of Jesus is proof that he was telling the truth. The New Testament writers unequivocally identify Jesus as the very God who created the universe. So the testimony of the Bible is consistent and clear.

But why would God choose to come into our world and live here as a human being? Why would God let his Son be crucified, and why would Jesus willingly go to the cross?

That's something we'll find out as we look further into the New Testament, and see how it explains Jesus' death and resurrection. For now, though, we can contemplate something that Jesus said:

KEY POINT

Jesus is the Son of God.

> *God so loved the world that he gave his one and only Son, that whoever believes in him shall not perish but have everlasting life* (John 3:16).

Jesus came because God loves us. And because Jesus came, everyone who believes in him can have everlasting life.

Something to Ponder

1. Who is the central figure in the New Testament?
2. Identify two of the four Old Testament passages that indicate the Messiah is to be God himself.
3. Identify two of the four passages which report Jesus' own claim to be God.
4. What New Testament passage teaches specifically that even though Jesus was God, he became a real human being?
5. What event proved that Jesus really was and is God?

CHAPTER WRAP-UP

- The Apostles' Creed is an early statement of the Christian's belief that Jesus is God.

- The prophet Isaiah predicted that a virgin would have a child, and that her child would be *God with us*. (Isaiah 7:14)

- The prophet Micah predicted that the Christ would be born in Bethlehem but that his origins would be *from days of eternity*. (Micah 5:1)

- Jesus claimed to be the *I AM*—the God—of the Old Testament. (John 8:58)

- The resurrection of Jesus proved that he really was the Son of God. (Romans 1:3)

- Hebrews says that Jesus is the *exact representation* of God's being. (Hebrews 1:3)

- Jesus said that love motivated God to send his Son into the world, to give everlasting life to those who believe in Jesus. (John 3:16)

13 THE LIFE OF CHRIST (1)

Matthew
Mark
Luke
John

Let's Get Started

The New Testament begins with four **gospels**. Each gospel is an account of Jesus' life on earth. The first three gospels are called **synoptic** gospels, because they are each organized chronologically. In this chapter we'll look briefly at each of the four gospels, and begin to trace the story of Jesus' life on earth.

gospel: "good news"

synoptic: a summary, telling the story of Jesus' life in chronological order

All About Jesus

Each gospel tells the same story, often describing the same events in almost the same words. Why then are their four accounts of Jesus' life in the New Testament? The reason is that each of the gospel writers shapes his account of Christ's life for a *different* group of people in the first century **Roman Empire**. Matthew shaped his account for the Jewish reader, emphasizing how Jesus fulfilled the Old Testament's prophecies about the Messiah. Mark shaped his account for the Romans, to show that Jesus was a man of action. Luke shaped his account for the Greeks, to show that Christ was the ideal human being. John's gospel emphasizes Christ's deity, and was written to stimulate saving faith in Jesus, the Son of God.

Roman Empire: In the first century, Europe, England, Egypt, Asia Minor, and the whole Middle East were part of Rome's empire

MATTHEW

. . . good news for the Jews

WHO	The disciple Matthew
WHAT	wrote this account of Jesus' life
WHERE	in the **Holy Land**
WHEN	around 60 A.D.,
WHY	to prove to the Jews that Jesus is the promised Messiah of the Old Testament.

Holy Land: modern-day Israel and Palestine

Just the FACTS

Matthew

*written for the Jews
focuses on Jesus'
fulfillment of Old
Testament prophecies*

**Dig
Deeper**

**Just the
FACTS**

Mark

*written for the Romans
focuses on Jesus'
actions, rather than
on his teachings*

pragmatic: *practical*

MATTHEW: Matthew was a tax collector—a collaborator with the Romans in exploiting his own people. When Jesus called him to become a disciple, Matthew immediately left his despised occupation and committed himself to follow Christ.

What's Special About Matthew's Gospel?

Over and over again Matthew quotes or refers to the Old Testament to show how Jesus fulfilled its prophecies concerning the Messiah. Highlights in Matthew's gospel, which are emphasized more than in the other gospels, are:

- Jesus' Sermon on the Mount (Matthew 5–7)
- Jesus' parables of the Kingdom (Matthew 11–13)
- Jesus' teaching about the future (Matthew 24–25)

MARK

. . . good news for the Romans

WHO	John Mark
WHAT	wrote this account of Jesus' life
WHERE	in Rome
WHEN	around 55 A.D.,
WHY	to present Jesus to the Romans as a man of authority and action.

MARK: Mark was a young person when Jesus died. After Jesus' resurrection Mark became one of the apostles in Peter's missionary team. His gospel records Peter's eye witness stories of Jesus' life and ministry.

What's Special About Mark's Gospel?

Mark is the shortest of the gospels. It focuses on Jesus' actions, rather than on his teachings, in order to demonstrate his authority which appealed to the **pragmatic** Roman. About a third of the book is about Jesus' last week on earth, ending with Christ's death and resurrection.

LUKE

. . . good news for the Greek

WHO	The physician Luke
WHAT	wrote this account of Jesus' life
WHERE	in Caesarea
WHEN	around 58 A.D., while Paul was in prison,
WHY	to present Jesus as an ideal human being who came to seek and to save the lost.

LUKE: Luke was a medical doctor who was converted on the Apostle Paul's first missionary journey, and who became a member of Paul's missionary team. His writing style shows him to have been a highly educated man. Luke traveled with Paul until the apostle was executed. He also wrote the book of Acts, an account of the spread of the gospel after Jesus' resurrection.

What's Special About Luke's Gospel?

Luke is the longest of the gospels, written after he *carefully investigated everything from the beginning* (Luke 1:3) by interviewing eyewitnesses to the events of Jesus' life. Luke was particularly interested in showing Jesus' concern for women, the poor, and the oppressed. While Luke follows the same chronological plan of Matthew and Mark, Luke includes six miracles and 19 parables that are not found in the other gospels.

JOHN

. . . good news for all!

WHO	The Apostle John
WHAT	wrote this theological account of Jesus' acts and teachings
WHERE	in Ephesus of Asia Minor
WHEN	from 80 A.D. to 90 A.D.
WHY	to inspire saving faith in Jesus Christ.

JOHN: John was a partner in a successful fishing business with his brothers James and Peter when all three were invited by Jesus to follow him. John lived well into his 90's. He also wrote three of the New Testament epistles and the book of Revelation.

Luke

written for the Greeks
focuses on Jesus'
*   concern for women,*
*   the poor, and the*
*   oppressed*

☞ **Check It Out:**

Luke 7:36–50;
  10:25–42

Dig Deeper

harmony: comparing side by side

Remember This . . .

What's Special About The Gospel Of John?

John's gospel is not organized chronologically. Instead, John selects miracles and teachings of Jesus that emphasize key theological themes, such as New Birth (John 3), Everlasting Life (John 5), Truth (John 8), Life (John 11), and Belief and Unbelief (John 4, 7, 12). Also, all of the events reported by John take place in Judea and Jerusalem. John does not report events that took place in Galilee (see Illustration #13, page 173).

Highlights in John's gospel, which are not found in any of the others, include:

- Jesus' raising of Lazarus (John 11)
- Jesus' last teachings to his disciples (John 13–16)
- Jesus' prayer for believers (John 17)

They All Flow In Harmony

One way to review the life of Christ is to study each gospel separately. Another way is to follow the chronological order set in the first three gospels, and to draw from each gospel. We'll follow the second approach. Here's an outline.

Overview of the Life of Jesus Christ

Chapter 13*	Jesus' miraculous birth
	John the Baptist
	Jesus' baptism
	Jesus' temptation
Chapter 14*	Jesus demonstrates his authority
	Jesus' teachings about God
	Jesus' involvement in controversies
Chapter 15*	Jesus' instructions to his disciples
	Jesus faces opposition
Chapter 16*	Jesus' presentation as Israel's king
	Jesus' rejection and death
	Jesus' resurrection

---

*Chapters from this book, *The Bible—God's Word for the Biblically-Inept*™

Away In A Manger

THE BIG PICTURE 🔍

> **Jesus' Birth** When Jesus was born, the Roman Empire (under the Emperor Augustus) dominated the Mediterranean world. The Holy Land was governed by King Herod the Great, who ruled for Rome. The first hint that the long-awaited age of the Messiah was about to dawn, was a series of angelic visitations to a couple of surprisingly ordinary people. But both met one vital criteria: They were both descendants of King David, from whose line the prophets said the Messiah would come.

☞ **Check It Out:**

Matthew 1–2

Luke 1–3

MARY: At the time Jesus was born Mary was a teenage girl of modest means, engaged to a carpenter named Joseph. Mary's simple and complete faith in God was displayed when she accepted the role as Christ's mother, even though she was a virgin and her pregnancy would be misunderstood.

Who's Who

JOSEPH: Joseph the carpenter was engaged to Mary. When he heard she was pregnant he planned to break the engagement, but was visited by an angel who told him that Mary had not been unfaithful to her engagement commitments.

Who's Who

HEROD THE GREAT: The powerful king of the Jews was aged and dying when Jesus was born. Yet when he heard that a *King of the Jews* had been born, Herod tried desperately to murder the young child.

Who's Who

What's Special About The Story Of Jesus' Birth?

1 *Christ was God the Son before Jesus was born (John 1:1–14).* John 12 shows that in the Old Testament, Jesus himself, and the New Testament, all teach that Jesus Christ is God the Son, who existed from eternity. Christ's life did not begin when Jesus was born!

☞ **Check It Out:**

John 1:1–3

2 *Jesus' two genealogies prove he descended from David (Matthew 1:2–17; Luke 3:23–37).* The Old Testament stated that the promised Messiah would be a descendant of David. Both Matthew and Luke trace Jesus' ancestry, naming only the most significant individuals. Both include David, but the two lists do not name all the same ancestors! Is the Bible wrong? The an-

swer is that one genealogy is that of Mary, Jesus' mother, while the other is that of Joseph, whom neighbors supposed was Jesus' father!

What Others are Saying:

Graham Scroggie: The Davidic descent of Jesus was never questioned. The claim to be the Messiah was never contested on the ground that his descent from David was doubtful. Those who did not accept the virgin birth would know that Jesus' title was determined by Joseph's line, and those who did accept the virgin birth must have had some reason for believing that Mary was of Davidic descent.[1]

J. Dwight Pentecost: Even though Joseph was not the physical father of Jesus, the fact that he married Jesus' mother would confer on Mary's son the rights of inheritance that he had received from the Davidic line.[2]

☞ **Check It Out:**

Luke 1:5–23; 1:26–38; 2:8–19

Matthew 1:18–25

angel: *spirit beings who serve God*

Gabriel: *an archangel; the most powerful of angels*

archangel: *a leader or angel of the highest rank*

betrothed: *engaged to be married*

3 *Angelic visitations are associated with Jesus' birth!* While every child's birth is special, they are not normally announced by **angels**! Yet the gospels record no less than six angelic visitations linked with the birth and infancy of Jesus! Jesus was special indeed.

1) The angel **Gabriel** foretold the birth of John the Baptist. The Old Testament predicted that God would send a messenger like Elijah to his people just before the Messiah appeared (Malachi 4:5–6). Gabriel appeared to a priest named Zechariah and announced he would have a son named John who would fulfill this prophecy.

2) The angel Gabriel appeared to a young virgin named Mary and announced she would have a child who would be the Messiah and also the *Son of the Most High.*

3) The angel Gabriel appeared to Joseph, who was **betrothed** to Mary, and told him that Mary's child was the son of God the Holy Spirit. The angel told Joseph to name the child Jesus, *because he will save his people from their sins.*

4) The night Jesus was born a host of angels appeared to shepherds in fields near Bethlehem, announcing that *a Savior has been born to you, he is Christ the Lord* (Luke 2:11).

5) Later, an angel warned Joseph to leave Bethlehem and take his son to Egypt (Matthew 2:13).

6) Still later, another angel told Joseph it was safe to return to his Jewish homeland (Matthew 2:19–21).

Alfred Edersheim: From the moment Mary was the betrothed wife of Joseph, the relationship was sacred, as if they had already been wedded. Any breach of it would be treated as adultery; nor could the bond be dissolved except, as after marriage, by regular divorce.[3]

4 *Jesus' birth and childhood fulfilled Old Testament prophecies.* Matthew, who was especially concerned with showing Jesus to be the Messiah promised in the Old Testament, notes a number of prophesies that were fulfilled by Jesus birth:

Dig Deeper

Prophecy	Given in . . .	Fulfilled in . . .
He was born of a virgin.	Isaiah 7:14	Matthew 1:20
He was born in Bethlehem.	Micah 5:2	Matthew 2:3–6
Herod murdered infants in an attempt to kill Jesus.	Jeremiah 31:15	Matthew 2:16–18
He was then taken to Egypt.	Hosea 11:1	Matthew 2:13
He grew up in Nazareth.	Isaiah 40:3	Matthew 2:21–23

J. W. Shepherd: Matthew desiring to link the person of the Messiah with ancient prophecy gave his own independent account. Luke narrates in simplicity and brevity, with consummate art the circumstances of the birth, and adds the testimony of various divinely chosen witnesses, who give the interpretation and worldwide significance of the event. Matthew adds to this testimony of universal interest, introducing the narrative of the Magi, the providential flight into Egypt and return to Nazareth in fulfillment of God's plan revealed in prophecy.[4]

KEY Symbols:

5 *Witnesses confirm the identity of Jesus (Matthew 2:1–12; Luke 2:12–38).* Matthew and Luke report other witnesses who confirm the uniqueness of Jesus. Two of the witnesses gave their testimony publicly when Mary, following Old Testament Law, came to the Temple with Jesus to offer a sacrifice for her purification. The other witnesses appeared when Jesus was about two years old. These witnesses are:

Jesus
God the Son
born of a virgin
came from the line of David
angelic visitations surrounded his birth
fulfillment of Old Testament prophecies

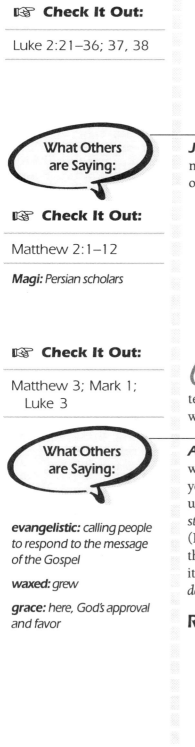

☞ **Check It Out:**

Luke 2:21–36; 37, 38

What Others are Saying:

☞ **Check It Out:**

Matthew 2:1–12

Magi: *Persian scholars*

☞ **Check It Out:**

Matthew 3; Mark 1; Luke 3

What Others are Saying:

evangelistic: *calling people to respond to the message of the Gospel*

waxed: *grew*

grace: *here, God's approval and favor*

1) Simeon, a devout Jew who had been promised he would see the Messiah before he died. God led him to the Temple and to the infant Jesus.

2) Anna, a prophetess who served God in the Temple after her husband died. The day of her husband's death Anna identified Jesus as the Messiah *to all who were looking forward to the redemption of Jerusalem.*

J. Dwight Pentecost: From the mouths of these two witnesses [Simeon and Anna] the nation Israel heard of the arrival of the Messiah.[5]

3) *The wise men (Matthew 2:1–12).* They are called **Magi** by Matthew. They saw a special star that indicated a "King of the Jews" had been born, and they traveled westward from Persia to Jerusalem. Although the story is told at Christmas, Jesus was about two years old when the wise men appeared. The gifts they brought were rich ones, and financed the family's flight to Egypt when King Herod tried to have Jesus killed.

6 *Jesus lived and grew up as an ordinary child (Luke 2:40–51).* The only incident from Jesus' childhood reported in the Bible tells how at age 12 he showed an understanding of God and his ways that amazed adult teachers.

Alfred Edersheim: Of the many years spent in Nazareth, during which Jesus passed from infancy to childhood, from childhood to youth, from youth to manhood, the **evangelistic** narrative has left us but briefest notice. Of his childhood: that *he grew and **waxed** strong in spirit, filled with wisdom, and the **grace** of God was upon him* (Luke 2:40); of his youth: besides the account of his questioning the Rabbis in the Temple, the year before he attained Jewish majority—that *he was subject to his parents' and that he increased in wisdom and stature, and in favour with God and man* (Luke 2:52).[6]

Repent!

THE BIG PICTURE 🔍

John the Baptist Jesus' cousin. His birth and mission had also been announced by an angel. When Jesus was about 30 years old, John the Baptist began to preach in the Jordan River valley. His message to Israel was "repent," because the promised Messiah was about to appear.

What's Special About John The Baptist's Mission?

1 John's ministry was predicted by Old Testament prophets (Luke 3:4–6). The gospel writers quote Isaiah 40:3–5 to describe John's role in preparing the way for Jesus. That prophecy says:

> A voice of one calling in the desert, "Prepare the way for the Lord, make straight paths for him. Every valley shall be filled in, every mountain and hill made low. The crooked roads shall become straight, the rough ways smooth. And all mankind will see God's salvation." (Luke 3:4–6)

2 John's message was one of repentance (Luke 3:7–14; Matthew 3:4–10; Mark 1:2–6). John urged those who came to hear him to repent, stop sinning, and seek forgiveness. John **baptized** those who confessed their sins and promised to change.

3 John's promise of the coming Savior (Matthew 3:11–12; Mark 1:7–8; Luke 3:15–18). When people asked if John might be the Messiah, John told them that Christ was coming. He baptized them with water. John told them the Messiah was far greater than he. He promised that the Messiah would baptize with *the Holy Spirit and with fire.*

J. Dwight Pentecost: The one who would give the Spirit as an identifying sign of relationship would be the true Messiah—not the one who gave the external preparatory sign. Messiah's baptism would not be external but internal. Fire was associated with judgment. When Messiah comes to rule, he will remove all that is worthless, useless, and lifeless; he will accept into his kingdom only what has life—the life which men have received from him.[7]

He Has Come

THE BIG PICTURE

Jesus' Baptism One day Jesus came to the riverside and asked John to baptize him. John refused at first, knowing that his cousin was not guilty of the sins against which he preached. Jesus insisted on being baptized to show his solidarity within John's message. When Jesus was baptized, John heard God speak from heaven identifying Jesus as *My beloved Son,* and the Holy Spirit settled on Christ in the form of a dove. John realized that Jesus was the Messiah he had been sent to announce, and told some of his own followers that Jesus was the one.

☞ **Check It Out:**

Luke 3:1–6

baptize: symbolizing the complete renewal and change in the believer's life

☞ **Check It Out:**

Luke 3:7–14

☞ **Check It Out:**

Luke 3:15–18

What Others are Saying:

KEY Symbols:

John the Baptist
his message
- repent
- stop sinning
- seek forgiveness

☞ **Check It Out:**

Matthew 3:13–17; Mark 1:9–11; Luke 3:21–23; John 1:19–34

What's Special About Jesus' Baptism?

1 *At the baptism Jesus was identified as the Messiah (John 1:29–34). God had told John that the Holy Spirit would descend visibly on the Messiah. The voice from heaven and the dove marked Jesus as the promised Messiah.*

What Others are Saying:

J. Dwight Pentecost: At the baptism Jesus the Son was officially recognized by God the Father as Israel's king. Jesus was anointed by the Spirit for the work that he had come to perform. The Father bore witness of the relationship between the Son and himself, saying, *you are my Son, whom I love.*[8]

☞ **Check It Out:**

John 1:29–35

2 *After the baptism John pointed Jesus out as the Messiah (John 1:35)*

What Others are Saying:

J. Dwight Pentecost: John had prepared the people for this momentous event. The Father had confirmed the appointment of the Son to the Messianic work. Now the Son was officially presented by the designated forerunner to the nation Israel with God's full approval of his person and work.[9]

I Dare You

☞ **Check It Out:**

Matthew 4:1–11

Mark 1:12, 13

Luke 4:1–13

☞ **GO TO:**

Genesis 3:1–7 (tempted)

THE BIG PICTURE 🔍

> **Jesus' Temptation** After Jesus was baptized he was led by the Holy Spirit into the wilderness. There he went without eating for 40 days. When he was physically weakened, Satan appeared and **tempted** Jesus three times. Jesus resisted each temptation and by so doing proved his moral right to be mankind's Savior. Only a sinless person could die for the sins of others. Only after Jesus had demonstrated his own ability to triumph over temptation did he begin to preach to others.

Who's Who

JESUS: Jesus, who is both fully human and truly God, faces each temptation using resources available to everyone who trusts God.

SATAN: Satan is the evil angel who tricked Eve into sinning in the Garden of Eden. Satan tries, but is unable to get Jesus to do anything that is out of the will of God.

 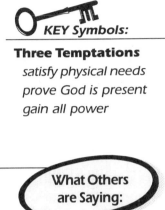

What's Special About The Temptation Of Jesus?

1 *The temptation to turn stones to bread (Matthew 4:1–4).* Physical needs and desires are one source of temptations that all human beings experience. When Jesus hungered, Satan challenged him to turn stones into bread. Jesus refused, quoting Deuteronomy 8:3, which teaches that human beings are not to live by bread alone *but by every word that comes from the mouth of God.* Human beings aren't animals who live by instinct. We can make choices, and our choices are to be guided by God.

KEY Symbols:

Three Temptations
satisfy physical needs
prove God is present
gain all power

G. Campbell Morgan: This perfect man declares that the strength of manhood lies in the absolute abandonment of his will to the will of God, that being the only right he possesses.[10]

What Others are Saying:

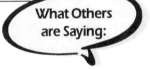

2 *The temptation to prove God is present (Matthew 4:5–7).* Satan took Jesus to the highest point of the Temple and challenged him to jump. Satan quoted Psalm 91:11, 12 to show that God would intervene and not let Jesus be hurt. Jesus quoted Deuteronomy 6:16, which says people are not to test God. Human beings are to live by faith, not by trying to make God prove he is there for us.

abyss: *chasm, depths*

G. Campbell Morgan: To have cast himself from the wing of the Temple into the **abyss** (see GWRV, page 253)would have been to tempt God, and in the last and final analysis would have demonstrated not trust, but lack of confidence. It is when we doubt a person that we make experiments to discover how far they are to be trusted. To make experiment of any kind with God, is to reveal the fact that one is not quite sure of him.[11]

What Others are Saying:

3 *The third temptation (Matthew 4:8–11).* Satan then offered Jesus immediate control of all the kingdoms of the world— if only Jesus would worship him. In the end Jesus would rule over the universe, but this would only happen after he went to the cross. Jesus refused to avoid the suffering that lay ahead. He would worship and serve God alone.

KEY POINT

We are to live by faith, not by trying to make God prove he is there with us.

J. Dwight Pentecost: God's will was to bring the Son to a throne but by way of the cross. The devil implied that Jesus might have what the Father promised without going to the cross.[12]

4 *Jesus used Scripture in meeting each temptation.* In the Old Testament Scriptures Jesus found an answer to each of Satan's temptations. God's Word can help us overcome our temptations too, but we must use the Bible the same way Jesus did. Christ did not just quote a Bible verse, he acted on what that verse taught. When we commit ourselves to do what the Bible teaches, we too will be well on our way to overcoming our temptations.

KEY POINT

When we commit ourselves to do what the Bible teaches, we too will be well on our way to overcoming our temptations.

Study Questions

1. Who wrote the gospel directed to the Jews?
2. Who wrote the gospel directed to the Romans?
3. Which gospel does not tell the story of Jesus' life in chrono-logical order?
4. Why are the two genealogies of Jesus different?
5. What marked Jesus' birth as special and unusual?
6. What was the message of John the Baptist?
7. What happened at Jesus' baptism that showed he was the promised Messiah?
8. Why was it important that Jesus not surrender to Satan's temptations?

CHAPTER WRAP-UP

- The four gospel accounts of Jesus' life on earth were shaped to appeal to the major groups of people in the first century Roman Empire.

- John's gospel is the "universal gospel." It emphasizes the fact that Jesus came and died to save all human beings, whatever their ethnic backgrounds.

- Jesus' birth was unique in that (1) it was announced several times by angels, (2) it was a fulfillment of several Old Testament prophecies, and (3) he was born of a virgin without a human father. (Matthew 1, 2; Luke 1–3)

- John the Baptist fulfilled the prophecy of Isaiah, that a prophet would announce the Messiah's appearance. (Isaiah 40:1–3)

- God identified Jesus as the Messiah when he was baptized by John. (Matthew. 3; Luke 3)

- Jesus proved his moral right to be the Savior by overcoming Satan's temptations. (Matthew 4; Luke 4)

14 THE LIFE OF CHRIST (2)

Matthew
Mark
Luke
John

Let's Get Started

After Jesus' baptism and triumph over temptation he began to instruct and preach in Galilee and Judea (see Illustration #13, this page). He was quickly labeled different from other teachers when he performed miracles that stunned those who came to hear him. He taught as if he spoke with God's own authority. The religious leaders felt threatened by this wonder-worker, so they opposed him, even though ordinary people flocked to hear him. But everyone remained at least a little uncertain about who Jesus really was.

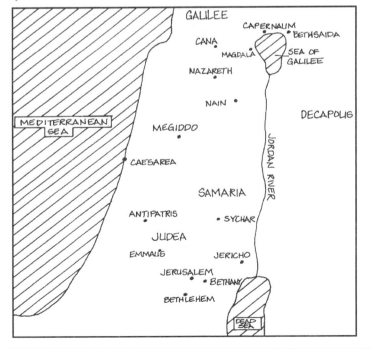

Illustration #13

First-century **Palestine**—Jesus taught and performed miracles in Galilee and in Judea for about three years. Nearly everyone in the tiny Jewish homeland would have had a chance to hear him and to see the miracles he performed.

Palestine: *the Holy land*

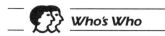

THE DISCIPLES: Several significant groups appear in the gospel stories about Jesus. The most important are Jesus' disciples and the religious leaders who opposed him.

Jesus chose twelve men to travel with him. He was training them to continue his work when he was gone. While the word *disciple* is sometimes used to describe anyone who followed Jesus, *the disciples* refers to these twelve. Of the twelve, Peter, James, and John were closest to Jesus. The twelve disciples were:

Peter	Andrew	Matthew	Thaddaeus
James	Philip	Thomas	Simon
John	Bartholomew	James (the less)	Judas

THE PHARISEES: The Pharisees were a small but influential group of men who claimed to follow every detail of God's Law. They believed that both the Scriptures and the **rabbis'** interpretations of Scripture were equally binding. Jesus followed the Scripture but ignored the interpretations of the rabbis. The Pharisees quickly became Jesus' enemies.

THE SADDUCEES: The Sadducees were wealthy men who controlled the priesthood. They were rivals of the Pharisees, and recognized only the first five books of the Old Testament as Scripture. But they joined the Pharisees in opposing Jesus, who they saw as a threat to their wealth and power.

Miracles From On High

THE BIG PICTURE 🔍

> **Miracles** The gospels contain many accounts of miracles that Jesus performed. These miracles made it clear that Jesus was a messenger from God. As a man who had been blind from birth (until Jesus gave him sight) stated, *If this man were not from God, he could do nothing* (John 9:33). Even more significantly, the healing miracles that Jesus performed had never been done before, and the Old Testament identified them as miracles that would be done by <u>the promised Messiah</u>. The miracles of Jesus were evidence of his authority—as God's spokesman, as Messiah, and as God the Son!

Charles C. Ryrie: Some characteristics of Christ's miracles:

1) They were performed for high purposes. He did not use them for his personal convenience (remember his temptation) but to meet definite needs of others.

2) They were not confined to a single sphere of life, so they could never be considered trickery. They were done on nature, on human beings, and on demons.

3) They were done openly in front of spectators and witnesses. When the gospels were written, there would have been many persons living who had seen his miracles and who would have known and objected if the gospel writers had not accurately recorded the stories.[1]

What's Special In The Miracle Stories Of The Gospels?

1 *Jesus' first miracle produced faith (John 2:1–11).* After Jesus was baptized he returned to Galilee with five of the men who later became his disciples. They stopped off at a wedding in Cana. Wedding parties often lasted for days. When the wine ran out, Jesus turned water into wine. Jesus' companions saw him perform this miracle *and his disciples put their faith in him.*

2 *Jesus' miracles showed his authority over nature (Matthew 4:18–22; Mark 1:16–20; Luke 5:1–11).* Jesus told several fishermen who later became his disciples to go out in their boats and let down their nets. Fishing was done at night, so the experienced Peter thought it would do no good, but said *because you say so, I will let down the nets.* Such a large school of fish swam into their nets that the nets began to break, and the boats began to sink. Jesus controlled the course of fish in the sea!

Astonished, Peter begged Jesus to go away *because I am a sinful man.* Instead, Jesus invited Peter to follow him. Jesus' miracles amazed people, but were intended to draw others to him rather than drive them away.

Other Miracles—Authority Over the Forces of Nature

Jesus stops a storm	Matthew 8:23–27; Mark 4:35–41; Luke 8:22–25
Jesus feeds 5,000	Matthew 14:31–21; Mark 6:31–44; Luke 9:10–17; John 6:1–13

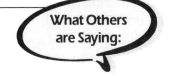

What Others are Saying:

KEY Symbols:

Jesus' Miracles
produced faith

☞ **Check It Out:**

John 2:1–11

☞ **Check It Out:**

Luke 5:1–11

Dig Deeper

Jesus walks on water	Matthew 14:22–33; Mark 6:45–52; John 6:14–21
Jesus feeds 4,000	Matthew 15:32–39; Mark 8:1–10;
Jesus withers a fig tree	Matthew 21:18–22; Mark 11:12–26
Coin in fish's mouth	Matthew 17:24–27
Another catch of fish	John 21:1–17

What Others are Saying:

☞ **Check It Out:**

Luke 4:31–37

demons: *evil spirits, the fallen angels who follow Satan*

J. Dwight Pentecost: The One who had performed the miracle was indeed the Creator[2]

3 *Jesus' miracles showed his power over **demons** (Mark 1:21–28; Luke 4:31–37).* The gospels frequently mention individuals who were possessed by demons. In this situation the demon had gained a grip and tormented the victim by simulating a painful disease or handicap.

The demons who victimized people with whom Jesus came in contact recognized him as *the Holy One of God* (Luke 5:34). Jesus invariably ordered demons to leave their victims. And the demons were forced to obey him.

Jesus' obvious authority over demons amazed those who witnessed these miracles. As Luke notes, *All the people were amazed and said to each other, . . . "with authority and power he gives orders to evil spirits and they come out! (Luke 4:36)"*

What Others are Saying:

J. Dwight Pentecost: The violent convulsion the man experienced together with the loud shriek the demon emitted suggested that the demon was fiercely resisting the command of Christ. Unable to resist, the demon came out of the man. The miracle immediately affected those who witnessed it. The deliverance from the demon was, first, an authentication of Christ's teaching and, second, an evidence of his great authority.[3]

Other Incidents—Authority Over Demons

Dig Deeper

Jesus and a deaf/blind man	Matthew 12:22–37; Mark 3:22, 30; Luke 11:14–23
Jesus and demoniacs of Gadara	Matthew 8:28–34; Mark 5:1–20; Luke 8:26–39
Jesus and a mute	Matthew 9:32–34

A woman's daughter	Matthew 15:21–28; Mark 7:24–30
Jesus and an epilleptic boy	Matthew 17:14–21; Mark 9:14–29; Luke 9:37–43
Jesus and a bent woman	Luke 13:10–17

4 *Jesus' miracles showed his authority over sickness (Matthew 8:14–17; Mark 1:29–34; Luke 4:42–44).* A number of passages mention occasions on which Jesus *healed many.* These passages describe one healing which led to many others. Mark's version reads:

> As soon as they left the synagogue, they went with James and John to the home of Simon and Andrew. Simon's mother-in-law was in bed with a fever, and they told Jesus about her. So he went to her, took her hand and helped her up. The fever left her and she began to wait on them.
>
> That evening after sunset the people brought Jesus all the sick and demon-possessed . . . and Jesus healed many who had various diseases. (Mark 1:29–34)

Charles C. Ryrie: Why was she [Simon's mother-in-law] miraculously cured? So she might serve the Lord. Here is the clue to why God permitted her to be sick as well as many others of his children: so that we might learn that life and health and strength are given to us that we might serve. Sickness can be used to teach us what we should do with our health.[4]

☞ **Check It Out:**

John 9:1–41

🔑 *KEY Symbols:*

Jesus' Miracles
showed his authority over
- nature
- demons
- sickness
- death

What Others are Saying:

Other Healing Miracles that Jesus Performed:

An officer's son	John 4:43–54
A leper	Matthew 8:2–4; Mark 1:40–45
A paralyzed man	John 5:1–23
A paralyzed man	Matthew 9:1–8; Mark 2:1–12; Luke 5:17–26
A withered hand	Matthew 12:9–14; Mark 3:1–5; Luke 6:6–11
A centurion's servant	Matthew 8:5–13; Luke 7:1–10
A hemorrhaging woman	Matthew 9:20–22 Mark 5:25–34 Luke 8:43–48

Dig Deeper

Two blind men	Matthew 9:27–31
A mute	Mark 7:31–37
A man born blind	John 9:1–41
A man with dropsy	Luke 14:1–6
Ten lepers	Luke 17:11–19
Blind Bartimaeus	Matthew 20:29–34; Mark 10:46–52; Luke 18:35–43
Malchus' ear	Matthew 26:51–54; Mark 14:46–47; Luke 22:49–51; John 18:10–11

☞ **Check It Out:**

John 11

KEY Symbols:

Jesus' Miracles
showed his authority to forgive sins

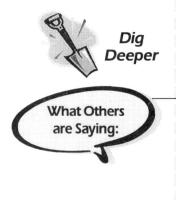

Dig Deeper

What Others are Saying:

5 *Jesus' miracles showed his authority over biological death (Mark 5:35–43; Matthew 9:18–26; Luke 8:41–56).* Jesus was called to the home of a religious leader whose daughter was ill. Before he arrived the girl died. Those who had gathered for the funeral, which in first century Judaism took place immediately, ridiculed Jesus when he reassured the parents. But Mark reports:

> *After he put them all out, he took the child's father and mother and the disciples who were with him, and went in where the child was. He took her by the hand and said to her, "Talitha koum!" (which means, "Little girl, I say to you, get up!"). Immediately the girl stood up and walked around (she was about twelve years old). At this they were completely astonished.* (Mark 5:40–42)

The gospels report two other persons whom Jesus raised from the dead. The most significant was Lazarus, who had been dead for three days when Jesus called him back to life. Here is where these stories can be found:

| Raising a widow's son | Luke 7:11–16 |
| Raising Lazarus | John 11:1–44 |

J. Dwight Pentecost: For men, physical death is irreversible. But for God it is only a state from which every individual will eventually awaken.[5]

6 *Jesus' miracles showed his authority to forgive sin (Matthew 9:1–8; Mark 2:1–12; Luke 5:17–26).* When the friends of a paralyzed man literally dug through the roof of a house in which Jesus was teaching, Christ said to the paralytic, *Friend, your sins are forgiven.* This pronouncement scandalized the religious

leaders, who thought to themselves, *Who can forgive sins but God only* (Luke 5:20–21).

Jesus knew what they were thinking, and challenged them. Was it easier to pronounce sins forgiven, or to tell a paralyzed man to get up and walk? It is of course easier to say "your sins are forgiven." If a person tells a paralytic to "get up and walk," everyone will know for sure he possesses the power to heal! So Jesus, to prove he had authority to forgive sins, told the paralyzed man to get up and walk. And he did!

J. Dwight Pentecost: Christ demonstrated by this miracle of healing that he was God and had the authority to forgive sin. The miracle silenced the Pharisees and the teachers of the Law, who had resisted Christ's claim that he was God and could forgive sin.[6]

What Others are Saying:

The Heart First

THE BIG PICTURE

Sermon on the Mount As Jesus performed miracles he also taught the crowds that gathered to see him. Two sermons from the early ministry of Jesus are recorded for us. Jesus spoke about the same subjects in what is called the Sermon on the Mount, recorded by Matthew, and the Sermon on the Plain, recorded by Luke. Jesus must have preached these sermons often as he traveled and spoke to crowds in Galilee and in Judea. Jesus' Sermon on the Mount highlights important truths that Christ emphasized to his first century listeners.

What's Special In Jesus' Sermon On The Mount?

1 *Jesus taught values (Matthew 5:3–10).* The **Beatitudes** present a set of values which Jesus expects his followers to adopt, because they are important to God. These are not the values most people think of as important.

Blessed are the poor in spirit, for theirs is the kingdom of heaven. Blessed are those who mourn, for they will be comforted.

KEY POINT

The miracles of Jesus were truly unique, and they fully supported his claim to be the promised Messiah, and his authority to teach about God.

☞ Check It Out:

Matthew 5:1–7:29;
Luke 6:17–42

Beatitude: a declaration of blessedness in the Sermon on the Mount

Something to Ponder

Blessed are the meek, for they will inherit the earth. Blessed are those who hunger and thirst for righteousness, for they will be filled. Blessed are the merciful, for they will be shown mercy. Blessed are the poor in heart, for they will see God.

Blessed are the peacemakers, for they will be called sons of God.

Blessed are those who are persecuted because of righteousness, for theirs is the kingdom of heaven. (Matthew 5:3–10)

God values . . .	People value the . . .
the poor in spirit	self-confident
	competent
	self-reliant
those who mourn	**hedonistic**
the meek	proud
	powerful
those who hunger	satisfied
for righteousness	well-adjusted
the merciful	practical
	successful
the pure in heart	"adult"
	sophisticated
	broad-minded
the peacemakers	assertive
	competitive
those persecuted because	popular
of righteousness	tolerant

*Remember
This . . .*

hedonistic: pleasure-seeking

What Others
are Saying:

☞ **Check It Out:**

Matthew 5:21–48

*Law and the prophets: the
entire Old Testament*

J. Dwight Pentecost: In these Beatitudes we see that Christ gave characteristics of true righteousness which was required for entrance into Messiah's kingdom. He promised blessing for those who show the characteristics of this righteousness.[7]

2 *Jesus explained the true intent of Old Testament Law (Matthew 5:17–47).* Jesus told his listeners that he had not come to abolish the **Law and the prophets** but to *fulfill* them. In the first century a teacher who fulfilled the Law explained its deepest and true meaning. Jesus explained what God had intended people to understand from the laws God had given to Israel.

When Jesus did this it became clear why he called for a *righteousness* [that] *surpasses that of the Pharisees and the teachers of the Law* (Matthew 5:20). The Pharisees focused on the behavior the Law described. But Jesus made it clear that God is concerned with the heart, not just with behavior.

In a series of illustrations Jesus contrasted both scriptural commandments and rabbinic interpretations with the inner righteousness which God requires.

KEY Symbols:

Pharisees
focused on behavior

Jesus
focused on the heart

What Jesus Taught about True Righteousness

Matthew 5:	21–26	27–30	31–32	33–35	38–48
Behavior (Pharisees)	Do not murder	Do not commit adultery.	Give legal divorce.	Keep oaths.	Hate enemies.
Source	Old Testament Law	Old Testament Law	Old Testament Law	Rabbis	Rabbis
Righteousness (Jesus)	Do not even be angry.	Do not even lust.	Do not divorce, be faithful.	Do not have need of oaths; always be truthful.	Do good to your enemies; love them.

Warren Wiersbe: Jesus made it clear that he had come to honor the Law and help God's people love it, learn it, and live it. He would not accept the artificial righteousness of the religious leaders. It was artificial. It made them proud, not humble; it led to bondage, not liberty.[8]

What Others are Saying:

3 *Jesus emphasized the personal nature of a relationship with God (Matthew 6:1–8).* Jesus went on to contrast those who truly love God with those whose real love is a reputation for **piety**. Key phrases in Jesus' examples are *to be seen* and *in secret*. In reality, relationship with God is an *in secret*, internal thing. Both the **hypocrite** and the true believer will give **alms** and pray, but the motive and nature of their actions will differ. Jesus taught:

piety: reverence for God

hypocrite: an actor putting on a show to impress others

alms: money given to the needy

> So when you give to the needy, do not announce it with trumpets, as the hypocrites do in the synagogues and on the streets, to be honored by men. I tell you the truth, they have received their reward in full. But when you give to the needy, do not let your left hand know what your right hand is doing, so that your giving may be in secret. Then your Father, who sees what is done in secret, will reward you (Matthew 6:2–4)

Warren Wiersbe: A hypocrite deliberately uses religion to cover up his sins and promote his own gains. True righteousness must come first from within. We should test ourselves to see whether we are sincere and honest in our Christian commitment.[9]

John Wesley: The pure in heart are they whose hearts God has purified through faith in the blood of Christ.[10]

4 *Jesus taught how to approach God in prayer (Matthew 6:9–13). What we call the "Lord's Prayer" is found in Jesus' Sermon on the Mount. What is significant is not merely the words, but the attitudes that the words express. Jesus said, This is how you should pray . . .*

> *Our Father in heaven, hallowed be your name, your kingdom come, your will be done on earth as it is in heaven. Give us today our daily bread. Forgive us our debts as we also have forgiven our debtor. And lead us not into temptation, but deliver us from the evil one. (Matthew 6:9–13)*

Each Phrase of the Lord's Prayer is Significant

The Prayer	The significance
• Our Father	We need a personal relationship with God.
• in heaven,	We acknowledge him as Lord over all.
• hallowed be your name,	We honor God as real and powerful.
• your kingdom come,	We accept God's right to rule in our lives.
• your will be done . . .	We submit to God's will as our guide in life.
• Give us today	We acknowledge our dependence on God.
• our daily bread.	We rely on him to daily supply our basic needs.
• Forgive us our debts	We acknowledge our faults.
• as we also have forgiven our debtor	We commit to live as a forgiven and forgiving people.
• And lead us	We express dependence on God for direction.
• not into temptation,	We ask not to be tested.
• but deliver us from the evil one.	We express dependence on God for protection.

**What Others
are Saying:**

J. Dwight Pentecost: He was not giving them a form that is to be prayed repetitiously. Rather, he indicated the areas that may rightfully occupy a person in prayer and spoke of the different kinds of prayer.[11]

5 *Jesus taught personal priorities (Matthew 6:19–24).* Jesus taught that a person cannot focus on what can be gained in this world and truly serve God at the same time. His warning is summed up in Matthew 6:24: *You cannot serve both God and money.*

The importance of this teaching is explained a few verses earlier. Human beings are destined to exist eternally, long after physical death ends our life on this earth. It is only reasonable to give priority to the eternal and lasting, rather than the fleeting and temporary. So Jesus said . . .

> *Do not store up for yourselves treasures on earth, where moth and rust destroy, and where thieves break in and steal. But store up for yourselves treasures in heaven, where moth and rust do not destroy, and where thieves do not break in and steal. For where your treasure is, there your heart will be also.* (Matthew 6:19-21)

Something to Ponder

6 *Jesus taught trust in God as a loving Father (Matthew 6:25–34).* While the rabbis spoke of God as the Father, or source, of the Jewish people, they did not think of an individual's relationship with God as being like that between a child and his own daddy. Jesus taught that God is by nature a heavenly Father, and that he has a father's love for human beings. Anyone who has a personal relationship with God, has God for a Father, and this means that God is committed to caring for him or her.

Jesus expressed this revolutionary teaching in a familiar passage which emphasizes freedom from anxiety for the person who knows God as Father.

> *Therefore I tell you, do not worry about your life, what you will eat or drink; or about your body, what you will wear. Is not life more important than food, and the body more important than clothes? Look at the birds of the air; they do not sow or reap or store away in barns, and yet your heavenly Father feeds them. Are you not much more valuable than they? Who of you by worrying can add a single hour to his life?*
>
> *And why do you worry about clothes? See how the lilies of the field grow. They do not labor or spin. Yet I tell you that not even Solomon in all his splendor was dressed like one of these. If that is how God clothes the grass of the field, which is here today and tomorrow is thrown into the fire, will he not much more clothe you, O you of little faith? So do not worry, saying, 'What shall we eat?' or*

KEY POINT

But seek first his Kingdom and his righteousness, and all these things will be given to you as well. Therefore do not worry about tomorrow, for tomorrow will worry about itself.

Something to Ponder

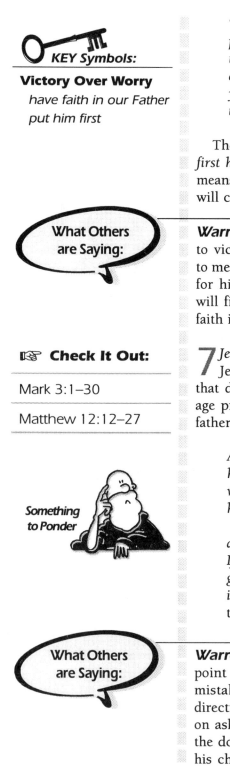

KEY Symbols:

Victory Over Worry
*have faith in our Father
put him first*

'What shall we drink?' or 'What shall we wear?' For the pagans run after all these things, and your heavenly Father knows that you need them. But seek first his Kingdom and his righteousness, and all these things will be given to you as well. Therefore do not worry about tomorrow, for tomorrow will worry about itself. (Matthew 6:25–34)

The key to understanding this teaching is in the phrase *seek first his Kingdom and his righteousness.* To trust God as Father means to put pleasing him first. Because God is our Father, he will care for us when we put him first.

What Others are Saying:

Warren Wiersbe: Three words in this section point the way to victory over worry: (1) *faith* (Matthew 6:30), trusting God to meet our needs; (2) *Father* (Matthew 6:32), knowing he cares for his children; and (3) *first,* (Matthew 6:33), putting God's will first in our lives so that he might be glorified. If we have faith in our Father and put him first, he will meet our needs."[12]

☞ **Check It Out:**

Mark 3:1–30

Matthew 12:12–27

7 *Jesus taught coming to God with our needs (Matthew 7:7–11). Jesus encouraged conscious dependence on God. One way that dependence on God is expressed is in prayer. To encourage prayer, Jesus drew an analogy between the love of human fathers and the love of our Heavenly Father.*

Something to Ponder

Ask and it will be given to you, seek and you will find, knock and the door will be opened to you. For everyone who asks receives; he who seeks finds; and to him who knocks, the door will be opened.
   Which of you, if his son asks for bread, will give him a stone? Or if he asks for a fish, will give him a snake? If you, then, though you are evil, know how to give good gifts to your children, how much more will your Father in heaven give good gifts to those who ask him! (Matthew 7:7–11)

What Others are Saying:

Warren Wiersbe: Why did our Lord discuss prayer at this point in his message? You and I are human and fallible; we make mistakes. Therefore we must pray and seek his wisdom and direction. If we are to have spiritual discernment, we must keep on asking God, keep on seeking his will, keep on knocking at the door that leads to greater ministry. God meets the needs of his children.[13]

8 *Jesus taught life-building (Matthew 7:24–27).* When Jesus' sermon drew to a close, he summed up the choice each hearer would have to make. As Christ often did, he used a story to emphasize his point. In this case it was the story of two men who were building houses. The one built on a foundation of solid rock; the other built on a foundation of sand.

> *Therefore everyone who hears these words of mine and puts them into practice is like a wise man who built his house on the rock. The rain came down, the streams rose, and the winds blew and beat against that house; yet it did not fall, because it had its foundation on the rock. But everyone who hears these words of mine and does not put them into practice is like a foolish man who built his house on sand. The rain came down, the streams rose, and the winds blew and beat against that house, and it fell with a great crash.* (Matthew 7:24–27)

To be able to weather the storm of life we need to hear and to practice the teachings of Jesus Christ.

Trouble On The Way

THE BIG PICTURE

Controversy Jesus' miracles and teaching brought the issue facing Israel into clear focus. Would God's people accept Christ as the Messiah and Son of God? At first it seemed they might. But the religious leaders, who could not and did not deny Christ's miracles, began to challenge Christ and to publicly oppose him. Their fierce opposition led to rising doubt and uncertainty. Both Matthew and Mark describe a critical confrontation.

> *Then they brought him a demon-possessed man who was blind and mute, and Jesus healed him, so that he could both hear and see. And all the people were astonished and said, "Could this be the Son of David?"*
> *But when the Pharisees heard this, they said, "It is only by Beelzebub, the prince of demons, that this fellow drives out demons."* (Matthew 12:22–24)

☞ **Check It Out:**

Matthew 12:22–29

Something to Ponder

Remember This . . .

KEY Symbols:

Ask
 it will be given

Seek
 you will find

Knock
 the doors will be opened

KEY Symbols:

Beelzebub
SATAN

☞ **GO TO:**

Matthew 12:26–29
(Kingdom)

KEY Symbols:

Jesus Taught

God's values

the real meaning of Old Testament Law

a personal relationship with God

how to pray

putting priorities in the right place

God is our loving "Father"

asking God for our needs

building a solid foundation in life

Jesus pointed out the foolishness of their theory. If Jesus' powers were demonic, that would mean Satan was fighting against himself. Such a spiritual civil war would lead to the destruction of Satan's kingdom. It was far more reasonable to assume that Jesus drove out demons by the power of God, in which case Christ was greater than Satan, and <u>God's Kingdom really was at hand</u>.

The issue was clear. But the people, used to following their leaders, were confused. As the controversy over who Jesus was grew, the story of the wise and foolish builder became more and more significant. Would God's Old Testament people build their future on the solid foundation of Jesus' words, or would they turn from him and build on sand?

Study Questions

1. Who were Jesus' disciples, how many of them were there, and what made them special?
2. Who were the Pharisees and Sadducees?
3. Jesus' miracles proved he spoke with divine authority. What kinds of miracles did Jesus perform?
4. What are the Beatitudes about?
5. How did Jesus fulfill the Law and the prophets?
6. Why was Jesus' insistence that God is a Father so important?
7. Why weren't the people convinced by Jesus' miracles and teaching that he really was the Christ?

CHAPTER WRAP-UP

- Jesus performed many miracles in Galilee and Judea.
- Jesus' miracles demonstrated his authority over nature, over demons, over sickness, over death, and his authority to forgive sin.
- Jesus taught the people as well as performed miracles. He tried to help them understand the meaning of a personal relationship with God.
- Jesus taught about God's values, the real meaning of God's Law, how to pray, and how to trust God as a loving Father.
- In all that Jesus did and said, he showed himself to have authority. But opposition to Jesus by the religious leaders led to controversy and confusion about who Jesus really was.

15 THE LIFE OF CHRIST (3)

Matthew
Mark
Luke
John

Let's Get Started

As the religious leaders' opposition became more and more overt, it became clear that the nation would not hail Jesus as Messiah and King. Therefore, he began to teach in parables, and to give private instruction to the disciples, who did believe in him.

We'll Get You Somehow

The Pharisees had accused Jesus of drawing on Satan's power to perform miracles. As their opposition to Jesus hardened, the religious leaders took every opportunity to challenge him and to undermine his appeal to the people.

Chapters 7 through 9 of John's gospel describe what happened one year during the **Feast of Tabernacles** (see GWRV, page 85). John sets the scene for us, describing the tension as everyone waited for Jesus to appear in Jerusalem.

> Now at the Feast the Jews were watching for him and asking, "Where is that man?" Among the crowds there was widespread whispering about him. Some said "He is a good man." Others replied, "No, he deceives the people." But no one would say anything about him for fear of the Jews [the religions leaders] (John 7:11–13).

☞ **Check It Out:**

John 7–9

Luke 11

Feast of Tabernacles: the greatest of Hebrew feasts; lasted seven days

What Happened When Jesus Arrived At The Festival?

1 *The leaders attacked Jesus' authority (John 7:11–15).*

> *Not until halfway through the Feast did Jesus go up to the Temple courts and begin to teach. The Jews were amazed and asked, "How did this man get such learning without having studied?" Jesus answered, "My teaching is not my own. It comes from him who sent me. If anyone chooses to do God's will, he will find out whether my teaching comes from God or whether I speak on my own.* (John 7:14–17)

In the first century a person had to study for years with a recognized rabbi to be accepted as a teacher of religion. How could Jesus be a teacher without having served such an apprenticeship? The implication was that Jesus had no authority to teach.

Jesus answered that his teaching came directly from God. Anyone who was committed to do God's will would realize Jesus was teaching the true Word of God.

What Others are Saying:

Warren Wiersbe: When I teach the Word of God, I can claim authority for the Bible, but not for all of my interpretations of the Bible. Jesus rightly could claim absolute authority for everything he taught.[1]

2 *The leaders attacked Jesus' person (John 7:25–29).*

> *At that point some of the people of Jerusalem began to ask, "Isn't this the man they are trying to kill? Here he is, speaking publicly, and they are not saying a word to him. Have the authorities really concluded that he is the Christ? But we know where this man is from; when the Christ comes, no one will know where he is from."*
>
> *Then Jesus, still teaching in the Temple courts, cried out, "Yes, you know me, and you know where I am from. I am not here on my own, but he who sent me is true. You do not know him, but I know him because I am from him and he sent me."*
>
> *At this they tried to seize him, but no one laid a hand on him, because his time had not yet come. (John 7:25–29)*

The leaders' opposition to Jesus, and their desire to see him dead, was common knowledge. The crowds could not understand why the leaders didn't simply arrest him. But at the same time, they had accepted their leaders' argument that Jesus couldn't be the Messiah because he was from Nazareth. If they had checked the genealogical records, they would have found *he was born in* <u>Bethlehem</u>, where Micah 5:2 said the Messiah would be born.

But Jesus focused on the central issue. He had come directly from God! And this the nation was not ready to accept.

☞ **GO TO:**

Micah 5:2
(Bethelehem)

F. F. Bruce: Jesus asserts afresh his unique relation to the Father, and his hearers cannot miss the implication of his words.[2]

What Others are Saying:

3 *The leaders attempted to trap Jesus (John 8:3–11).*

> *The teachers of the Law and the Pharisees brought in a woman caught in adultery. They made her stand before the group and said to Jesus, "Teacher, this woman was caught in the act of adultery. In the Law Moses commanded us to stone such women. Now what do you say?" They were using this question as a trap, in order to have a basis for accusing him. (John 8:3–6)*

J. Dwight Pentecost: They hoped to show that the Law was so harsh it must be reinterpreted and that their reinterpretation in their traditions was therefore valid. John specifically stated that the Pharisees were not concerned with righteousness or justice. They hoped to trap Christ into saying that the Law was too harsh to be accepted as written and must be reinterpreted.[3]

What Others are Saying:

Instead Jesus challenged the accusers. Let the one who is without sin throw the first stone, he said, and one by one the woman's accusers left. Jesus said, *Neither do I condemn you. Go now and leave your life of sin* (John 8:11). The Law was valid, but Jesus came bringing a forgiveness so transforming that those who accepted him would be able to leave their life of sin.

4 *The leaders rejected conclusive evidence of Jesus' authority (John 9:1–41).* Additional incidents depicting opposition to Jesus culminate in the story of when Jesus gave sight to a man who was born blind. When the miracle is brought to the attention of

the Pharisees, at first they try to deny the miracle. But when many witnesses come forward to testify that the man really was born blind, the Pharisees desperately try to discredit Jesus.

Upon learning that Jesus had made mud and put it on the man's eyes on the Sabbath, they announced: *This man is not from God, for he does not keep the Sabbath (I John 9:16)*. But the problem with this theory was expressed by others: *How can a sinner do such miraculous signs?*

Finally the Pharisees bluntly rejected the evidence before them, and railed at the man whom Jesus had healed.

> *Then they hurled insults at him and said, "You are this fellow's disciple! We are disciples of Moses! We know that God spoke to Moses, but as for this fellow, we don't even know where he comes from."*
>
> *The man answered, "Now that is remarkable! You don't know where he comes from, yet he opened my eyes. We know that God does not listen to sinners. He listens to the godly man who does his will. Nobody has ever heard of opening the eyes of a man born blind. If this man were not from God, he could do nothing."*
>
> *To this they replied, "You were steeped in sin at birth; how dare you lecture us!" And they threw him out.* (John 9:28–34)

What Others are Saying:

maxim: *a saying of truth*

publican: *Roman tax collector*

F. F. Bruce: Without knowing it, the man anticipates a rabbinical **maxim** later expressed in the form: "Every one in whom is the fear of heaven, his words are heard." A miracle of this magnitude must be recognized as an answer to prayer; the man who received this answer must be no ordinary man.[4]

Warren Wiersbe: The religious leaders officially excommunicated this man from the local synagogue. This meant that the man was cut off from friends and family and looked on by the Jews as a "**publican** and sinner."[5]

The religious leaders were now so firm in their opposition to Jesus that when argument failed, they used their power to oppress those who acknowledged Jesus as the Christ. It became increasingly clear that the religious leaders had succeeded in preventing the nation from acclaiming Jesus as Messiah and King.

You Won't Understand

As the controversy over Jesus grew, Christ began to teach in **parables**. When Jesus' disciples asked why he spoke to the crowds in parables, Jesus gave a surprising answer:

> *The knowledge of the secrets of the kingdom of heaven has been given to you, but not to them. . . . This is why I speak to them in parables: "Though seeing, they do not see: though hearing they do not hear or understand."* (Matthew 13:11, 13)

J. Dwight Pentecost: The leaders had already indicated their purpose to reject the person of Christ and to discount his miracles because they believed his miracles were done by Satan's power. On the other hand, some had believed his word and accepted his person, and these needed instruction. Christ did not attempt to separate the unbelievers from the believers and then instruct only the believers. He constructed his teaching in such a way that those who had believed would understand, and those who had rejected, even though they heard, would not understand.[6]

What's Special About Jesus' Parables?

1 *The parables concerned the **kingdom of heaven***. Jesus said that his parables concerned the *secrets of the kingdom of heaven*. The phrase *kingdom of heaven* means *the rule of heaven,* and thus how God exercises his authority in our world. What Jesus revealed in his parables were secrets, in that what he now taught had not been revealed in the Old Testament.

2 *The parables contrast the expected form of God's kingdom with a "secret" form that Jesus revealed (Matthew 13:1–50).* The Old Testament prophets pictured a visible kingdom of God on earth. That kingdom (see GWRV, pages 307–324) will exist one day, but because Israel rejected her Messiah King, God introduced an unexpected form of his kingdom. This *secret* form of God's kingdom will exist until the crucified and resurrected Savior returns to earth.

J. Dwight Pentecost: In view of Israel's rejection of the person of Christ, he announced the introduction of a new form of the kingdom. This present age with its new form of the king-

☞ **Check It Out:**

Matthew 13

Mark 4

parable: *a story teaching a lesson*

What Others are Saying:

☞ **GO TO:**

Matthew 13:11 (kingdom)

KEY Symbols:

Kingdom of Heaven
rule of heaven

What Others are Saying:

Kingdom Parables

The parable	The expected form of God's kingdom	The secret form of God's kingdom
1. The sower (Matthew 13:2–9, 18–23)	Messiah turns all Israel and nations to himself.	Individuals respond differently to the Word of the Messiah.
2. Wheat and tares (Matthew 13:24–30, 27–43)	The kingdom's righteous citizens rule the world with the king.	The kingdom's citizens live among the men of the world, growing together until God's harvest.
3. Mustard seed (Matthew 13:31–32)	The kingdom begins in majestic glory.	The kingdom begins in insignificance, its greatness comes as a surprise.
4. Leaven (Matthew 13:33)	Only the righteous enter the kingdom; other "raw material" is excluded.	The kingdom begins with corrupt "raw material" and grows to fill the believer with righteousness.
5. Hidden treasure (Matthew 13:44)	The kingdom is public, and for all.	The kingdom is hidden, for individual "purchase."
6. Priceless pearl (Matthew 13:45, 46)	The kingdom brings all good things to men.	The kingdom demands we abandon all other values (Matthew 6:33).
7. Dragnet (Matthew 13:47–50)	The kingdom begins with separation of the righteous from the unrighteous.	The kingdom ends with separation of the righteous from the unrighteous.

dom is characterized by the sowing of the Word to which there will be varying responses.[7]

How important it is that we respond to Jesus, and through faith in him enter that secret kingdom of his today.

For You Alone

Something to Ponder

☞ **Check It Out:**

Matthew 16

Luke 15

John 13–16

When Jesus came to the region of Caesarea Philippi, he asked his disciples, "Who do people say the Son of Man is?" They replied, "Some say John the Baptist, others say Elijah; and still others, Jeremiah or one of the prophets? "But what about you," he asked, "Who do you say that I am?" (Matthew 16:13–15)

With this event a significant change took place in Jesus' ministry. Although the people recognized Jesus as a prophet, they failed to accept him as the Messiah. However, as Peter's answer to Christ's question *What about you?* showed, the disciples did recognize Jesus as both the Christ and the Son of God. From this point on, Jesus focused on instructing his disciples.

There is much in each gospel that reflects the private teaching Jesus gave to those who did believe in him. We'll sample some of that private and personal instruction now.

What's Special In Jesus' Instruction Of His Disciples?

1 *The instruction is for those who believe in Jesus as the Christ, the Son of God.*

> "But what about you?" he [Jesus] asked. Who do you say that I am?"
> Simon Peter answered, "You are the Christ, the Son of the living God."
> Jesus replied, "Blessed are you, Simon son of Jonah, for this was not revealed to you by man, but by my Father in heaven. And I tell you that you are Peter, and on this rock I will build my church, and the gates of **Hades** will not overcome it." (Matthew 16:15–18)

Today we define a disciple or follower of Jesus by his or her trust in Jesus as *the Christ, the Son of the living God.* Jesus' private instruction in the gospels is addressed to all who share Peter's belief.

Some have thought Christ was saying that Peter was the rock on which Jesus would build his Church. In fact, the rock is Christ himself. Jesus is the Christ, the Son of God; he is the foundation on which Christianity rests.

Warren Wiersbe: Jesus Christ is the foundation rock on which the church is built. The Old Testament prophets said so (Psalm 118:22; Isaiah 28:16). Jesus himself said this (Matthew 21:42), and so did Peter and the other apostles (Acts 4:10–12). Paul also stated that the foundation for the church is Jesus Christ (I Corinthians 3:11).[8]

KEY Symbols:

The Rock
Jesus Christ
the foundation

Hades: *Greek term for place of the dead*

What Others are Saying:

2 Jesus began to speak of his coming crucifixion.

> *From that time on Jesus began to explain to his disciples that he must go to Jerusalem and suffer many things at the hands of the elders, chief priests and teachers of the Law, and that he must be killed and on the third day be raised to life.* (Matthew 16:21)

Until there was clear evidence that the nation would reject Jesus as the Messiah, Christ had not mentioned the cross. When it was clear that the people would not acknowledge him, Jesus began to tell his followers of his coming **crucifixion** (see Illustration #14, page 207) and **resurrection**.

3 Jesus taught his disciples what it would mean to follow him.

> *Then Jesus said to his disciples, "If anyone would come after me, he must deny himself and take up his cross and follow me. For whoever wants to save his life will lose it, but whoever loses his life for me will find it. What good will it be for a man if he gains the whole world, yet forfeits his soul? Or what can a man give in exchange for his soul?* (Matthew 16:24–26)

KEY Symbols:

Old Life
   life apart from God

New Life
   a life of love, joy, and
      fulfillment
   eternal life

Remember This . . .

A Disciple of Jesus is to

1) deny himself and
2) take up his cross; in so doing he will
3) lose his life, but at the same time he will
4) find it.

What was Jesus saying? In Scripture the cross represents Jesus' crucifixion, but it also represents God's will for Jesus. A disciple's cross represents God's will for the disciple. Jesus expects disciples to do God's will, even when that means denying something they would rather do.

The life that the disciple loses is his or her old life, lived apart from God. The life that the disciple finds is the new life that Jesus gives to his followers—a life of love, joy, and fulfillment—that lasts eternally.

☞ **Check It Out:**

Luke 15:11–27

4 Jesus taught his disciples about God's attitude toward sinners.
Luke 15 records three stories Jesus told to illustrate God's

attitude toward sinners: God is like a shepherd who seeks a lost sheep, and rejoices when it is found; God is like a woman who loses a coin, and celebrates when it is found; God is like a father who rejoices at the return of a son, even though the son has sinned and abused his father's love.

What Others are Saying:

J. Dwight Pentecost: Jesus taught that God loves sinners and searches for them; all heaven rejoices with God at the return of the lost. This teaching was in stark contrast to the attitude of the Pharisees, who in self-righteousness hated sinners and did not rejoice when tax collectors and sinners came to Christ and were restored to fellowship with God.[9]

☞ **Check It Out:**

Matthew 20:17–28

5 *Jesus taught his disciples about servanthood.* Shortly after Jesus had again foretold his coming death and resurrection, James and John, two of the disciples, had their mother ask Christ for the two most important posts in his future kingdom. When the other disciples heard this, they were upset and angry. Jesus used the opportunity to teach them about greatness.

> *You know that the rulers of the Gentiles lord it over them, and their high officials exercise authority over them. Not so with you. Instead, whoever wants to become great among you must be your servant, and whoever wants to be first must be your slave—just as the Son of Man did not come to be served, but to serve, and to give his life as a ransom for many.* (Matthew 20:25–28)

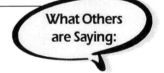
What Others are Saying:

John Wesley: Do all the good you can, by all the means you can, in all the ways you can, in all the places you can, at all the time you can, to all the people you can and as long as you can.[10]

6 *Jesus taught his disciples to love each other.* One of the most intimate and private of Christ's times with his disciples is described in John 13–16, when the disciples shared a meal with Jesus the evening before he was crucified. Jesus began that evening's teaching by giving his disciples what Christ called a *new commandment.*

KEY Symbols:

A New Commandment
*love one another
given at the Last Supper*

> *A new command I give you: Love one another. As I have loved you, so you must love one another. By this all men will know that you are my disciples, if you love one another.* (John 13:34, 35)

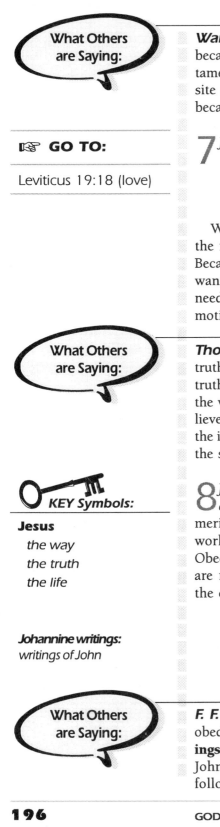

**What Others
are Saying:**

☞ **GO TO:**

Leviticus 19:18 (love)

**What Others
are Saying:**

🔑 **KEY Symbols:**

Jesus
  the way
  the truth
  the life

Johannine writings:
writings of John

**What Others
are Saying:**

Warren Wiersbe: The word *new* does not mean *new in time*, because <u>love has been important to God's people</u> from Old Testament times. It means *new in experience, fresh.* It is the opposite of *worn out.* Love would take on new meaning and power because of the death of Christ on the cross.[11]

7 *Jesus taught his disciples that he alone provides access to God.*

> *Jesus answered, I am the way and the truth and the life. No one comes to the Father except through me.* (John 14:6)

While Jesus' claim is exclusive, and a decisive rejection of the notion that "all religions lead to God," it is also inclusive. Because Jesus is the way, the truth, and the life, any one who wants to can come to the Father through him! The disciples needed to grasp this truth firmly, not just for themselves, but to motivate them to share Christ with others.

Thomas a' Kempis: "Follow thou me. I am the way and the truth and the life. Without the way there is no going; without the truth there is no knowing; without the life there is no living. I am the way which thou must follow; the truth which thou must believe; the life for which thou must hope. I am the inviolable way; the infallible truth; the never-ending life. I am the straightest way; the sovereign truth; life true, life blessed, life uncreated."[12]

8 *Jesus taught his disciples that only love can motivate true obedience.* The rabbis of Christ's day taught that a person gained merit by obeying God's Law, and could thus earn a place in the world to come. Jesus offered eternal life to sinners as a free gift. Obedience is a product of salvation, not a means to it. People are not saved because they obey, but obey because they love the one who has saved them.

> *Jesus replied, "If anyone loves me, he will obey my teaching. My Father will love him, and we will come to him and make our home with him. He who does not love me will not obey my teaching."* (John 14:23, 24)

F. F. Bruce: The vital link between their love for him and their obedience to him is a recurring theme in the **Johannine writings**. *This is the love of God, that we keep his commandments* (I John 5:3), and chief among these is the commandment that the followers of Jesus should love one another; indeed, *we know* *that we love the children of God, when we love God and obey his commandments* (I John 5:2). To love the Father is to love his children; to love the Son is to love his followers; for them to love one another is to love the Father and the Son.[13]

9 *Jesus taught his disciples that to be fruitful they must stay close to him.* One of the New Testament letters describes the fruit that God produces in the believer's life as *love, joy, peace, patience, kindness, goodness, faithfulness, gentleness and self-control* (Galatians 5:22, 23). But Jesus warned his followers that these gifts would be theirs only if they stayed close to him. In the private instruction he gave his disciples the night before he was crucified, Jesus used the image of a vine and its branches to convey this important message.

> *I am the true vine and my Father is the gardener. . . . Remain in me, and I will remain in you. No branch can bear fruit by itself; it must remain in the vine. Neither can you bear fruit unless you remain in me. . . .*
>
> *I am the vine; you are the branches. If a man remains in me and I in him, he will bear much fruit; apart from me you can do nothing. . . .*
>
> *As the Father has loved me, so have I loved you. Now remain in my love. If you obey my commands, you will remain in my love, just as I have obeyed my Father's commands and remain in his love. I have told you this so that my joy may be in you and your joy may be complete.* (John 15:1, 4, 5, 9–11)

J. Dwight Pentecost: Christ used the illustration of the branch and the vine to show what it meant to remain in him. The branch has no life in itself; it draws its life from the vine. The branch is nourished and sustained by the life of the vine. As long as there is an uninterrupted flow of life from the vine into the branch, the branch is capable of bearing fruit. The moment the branch is severed from the life of the vine, it is rendered incapable of bearing fruit. What was true in the natural realm was most certainly true of these men in their forthcoming ministry.[14]

10 *Jesus commissioned his disciples to **testify** about him.*

You also must testify, for you have been with me from the beginning. (John 15:27)

Something to Ponder

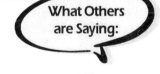

What Others are Saying:

F. F. Bruce: The witness which Jesus had borne, by his words and works, to the grace and truth of God would not come to an end when he was no longer in the world.[15]

The private instruction that Jesus gave his disciples is recorded in Scripture to guide Jesus' followers today. Christians today are defined by the conviction stated by Peter, that Jesus is the Christ, the Son of the Living God. For following Jesus means submitting to God's will, having a concern for the sinners God loves and yearns to save, and seeking to serve others.

Christians committed to Jesus will love each other as he commanded, be moved by love to obey God, maintain that intimate relationship with Jesus which is required for fruitfulness, and tell others about the love and grace of God expressed in Jesus Christ.

KEY Symbols:

Committed Christians

love each other
obey God
are fruitful
tell others

Study Questions

1. Who brought the charge that Satan was behind the miracles Jesus performed?
2. Why was the charge that Jesus had not "studied" important?
3. What argument of the blind man did the Pharisees reject in order to condemn Jesus?
4. Why did Jesus begin to use parables in speaking to the crowds?
5. What was the subject of the parables of Jesus?
6. What belief marks a person as a true disciple of Jesus?
7. What is the key to greatness for a disciple of Jesus?
8. What was Jesus' *new commandment* to his disciples?

CHAPTER WRAP-UP

- The Pharisees and other religious leaders openly attacked and tried to undermine Jesus.
- The Pharisees and other religious leaders used their powers of excommunication to punish those who supported Jesus.
- When it became clear that the nation would not accept Jesus as the Messiah and Son of God, he began to teach in parables.
- Jesus' parables were about a form of God's rule on earth that had not been predicted in the Old Testament.
- Jesus gave private instruction to the disciples, who did believe in him as Christ, the Son of God.
- Jesus taught his disciples to choose God's will, to love each other, and to serve others.
- Jesus taught that love for him would produce obedience, and that disciples who obey him will live fruitful, productive lives.

16 THE LIFE OF CHRIST (4)

Matthew
Mark
Luke
John

CHAPTER HIGHLIGHTS

- Triumphal Entry
- Gethsemane
- The Cross
- Victory Over Death

Let's Get Started

During the last week of his life, Jesus again went to Jerusalem for the Passover Festival. When he entered the city he was loudly acclaimed the Messiah. But within a few days he was arrested, tried before religious and Roman courts, condemned to death, and executed. The hopes of his followers were dashed. But within three days, Jesus rose from the grave!

A King On A Donkey?

THE BIG PICTURE 🔍

> **Final Week** The week began when Jesus entered Jerusalem riding on a donkey. He was praised as the *Son of David* by the crowds who had come for the festival. The leaders reacted by unsuccessfully trying to trap him. Jesus finally, openly condemned them. But Jesus privately instructed his disciples about what to expect in the future.

☞ **Check It Out:**

Matthew 21–25; Mark 11–13; Luke 19–21; John 12

What Was Special About Jesus' Last Week On Earth?

1 *The triumphal entry (Matthew 21:1–17; Mark 11:1–11; Luke 19:28–44).* Some 400 years earlier the prophet Zechariah had announced that Israel's king would enter Jerusalem *gentle and riding on a donkey, on a colt, the foal of a donkey* (Zechariah 9:9). Matthew describes the scene in Jerusalem on what we call "Palm Sunday."

> [The disciples] *brought the donkey and the colt, placed their cloaks on them and Jesus sat on them. A very large crowd spread their cloaks on the road, while others cut branches from the trees and spread them on the road. The crowds that went ahead of him and those that followed shouted,*
>
> > *"**Hosanna** to the Son of David!"*
> > *"Blessed is he who comes in the name of the Lord!"*
> > *"Hosanna in the highest!"*
>
> *When Jesus entered Jerusalem, the whole city was stirred and asked, "Who is this?"*
>
> *The crowds answered, "This is Jesus, the prophet from Nazareth in Galilee."* (Matthew 21:7–11)

Hosanna: *a Hebrew expression meaning "Save!"*

What Others are Saying:

J. Dwight Pentecost: This was the day of Christ's official presentation of himself as Messiah to Israel. Christ was identified before the nation as the Messiah at his baptism. He was authenticated as Messiah at his temptation. But it was at this triumphal entry that Christ made an official presentation of himself as Messiah to the nation.[1]

2 Jesus drove merchants out of the Temple (Matthew 21:12–17; Mark 11:12–17). Jewish pilgrims who came to worship God at the Temple were forced by the chief priests to use only "Temple money" to pay a tax that Old Testament Law required. "Money changers" had set up tables in the Temple where the correct coins, Tyran Duodrachma, could be purchased at an exorbitant price. Other merchants sold sacrificial animals that had been certified by the priests as being without blemish, again charging high rates. The chief priests received a percentage of the income. After coming into the city . . .

KEY Symbols:

Temple Money
Tyran Duodrachma
- tax money

> *Jesus entered the Temple area and drove out all who were buying and selling there. He overturned the tables of the money changers and the benches of those selling doves. "It is written," he said to them, "'My house shall be called a house of prayer,' but you have made it a 'den of robbers.'"* (Matthew 21:12, 13)

What Others are Saying:

Warren Wiersbe: The dealers charged exorbitant prices and no one could compete with them or oppose them. Historians tell us that Annas, the former High Priest, was the manager of this enterprise, assisted by his sons. The purpose of the Court of the Gentiles (see GWRV, Illustration #5, page 153) in the Temple was to give the 'outcasts' an opportunity to enter the Temple and learn from Israel about the true God. But the presence of this 'religious market' turned many sensitive Gentiles away from the witness of Israel. The Court of the Gentiles was used for mercenary business, not missionary business.[2]

3 *Jesus exposed the motives of the religious leaders when they challenged his authority (Matthew 21:22–27; 33–45; Mark 11:27–12:12).* In driving the merchants from the Temple Jesus had directly challenged the chief priests. A delegation of priests, with teachers of the Law and elders, demanded that Jesus tell them who gave him the authority to do what he had done. Jesus refused, and told a story about tenants who were left to tend their owner's vineyard. When the owner sent servants to collect his share, the tenants beat some and killed others. Finally the owner sent his son.

Jesus concluded . . .

> But the tenants said to one another, "This is the heir. Come, let's kill him and the inheritance will be ours." So they took him and killed him and threw him out of the vineyard. What then will the owner of the vineyard do? He will come and kill those tenants and give the vineyard to others. (Mark 12:7–9)

The religious leaders realized that Jesus was speaking about them. They were the tenants, left in charge of God's vineyards. The servants were the prophets God had sent their forefathers; Jesus was the son. They wanted desperately to arrest Jesus, but they feared the reaction of the crowd.

Later at midnight they would seize Jesus . . . and by dawn they would condemn him to death.

4 *The leaders tried desperately to turn the people against Jesus (Matthew 22:15–22; Mark 12:13–17; Luke 20:20–26).* The most dangerous trap was set by a group of Pharisees and **Herodians**. They asked Jesus the question, *Is it right to pay taxes to **Caesar** or not? Should we pay or shouldn't we?* (Matthew 22:17)

Alfred Edersheim explains why the Pharisees were convinced that this question would bring Jesus down.

☞ **Check It Out:**

Mark 11:27–12:12

KEY Symbols:

Parable of the Tenants and the Vineyard

vineyard
- God's

tenants
- religious leaders

servants
- God's prophets

heir
- Jesus
- killed by the tenants

Herodians: *a political party that supported the royal family of King Herod*

Caesar: *Augustus; Emperor of Rome; here, it is a symbol for civil authority*

**What Others
are Saying:**

Alfred Edersheim: There was a strong party in the land, with which, not only politically but religiously, many of the noblest spirits would sympathize, which maintained, that to pay the tribute-money to Caesar was virtually to own his royal authority, and so to disown that of Jehovah, who alone was Israel's king. They would argue, that all the miseries of the land and people were due to this national unfaithfulness. Indeed, this was the fundamental principle of the Nationalist movement.

To have said No, would have been to command rebellion; to have said simply Yes, would have been to give a painful shock to deep feeling, and, in a sense, in the eyes of the people, the lie to his own claim of being Israel's Messiah King.[3]

Jesus stunned his opponents by asking them for a coin, and then asking whose portrait was on it. When the Pharisees answered, *Caesar's,* Jesus said *Give to Caesar what is Caesar's and to God what is God's* (Mark 12:17).

This, with other attempts to trap Jesus on that last week, failed utterly.

5 *Jesus successfully exposed the hypocrisy of the religious leaders (Matthew 22:41–46; Mark 12:35–37; Luke 20:41–44).* Jesus exposed the hypocrisy of the leaders when he asked the Pharisees a question about Old Testament teaching on the Christ.

> *"Whose son is he?"*
> *"The son of David," they replied.*
> *He said to them, "How is it then that David, speaking by*
>   *the Spirit, calls him 'Lord'? For he says,*
> *'The Lord said to my Lord:*
>   *Sit at my right hand*
> *until I put your enemies*
>   *under your feet.'*
> *If then David calls him 'Lord,' how can he be his son?"*
> (Matthew 22:42–45)

**What Others
are Saying:**

J. Dwight Pentecost: Psalm [110] was universally recognized as messianic. The one invited to sit at the Lord's right hand was the Messiah. The 'Lord' who invited him to sit at his right hand was the God of Abraham. The Messiah was referred to as 'my Lord.' With this interpretation the Pharisees would have been in agreement. Christ addressed this question to them: If the Messiah was the 'son,' or descendant, of David, "How is it then that David, speaking by the Spirit, calls him 'Lord'?" It was not natural for one to call his own son "my Lord." The fact that Messiah was David's son testified to Messiah's true humanity, but the fact that David called him "my Lord" testified to his true and undiminished deity, for "Lord" was a title for Deity. . . . It was just such a claim as the psalmist foretold of Messiah that Jesus made for himself. If the Pharisees answered that David called him his Lord because he is God, then they could not object to Christ, David's son according to the flesh, claiming to be the Son of God. If they agreed that Messiah was to be truly human and truly God, they must cease their objections to Christ's claim concerning his person. The Pharisees realized the dilemma that faced them and refused to answer.[4]

The incident proved that the Pharisees knew the rightness of Jesus' claims—and hated him anyway. The religious leaders who claimed the right to interpret God's Word were rebellious tenants, who rather than submit to the authority of God's Son would seek any excuse to kill him.

With this established, Jesus openly and forcefully condemned the *teachers of the Law and Pharisees* as hypocrites.

6 *Jesus then taught his disciples about the future (Matthew 24–25; Mark 13; Luke 21:5–36).* Jesus was well aware that the religious leaders were determined to kill him. That last week he took the time to speak with his disciples privately about what would happen after his death and resurrection. Included in Jesus' teaching were three key points.

First, Jesus himself would return to earth in power and glory.

> *They will see the Son of Man coming on the clouds of the sky, with power and great glory. And he will send his angels with a loud trumpet call, and they will gather his elect from the four winds, from one end of the heavens to the other.* (Matthew 24:30–31)

Second, no one would be able to predict when he would return.

> *No one knows about that day or hour, not even the angels in heaven, nor the Son, but only the Father.* (Matthew 24:36)

Third, until he does come, Jesus' followers are to watch for him and serve him faithfully.

☞ **Check It Out:**

Matthew 23:1–37

KEY Symbols:

Three Key Points
Jesus will return
no one knows when
watch and serve him
faithfully

Caiaphas: High Priest at the time of Jesus' crucifixion

☞ **Check It Out:**

Matthew 26:17–27:31;
Mark 14:12–15:16;
Luke 22:1–23:23;
John 13:1–19:16

Dig Deeper

Therefore keep watch, because you do not know on what day your Lord will come. . . . So you also must be ready, because the Son of Man will come at an hour when you do not expect him. (Matthew 24:42, 44)

7 *Even while Jesus was speaking to his disciples, the leaders were plotting to kill him (Matthew 26:3–5).*

*Then the chief priests and the elders of the people assembled in the palace of the High Priest, whose name was **Caiaphas**, and they plotted to arrest Jesus in some sly way and kill him. "But not during the Feast," they said, "or there may be a riot among the people." (Matthew 26:3–5)*

Jesus' Last Day on Earth

Events	Matthew	Mark	Luke	John
Jesus prays in Gethsemane.	26:36–46	14:32–42	22:39–46	18:1
Jesus is arrested there.	26:47–56	14:43–52	22:47–53	18:2–12
Jesus is tried before Annas.	–	–	–	18:12–23
Jesus is tried before Caiaphas.	26:57–68	14:53–65	22:54–65	18:24
Peter denies Jesus.	26:69–75	14:66–72	22:54–62	18:15–27
Jesus is condemned by Sanhedrin.	27:1	15:1	22:66–71	–
Judas commits suicide.	27:3–10	–	–	–
Jesus is tried by Pilate.	27:11–14	15:2–5	23:1–5	18:28–38
Jesus is tried by Herod.	–	–	23:6–12	–
Jesus is condemned by Pilate.	27:15–26	15:6–15	23:13–25	18:39–19:16
Jesus is mocked and scourged.	27:27–30	15:16–19	–	19:2–3
Jesus is led to Calvary.	27:31–34	15:20–23	23:26–33	19:16–17

Tomorrow Doesn't Look Good

☞ **GO TO:**

John 17 (prayer)

Each of the gospels gives a detailed account of Jesus' last day on earth which, according to Jewish reckoning, began at sundown. But not each gospel account includes every feature of that final, fateful day. As evening approached several disciples made arrangements to share a meal with Jesus (the Last Supper), even as Judas arranged with the High Priest to betray Jesus for 30 pieces of silver. John's gospel describes the meal and the conversation there, and records <u>a prayer that Jesus offered for all believers</u>. Other events followed, in this order:

What's Special In Jesus' Last Day?

1 *Jesus' prayer in Gethsemane (Matthew 26:36–46; Mark 14:32–42; Luke 22:39–42).* Gethsemane was an olive grove, that grew on a hill across the Kedron Valley from Jerusalem.

> *They went to a place called Gethsemane, and Jesus said to his disciples, "Sit here while I pray." He took Peter, James and John along with him, and he began to be deeply distressed and troubled. "My soul is overwhelmed with sorrow to the point of death," he said to them. "Stay here and keep watch."*
>
> *Going a little further, he fell to the ground and prayed that if possible the hour might pass from him. "**Abba**, Father," he said, "everything is possible for you. Take this cup from me. Yet not what I will, but what you will." (Mark 14:32–37)*

Abba: *"daddy" in Aramaic, the language Jesus spoke!*

The prayer of Jesus has puzzled many. Did Jesus really beg to avoid the crucifixion? He had said earlier that he had come to earth *not to be served, but to serve, and give his life as a ransom for many* (Matthew 20:28). Pentecost gives the best explanation of Christ's prayer.

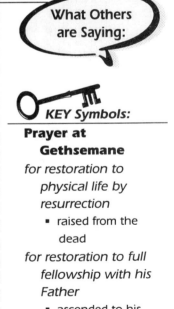

What Others are Saying:

J. Dwight Pentecost: Christ prayed that God might accept his death as full payment of the sin of sinners and bring him out of death and restore him to life again. Thus the prayer should be understood as a prayer for restoration to physical life by resurrection, and a restoration to full fellowship with his Father out of the spiritual death into which he would enter. The evidence that God answered Jesus' prayer is seen, first, in the fact that Christ was raised from the dead on the third day and given a glorified body. Second, it is seen in the fact that on the fortieth day he ascended to the Father to be seated at his right hand in glory.[5]

KEY Symbols:

Prayer at Gethsemane

for restoration to physical life by resurrection
- raised from the dead

for restoration to full fellowship with his Father
- ascended to his Father

2 *Jesus' arrest (Matthew 26:47–56; Mark 14:43–52; Luke 22:47–53; John 18:2–12).* Judas led a mob sent by the High Priest to seize Jesus. When one of the disciples tried to resist, Jesus said something that showed he remained in full control of the situation.

KEY POINT

Blasphemy would not
do so they had to find
another reason—
political reasons

☞ Check It Out:

John 18:28–19:16

*Do you think I cannot call on my Father, and he will at
once put at my disposal more than twelve **legions** of angels? But how then would the Scriptures be fulfilled that
say it must happen this way?* (Matthew 26:53, 54)

3 *Jesus was examined at night by three religious **tribunals** (Matthew 27:57–68; Mark 14:53–65; Luke 2:54–71; John 18:12–27).*
The critical point was reached near dawn when the High Priest
asked Jesus a question to which he knew Christ's answer.

> *The High Priest said to him, "I charge you under oath by
> the living God: Tell us if you are the Christ, the Son of God."*
>
> *"Yes, it is as you say," Jesus replied. "But I say to all of
> you: In the future you will see the Son of Man sitting at the
> right hand of the Mighty One and coming on the clouds of
> heaven."*
>
> *Then the High Priest tore his clothes and said, "He has
> spoken **blasphemy**! Why do we need any more witnesses?
> Look, now you have heard the blasphemy. What do you
> think?"*
>
> *"He is worthy of death," they answered.* (Matthew
> 26:63–66)

The problem was that no first century Jewish court had the
authority to impose a death sentence. That right was reserved to
Roman courts alone. While the charge of blasphemy might call
for the death penalty in Judaism, it was not a capital crime to the
Romans. They would have to charge Jesus with a crime other
than the one they had convicted him of!

4 *Jesus was then accused of political crimes (Matt. 27:11–26; Mark
15:2–19; John 18:28–19:16).* John's gospel describes in detail
Jesus' trial before the Roman governor Pilate. The charge was political: in presenting himself as the Christ, Jesus had laid claim to
being the *King of the Jews*, for the Messiah was to be a king.

Pilate saw through the **subterfuge**, but finally gave in and ordered Christ be crucified. The pressure to which Pilate finally
submitted is expressed in John 19:12.

> *From then on, Pilate tried to set Jesus free, but the Jews kept
> shouting, "If you let this man go, you are no friend of Cae-
> sar. Anyone who claims to be a king opposes Caesar.*

In Rome the man who had sponsored Pilate, a commander of the emperor's **Praetorian Guard**, a man named Sejanus, had recently been executed by the Emperor Tiberius. Many of Sejanus' government appointees had been executed or exiled as well. Pilate knew he was vulnerable, and was terrified that the Jewish leaders might accuse him to the Emperor. In the end Pilate, knowing that Jesus was innocent, decided to have Jesus crucified rather than run any personal risk!

Later in a sermon the Apostle Peter would say, *this is how God fulfilled what he had foretold through all the prophets, saying that his Christ would suffer (Acts 3:18).* God providentially arranged distant events to bring about what he had foretold through the prophets.

Nailed To A Cross

The Nelson Illustrated Bible Handbook describes crucifixion this way:

Crucifixion (see Illustration #14, this page) was practiced as a method of torture and execution by the Persians before it was adopted by the Romans. Roman law allowed only slaves and criminals to be crucified. Roman citizens were not crucified. The victim's arms are stretched out above him, fas-

☞ **Check It Out:**

Matthew 27:32–66; Mark 15:21–47; Luke 23:26–56; John 19:16–42

Praetorian Guard: the bodyguard of the Roman emperor

Something to Ponder

Remember This . . .

tened to a cross bar fixed near the top of a stake slightly taller than a man. Suspended this way, blood is forced to the lower body. The pulse rate increases, and after days of agony the victim dies from lack of blood circulating to the brain and heart. The Romans often placed a **titulus** above the sufferer naming his crime. **Scourging** before crucifixion hastened death, as did breaking a victim's legs.[6]

By examining the account of Jesus' crucifixion given in the four gospels, the details of what happened and Jesus' words from the cross can be reconstructed.

Mark describes the end of that fateful day:

Dig Deeper

Crucifixion Events at Calvary

Event	Matthew	Mark	Luke	John
Jesus refuses drugs.	27:3	–	–	–
Jesus is crucified.	27:35	–	–	–
"Father forgive them."	–	–	23:34	–
Soldiers gamble for clothing.	27:35	–	–	–
Jesus is mocked by observers.	27:39–44	15:29	–	–
Jesus is ridiculed by thieves.	27:44	–	–	–
One thief believes.	–	–	23:39–43	–
"Today you will be with me."	–	–	23:43	–
To Mary: "Behold, your son."	–	–	–	19:26–27
Darkness falls.	27:45	15:33	23:44	–
"My God, my God . . ."	27:46–47	15:34–36	–	–
"I thirst."	–	–	–	19:28
"It is finished."	–	–	–	19:30
"Father, into your hands . . ."	–	–	23:46	–
Jesus releases his spirit.	27:50	15:37	–	–

*It was **Preparation Day** (that is, the day before the Sabbath). So as evening approached, Joseph of Arimathea, a prominent member of the Council, who was himself waiting for the kingdom of God, went boldly to Pilate and asked for Jesus' body. Pilate was surprised to hear that he was already dead. Summoning the **centurion**, he asked him if Jesus had already died. When he learned from the centurion that it was so, he gave the body to Joseph. So Joseph bought some linen cloth, took down the body, wrapped it in the linen, and placed it in a tomb cut out of rock. Then he rolled a stone against the entrance of the tomb. (Mark 15:42–47)*

Matthew adds that the next day the chief priests and Pharisees asked Pilate for permission to secure the tomb (see GWDN, pages 160–161).

> *"Take a guard," Pilate answered. "Go, make the tomb as secure as you know how." So they went and made the tomb secure by putting a seal on the stone and posting a guard."* (Matthew 27:65, 66)

What Is The Significance Of Jesus' Death On The Cross?

The Bible makes it clear that Jesus' death on the cross was always an essential element in God's plan. The crucifixion was prophesied in the Old Testament. Jesus informed his disciples beforehand of what would happen, and rather than call on the Father for angelic armies, Jesus chose to let himself be executed.

Here are some of the passages from the Old and New Testaments that explain the significance of Jesus' death:

1 *He was pierced for our transgressions (Isaiah 53:4–6).* Writing 700 years before Jesus was born, God announced through the prophet Isaiah:

> *Surely he took up our **infirmities**
>   and carried our sorrows,
> yet we considered him stricken by God,
>   smitten by him, and afflicted.
> But he was pierced for our **transgressions**,
>   he was crushed for our **iniquities**;
> the punishment that brought us peace was upon him,
>   and by his wounds we are healed.
> We all, like sheep, have gone astray,
>   each of us has turned to his own way;
> and the Lord has laid on him
>   the iniquity of us all. (Isaiah 53:4–6)*

2 *Christ died for us (Romans 5:8, 9).* Writing to the Romans the Apostle Paul explained the reason for Jesus' death in these words:

> *God demonstrates his own love for us in this: While we were still sinners, Christ died for us. Since we have now been **justified** by his blood, how much more shall we be saved from wrath through him? (Romans 5:8, 9)*

KEY POINT

We all, like sheep, have gone astray, each of us has turned to his own way; and the Lord has laid on him the iniquity of us all.

infirmities: *moral weaknesses*

transgressions: *violations of the law; sin*

iniquities: *wicked acts*

justified: *pronounced not guilty*

John Stott: What is written is that *while we were sinners Christ died for us* (Romans 5:8), and whenever sin and death are coupled in Scripture, death is the penalty or *wage* of sin. This being so, the statement that *Christ died for sinners*, that though the sins were ours, the death was his, can mean only that he died as a sin offering, bearing in our place the penalty that our sins deserved.[7]

KEY Symbols:

Sin
death is the penalty

Max Lucado: The cross did what sacrificed lambs could not do. It erased our sins not for a year, but for eternity. The cross did what man cannot do. It granted us the right to talk with, love, and even live with God.[8]

KEY Symbols:

Old Testament
sacrificed lambs
- temporary forgiveness

New testament
Jesus' sacrifice
- eternal forgiveness
- the Lamb of God

3 *God made him . . . sin for us* (II Corinthians 5:21). The Apostle Paul explained further when writing a second letter to the Corinthians. At the cross an amazing transaction took place. Jesus took our sins on himself; his death took the penalty that our sins deserved. And, wonder of wonders, God then credited the righteousness of Jesus to us! With sin paid for, there was no longer a barrier between human beings and God. With Jesus' own righteousness credited to our account, we are welcome to enter God's presence. As Paul wrote,

> *God made him who had no sin to be sin for us, so that in him we might become the righteousness of God.* (II Corinthians 5:21)

KEY POINT

The love of God is limitless; it embraces all mankind.

In these and many other similar words, the New Testament shares its good news. Jesus' death was a payment for our sins—a promise of forgiveness to all who will trust God and take him at his word.

As Jesus had told one of the Pharisees at the beginning of his ministry,

> *For God so loved the world that he gave his one and only Son, that whoever believes in him shall not perish but have eternal life. . . . Whoever believes in him is not condemned, but whoever does not believe stands condemned already because he has not believed in the name of God's one and only Son.* (John 3:16, 18)

F. F. Bruce: If there is one sentence more than another which sums up the message of the fourth gospel [John], it is this. The love of God is limitless; it embraces all mankind. No sacrifice was too great to bring its unmeasured intensity home to men and women; the

Appearances of Jesus

Event	Matthew	Mark	Luke	John
Resurrection Morning				
Three women set out for the tomb.	–	–	23:55; 24:1	–
The stone has been rolled away.	–	–	24:2–9	–
Mary Magdalene leaves to tell Jesus' disciples.	–	–	–	20:1–2
Jesus' mother Mary sees angels.	–	–	–	20:1–2
Peter & John come and look in tomb.	–	–	–	20:3–10
Jesus' mother Mary returns with other women.	–	–	24:1–4	–
These women see angels.	–	16:5	24:5	–
The angel says Jesus is risen.	28:6–8	–	–	–
Departing, they meet Jesus.	28:9–10	–	–	–
Additional Appearances of Jesus				
To Peter, the same day	–	–	24:35	–
To disciple on Emmaus road	–	–	24:13–31	–
To the apostles (but not Thomas)	–	–	24:36–45	20:19–24
To the apostles (with Thomas)	–	–	–	20:24–29
To seven at Lake Tiberius	–	–	–	21:1–23
To some 500 in Galilee	I Corinthians 15:6	–	–	–
To James in Jerusalem	I Corinthians 15:7	–		
To many at Jesus' ascension	Acts 1:3–12	–		
To Stephen when he was stoned	Acts 7:55	–		
To Paul near Damascus	Acts 9:3–6	–		
To Paul in the Temple	Acts 22:17–19	–		
To John on Patmos	Revelation 1:10–19	–		

Dig Deeper

best that God had to give, he gave—his only son, his well-beloved. The gospel of salvation and life has its source in the love of God. The essence of the saving message is made unmistakably plain.[9]

Billy Graham: There is only one way you can be forgiven, and that is through Christ.[10]

Up From The Grave He Arose

Jesus was buried late Friday afternoon in the garden tomb of Joseph of Arimathea, and his body remained there all of Saturday. Early Sunday—by normal Jewish reckoning, the third day—Jesus rose from the dead.

The four gospels each give an account of the events of that day. Working from all four, we can reconstruct the events.

Looking back on the resurrection of Jesus from the dead, the Apostle Paul sees it as God's powerful and ultimate declaration that he truly was and is the <u>Son of God</u>.

What Others are Saying:

☞ **Check It Out:**

Matthew 28; Mark 16; Luke 24; John 20–21

☞ **GO TO:**

Romans 1:3 (Son of God)

And what significance does the resurrection of Jesus have for you and me? The resurrection is both proof and promise that death is not the end . . . for anyone.

Peter Marshall: The glorious fact that the empty tomb proclaims to us is that life for us does not stop when death comes. Death is not a wall, but a door. And eternal life which may be ours now, by faith in Christ, is not interrupted when the soul leaves the body, for we live on . . . and on.

There is no death to those who have entered into fellowship with him who emerged from the tomb. Because the resurrection is true, it is the most significant thing in our world today. Bringing the resurrected Christ into our lives, individual and national, is the only hope we have. Because I live, ye shall live also. (John 14:19)[11]

Study Questions

1. What event began Jesus' last week on earth?
2. What did Jesus do in the Temple that offended the chief priests?
3. Why was the Pharisees' question about paying taxes a trap, and how did Jesus answer them?
4. According to Matthew 23, what did Jesus say that the Pharisees and teachers of the Law were?
5. How did God answer the prayer Jesus made in Gethsemane?
6. What was Jesus charged with in the Jewish courts? What was Jesus charged with in Pilate's court?
7. What happened to Jesus' body after he was crucified?
8. How does the Bible explain the significance of Jesus' death?
9. What does the fact of Jesus' resurrection mean for us today?

CHAPTER WRAP-UP

- When Jesus entered Jerusalem on Palm Sunday, he was acclaimed as the Messiah.
- Jesus exposed the hypocrisy of the leaders and openly condemned them.
- The religious leaders determined to kill Jesus in order to maintain their own power and position.
- Jesus told his disciples that he would be crucified, but that afterward he would come to earth again to rule.
- Jesus was seized at night, tried, and condemned by the Jewish Sanhedrin for claiming to be the Son of God.
- Jesus was crucified by the Romans as *King of the Jews*.
- Jesus died and was buried, but on the third day he rose from the grave and was seen by many witnesses.

17 THE SPREADING FLAME

Acts

CHAPTER HIGHLIGHTS

- The Holy Spirit
- Pentecost
- Tell All the World
- The Apostle Paul
- Trouble Brewing

Let's Get Started

The raising of Jesus marked the beginning of Christianity. The disciples began to proclaim Christ as resurrected Lord. Many in Jerusalem believed their message, and a vital community of believers was formed. Acts traces the early expansion of Christianity from its Jewish roots to a faith spread throughout the Roman Empire (see Illustration #15, page 214).

ACTS

. . . the spread of the Gospel

WHO	Luke, a physician and companion of Paul on his missionary journeys,
WHAT	wrote this book of history about the early Church
WHERE	in Rome
WHEN	about 63 A.D.,
WHY	to record the spread of the **Gospel** throughout the Roman world between 33 A.D. and 63 A.D.

Up, Up And Away

The first chapter of Acts is a prelude to the New Testament. It presents three keys to understanding Christianity in the first century—and today!

KEY Symbols:

Events in Acts	A.D.
Resurrection	33
Paul Converted	36
Paul's 1st Mission	48
Jerusalem Council	49
Paul's 2nd Mission	49–52
Paul's 3rd Mission	53–57
Paul Arrested	57
Paul in Caesarea	57–60
Paul in Rome	61–63

Just the FACTS

Gospel: "good news" about Jesus as Savior

☞ **Check It Out:**

Acts 1

Illustration #15

The Roman Empire—Within 30 years of Jesus' resurrection the Gospel had spread throughout the Roman Empire. There were Christian groups in most of its major cities. The rapid spread was made possible because Rome maintained good roads, and had wiped out the pirates who had made sea travel unsafe. Everyone in the Roman Empire spoke a common tongue, Greek, which made it possible to share the Gospel in different countries. And the New Testament **epistles**, written in Greek, could be read by all.

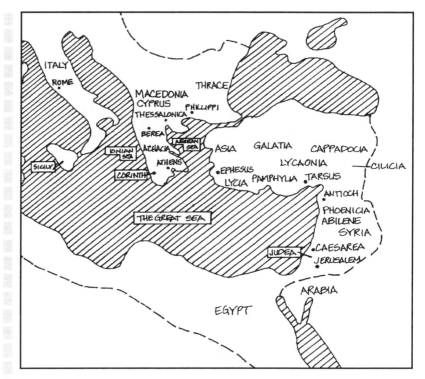

epistles: New Testament letters written by apostles

Holy Spirit: God, the third person of the Trinity

What Others are Saying:

KEY Symbols:

Key #1
Jesus sent his Holy Spirit

Key #1

But you will receive power when the Holy Spirit comes on you.(Acts 1:8)

The first key to understanding Acts and the New Testament is that when Jesus returned to heaven, he sent the Holy Spirit to provide power for Christian living and Christian witness. The book of Acts is the story of the works of the Holy Spirit in and through believers in Jesus.

Lawrence O. Richards: The New Testament reveals the Spirit to be a person, one with the Father and Son (Matthew 28:19; John 15:26). He is also given a personal name in the New Testament: *Comforter.* While the Spirit is mentioned in the Old Testament, the full revelation of his personality comes in the New.

Three New Testament lines of teaching about the Spirit are important to us. First, the Spirit is seen in the gospels as the one who oversees the birth of Christ, and who is the source of Jesus' strength and power in ministry (Matthew 12:28; Luke 4:18; John 3:34). Second, the Spirit is promised to Jesus' followers and spoken of as the source of our power (John 14:16, 17; 16:5–15; Acts 1:8). Third, the epistles go into great detail about the role of the Spirit in the life of the individual believer and the Christian community. It is the Holy Spirit who **empowers** individuals for ministry today. The vitality of our personal Christian life depends on the person and work of the Spirit, whom God has given to be with us, and filling our lives with his power.[1]

Key #2

After he said this, [Jesus] was taken up before their very eyes, and a cloud hid him from their sight. They were looking intently up into the sky as he was going, when suddenly two men dressed in white stood beside them. "Men of Galilee," they said, "why do you stand here looking into the sky. This same Jesus, who has been taken from you into heaven, will come back in the same way you have seen him go into heaven." (Acts 1:9–11)

Forty days after the resurrection Jesus was taken up into heaven. He will remain there until, as the angels promised, he comes back again. But what is Jesus doing now?

The New Testament tells us:

1. Jesus is preparing a place for us.   John 14:2
2. Jesus is interceding (praying) for us.   Romans 8:34
    Hebrews 7:25
5. Jesus is our **advocate** when we sin.   I John 2:1
4. Jesus is guiding and directing us.   Ephesians 1:22

Ephesians adds that *all things* have been placed *under his feet* (Ephesians 1:22). Today Jesus is the ultimate authority in the universe, and is actively working out God's plan for individuals and the world. While not physically present on earth, Jesus is at work within and for those who trust him.

Key #3

*You will receive power when the Holy Spirit comes upon you and you will be my **witnesses** . . . to the ends of the earth. (Acts 1:8)*

KEY Symbols:

The Spirit
oversees the birth of Christ and is the source of Jesus' strength and power in his ministry
promised to Jesus' followers and source of our power
gives us vitality in our Christian life and ministry

KEY Symbols:

Key #2
Jesus ascended into heaven

Remember This . . .

advocate: *a person who pleads the cause of another*

witnesses: *those who testify to what they have experienced*

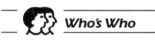
Who's Who

deacon: a church officer; a servant

☞ **Check It Out:**

Acts 2:1–21

KEY Symbols:

Pentecost
*rushing wind
tongues of fire
miraculous translation
of many languages*

What Others
are Saying:

The men identified as Jesus' disciples in the gospels become his apostles in Acts, and testify to the reality of Jesus' resurrection. Although Acts emphasizes the ministry of two apostles, the privilege of being Jesus' witness is given to every believer.

Rushing Wind And Tongues Of Fire

THE BIG PICTURE 🔍

The Church Grows The promised coming of the Holy Spirit did empower the apostles. This section of Acts records two powerful sermons of Peter, and describes the response. Although the leaders who had conspired to have Jesus crucified threatened the apostles, and through disputes threatened the unity of the young Christian community, the church in Jerusalem multiplied rapidly.

PETER: Peter was the leading disciple and apostle, who preaches the first gospel sermons.

STEPHEN: Stephen was the **deacon** and vibrant Christian witness, who was stoned to death for his witness to Christ in Jerusalem.

What's Special In Acts 2–7?

1 *The Holy Spirit filled and empowered Jesus' followers (Acts 2:1– 21).* Fifty days after the resurrection, during, a Jewish festival called Pentecost, the Holy Spirit filled Jesus followers, who had been gathered for prayer. This initial coming of the Spirit was marked by visible signs: the sound of rushing wind, tongues of fire above the believers' heads, and the miraculous translation of what the believers said, so that each foreign visitor to Jerusalem *heard them speaking in his own language* (Acts 2:6).

Peter explained the phenomenon by referring to an Old Testament prophecy in which God promised, *I will pour out my Spirit on all peoples* (Acts 2:17).

Warren Wiersbe: Peter did not say that Pentecost was the fulfillment of the prophecy of Joel 2:28–32. When you read Joel's prophecy in context, you see that it deals with the nation of Israel in the end times, in connection with the *Day of the Lord.* However, Peter was led by the Spirit to see in the prophecy an application to the **Church**. He said, *This is the same Holy Spirit that Joel wrote about. He is here!*[2]

Church: consists of the followers of Jesus Christ, as opposed to a church which is the building where people meet to worship

2 *History's first two gospel sermons (Acts 2:22–3:26).* Acts records two of Peter's sermons preached to crowds gathered in Jerusalem (Acts 2:22–39; 3:12–26). The truths of these sermons remain the central truths on which Christianity rests.

As Acts 2 and 3 report, the early preaching of the apostles was accompanied by miracles, authenticating their message of Jesus and his continuing power as Lord.

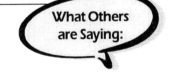

Dig Deeper

The Truths Preached about Jesus	First Sermon	Second Sermon
The historic person	2:22	–
Was crucified and raised from the dead	2:23, 24	3:15–15
As prophecy foretold	2:25–35	3:18
He is God's Messiah	2:36	3:20
All who believe in him will receive **remission** of sins, and be given the Holy Spirit	2:37, 38	3:19, 21–26

3 *The overwhelming response to the gospel message (Acts 2:41; 6:7).* After Peter's first sermon some 3,000 people responded to the Gospel and trusted Jesus as Savior.

remission: release from guilt or penalty of sin

> *So the Word of God spread. The number of disciples in Jerusalem increased rapidly, and a large number of priests became obedient to the faith.* (Acts 6:7)

F. F. Bruce: The disciples' public witness met with widespread acceptance in Jerusalem, and their following increased rapidly. They also won over a number of Pharisees, and even a considerable body of priests. The one group that showed direct hostility to the new community was the Sadducean party [the Sadducees], especially the chief priests and Temple authorities.[3]

What Others are Saying:

4 *Acts describes the early Church as a close and loving fellowship of believers (Acts 2:42–47; 4:32–35).* These two passages are often quoted as picturing an "ideal" church family. When looking for a church today, it is wise to seek one devoted to the apostles' teaching, to caring fellowship, and prayer.

☞ **GO TO:**

Acts 2:42–47; 4:32–35

5 Even the "ideal" Jerusalem church faced external and internal challenges (Acts 4–7). These chapters describe two external and two internal challenges that the Jerusalem church faced. Check out one of each of the following:

External	Challenge	Response
Acts 4:1–31	Peter and John are threatened.	The church gathers to pray.
Acts 6:8–7:60	Stephen is stoned by a mob.	Stephen prays for his killers.

Internal		
Acts 5:1–11	Two people lie to God and the apostles.	God publicly judges them.
Acts 6:1–7	There are complaints of unfair treatment.	Deacons are appointed to oversee.

Go Tell It On The Mountain

THE BIG PICTURE 🔍

☞ **Check It Out:**

Acts 8–12

Expansion After the stoning of Stephen, the Christians in Jerusalem were persecuted, and most were forced to leave the city. But as the new believers traveled, they shared the Gospel with others. Soon the message spread to Judea and even to Samaria (see map on page 173), where Samaritans also accepted Christ as Savior. The great surprise for the early Jewish Christians took place when a retired Roman centurion named Cornelius was converted, and it dawned on all that the message of salvation was for all people, not just for God's covenant people, the Jews.

 **Who's Who**

PHILLIP: One of the first deacons, who launches a revival in Samaria.

 **Who's Who**

SAUL: A young Pharisee who after his conversion will gain fame as the Apostle Paul.

 **Who's Who**

BARNABAS: An early convert who became a leader in the first gentile church, and Paul's companion on his first missionary journey.

 **Who's Who**

CORNELIUS: A Roman centurion who believes in Israel's God, and becomes the first gentile convert to Christianity.

What's Special In Acts 8–12?

1 *When Philip begins to preach Christ in Samaria, many are converted (Acts 8:1–25).* The Samaritans were a foreign people who had been settled in Israel by the Assyrians after the Jews were deported in 722 B.C. While they worshiped Israel's God, the Jews considered their religion corrupt and would have nothing to do with them. But Philip's preaching and the miracles he performed in Jesus' name convinced many to trust Christ.

In this case God delayed giving the Holy Spirit to believing Samaritans until the apostles Peter and John came from Jerusalem. This established the authority of the apostles and the fact that the church is one.

☞ **Check It Out:**

Acts 8:1–25

2 *Philip is called away from Samaria to share the Gospel with one individual (Acts 8:26–40).* The Holy Spirit took Philip from a ministry of thousands to share the Gospel with one individual, an Ethiopian **Eunuch**. God is as concerned with the salvation of a single individual as he is with thousands.

Eunuch: by the first century the title of a high official in some lands

3 *The conversion of Saul (Acts 9).* In the Roman Empire non-citizens were governed by the law of their homeland. This gave the Sanhedrin in Jerusalem authority over Jews anywhere in the empire. Saul was authorized by the Sanhedrin to arrest Christian Jews in Damascus, another country in the empire. On the way Christ spoke to Saul, and the encounter led to Saul's **conversion**.

Immediately this persecutor of the Church began to promote the faith he had tried to stamp out!

☞ **Check It Out:**

Acts 9:1–31

conversion: a person's turning to God

Warren Wiersbe: Saul of Tarsus became Paul the Apostle, and his life and ministry have influenced people and nations ever since. Even secular historians confess that Paul is one of the most significant figures in world history.[4]

What Others are Saying:

4 *Peter's vision (Acts 10:9–22).* The Jews considered **Gentiles** unclean. This meant that contact with a Gentile could disqualify a Jew from participating in worship at God's Temple. God gave Peter a vision, and a voice from heaven told Peter to kill and eat unclean animals. Shocked, Peter refused. Peter was then told not to regard as impure anything that God had made clean. Immediately afterward messengers came from Cornelius, a retired Roman officer, inviting Peter to his house. Peter realized that God intended him to go, despite the fact that the Jews regarded Gentiles as unclean.

☞ **Check It Out:**

Acts 10:9–22

Gentile: any non-Jew

☞ **GO TO:**

Leviticus 11 (unclean)

5 *The conversion of Cornelius (Acts 10–11).* When Peter shared the Gospel at the house of Cornelius, all who gathered there believed, and began to speak in tongues. Peter saw this as a sign that God had accepted Gentiles into the church. When he reported what happened, the Jerusalem Christians praised God, saying *So then, God has even granted the Gentiles repentance unto life* (Acts 11:18).

What Others are Saying:

Craig S. Keener: Until now no one had believed that Gentiles could be saved on the same terms as Jewish people, who had been chosen for salvation by God's sovereign grace.[5]

6 *The first predominantly gentile church is established in Antioch (Acts 11:1–30).* News reached Jerusalem that a church made up of Gentiles existed in Antioch (see Illustration #15, page 214). Soon thereafter, the apostles sent Barnabas to Antioch, who became a leader there. He also brought Saul of Tarsus into the leadership team.

☞ **Check It Out:**

Acts 12

7 *Peter is freed from prison by an angel (Acts 12).* King Herod Antipas, a grandson of Herod the Great, executed the Apostle James. When he saw that this pleased the Jewish leaders, he arrested Peter. But an angel freed Peter from prison and later struck Herod with a fatal sickness. God was protecting his Church.

In Acts this is the last we hear of Peter. Church history tells us that Peter ministered primarily to Jewish Christians throughout the Roman Empire, and that he was crucified in Rome under the Emperor Nero around 66 B.C.

Off We Go (46–57 A.D.)

THE BIG PICTURE 🔍

☞ **Check It Out:**

Acts 13–20

Paul's Journey These chapters in Acts briefly summarize the Apostle Paul's three missionary journeys (see Appendix A) to major cities of the Roman Empire. Paul and his companions established churches in these population centers. The new Christians then spread the Gospel to the surrounding villages and countryside. Later, Paul revisited these churches to give them additional teaching. Paul also wrote letters of instruction to the young churches. His letters were collected and distributed to churches everywhere. Thirteen of Paul's letters are in the New Testament.

PAUL: Becomes the leader of the **missionary** team and spearheads the spread of the Gospel throughout the Roman Empire.

BARNABAS: Paul's friend and companion on his first journey.

SILAS: Silas was Paul's partner on the second and third journeys.

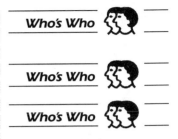

Who's Who ____

Who's Who ____

Who's Who ____

missionary: *a person sent by a church to carry on religious work*

What's Special In Acts 13–20?

1 *Paul's missions strategy (Acts 13–14).* On entering a city Paul went first to the Jewish synagogue to teach about Jesus. Jewish synagogues in pagan cities often attracted *God-fearers*—persons who were attracted to the God and the high moral standards of Judaism but who had not converted and adopted a Jewish lifestyle. Many of these God-fearers responded to the Gospel and with Jewish converts formed the core of Christian churches.

The Cities Paul and His Team Visited

Psidian Antioch	(Acts 13:13–52)
Iconium	(Acts 14:1–60)
Lystra and Derbe	(Acts 14:8–20)
Thessalonica	(Acts 17:1–9)
Berea	(Acts 17:10–18)
Corinth	(Acts 18:1–28)

Dig Deeper

2 *The Jerusalem Council in 49 A.D. (Acts 15).* Paul's success in establishing predominantly Christian churches in major cities of the Roman Empire led to a theological dispute. Some Jewish Christians were convinced that the gentile believers should keep the Law of Moses and be circumcised. That is, they must believe in Jesus and follow Jewish customs.

To the Apostle Paul this was a corruption of the Gospel, which offers salvation to sinners solely on the basis of faith in Jesus, who died for mankind's sins. Peter agreed, arguing that God saved Jew and Gentile alike who trusted in Christ. After a lengthy discussion, James, the brother of Jesus, summarized the council's conclusion, quoting the prophet Amos to show that Gentiles would be converted as Gentiles. All the council asked of the Gentiles was that they refrain from practices which would make it difficult for Jewish believers to fellowship with them.

Although the Jerusalem Council agreed that salvation was

☞ **Check It Out:**

Acts 15:1–21

KEY POINT

Salvation comes by faith in Jesus Christ not by works or keeping the Law.

not linked to keeping the Law of Moses, the early Church continued to be troubled by Jewish Christians who visited Gentile churches and taught that salvation came from faith plus keeping God's Law. The Apostle Paul deals with this issue in his letters to the Romans and to the Galatians.

What Others are Saying:

purview: range of operation

F. F. Bruce: It was not contemplated that Jewish Christians should be liberated from the obligation to maintain the Jewish way of life. The decree did not take them into it's **purview**. The majority of Jewish Christians at this time were far from sharing the emancipated attitude of Paul, who was equally happy to live as a Gentile in a Gentile environment and to follow the Jewish way of life in the company of Jews. To him it was religiously indifferent which way of life he followed; these things were completely subordinate to the main purpose of his life and to the spiritual health of the people in whose society he found himself.[6]

☞ **Check It Out:**

Acts 16:16–40; 19:1–51

3 *The challenges of missionary life (II Corinthians 11:23–28).* Reading in Acts 16 and 19 it is clear that Paul and his team faced many challenges and difficulties spreading the Gospel throughout the Roman Empire. Paul sums up 20 years of missionary experience in II Corinthians 11:

Something to Ponder

I have worked much harder, been in prison more frequently, been flogged more severely, and been exposed to death again and again. Five times I received from the Jews the forty lashes minus one. Three times I was beaten with rods, once I was stoned, three times I was shipwrecked. I spent a night and a day in the open sea, I have been constantly on the move. I have been in danger from rivers, in danger from bandits, in danger from my own countrymen, in danger from Gentiles; in danger in the city, in danger in the country, in danger at sea; and in danger from false brothers. I have known hunger and thirst and have often gone without food; I have been cold and naked. Besides everything else, I face daily the pressure of my concern for all the churches. (II Corinthians 11:23–29)

Remember This . . .

What drove Paul and other early Christians was not any profit they might make from the Gospel, but the conviction that people everywhere needed to hear of the forgiveness of sins God offers to all who simply trust in his Son.

Cornered (57–63 A.D.)

THE BIG PICTURE

> **Paul's Trial** In 57 A.D. Paul felt led to return to Jerusalem. When a riot broke out there, Roman soldiers rescued him and he claimed protection as a Roman citizen. The Jews claimed Paul was a political agitator and religious renegade. The Roman governor kept Paul in Caesarea (see Illustration #15, page 214) for two years, hoping for a bribe. Then when a new governor was appointed, Paul exercised his right as a Roman citizen. He appealed to Caesar to have his case decided in Rome. Acts tells the story of Paul's journey to Rome (see Appendix A) and even includes information about a shipwreck along the way, but the book concludes before Paul goes to trial.

☞ **Check It Out:**

Acts 21–28

FELIX: The Roman governor of Palestine who hoped Paul would offer him a bribe.

Who's Who

FESTUS: The new Roman governor who asked Paul to go to Jerusalem for trial.

Who's Who

KING AGRIPPA (Herod Agrippa II): The administrator of Judea under the Romans, who heard Paul's defense with Festus.

Who's Who

What's Special In Acts 21–28?

1 *The Jerusalem riot and Paul's arrest (Acts 21:17–22:29).* Prominent signs were posted in the Jerusalem Temple, warning Gentiles not to enter on pain of death. The riot broke out when Jews who recognized Paul falsely accused him of bringing Gentiles into the Temple.

After being rescued, Paul asked to speak to the crowd. He recited his training under a famous rabbi, and told the story of his conversion. But when Paul reported that the Lord told him to go to the Gentiles, the crowd rioted again.

☞ **Check It Out:**

Acts 22:1–29

Warren Wiersbe: Paul was about to explain why he was involved with the Gentiles, but the Jews in the Temple would not permit him to go on. No devout Jew would have anything to do with the Gentiles! Had Paul not uttered that one word, he might have later been released; and perhaps he knew this. However, he had to be faithful in his witness, no matter what it cost him.[7]

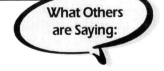

What Others are Saying:

☞ **Check It Out:**

Acts 24:1–27

☞ **Check It Out:**

Acts 24, 25

KEY Symbols:

The Way
*early name of
Christianity*

*acquitted: declared not
guilty*

2 *The trial before Felix (Acts 24:1–27).* The Roman historian Tacitus described Felix as a person who "had the power of a tyrant and the temper of a slave," and says that he was known for his lust and cruelty. Luke describes Felix as *well acquainted with the Way,* the early name of Christianity. Paul's bold witness frightened but also fascinated Felix, who kept Paul under house arrest for two years in hopes of getting a bribe.

3 *The trial before Festus (Acts 25–26).* On arriving to govern the province that included Judea and Jerusalem, Festus considered sending Paul to Jerusalem for trial. Rather than agree, Paul exercised his right as a Roman citizen to *appeal to Caesar,* to be tried in Rome by an imperial court.

Later Festus discussed Paul's case with King Agrippa, who asked to hear Paul's defense. First century gossip held that Bernice, who was Agrippa's sister, was also his mistress. For the third time recorded in Acts, Paul tells the story of his conversion, this time to a room filled with high officials.

Paul's position seemed like madness to the Roman, but King Agrippa, who believed the prophets, understood the message. There is no historical record of his becoming a believer.

4 *The voyage to Rome (Acts 27, 28).* Acts concludes with Luke's account of a terrible storm that wrecked the ship on which Paul and other prisoners were being taken to Rome. When they arrived in Rome no charges had been forwarded from Jerusalem. Paul lived there under guard for two years, freely sharing the Gospel with visitors and with the soldiers who guarded him.

What Happened To Paul?

Acts ends before Paul goes to trial. Tradition tells us that he was **acquitted**, and continued his missionary work by going to Spain. Later, during the reign of Nero, again Paul was arrested. This time the faithful apostle, like Peter, was put to death in Rome.

But the Gospel message he had carried throughout the Roman Empire had taken root in the hearts and lives of many. Just a few centuries later, Justin Martyr, an early Church father, would write that in Africa Christians were "all but a majority in every city!"

Study Questions

1. What kind of literature is Acts?
2. With what event does Acts begin?
3. What did the coming of the Holy Spirit provide the disciples?
4. What were two of the five basic truths emphasized in Peter's first two gospel sermons?
5. What two persons are the dominant figures in Acts?
6. What was important about the conversion of Cornelius?
7. How many missionary journeys of Paul are reported in Acts?
8. Why was the Jerusalem Council significant?
9. When Acts ends, where is the Apostle Paul?

CHAPTER WRAP-UP

- Acts is a history of the expansion of Christianity during the 30 years following Jesus' resurrection.

- Jesus ascended to heaven, where today he intercedes for believers and guides his Church.

- Jesus sent the Holy Spirit to empower his disciples to be witnesses of him throughout the world.

- Peter was the first to preach the Gospel message to the Jews. He was also the first to preach to any Gentile.

- After his conversion Saul of Tarsus became Paul the Apostle, who spearheaded bringing the Gospel to the gentile world.

- In three missionary journeys over a span of 11 years the Apostle Paul established churches in many of the major cities of the Roman Empire.

- Paul's arrest and trial gave him opportunities to present the Gospel to important government officials in Palestine and in Rome itself.

18 EXPLAINING THE GOSPEL

Romans
Galatians

CHAPTER HIGHLIGHTS

- The Epistles
- Righteousness and Unrighteousness
- Divine Judgment
- God's Solution
- Rely on Grace

Let's Get Started

The last five chapters have covered Matthew through Acts, books of the Bible that consist of stories, or *historical narrative*, about Jesus and about Jesus' followers. This chapter will cover the first two books of a different kind of writing—epistles. The epistles are letters of correspondence that were written by Jesus' apostles, sometimes to churches and sometimes to individuals. There are 21 of them in the New Testament, and each is designed to instruct believers through the ages. Eventually the letters were copied and circulated to all the churches. Collections of the epistles were valued in the first century and recognized as Scripture—the authoritative Word of God, transmitted through men, but **inspired** by the Holy Spirit.

There are two major collections of letters: the *Pauline Epistles,* and the *General Epistles.* The Pauline Epistles were written by Paul, and the General Epistles were written by Peter, John, Jude, James, and the unknown author of Hebrews.

We don't have enough space here to address each epistle from start to finish, but an outline of each will be provided, so that if you want to "dig deeper" into Scripture, you will have a guide along the way. We will, however, look at a sampling of each epistle, and then we'll discuss the key thought that sums up each book's main focus.

KEY Symbols:

Epistles
letters
instruct believers

inspired: God-guided

KEY Symbols:

Pauline Epistles
Paul
General Epistles
Peter, John, Jude, James, and the author of Hebrews

**What Others
are Saying:**

KEY Symbols:

The Authors
explain
argue
illustrate
exhort
instruct

exhort: *to urge, advise,
caution earnestly*

**Remember
This . . .**

**Just the
FACTS**

Lawrence O. Richards: We study the epistles differently than we study the Old Testament and New Testament books of history. In narrative portions of our Bible, the authors have carefully arranged the sequence of incidents they report to illustrate their themes. We study such histories by watching unfolding events and listening for statements of truth which help us interpret their meaning. In the epistles, a more direct approach is taken. The authors explain, argue, illustrate, **exhort**, and instruct. To study the New Testament epistles we should carefully trace the "argument"—the flow of thought—of each writer.[1]

We will group the epistles according to common themes as charted below.

Chapter	The Epistles	Common Theme
18	Romans, Galatians	Paul's letters which explain the Gospel
19	I, II Corinthians I, II Thessalonians	Paul's letters written to clear up misunderstandings
20	Ephesians, Colossians, Philippians	Paul's letters written from prison in Rome
21	I, II Timothy, Titus, Philemon	Paul's letters written to individuals
22	Hebrews	Christ's superiority to Judaism
23	James, I, II Peter, I, II, III John, Jude	Letters written by other apostles on various themes

In these chapters we'll find out what each letter is about, and look at particular sections in depth. Future books in the *God's Word for the Biblically-Inept*™ series will help you master each epistle.

ROMANS

. . . God's gift of righteousness

WHO	The Apostle Paul
WHAT	carefully explained the Christian Gospel
WHERE	to Christians in Rome
WHEN	about 57 A.D.,
WHY	so that they would understand the relationship between grace and righteousness.

Righteous Living

The Old Testament reveals God as a moral being, whose Law laid out standards of righteousness which God expected his people to maintain. Then the Christian Gospel burst on the scene, and Jesus' apostles announced that because Christ died for our sins, God would forgive the sins of all who simply trust in him. To some the gospel message seemed scandalous! What about righteousness? Isn't a salvation won by faith inconsistent with the very nature of a God who is righteous and who, as the Old Testament reveals, expects righteousness from his people?

In Romans Paul answers the very real questions about the Gospel that were asked in the first century, and that are often asked today.

KEY Symbols:

Argument
flow of thought

Everett F. Harrison: Romans satisfies the craving of the human spirit for a comprehensive **exposition** of the great truths of salvation set out in logical fashion, supported and illumined by Old Testament Scripture. The systematic element includes due attention to doctrine and life—in that order, because right relations must be established with God before one can live so as to please him and **mediate** his blessings to others.[2]

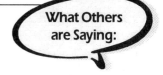

What Others are Saying:

exposition: *a detailed statement or explanation*

mediate: *to transfer*

Tracing Paul's Argument—His Flow Of Thought

The *argument* of a New Testament epistle is its *flow of thought*. When we trace the argument of Romans, we not only have a summary of its content, we have an outline of the book. Here's how Paul answers the questions about righteousness.

Introduction .... Romans 1:1–17
1. No one is righteous in God's sight: 1:18–3:20
    a. not the Gentiles,   1:18–32
    b. not the Jews,   2:1–3:8
    c. and Scripture proves this.   3:9–20
2. So God provided righteousness as a gift 3:21–5:21
    a. through the death of Christ.   3:21–31
    b. In fact, God has always accepted faith in place of righteousness,   4:1–25
        (1) as the experience of Abraham and David illustrates,   4:1–17
        (2) and as we can experience faith in Jesus today. 4:18–25

Dig Deeper

c. So sinners today can have peace with God through Christ,   5:1–11

d. who has reversed the curse that Adam's sin imposed on humankind.   5:12–21

3. What's more, faith in Christ makes it possible for saved sinners to live righteous lives, ... 6:1–39

a. because faith unites us with Jesus.   6:1–23.

b. We can't live up to the Law's demands in our own strength, so we do not look to the Law to help us. Instead,   7:1–25

c. we rely on the Holy Spirit who gives the power to please God here and now,   8:1–17

d. and who will totally transform us in bringing us to glory in eternity.   8:18–39

4. God is not being unrighteous in making this gift available now to Gentiles, because 9:1–11:36

a. setting Israel aside is just, and   9:1–10:21

b. God will yet keep the prophets' promises to Israel in the future.   11:1–36

5. So Christians today are called to live righteous lives, ... 12:1–15:13

a. as members together of a community of believers, 12:1–21

b. as citizens in a secular society,   13:1–14,

c. and as brothers and sisters who accept one another and glorify God together.   14:1–15:13

Personal greetings (closing) 15:14–16:27

KEY Symbols:

Unrighteous living
watch out for God's wrath

A Little Sample

To get a feel for the book of Romans, let's look together at verses from Section 1 of Paul's argument above. Paul speaks directly to the issue of human righteousness by pointing out that *no one* is righteous in God's sight. If salvation depends on our efforts to please God by doing what he requires, we are in trouble indeed! And our trouble all begins with our **alienation** from God! It is this alienation that has brought all human beings under the wrath of God.

alienation: separation

God's Wrath For The Unrighteous

Better Watch Out

> The **wrath** of God is being revealed from heaven against all the **godlessness** and wickedness of men who suppress the truth by their wickedness. (Romans 1:18).

God is not indifferent to unrighteousness. People who sin are objects of God's wrath, subject to eternal punishment. That truth is *being revealed* even now, in the corruption of morals and in the wickedness of those who *suppress the truth.*

I Don't Want To Hear It

> Since what may be known about God is plain to them, because God has made it plain to them. For since the creation of the world God's invisible qualities—his eternal power and divine nature—have been clearly seen, being understood from what has been made, so that men are without excuse. (Romans 1:19, 20)

The truth that human beings **suppress** is simply the fact that a Creator God exists. Paul's point is that the Creation is like a great radio transmitter, broadcasting the message of his existence. The Greek uses a different phrase in the clause, *God has made it plain to them.* What the Greek says is that God has made it plain "*in them.*" God not only shaped the universe to send the message that he formed all that exists; God also shaped human nature with a built-in receiver, tuned to God's station. Human beings who suppress the truth of God's existence are *without excuse,* because to reject or ignore God they must have willfully "turned down" their inner receiver. Human beings have willfully refused to accept the message God is broadcasting.

Warren Wiersbe: Human history is not the story of a beast that worshiped idols, and then evolved into a man worshiping one God. Human history is just the opposite: man began knowing God, but turned from the truth and rejected God.[3]

☞ **Check It Out:**

Romans 1:18–3:20

wrath: God's firm intent to punish sin and sinner

godlessness: failure to show reverence for God

KEY Symbols:

God's Invisible Qualities

his eternal power
his divine nature

suppress: purposefully ignore

KEY POINT

We say there is no God.

What Others are Saying:

Bow Down—No Way

glorify: to give God credit and praise for what he has done

The appropriate response to God's revelation of himself in creation is to give God credit for his works and to thank him. Rather than do this, humans have suppressed the truth that God exists and deserves our worship.

Gods That Can't Talk Back

. . . but their thinking became futile and their foolish hearts were darkened. Although they claimed to be wise, they became fools, and exchanged the glory of the immortal God for images made to look like mortal man and birds and animals and reptiles. (Romans 1:21–3)

KEY POINT

We make our own gods.

Everett F. Harrison: Man is a religious being, and if he refuses to let God have the place of preeminence that is rightfully his, then he will put something or someone in God's place.[4]

OK, Have It Your Way

Therefore God gave them over in the sinful desires of their hearts to sexual impurity for the degrading of their bodies with one another. They exchanged the truth of God for a lie, and worshiped and served created things rather than the Creator—who is forever praised. Amen. (Romans 1:24–25)

KEY POINT

God leaves us to our own destruction.

The phrase *gave them over* is repeated in Romans 1:26 and 1:28. Paul has said that God's wrath *is being* revealed from heaven (Romans 1:18). The sexual impurity and the other sins he describes in this chapter are clear evidence that God's wrath is directed against those who have rejected him. For the more morally corrupt a person or society becomes, the less peace, joy, and inner satisfaction human beings will experience. Sin may look attractive, but when indulged in, sins make us miserable! The misery that results from our sins is evidence of God's anger!

Warren Wiersbe: The lie is that man is his own god, and he should worship and serve himself and not the Creator.[5]

Max Lucado: God's highest dream is not to make us rich, not to make us successful or popular or famous. God's dream is to make us right with him. [6]

Men With Men, Women With Women

> Because of this, God gave them over to shameful lusts. Even their women exchanged natural relations for unnatural ones. In the same way the men also abandoned natural relations with women and were inflamed with lust for one another. Men committed indecent acts with other men, and received in themselves the due penalty for their **perversion**. (Romans 1:26, 27)

KEY POINT

God leaves us to our own perversion, wickedness, evil, greed, and depravity.

Wolfheart Pannenberg: The New Testament contains not a single passage that might indicate a more positive assessment of homosexuality than these Pauline statements. Thus, the entire biblical witness includes practicing homosexuality without exception among the kinds of behavior that give particularly striking expression to humanity's turning away from God. [7]

What Others are Saying:

perversion: wickedness

Wake Up, I'm Here

> They have become filled with every kind of wickedness, evil, greed and **depravity**. They are full of envy, murder, strife, deceit and malice. They are gossips, slanderers, God-haters, insolent, arrogant and boastful; they invent ways of doing evil; they disobey their parents; they are senseless, faithless, heartless, ruthless. (Romans 1:29–31)

depravity: fallenness

Genesis reveals the source of all that is good in human beings. God created humankind in his own image, with the capacity to love, to respond to love, to enjoy beauty and make beautiful things. Romans traces the origin of that which we all agree is evil. In abandoning God and suppressing the truth about him, human beings open themselves up to all that is evil. The very existence of such evils in society is evidence of man's abandonment of God, for where God is known and loved such behavior is unthinkable.

Remember This . . .

Warren Wiersbe: Paul names 24 specific sins, all of which are with us today. [8]

That's OK With Me

*righteous decree: God's
requirement that humans
do what is right*

*Although they know God's **righteous decree** that those
who do such things deserve death, they not only continue to do these very things but also approve of those
who practice them.* (Romans 1:32)

To understand what Paul is saying here we need only observe
those who defend what everyone knows is immoral behavior,
arguing for privacy rights and the freedom to do what we wish
without being subject to the morality of "religious bigots." Rather
than taking a stand for what is right, such persons insist that
others have the "right" to do what is wrong.

**What Others
are Saying:**

*allying: getting on the side
of*

*wanton: rampant and
unruly*

**Something
to Ponder**

Everett F. Harrison: The knowledge of God's righteousness,
innate in their very humanity, was sufficient to remind them
that the price of disobedience would be death. Yet men were
not deterred from their sinful ways by this realization. In fact,
they were guilty of the crowning offense of applauding those
who practiced wickedness in its various manifestations. Instead
of repenting of their own misdeeds and seeking to deter others,
they promoted wrongdoing by encouraging it in their fellows,
allying themselves with **wanton** sinners in defiant revolt against
God.[9]

In this first chapter, then, Paul argues that the sins in which
individuals and societies find themselves entangled, are in
fact evidence of God's wrath, directed against those who
have rejected a personal relationship with him. To argue
that human beings must act in righteous ways to please
God is to put the cart in place of the horse. What human
beings need is to reestablish a relationship with God that
will free them from their sins!

In Romans 2, Paul goes on to make it clear that all who have
sinned will be judged by God.

God's Principles Of Divine Judgment
You Do Evil, You'll Be Judged

*All who sin apart from the Law will also perish apart
from the Law, and all who sin under the Law will be
judged by the Law.* (Romans 2:12)

Because not everyone knows the divine standards as revealed in Moses' Law, it would hardly be fair to use the Ten Commandments to measure everyone's behavior. That is, the Jew, to whom the Law was given, can be judged by the Law, which he knows and accepts. But Gentiles, whose moral viewpoint has not been shaped by a knowledge of the divine Law, can hardly be judged by it. However, this does not acquit the person who is ignorant of God's standards: they too will perish.

Everyone Knows "Right" and "Wrong"

> *Indeed, when the Gentiles who do not have the Law, do by nature things required by the Law, they are a Law for themselves, even though they do not have the Law, since they show that the requirements of the Law are written on their hearts, their consciences also bearing witness, and their thoughts now accusing, now even defending them.* (Romans 2:14–15)

Paul's point is that everyone, even those ignorant of God's revealed standards, still recognizes that some things are morally right, and others morally wrong. For example, some cultures consider it moral to have as many as four wives. But in every culture some kinds of sexual behavior are labeled "wrong" and others "right." This points to the fact that human beings were created with a moral sense, so that all are evaluating actions as "right" or "wrong." Societies without access to God's standards create their own standards. Even more to the point, every person's conscience bears witness to the fact that he or she has violated *his own standards*, if not God's!

Because God is totally just and fair, God will not judge those who do not know his Law by that Law. Instead, he will judge them by their own moral standards! And when that happens every person will be judged "guilty!" for each of us is aware that we have not always done that which we ourselves believe is right.

Everett F. Harrison: Despite the great differences in laws and customs among people around the world, what unites them in a common humanity is the recognition that some things are right and others are wrong.[10]

☞ **Check It Out:**

Romans 2:1–3:8

KEY POINT

God judges us all whether we are Jews or Gentiles.

KEY Symbols:

We Are All Judged
Jews
  ▪ by Moses' Law
Gentiles
  ▪ by their own conscience

What Others are Saying:

THE NEW TESTAMENT — EXPLAINING THE GOSPEL   **235**

That Old Conscience Again

The Apostle Paul quotes the Old Testament as proof that all have sinned.

KEY POINT

We have all sinned.

> *We have already made the charge that Jews and Gentiles alike are all under sin. As it is written:*
>> *There is no one righteous, not even one;*
>> *there is no one who understands,*
>> *no one who seeks God."* (Romans 3:9–11)

Paul has argued that God's wrath is being expressed in the sins we see all around us. God's future judgment of sinners will be fair, for God will judge those who live under the Law by the Law, and judge others by their own standards of right and wrong. But whatever standard is used, our own consciences convict us.

Now Paul offers proof. God's Word says that *there is no one righteous, not even one.* When a human being stands before God to be judged by him, not one will be judged righteous.

What Others are Saying:

Warren Wiersbe: These verses indicate that the whole of man's inner being is controlled by sin; his *mind* (*no one who understands*), his *heart* (*no one who seeks after God*), and his *will* (*no one that does good*). Measured by God's perfect righteousness, no human being is sinless.[11]

The Law Won't Get You To Heaven

KEY POINT

The Law cannot save us, but through it we can become conscious of sin.

> *Now we know that whatever the Law says, it says to those who are under the Law, so that every mouth may be silenced and the whole world held accountable to God. Therefore no one will be declared righteous in his sight by observing the Law; rather, through the Law we become conscious of sin.* (Romans 3:19, 20)

The Law was never intended as a guide to show human beings how they might please God, or as a standard we are to live up to. The Law was intended to be a mirror, to show us how far short we fall of being what we ought to be!

No one will be declared righteous in God's sight by observing the Law. Through the Law we become conscious of sin.

But There's Hope!

Romans was written for those who were scandalized by a Gospel that offers salvation to sinners as a free gift. It was written for those who assumed that in promising to forgive sins, God was acting against his own nature as a righteous God.

Paul's response is profound. Those who assume such must first face a simple fact. No human being is or can become righteous. <u>All have sinned</u>. If salvation depends on human effort to do what is right, all are lost indeed!

Man's Problem:

The roots of sin are anchored in mankind's rejection of God.

God's Solution:

Jesus Christ died to pay the penalty for man's sin that through faith in him those who believe might not only be forgiven but reestablish a personal relationship with God! And just as man's rejection of God produced sins in individuals and society, the restoration of a personal relationship with God will produce righteousness in those who are joined to Jesus Christ!

Romans teaches us that the Gospel is about righteousness! God declares those who believe in Jesus to be righteous in his sight. And then God works in the believer's life to produce a righteousness that we could never demonstrate apart from him.

Max Lucado: Simply put: The cost of your sins is more than you can pay. The gift of your God is more than you can imagine. *A person is made right with God through faith*, Paul explains, *not through obeying the Law* (Romans 3:28).[12]

John Wesley: You are called to show by the whole tenor of your life and conversation that you are renewed in the spirit of your mind.[13]

☞ **GO TO:**

Romans 3:23 (sinned)

John 3:16 (save)

KEY POINT

Only Jesus can <u>save</u> us and make us righteous.

Something to Ponder

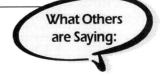

What Others are Saying:

GALATIANS

. . . the Law, or the Spirit?

WHO	The Apostle Paul
WHAT	wrote this letter
WHERE	to Christians in the province of Galatia
WHEN	about 49 A.D.,
WHY	to explain how freedom from the demands of Old Testament Law promotes righteous living and true goodness.

Rely On The Grace Of God, Not The Law

Acts reports that after Paul and Barnabas completed their first missionary journey, *men came down from Judea to Antioch (see Appendix A), and were teaching the brothers, 'Unless you are circumcised according to the custom taught by Moses, you cannot be saved* (Acts 15:1). These **Judaizers** insisted that gentile Christians be *required to obey the Law of Moses* (Acts 15:5). Many new Christians were confused. After all, the Old Testament was God's Word. Shouldn't Christians be responsible to keep its laws as well as to trust in Christ?

Judaizers: men who taught that Christians must keep Jewish laws

Paul saw this teaching as a critical distortion of the Gospel. He sent this letter to the Galatian churches to help them understand the limitations of the Law and the secrets of living in reliance on God's Holy Spirit.

What Others are Saying:

James Montgomery Boice: Galatians has been called the 'Magna Carta of Christian liberty,' and this is quite correct. For it rightly maintains that only through the grace of God in Jesus Christ is a person enabled to escape from the curse of his sin and of the Law and to a new life, not in bondage or license, but in genuine freedom of mind and spirit through the power of God.[14]

Tracing Paul's Argument

The Judaizers attacked Paul on three grounds. They claimed that (1) Paul is not really an apostle, (2) God authored the Law, and Paul shouldn't teach that it is set aside, and (3) Paul's teaching is a license to sin. Paul's letter to the Galatians responds to each of these charges. The outline below traces Paul's argument.

Greetings .... Galatians 1:1–5

1. Paul's apostleship rests on the fact that   1:11–2:21
   a. Jesus himself revealed the Gospel to Paul,   1:11, 12
   b. God himself called Paul to his ministry, and   1:13–24
   c. Jesus' apostles confirmed Paul's calling.   2:1–21
2. Paul's teaching distinguishes between Law
   and Faith. 3:1–4:31
   a. Law is unrelated to   3:1–18
      (1) how we receive spiritual life,   3:1–5
      (2) how Old Testament saints were made righteous,   3:6–9
      (3) how God fulfills his promises, and   3:10–14
      (4) how those promises function in our relation-
          ship with God.   3:15–18
   b. The Law's role has always been limited   3:19–4:7
      (1) by the fact it was temporary,   3:19, 20
      (2) by the fact it cannot give life,   3:21, 22
      (3) by the fact that Law points to faith,
          and   3:23, 24
      (4). by the fact that believers now have full rights as
          God's sons.   3:25–4:7
   c. The Law is an inferior way, that leads to   4:8–5:12
      (1) loss of joy,   4:8–19
      (2) loss of freedom, and   4:20–5:1
      (3) loss of power.   5:2–12
3. Paul's emphasis on freedom produces
   godliness that 5:13–25
   a. affirms love,   5:13–15
   b. relies on the Holy Spirit,   5:16–18
   c. releases one from the sinful nature, and   5:19–21
   d. produces spiritual fruit.   5:22–26

Closing exhortations and greetings 6:1–18

Dig Deeper

KEY POINT

What no human being can do on his own, God can and will do in those who know Jesus.

A Little Sample

Paul has argued that those who look to the Law as a means of producing righteousness fall into a trap. People who look to the Law and attempt to keep it in their own strength are sure to fail. Instead, Paul encourages believers to seek to love and serve others in the power of the Holy Spirit. What no human being can do on his own, God can and will do in those who know Jesus.

That Old Devil Is Still There

☞ **Check It Out:**

Galations 5:13–25

So I say, live by the Spirit and you will not gratify the desires of the sinful nature. For the sinful nature desires what is contrary to the Spirit, and the Spirit what is contrary to the sinful nature. They are in conflict with each other. . . . (Galatians 5:16–17)

What Others are Saying:

James Montgomery Boice: Some have maintained that there is no conflict within the Christian because of the supposition that the sinful nature has been eradicated. But this is not true according to this and other passages. Naturally, the sinful nature is to become increasingly subdued as the Christian learns by grace to walk in the Spirit. But it is never eliminated. So the Christian is never released from the necessity of consciously choosing to go in God's way. There is no escape from the need to depend on God's grace.[15]

KEY POINT

Depend on God's grace to defeat the devil daily.

Be Led By The Spirit Of God

But if you are led by the Spirit, you are not under the Law. (Galatians 5:18)

Life by the Spirit is neither legalism nor license. It is instead an openness to God's inner leading and a ready willingness to reach out to others in love.

KEY POINT

Live in openness and freedom in God's Spirit.

We Know And Can See The Difference

The acts of the sinful nature are obvious: sexual immorality, impurity and debauchery; idolatry and witchcraft; hatred, discord, jealousy, fits of rage, selfish ambition, dissensions, factions and envy; drunkenness, orgies and the like. I warn you, as I did before, that those who live like this will not inherit the kingdom of God. But the fruit of the Spirit is love, joy, peace, patience, kindness, goodness, faithfulness, gentleness, and self-control. Against such things there is no law. (Galatians 5:19–23)

KEY POINT

Thereby produce the Fruit of the Spirit in your life.

James Montgomery Boice: If one's conduct is characterized by traits on this first list, then he is either not a believer or else is a believer who is not being led by God's Spirit. The same standard of evaluation holds true for churches.[16]

Laws are passed against wrong behavior. They do not produce good behavior. When we understand the Christians' freedom from the Law as a freedom to follow the way of the Holy Spirit who has taken up residence in our lives, freedom is no longer frightening. When we respond to the Spirit's promptings, he produces only positive things in us.

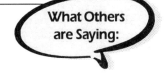

Warren Wiersbe: The contrast between works and fruit is important. A machine in a factory works, and turns out a product, but it could never manufacture fruit. Fruit must grow out of life, and, in the case of the believer, it is the life of the Spirit. The old nature cannot produce fruit; only the new nature can do that.[17]

Remember This . . .

Romans and Galatians thus find the key to both man's despair and man's hope in relationship with God. It is because of man's lost relationship with God that sin has gained its grip on individuals and society. And it is through the restored relationship with God offered to us in Jesus Christ that we have hope for living a truly good life.

Study Questions

1. What kind of literature is the New Testament epistles?
2. What does it mean to "trace the argument" of an epistle?
3. What is the theme of Paul's letter to the Romans?
4. What are three things Romans teaches about righteousness?
5. What is the root cause of sin in individuals and society?
6. How can God judge people who have never heard of his Law?
7. What is the true role of God's Law?
8. What is the theme of Paul's letter to the Galatians?
9. What are the two contrary principles operating in a Christian's life?
10. What is the difference between trying to relate to God through the Law, and being led by the Spirit?

CHAPTER WRAP-UP

- Many books in the New Testament were originally letters written by apostles to instruct Christians.
- The book of Romans was written to show how the Gospel relates to righteousness.
- Romans teaches that no human being is righteous, but that when God declares as righteous a sinner who believes in Jesus, God the Holy Spirit will enable that believer to lead a righteous life.
- Romans traces the root of human sin to mankind's alienation from God.
- Galatians emphasizes that both salvation and Christian living are experienced by reliance on the grace of God, not reliance on God's Law.

19 THE PROBLEM–SOLVING EPISTLES

I, II Corinthians
I, II Thessalonians

CHAPTER HIGHLIGHTS

- Problem-solving
- Then and Now
- Spiritual Principles
- Encouragement
- Misunderstandings

Let's Get Started

Paul's missionary team traveled from city to city spreading the Gospel. In each city a young church was established. Paul and his companions would spend a few months or even a year with most congregations, teaching the basic truths of the Gospel. The missionaries would then move on to another city and repeat the process.

Even though Paul and his team revisited the newly established churches whenever possible, the young believers often had unanswered questions. So when Paul heard about questions or problems in one of the churches he founded, he often sat down to write them. Some letters instructed a congregation on how to deal with a problem. Others clarified his earlier teaching. In this chapter we'll look at four letters of Paul that are clearly problem-solving epistles.

I CORINTHIANS
. . . getting back on track

WHO	The Apostle Paul wrote this letter
WHAT	in response to messengers who reported disputes that were tearing congregations apart
WHERE	in Corinth
WHEN	about 57 A.D.,
WHY	to show them how to rebuild a loving community.

Just the FACTS

☞ **Check It Out:**

Acts 18:1–18

Aphrodite: the Greek goddess of love and beauty

Something to Ponder

Dig Deeper

It Happened Then, Just Like It Does Now

First century Corinth (see Appendix A) was a busy city of some 250,000. Its population included native Greeks, a large number of Jews and other orientals, Roman settlers, government officials and businessmen. Priestess-prostitutes in Corinth's temple to **Aphrodite** helped create the climate of moral laxness for which Corinth was noted. Paul visited Corinth in 50 A.D., and stayed there for about 18 months, establishing a large body of believers there, with members from every strata of society.

Some five years after the church was founded, messengers from Corinth told Paul about the dissension and disputes that were tearing the congregation apart.

Commenting on these problems, the Nelson Illustrated Bible Handbook notes,

> the disturbing things which happened at Corinth still happen in modern congregations. There are still divisions, as believers exalt this or that human leader. There is still open immorality, for our society too is lax and wanton. Disputes between believers still lead to bitterness and law suits. Families break up. Pastors are caught in sin. And debates over doctrine divide our fellowship. Misunderstanding of basic truths still raises doubts and uncertainties. These facts make this letter of Paul to Corinth one of the most relevant of the New Testament epistles for us today.

Tracing Paul's Argument

The plan of Paul's first letter to the Corinthians is easy to follow, because the apostle simply addresses the problems one by one. Each new topic is introduced by a Greek phrase meaning "now concerning." Rather than give a short answer to problems in the church, Paul typically reviews basic truths the Corinthians need to understand, and then applies these truths to solve the problem.

To trace Paul's argument in this book we'll follow his plan, and

1) look at each problem,

2) explain the truths needed to resolve it, and

3) apply it to solve the problem.

Select any one of the problems that interests you, and follow along the three-part summary in your own Bible.

My Leader Is Better Than Yours

Divisions in the church (I Corinthians 1–4).

Greetings .... (I Corinthians 1:1–10).

1) The problem . . . (I Corinthians 1:10–17). The unity of the church is shattered by groups that quarrel over which leader they should be loyal to.

2) Instruction in basic Christian truth . . . (I Corinthians 1:18–3:23). Human wisdom, which relies on human reasoning, and God's wisdom, which is exhibited in the cross, are different in nature (I Corinthians 1:18–2:4). God's wisdom must be discerned by those who rely on the Spirit. The quarreling in Corinth shows that the believers there are **worldly** (I Corinthians 2:5–3:4). In truth, leaders are God's fellow workers, the Corinthians are God's building, and the foundation on which all must build is Jesus. So no more boasting about men (I Corinthians 3:5–23).

3) The solution . . . (I Corinthians 4:1–21). Human leaders are to be respected as servants entrusted with the secret things of God but not as founders of factions.

The Wicked Must Go

Impurity in the church (I Corinthians 5:1–6:20).

1) The problem . . . (I Corinthians 5:1–2). Sexual immorality goes on without confrontation by the church, and the Corinthians dare to be proud!

2) Instruction in basic Christian truth . . . (I Corinthians 5:3–6:20). Christians must not associate with other believers who practice sexual immorality (I Corinthians 5:3–13). Similarly, disputes between believers should be resolved by judges appointed within the church (I Corinthians 6:1–11). Sexual immorality of any kind is especially corrupting and must be avoided (I Corinthians 6:12–20).

3) The solution . . . (I Corinthians 5:13). *Expel the wicked man from among you.*

KEY Symbols:

Leaders
God's fellow workers

The Church
God's building

The Foundation
Jesus

worldly: *thinking and acting like those who do not know Christ*

KEY POINT

Human leaders are servants.

KEY POINT

The Church cannot tolerate wicked members.

Stay Hitched

Confusion about marriage (I Corinthians 7:1–39).

ascetic: *pertaining to rigorous self-denial*

1) The problem . . . (I Corinthians 7:1). Some had put an **ascetic** spin on Paul's comment that *it is good for a man not to marry.* A few of the married were refraining from sexual relations, others divorced, still others hesitated to wed.

2) Instruction in basic Christian truth . . . (I Corinthians 7:2–40). One purpose of marriage is to meet the sexual needs of each partner. A person with a strong sex drive should marry (I Corinthians 7:2–9). The married should not divorce, but if a non-Christian spouse leaves a believer, the Christian need not remain unmarried (I Corinthians 7:10–14). Paul generally advises people to remain in whatever state they were in when saved, but each person has his or her own calling, and each must follow his or her own leading (I Corinthians 7:15–40).

KEY POINT

Marry a believer.

3) The solution . . . (I Corinthians 7:5, 10, 36). The married should not give up sexual relations (I Corinthians 7:5) or divorce (I Corinthians 7:10). There are good reasons to remain single, but any unmarried person may wed without sinning (I Corinthians 7:36) as long as he or she weds another believer (I Corinthians 7:39).

Don't Offend Your Brother

Meat sacrificed to idols . . . (I Corinthians 8:1–11:1).

1) The problem . . . (I Corinthians 8:1–7). Most meat sold in the first century was from animals that had been sacrificed to pagan deity. Some Corinthians shopped in markets associated with pagan temples, convinced *that an idol is nothing at all.* Others were scandalized at this traffic with idolatry.

KEY POINT

If it means causing someone to stumble, don't do it.

2) Instruction in basic Christian truth . . . (I Corinthians 8:7–10:22). There is some truth in each party's argument. But this is an issue that should be approached on the basis of love, with consideration for the *weaker* brother who sees eating such meat as participating in idolatry (I Corinthians 8:7–13). Paul has himself set the example of giving up

perfectly legitimate "rights" out of concern for others (I Corinthians 9:1–27). At the same time all must remain aware of the fact that immorality and idolatry are closely associated, and so contact with idolatry is to be avoided (I Corinthians 10:1–22).

3) The solution . . . (I Corinthians 10:23–11:1). Apply the principle *everything is permissible—but not everything is beneficial* (I Corinthians 10:23). So, within the church, seek first the good of others. When eating with an unbeliever don't ask, but if the unbeliever makes a point of telling you the meat has been dedicated to an idol, don't eat for the sake of your host's conscience. Use your freedom to glorify God, not to cause others to stumble.

Cover Your Head

Disorderly public worship (I Corinthians 11:2–34).

1) The problem . . . (I Corinthians 11:5, 17–21). Women were praying and prophesying in public worship with their heads uncovered (I Corinthians 11:5), and the well-to-do were treating the **Lord's Supper** as a social event and making distinctions between wealthier and poorer classes.

2) Instruction in basic Christian truth . . . (I Corinthians 11:3–16; 23–32). The Creator made a distinction between male and female, and this is to be preserved in the Christian community. Christ himself established the pattern to be followed when we celebrate the Lord's Supper.

3) The solution . . . (I Corinthians 11:10, 23–26). Women are to wear the head coverings that mark them as female and that signify the authority Christian women now have to pray and prophesy in church. The Lord's Supper is to be celebrated as the simple ceremony Christ instituted, with full awareness of its significance.

Pentecost

Confusion about spirituality . . . (I Corinthians 12:1–14:39).

1) The problem . . . (I Corinthians 12:1–3; 14:2–3). In first century paganism, ecstatic utterances and even epileptic seizures were thought to indicate closeness to a god. The

Lord's Supper: Communion

KEY POINT

Worship is to praise God, not to do your own thing.

☞ **GO TO:**

Matthews 26:17–30 (Lord's Supper)

☞ GO TO:

I Corinthians 12:10
(tongues)

gift of tongues: speaking to
God in spiritual rather than
human language

spiritual gift: a supernatural
ability to minister to others

Body of Christ: all believers,
united to Jesus and each
other

KEY POINT

Everyone plays a part
with the gift God has
given them.

interpreting: translating

What Others
are Saying:

KEY POINT

Do the Lord's work
and let tomorrow take
care of itself.

young Christians in Corinth assumed that those who had
the **gift of <u>tongues</u>** were especially spiritual and closer to
God.

2) Instruction in basic Christian truth . . . (I Corinthians 12:1–
14:25). The Holy Spirit gives each believer a **spiritual gift**.
The gifts differ, but every gift is a sign of the Holy Spirit's
presence in the believer's life (I Corinthians 12:1–11).
Christians are like parts of a human body; the Spirit's gifts
fit each person for his or her role in the **Body of Christ**,
and every person has an important part to play (I
Corinthians 12:12–31). But the true test of spirituality is
not one's gift but one's love (I Corinthians 13:1–13). Don't
overemphasize tongues; unlike tongues, the intelligible
words spoken by a prophet instruct and build others up,
so this gift is more important (I Corinthians 14:1–25).

3) The solution . . . (I Corinthians 14:25–33). When you
meet together let everyone take turns contributing to
the service in an orderly way. And if someone with the
gift of **interpreting** tongues is present, those who speak
in tongues can take part too. Regarding the disruptive
women there—they should listen and learn quietly (I
Corinthians 14:34–40).

Billy Graham: According to the Bible, love is the dominant
principle of life.[1]

Don't Worry About Tomorrow

Uncertainty about resurrection (I Corinthians 15:1–58).

1) The problem . . . (I Corinthians 15:12). Some are saying
there is no resurrection.

2) Instruction in basic Christian truth . . . (I Corinthians
15:1–57). It is a historical fact, witnessed by many, that
Jesus rose from the dead (I Corinthians 15:1–11). If there
is no resurrection, Christ wasn't raised, and the Gospel is
utter nonsense (I Corinthians 15:12–19). But Christ indeed has been raised from the dead, and in the end will
destroy death itself (I Corinthians 15:20–28). The resurrection body awaiting us will be glorious, powerful, and
spiritual, and when we are clothed with immortality we
will experience the victory Christ has won.

3) The solution . . . (I Corinthians 15:58). Give yourselves fully to the work of the Lord, because you know that your labor in the Lord is not in vain.

Closing remarks .... (I Corinthians 6:1–29).

II CORINTHIANS
. . . *secrets of ministry*

WHO   The Apostle Paul wrote this letter

WHAT   sharing principles underlying his ministry

WHERE   to the Corinthian church

WHEN   about 58 A.D.,

WHY   to encourage any who were hurt by his first letter, and to warn those who were still rebellious.

Sorry To Be So Blunt

Paul's second letter to the Corinthians was written within a year of the first. Paul had heard encouraging reports that many responded to his rather blunt epistle by facing their sins and working to resolve problems. But a hostile minority remained determined to reject Paul's guidance. In this warm and revealing letter Paul opens his heart to share his love for the Corinthians and his vision of Christian ministry—and to warn those who still rejected his authority as an apostle of Jesus Christ.

Tracing Paul's Argument

This most personal of Paul's letters takes up three distinct topics. He begins with an explanation of his conduct and ministry (II Corinthians 1–7). Paul then encourages the Corinthians to give generously to a collection being taken up for the saints and for Jerusalem (II Corinthians 8–9). Finally Paul confronts and warns those who challenge his authority as an apostle (II Corinthians 10–13).

Let's imagine that the Apostle Paul made notes about what he wanted the Corinthians to understand about him and his ministry before writing this letter. His notes might have looked something like this.

**Dig
Deeper**

1. Me and my ministry .... II Corinthians 1:1–7:16
   A. Personal matters   1:1–2:11
      (1) I hurt for your benefit.   1:1–11
      (2) I really did plan to visit you but decided a visit
          then would have hurt rather than helped
          you.   1:12–2:4
      (3) (Oh yes. Tell them to forgive the man they
          disciplined. He's repented.)   2:5–11
   B. My ministry   2:12–6:2
      (1) Your transformation is proof that God called
          me and   2:12–3:6
      (2) proof that Jesus is real because we are being
          transformed, though we are not perfect.   3:7–16
      (3) Present failures don't cause us to lose heart.
          *What is seen is temporary, but what is unseen is
          eternal.*   4:1–18
      (4) (How neat it will be when we are with the Lord
          in eternity!)   5:1–10
      (5) For now though, I rely on the love God has
          planted in your hearts to bring your lives into
          harmony with his will.   5:11–6:2
   C. Getting personal again   6:3–7:16
      (1) It hasn't been easy, this ministry of mine, but
          I've been open with you.   6:3–11
      (2) (Warn them about getting tied up with unbe-
          lievers!)   6:12–7:1
      (3) I take such pride in you, especially in the way
          most of you responded to my earlier letter. *I am
          glad I can have complete confidence in you.*   7:2–15

2. As to your giving 8:1–9:15
   A. Be like the Macedonians: give yourselves first, then
      your money.   8:1–7
   B. God doesn't command giving, he invites us to follow
      Jesus' example.   8:8–12
   C. Really, giving is simply sharing so everyone will have
      enough.   8:13–15
   D. (Mention that Titus is coming to help, so they'll be
      ready with the collection.)   8:16–9:5
   E. *Whoever sows sparingly will also reap sparingly.*
      9:6–9
   F. Give freely, because God will provide freely.
      9:10–12
   G. Those who receive will praise God, and pray for
      you!   9:13–15

3. About apostles and authority 10:1–13:11
   A. The true apostle's arsenal is filled with powerful spiritual weapons.   10:1–6
   B. You've been fooled by **pseudo**-apostles because you evaluate by the wrong criteria.   10:7–18
   C. I wouldn't even let you support me   11:1–14
   D. Let them compare some of my meaningless "credentials"   11:15–33
   E. What really counts isn't even visions, but weaknesses which make it plain that anything accomplished is done by Christ's power.   12:1–10
   F. I really care about you, and I'm worried that when I come, some of you will not have repented and changed.   12:11–21
   G. Jesus is *not weak in in dealing with you*. Christ did give me authority to build you up. Respond, or Jesus will deal with you!   13:1–10

Final greetings 13:11–14

pseudo: false

A Little Sample

The false *super-apostles* (II Corinthians 11:5) who criticized Paul bragged about their strengths, and ridiculed Paul's weaknesses. Paul was hardly a compelling **orator**, nor was he an imposing figure physically. While Paul was given stunning revelations, he does not boast about them. In these verses Paul has a surprising response to his critics, and to his revelations.

> *To keep me from becoming conceited because of these surpassingly great revelations, there was given me a thorn in my flesh, a messenger of Satan, to torment me.* (II Corinthians 12:7)

Most believe the *thorn in the flesh* was a disfiguring and debilitating eye disease that made Paul even more vulnerable to ridicule by his opponents.

☞ **Check It Out:**

II Corinthians 12:7–10

orator: speaker

KEY Symbols:

Paul's "thorn in the flesh"
an eye disease

Warren Wiersbe: The Lord knows how to balance our lives. If we have only blessings, we may become proud; so he permits us to have burdens as well.[2]

What Others are Saying:

Three times I pleaded with the Lord to take it away from me. (II Corinthians 12:8)

KEY POINT

God kept Paul a humble, open channel.

Paul's response was appropriate. Like others with an illness or disability, Paul prayed. We're told by some that healing is guaranteed to believers who have enough faith. Certainly Paul was a man of faith, and prayed with utter confidence. But as the next verse tells us, God's answer was "No."

But he said to me, "My grace is sufficient for you, for my power is made perfect in weakness." (II Corinthians 12:9)

In Paul's case, God permitted the illness for more than one reason. First, the disability was to keep Paul from becoming conceited. Second, it was to make Paul a less cluttered channel through which God's power might flow.

What Others are Saying:

impediment: any physical defect that obstructs normal speech

Dwight L. Moody: When God delivered Israel out of Egypt he didn't send an army. God sent a man who had been in the desert for 40 years, and had an **impediment** in his speech. It is weakness that God wants. Nothing is small when God handles it.[3]

Therefore I will boast all the more gladly about my weaknesses, so that Christ's power may rest on me. (II Corinthians 12:9)

Paul understood God's message. His disability was a blessing, for it constantly reminded him to rely on God rather than on his own gifts and abilities.

What Others are Saying:

Martin Luther: Those whom God adorns with great gifts he plunges into the most severe trials in order that they may learn that they're nothing . . . and that he is all.[4]

I THESSALONIANS

. . . *encouragement for holy living*

Just the FACTS

WHO	Paul wrote this letter
WHAT	to encourage further commitment
WHERE	from believers in Thessalonica,
WHEN	about 51 A.D. or 52 A.D.,
WHY	toward holy living.

You're Doing Good

The city of Thessalonica (see Appendix A)was the capital of the Roman province of Macedonia. Rome maintained a great naval base there, and it was also a prosperous commercial center. Paul and his team spent only a brief time there, due to opposition aroused by Jews who were angry about the Gentiles' response to Paul's message. While Paul spent less than three months in Thessalonica, a flourishing church was planted there. This first letter to the church was written after Timothy visited the city and brought back a positive report to Paul.

This letter is probably the first of Paul's epistles. It is notable that the apostle mentions the return of Jesus in each of its five chapters.

☞ **Check It Out:**

Acts 17:1–9

Tracing Paul's Argument

Paul had three chief aims in writing this epistle: (1) to express thanks to God for the healthy spiritual condition of the church (I Thessalonians 1:2–10), (2) to reaffirm his affection for the congregation (I Thessalonians 2:1–3:13), and (3) to encourage them to continue in their commitment to godly living (I Thessalonians 4:1–5:23).

☞ **Check It Out:**

I Thessalonians 4:13–18

Greetings .... I Thessalonians 1:1

1. We thank God, for you   1:2–10
    A. responded to the Gospel, and   1:2–7
    B. are spreading the Gospel.   1:8–10

2. Remember how 2:1–3:12
    A. open we were with you,   2:1–6
    B. how much we loved you,   2:7–9
    C. how we parented each of you,   2:10–13
    D. and how you've responded despite the suffering it has cost you.   2:14–16
    F. I still long to see you,   2:17–20
    G. but I had to send Timothy instead   3:1–5
    H. and am overjoyed at his report!   3:6–13

3. Now I urge you to keep on growing 4:1–5:24
    A. Exercise self-control and avoid immorality.   4:1–8
    B. Keep on loving one another.   4:9–10
    C. Live quiet, responsible lives.   4:11–12
    D. Encourage each other with the promise of Jesus' coming.   4:13–18
    F. Keep focused on serving Jesus now.   5:1–11

Dig Deeper

G. And do all those "little things" that are to mark Jesus' people. 5:12–27

Grace to you! 5:28

A Little Sample

A few Thessalonian Christians had died, and some were devastated. They were certain the dead had missed the blessings Paul had taught were linked with the return of Jesus. Paul penned this famous passage to clarify what the future holds for all believers:

> *Brothers, we do not want you to be ignorant about those who **fall asleep**, or to grieve like the rest of men, who have no hope. We believe that Jesus died and rose again and so we believe that God will bring with Jesus those who have fallen asleep in him.* (I Thessalonians 4:13, 14)

II Corinthians 5:8 says that the Christian who has died and is *away from the body* [is] *at home with the Lord.* Biological death closes the door on this world, but opens the door to heaven for the Christian. We pass through the curtain fully conscious and aware. But God has even more in store for his own.

> *According to the Lord's own word, we tell you that we who are still alive, who are left till the coming of the Lord, will certainly not precede those who have fallen asleep.* (I Thessalonians 4:15)

Those living when Jesus returns have no special advantage over believers who have died!

> *For the Lord himself will come down from heaven, with a loud command, with the voice of the archangel and with the trumpet call of God, and the **dead in Christ** will rise first.* (I Thessalonians 4:16)

When Jesus does return, the first event will be the resurrection of Christians (see GWRV, page 298) who have died.

> *After that, we who are still alive and are left will be **caught up** with them in the clouds to meet the Lord in the air. And so we will be with the Lord forever. Therefore encourage each other with these words.* (I Thessalonians 4:17, 18)

fall asleep: died; appropriate for Christians who die and will awake.

dead in Christ: Christians who have died

*caught up: taken up to heaven in the **Rapture** (see GWRV, pages 63–67)*

Rapture: when the Church is removed from the earth

Then, together, the living and those who have died, transformed and in resurrection bodies like his own, will be caught up to be with the Lord forever.

Remember This . . .

What Others are Saying:

Robert L. Thomas: Only *after that* will living Christians be *caught up* for the meeting with Christ. The interval separating the two groups will be infinitesimally small by human reckoning. Yet the dead in Christ will go first. They will be the first to share in the glory of his visit. In this rapid sequence the living will undergo an immediate change from mortality to immortality (I Corinthians 15:52, 53), after which they will be insusceptible to death.[5]

II THESSALONIANS

. . . more on the Second Coming

WHO	The Apostle Paul wrote this letter
WHAT	sharing more about Jesus' return
WHERE	to the Thessalonians
WHEN	within a few months of his first letter,
WHY	to encourage those who were being persecuted and to correct misunderstandings.

Just the FACTS

We're Not There Yet

Paul's first letter hadn't cleared up all the Thessalonians' confusion about the future. In particular the Thessalonians were under the impression that the persecution they were experiencing was part of the <u>great tribulation</u> (see GWRV, pages 85–292) Paul had told them was linked to history's end. Paul explains that this can't be, and reminds them that he told them about a **man of lawlessness** (see GWDN, page 292) the prophet Daniel and Jesus himself said would appear first.

This individual whose appearance will mark the beginning of history's end, also called the Antichrist (Against- or Counterfeit-Christ), is described by Paul as *one who will oppose and will exalt himself over everything that is called God or is worshiped, so that he sets himself up in God's Temple, proclaiming himself to be God* (II Thessalonians 2:4).

☞ **GO TO:**

Daniel 9:23–27 (Tribulation)

man of lawlessness: the Antichrist

KEY Symbols:

Great tribulation
TRIBULATION PERIOD

DAY OF THE LORD

Man of Lawlessness
ANTICHRIST

Tracing Paul's Argument

Paul's brief letter is intended to help the Thessalonians put their troubles in perspective as well as correct misunderstandings. Compared to the awful judgment God will visit on the lost, present persecutions are nothing.

Greetings .... II Thessalonians 1:2

1. About present persecutions, ... 1:3–12
   I thank God for your perseverance,   1:3–4
   which is evidence that God's terrible   1:5–10
   future judgment of sinners is just, so I keep on praying
      Jesus will be glorified in you.   1:11–12

2. Concerning Christ's coming for us, ... 2:1–17
   first, the Day of the Lord has not come,   2:1–4
   for the power of lawlessness is being   2:5–7
   temporarily restrained by the Holy Spirit. When the
      lawless one does come, Satan will   2:8–12
   produce false miracles, and the world will follow the
      lawless one. Stand firm in the Gospel and be en-
      couraged.   2:13–17

3. For now, ... 3:1–15
   pray for us,   3:1–5
   and don't sit around waiting for Jesus; work and take
      care of yourselves.   3:6–15

Goodbye 3:16–18

What Others are Saying:

Calvary: the site in Jerusalem where Jesus died

KEY POINT

Concentrate on today! Tomorrow will <u>take care of itself.</u>

☞ GO TO:

Matthew 6:34 (take care)

C. S. Lewis: In the long run the answer to all those who object to the doctrine of hell, is itself a question: "What are you asking God to do?" To wipe out all their past sins and, at all costs, to give them a fresh start, smoothing away every difficulty and offering every miraculous help? But he has done so, on **Calvary.** To forgive them? They will not be forgiven. To leave them alone? Alas, I am afraid that is what he does.[6]

1. Name Paul's four problem-solving epistles.
2. What solution did Paul give to the problem of immorality in the church?
3. What was wrong about the Corinthians' emphasis on the gift of tongues?
4. What are two reasons why Christians should be generous givers?
5. What were two reasons why God did not answer Paul's prayers for healing?
6. Why aren't Christians to grieve the death of loved ones in the same way unbelievers grieve?
7. How will God repay those who persecute believers?

CHAPTER WRAP-UP

- When Paul heard of problems in the churches he founded, he often wrote letters of instruction and encouragement.

- Many of the problems addressed in Paul's first letter to the Corinthians are common in modern churches as well.

- Paul's second letter to the Corinthians explains the spiritual principles on which his ministry was based.

- Paul wrote I Thessalonians to encourage the committed but persecuted Christian community, and to help them understand their future.

- In II Thessalonians Paul corrected misunderstandings about Christ's return to earth, and urged holy living during the interim.

20 PAUL'S PRISON EPISTLES

Ephesians
Philippians
Colossians

CHAPTER HIGHLIGHTS

- The Living Church
- Working Out Salvation
- God Becomes Man
- Importance of Daily Living

Let's Get Started

Acts ends with Paul in a Roman prison awaiting trial. For two years Paul lived there under guard in a rented house, and was free to receive visitors. Often the visitors were from churches Paul had founded. In this way Paul was able to keep in close touch with Christians throughout the empire, and even to send letters of instruction to churches. The New Testament books of Ephesians, Philippians, and Colossians are letters written to churches during this time. Thus they are called the "prison epistles."

EPHESIANS

. . . the true church

WHO	The Apostle Paul wrote this letter,
WHAT	exploring the true nature of Christ's Church
WHERE	with the Christians in Ephesus
WHEN	about 62 A.D.,
WHY	to contrast Christianity with religion of that great temple city.

Just the FACTS

The Church Is You And Me

When the Apostle Paul and his missionary team first reached Ephesus (see Appendix A), it was the leading city in Asia Minor made rich by the pilgrims who flocked to the city to visit the

Illustration #16

Temple of Diana at Ephesus—*Thousands of people came to the temple of Diana at Ephesus each year, and the city's prosperity depended on these visitors. The temple also served as a bank, in which individuals and rulers deposited vast sums.*

pagan: *someone who observes* **polytheistic** *religion*

polytheistic: *many gods*

KEY Symbols:

The Church
  a living organism not an institution

magnificent temple of Diana, or Artemis (see Illustration #16, this page). Despite the success of Ephesus' religious institution, the population of the city was spiritually hungry, and deeply involved in dark occult practices. Paul's presentation of the Gospel was so effective that it literally threatened the livelihood of citizens who depended on the sales of religious medals and on feeding and housing visitors.

Some years later, Paul wrote to the Ephesians to emphasize a vital difference between Christian faith and **pagan** "religion." Christianity is no institutional faith that finds expression in magnificent buildings or silver trinkets. Christianity is a relational faith. The "Church" is not a building but people who know God, who express his love in the way they live with one another, and who display his character in the holiness of their daily lives.

THE BIG PICTURE

Ephesians The basic message of Ephesians is that Christ's Church is a living organism, not an institution. Father, Son, and Holy Spirit were each intimately involved in forming the New Testament community of faith, which can be understood as a living temple, as the Body of Christ, and as the family of God the Father.

Ephesians can be divided into two main sections, as follows:

Greetings .... Ephesians 1:1–2

1. Understanding the Church 1:3–3:21
   A. As God's creation   1:4–23
   B. As one people   2:1–22
   C. As the family of God   3:1–21

2. Living as the Church 4:1–6:20
   A. In ministry   4:1–16
   B. In purity   4:17–5:20
   C. In every relationship   5:21–6:9
   D. Enabled by God   6:10–20

Farewell.. 6:21–24

Dig Deeper

What's Special In Ephesians?

1 *What God has done for believers in Christ (Ephesians 1:3–14).* Paul writes that God has blessed believers with *every spiritual blessing in Christ.* He then goes on to show how each Person of the Trinity has been actively involved in providing the blessings Christians now enjoy. Note that . . .

☞ **Check It Out:**

Ephesians 1:3–14

God the Father	Christ the Son	The Holy Spirit
chose us to be holy and blameless	provided **redemption** through his blood	marked us by his presence in us
predestined us to be adopted		guarantees our inheritance
made his will known to us	provided forgiveness of our sins	
put his plan into effect at the right time		

Warren Wiersbe: Nowhere in the Bible are we taught that people are *predestined* to hell, because the word refers only to God's people. The word simply means 'to ordain beforehand, to predetermine.' Election seems to refer to people, while predestination refers to purposes. The events connected with the crucifixion of Christ were predestined.[1]

What Others are Saying:

predestined: *chosen beforehand*

redemption: *the payment of a price to free sinners*

2 *Paul's prayers for the Ephesians (Ephesians 1:15–22; 3:14–20).* Paul's prayers are a major feature of the prison epistles. In his first prayer for the Ephesians Paul asks God to help him know him better, and to realize that his incomparably great power is at work in and for them. In his second prayer for the

Ephesians, Paul asks God to so root the Ephesians in love for one another as members of the Father's family, that they may experience Christ's love, which surpasses knowledge.

3 *The true relationship between faith and* **works** *(Ephesians 2:1–10).* The raw material with which God constructed his Church is human beings who are spiritually *dead in* [their] **trespasses** *and sins.* By nature every human impulse is to satisfy the cravings of the sinful nature. To form Christ's Church, God made such persons *alive in Christ.* The new life God provides is entirely a gift of divine **grace**, not something anyone can earn by doing good.

Yet once a person has trusted Christ and received the gift of life, he or she discovers a desire to do good out of gratitude to God.

What Others are Saying:

Something to Ponder

☞ **Check It Out:**

Ephesians 4:22–5:2

Lewis Smedes: Realistic common sense tells you that you are too weak, too harassed, too human to change for the better; grace gives you the power to send you on your way a better person[2]

Only after a person has experienced God's grace and been made alive through faith in Christ can he or she do anything to please God.

4 *The Christian's new self (Ephesians 4:20–5:7).* In Ephesians 2:10 Paul calls Christians *God's workmanship, created in Christ Jesus.* Now Paul applies this truth. God's creation is a *new self* which was *created to be like God in true righteousness and holiness* (Ephesians 4:24). It follows that we are to get rid of such things as bitterness and anger and malice which are associated with the old self, and to be kind, compassionate, and forgiving. Paul sums up the Christian's calling by saying, *Be imitators of God, therefore, as dearly loved children, and live a life of love, just as Christ loved us and gave himself up for us. . . .* (Ephesians 5:1, 2).

5 *What it really means to be "head of the house" (Ephesians 5:21–32).* The stereotype portrays the Christian husband as a dictator who demands that his wife **submit** by giving up her rights in order to serve him. But no one could read Paul's description of the man as head of the house and come up with such a notion. As head of the house, the Christian husband is to model himself on Jesus Christ, the head of the Church. As Christ loved the Church and gave himself for it, a husband is to love his wife, intent on caring for her and helping her achieve her full potential as a person. This kind of love makes it easy for a wife to respect her husband, and to be responsive to him.

Larry Christianson: Those who stubbornly hold that their own happiness and convenience are the highest goals of family life will never understand God's plan for marriage and the family.[3]

What Others are Saying:

PHILIPPIANS

. . . *testimony to joy*

WHO	The Apostle Paul wrote this letter
WHAT	to share the joy he experienced
WHERE	with the Christians in Philippi,
WHEN	about 62 A.D.
WHY	in the hopes of relieving their distress over his imprisonment in Rome.

Just the FACTS

Joy In the Midst of Trials

Paul's imprisonment in Rome caused deep concern in many of the churches he had founded. The Christians in Philippi (see Appendix A) felt especially close to Paul, and had often sent him funds to help with his mission. In this very personal epistle Paul shares his own feelings about being incarcerated. Rather than seeing his imprisonment as a setback for the Gospel, Paul believes it will motivate believers throughout the empire to be even more bold in sharing the good news of Jesus Christ.

One striking feature of Philippians is the frequency with which Paul expresses his own sense of joy and rejoicing. How striking that in prison, where few would believe it is possible to be happy, the apostle finds so many sources of joy.

☞ **Check It Out:**

Acts 16:11–40

THE BIG PICTURE

Philippians Philippi was a Roman colony city, settled by discharged army veterans. It had no Jewish community, but it did have a strong gentile Christian church to which Paul had strong, loving ties. One of the major features of this book is a powerful poetic passage which describes the humility of Jesus, who surrendered the **prerogatives** of deity to become a human being and die for us. Christ's subsequent exaltation is a reminder to believers everywhere that the way up is down, and that it is the path of selfless giving which leads to personal fulfillment.

KEY POINT

The way up is down, and selfless giving leads to personal fulfillment.

prerogative: a particular right to do something

Here's help for following Paul's thoughts in this personal and newsy letter:

Dig Deeper

Very personal greetings .... Philippians 1:1–11

1. News and instructions 1:12–2:30

2. News about Paul 1:12–26

3. Instructions for the church 1:27–2:18
   A. On stability   1:27–30
   B. On humility   2:1–11
   C. On obedience   2:12–18

4. News about friends 2:19–30

5. Warning against false teaching 3:1–21
   A. Against Judaizers   3:1–11
   B. Against perfectionists   3:12–17
   C. Against imitation   3:18–21

6. Exhortations 4:1–9

7. Gratitude 4:10–20

Farewell 4:21–23

What's Special In Philippians?

1 *The many sources of Paul's joy.* In Philippians Paul identifies a number of sources for his joy; sources which can provide joy for us as well. Reading one or two of the following verses will provide an introduction to the different sources of Christian joy.

Dig Deeper

Paul finds joy . . .	Philippians
in partnering with others to share the Gospel	1:4
in stimulating others to share the Gospel	1:18
in the prayers of others for him	1:19
in the unity and love of the Philippians	2:2
in the privilege of suffering for others	2:17
in the Lord himself	3:1; 4:4
in fellow believers he loves	4:1
in the love others show him	4:10

2 *Paul's inner conflict over dying (Philippians 1:23).* If the Roman court were to rule against Paul, he would be executed. In facing this reality Paul's inner conflict was not motivated by a fear of death. He writes, *I desire to depart and be with Christ, which is better by far; but it is more necessary for you that I remain in the body* (Philippians 1:23). Unselfishly, Paul expresses his willingness to continue living in this world, but only because he might be of further help to the churches he has planted.

How few realize what Paul realized—heaven is the soul's true home.

Something to Ponder

3 *Working out salvation is different than working for salvation (Philippians 2:12, 13).* Paul encourages the Philippians to *work out their salvation* and reminds them that it is *God who works in you to will and to act according to his good purposes* (Philippians 2:13). The salvation Christians enjoy can be *worked out* only in those who already possess it!

Pope John Paul III: Every Christian—as he explores the historical record of Scripture and tradition and comes to a deep, abiding faith—experiences that Christ is the risen one and that he is therefore the eternally living one. It is a deep, life-changing experience. No true Christian can keep it hidden as a personal matter. For such an encounter with the Living God cries out to be shared—like the light that shines, like the yeast that leavens the whole mass of dough[4]

What Others are Saying:

4 *A vivid description of the confident Christian (Philippians 3:2–11).* Paul warns the Philippians against false Jewish teachers who brag about their credentials. Paul quotes his own qualifications, which are more impressive than theirs, and then consigns his credentials to the rubbish heap! What counts is knowing Christ. Paul's confidence is based on the fact that Christ's resurrection power can be experienced here and now by the believer whose earnest desire is to know Jesus better.

The confident Christian does not see himself or herself as perfected, but eagerly presses on to *take hold of that for which Christ Jesus took hold of me* (Philippians 3:12). Our confidence is not in ourselves or in our achievements, but in his power to constantly lift us beyond ourselves.

KEY POINT

Our confidence as Christians is in God's power to lift us beyond ourselves.

5 *Freedom from anxiety is ours to claim (Philippians 4:6–7).* Paul's obvious sense of joy seems strangely out of place. Most of us in a similar situation would be worried and anxious. But Paul shares his secret with us: in everything, and with thanksgiving, he presents his requests to God. In return God floods his heart with a peace that transcends all understanding. Paul has turned his problems over to the Lord, and they no longer trouble him!

6 *The secret of contentment in all circumstances (Philippians 4:12–13).* The trouble with difficult circumstances is that they seem to rob us of our freedom of choice. The slave can't go where he wishes; the cripple can't run and jump. Paul however is *content in any and every situation.* He simply doesn't let circumstances bother him.

How can this be? Paul says *I can do everything through him who gives me strength* (Philippians 4:13). Circumstances have no power over Paul. God gives the strength needed to do whatever needs to be done in the situation. Confident in God's presence and power, you and I, like Paul, can be content.

A Little Sample

Philippians 2 is one of the most profound passages in the Bible. Paul urges the Philippians to maintain unity of heart and purpose by doing *nothing out of selfish ambition or vain conceit, but in humility consider others better than yourselves* (Philippians 2:3). This will be possible only if the Christians in Philippi adopt the attitude displayed by Jesus Christ when he entered our world and went to the cross.

As Paul traces the course which Jesus followed in setting aside the prerogatives of deity, he reminds us that Christ's path led to even greater glory.

> *Who, being in very nature God,*
> *did not consider equality with God*
> *something to be grasped,*
> *But made himself nothing,*
> *taking the very nature of a servant,*
> *being made in human likeness.*
> *And being found in appearance as a man,*
> *he humbled himself,*
> *and became obedient to death—*
> *even death on a cross.*

Something to Ponder

Therefore God exalted him to the highest place,
and gave him the name that is above
every name, that at the name of Jesus every knee should bow,
in heaven and on earth and under the earth,
and every tongue confess that Jesus
Christ is Lord,
to the glory of God the Father.
(Philippians 2:6–11)

Rather than suffer loss when we surrender our own interests to meet the needs of others we, like Christ, can only gain.

Remember This . . .

COLOSSIANS

. . . *God in daily life*

WHO	The Apostle Paul
WHAT	wrote this letter
WHERE	from prison to the Christians in Colosse (see Appendix A),
WHEN	about 62 B.C.,
WHY	to clear up their confusion, which was the result of false teachers who divorced spirituality from daily life.

God Is By My Side, All The Time

heresies: false teachings

One of the early **heresies** that confused early Christians is demonstrated here in Colossians. Some people argued that all matter was evil. Only the "spiritual" and immaterial can be "good." If so, it follows that God could have nothing to do with the material universe. It must have been created by lesser beings far removed from God. What's more, if Jesus were God he could not have taken on a real human body. Conversely, if Jesus had a real human body, he could not be God. According to this heresy, it also follows that what Christians do in their daily lives has nothing to do with spirituality, for daily life is conducted in the material world.

Paul's letter to the Colossians confronts this notion and presents Jesus Christ as God come in the flesh.

Colossians Curtis Vaughn, writing in the Expositor's Bible Commentary, sketches the leading features of the heresy Paul combats in Colossians. "(1) It professed to be a 'philosophy,' but Paul, refusing to recognize it as genuine, called it a 'hollow and deceptive philosophy' (Colossians 2:8). (2) It placed too much emphasis on ritual circumcision, dietary laws, and the observance of holy days (Colossians 2:11, 14, 16, 17). (3) Affirming the mediation of various supernatural powers in the Creation of the world and the whole process of salvation, the false teaching insisted that these mysterious powers be **placated** and worshiped (Colossians 2:15, 18, 19). As a result of this, Christ was relegated to a relatively minor place in the Colossian system. (4) Some of the errorists were ascetic (Colossians 2:20–23), teaching that the body is evil and must be treated as an enemy. (5) The advocates of this system claimed to be Christian teachers (Colossians 2:3–10)."

placate: to appease

To counter this false teaching, Paul presents a powerful portrait of Jesus Christ and his work on our behalf. He also offers an appealing description of the life by which Christians can honor him.

Dig Deeper

Greetings .... Colossians 1:1, 2

1. Thanksgiving and prayer 1:3–14

2. The real Jesus 1:15–2:7
   A. Christ is supreme   1:15–23
   B. Paul ministers Christ   1:24–2:7

3. Warning against errors 2:8–23
   A. Against deceptive philosophy   2:8–15
   B. Against legalism   2:16, 17
   C. Against angel worship   2:18, 19
   D. Against asceticism   2:20–23

4. Living the Christian life... 3:1–4:6
   A. Its heavenly source   3:1–4
   B. Guidelines   3:5–4:6
      (1) Abandon sins   3:5–11
      (2) Cultivate virtues   3:12–17
      (3) Strengthen the family   3:18–4:1
      (4) Pray and witness   4:2–6

5. Conclusion 4:7–18
    A. Commendations 4:7–9
    B. Greetings 4:10–15
    C. Instructions 4:16–17
    D. Benediction 4:18

What's Special In The Book Of Colossians?

1 *Paul's prayer points the way to spiritual growth (Colossians 1:9–11).* Paul's prayer outlines a step-by-step plan for anyone who wants to grow spiritually and deepen his or her personal relationship with God.

Step	Description	Action to Take
1	Fill up with the knowledge of God's will.	Study Scripture where his will is revealed.
2	Exercise spiritual wisdom and insight.	Seek to apply what you learn to daily life.
3	Live a life worthy of the Lord.	Act on what you learn, desiring to please him.
4	Bear fruit in every good work.	Bear fruit and God will produce fruit and good works.
5	Grow in the knowledge of God.	Grow and you will experience God's very presence.

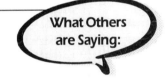

Edmund P. Clowney: Wisdom starts in heaven but works at street level, where we bump shoulders with others. It isn't satisfied with information retrieval: You can't access wisdom by the megabyte. Wisdom is concerned with how we relate to people, to the world, and to God.[5]

2 *The real Jesus is both fully God and truly man (Colossians 1:15–23).* The Bible makes absolutely clear who Jesus is. This brief passage (Colossians 1:15–23) is one of the clearest in Scripture.

Biblical Descriptions	Characteristics
The image of the invisible God	Seeing Jesus is seeing God.
The firstborn over all creation	The heir to all that exists.
By him all things were created	He is the Creator God.
All things were created by and for him	He is the beneficiary of Creation.
In him all things hold together	His power holds the universe together even now!
He is the head of the Church	He guides, directs his people.
He is the firstborn from the dead	He is our living Lord.
All God's fullness dwells in him	He is fully, completely God.

preeminent: first of all

*reconciled: brought into
harmony*

*Remember
This . . .*

*legalism: trying to please
God by keeping the Law*

Warren Wiersbe: To many people, Jesus Christ is only one of a several great religious teachers, with no more authority than they. He may be *prominent*, but he is definitely not **preeminent**. They may not be denying him, but they are dethroning him and robbing him of his rightful place.[6]

3 *What Jesus did in our world makes all the difference (Colossians 1:22).* Paul challenges the notion that the material universe is irrelevant. He writes *"now [God] has **reconciled** you by Christ's physical body through death to present you holy in his sight"* (Colossians 1:22). God the Son took on a flesh-and-blood human body, and in that body Christ died on the cross. In that act of self-sacrifice, Jesus paid for all our sins, bringing us back into conformity with God by making us holy in his sight. No one, realizing what Jesus has done, can ever claim that what human beings do in this world of space and time is irrelevant to God.

4 *Will the real Christian please stand up? (Colossians 2:20–23; 3:12–17).* Some people have a peculiar idea about what real Christians are like. Two passages in Colossians contrast the fake and the real Christian lifestyle. Compare them side by side:

Fake Christians . . .	Real Christians . . .
make up rules	are kind and compassionate
emphasize don'ts	forgive and love
look pious	enjoy worship
punish themselves	honor God in all they do

Warren Wiersbe: People who religiously observe diets and days give an outward semblance of spirituality, but these practices cannot change hearts. **Legalism** is a popular thing because you can 'measure' your spiritual life—and even brag about it. But this is a far cry from measuring up to Christ.[7]

1. What is the theme of Ephesians?
2. According to Ephesians 2, what is the relationship between faith and works?
3. What are responsibilities of the husband as "head of the house"?
4. What key words recur again and again in Philippians?
5. What can a Christian do to gain freedom from anxiety?
6. What heresy is Paul combatting in Colossians?
7. What passage in Colossians makes it absolutely clear that Jesus is God?
8. What are two characteristics of "fake" Christians? What are two characteristics of "real" Christians?

CHAPTER WRAP-UP

- While imprisoned in Rome the Apostle Paul wrote letters of instruction to several churches he had founded.

- In Paul's letter to the Ephesians he contrasts Christianity with "religion," and Christ's living church with mere buildings.

- To create the Church God gave spiritual life to persons who were dead to God because of their sins.

- Paul urged the Philippians to work out or express the salvation that God had given them in Christ.

- Philippians Chapter 2 shows how Christ surrendered the prerogatives of deity to become a human being and die on the cross.

- Paul's letter to the Colossians emphasizes the fact that Jesus Christ is God, who took on a real human body.

- Colossians reminds us that the way we live our daily lives is important to God, and that what we do daily can glorify him.

21 PAUL'S LETTERS TO INDIVIDUALS

I, II Timothy
Titus
Philemon

CHAPTER HIGHLIGHTS

- Be an Example
- Godly Leaders
- False Teachers
- Good Works
- Slavery

Let's Get Started

Most of the New Testament letters of Paul were written to churches, but four were written to individuals.

Timothy and Titus were both young leaders who traveled from church to church. Their ministry was to correct false teaching and set local congregations on the path of godly living. The letters Paul wrote to them are filled with practical advice. The two letters to Timothy and the one letter to Titus are called the "pastoral epistles." The short letter to Philemon has another purpose entirely. In it Paul encourages a well-to-do Christian to welcome back a runaway slave who had become a Christian through Paul's witness.

KEY Symbols:

Pastoral Epistles
to young leaders in the Church
- Timothy
- Titus

I TIMOTHY

. . . the healthy local church

Who	The Apostle Paul
What	wrote this letter of advice
Where	to Timothy, who was on a mission for Paul in Ephesus,
When	around 64 A.D.,
Why	to correct problems in the church and to restore spiritual health.

Just the FACTS

TIMOTHY: Timothy had been a member of Paul's missionary team. He was a young man whose father was Greek and whose mother was Jewish. Paul had sent him on several missions (I Corinthians 4:17; 16:10; Acts 19:22; II Corinthians 1:1, 19), and he had not always been successful. While aware of Timothy's weaknesses, Paul encourages as well as guides this younger man who will be one of the Church's leaders when Paul dies.

Looking For A Church?

Despite the fact that he had been taught the Scriptures by his mother and grandmother from childhood (II Timothy 1:5–6) and had been trained by Paul himself, Timothy remained shy and unassertive. Also, he was young to be a leader in a culture that respected age and maturity. Despite this, Paul treated Timothy as a son and recognized his potential as a leader of the next generation of Christians. At the time Paul wrote, Timothy was in Ephesus, sent there to resolve problems that had emerged in the church and to establish stronger local leadership. It was a challenging mission, and Paul outlines many of the steps Timothy would need to take. This letter can be particulary valuable today. Paul's instructions to Timothy paint a picture of the ideal church—a picture which may prove valuable to present-day Christians who are looking for a local congregation to join.

KEY Symbols:

False Doctrine

promotes

- controversy
- ungodliness

**Sound Doctrine
(God's Truth)**

produces

- love which comes from a pure heart and a good conscience and a sincere faith

THE BIG PICTURE

> **I Timothy** In this letter Paul describes the strong and healthy church which he expects Timothy to help establish in Ephesus. In addition Paul gives Timothy guidelines to follow.

Paul's letter takes up a variety of topics:

Greetings .... I Timothy 1:1–2
1. Correct false teaching with sound doctrine 1:3–20
   A. (See what the truth has done for me!)   1:12–17
   B. Fight the good fight.   1:18–20
2. Keep the focus on the Lord during worship 2:1–15
3. Remember that leaders are to model godliness ... 3:1–16
4. Identify false teaching and false teachers 4:1–16
   while serving as an example of godliness 4:12–16

Dig Deeper

5. Treat everyone with respect. 5:1–6:10
   A. Don't forget the "widows' corps." 5:3–17
   B. Show respect to church elders. 5:18–25
   C. Remind slaves to respect their masters 6:1–2
   and warn against a love of money. 6:3–10

6. As for you, Timothy, pursue righteousness. 6:11–21
   A. Oh yes, warn the wealthy, and 6:17–19
   B. guard what has been entrusted to you. 6:20–21

J. Vernon McGee: In I Timothy we deal with the nitty-gritty of the local church, with the emphasis that it is the character and caliber of her leaders that will determine whether the church is really a church of the Lord Jesus Christ.[1]

What Others are Saying:

What's Special In I Timothy?

1 *The vital importance of* **sound doctrine** *(I Timothy 1:3–11).* Paul gives an important reason why Timothy is to confront those who teach false doctrine. God's truth will produce *love, which comes from a pure heart and a good conscience and a sincere faith (I Timothy 1:5).* False doctrine promotes controversy and ungodliness.

In the next paragraphs (I Timothy 1:12–17) Paul points out that he himself was once the worst of sinners, a persecutor and a violent man. But the gospel message of the love and grace of God transformed Paul completely.

sound doctrine: healthy, correct teaching

William Barclay: The Christian's dynamic comes from the fact that he knows sin is not only breaking God's Law but also breaking his heart. It is not the Law of God but the love of God which constrains us.[2]

What Others are Saying:

2 *One God and one* **mediator** *between God and man (I Timothy 2:1–5).* The Bible never apologizes for presenting faith in Christ as the only way that a person can establish a personal relationship with God. The common notion that all religions lead to the same God is, quite simply, false. Jesus Christ died to pay the price of sin for all human beings, and trust in him is the only avenue that leads to God.

I am the way and the truth and the life. No one comes to the Father except through me. (John 14:6)

☞ **Check It Out:**

I Timothy 3:1–7

mediator: a go-between who brings parties together

Remember
This . . .

KEY POINT

Character is of more importance than training or spiritual gifts in a leader.

3 *Qualifications for church leaders (I Timothy 3:1–16).* It is striking that the list of qualifications for church leaders, whether elders, deacons, or deaconesses, emphasize character rather than training or even spiritual gifts. The reason is that leaders are to be mature Christians who model the godly Christian character that the Holy Spirit seeks to produce in all believers. We see this clearly when we compare the words Paul used to describe the Christian way of life with those he used to describe the qualifications of a leader.

Christian leaders are to be . . .	The Christian lifestyle involves . . .
above reproach	godliness
temperate	temperance
self-controlled	self-control
respectable and upright	trustworthiness
hospitable	love
not alcoholics	self-discipline
not competitive but gentle	gentleness
not quarrelsome	being considerate
not quick-tempered	being peaceable
not materialistic	generosity
respected by unbelievers	integrity
lovers of goodness	dedication to goodness, faith, and endurance

4 *Advice for every young believer (I Timothy 4:12).* Paul's advice to Timothy is ideal for any believer, whether young in years or young in the faith.

Don't let anyone look down on you because you are young, but set an example for the believers in speech, in life, in love, in faith, and in purity. (I Timothy 4:12)

What Others are Saying:

J. Vernon McGee: The important thing is not your age, but whether you are an example.[3]

5 *The widows' corps (I Timothy 5:3–16).* The New Testament Church, like the Jewish community, demonstrated a real concern for widows and the fatherless by providing support for them. With no occupations open to women in the first century, Paul advised younger widows to remarry. Those widows with adult children should be supported by their families (I Timothy 5:16).

But the church which supported widows also gave a special ministry to older widows who had demonstrated solid Christian character (I Timothy 5:9, 10). That ministry, described in Titus 2:4–5, was to *train the younger women to love their husbands and children, to be self-controlled and pure, to be busy at home, to be kind, and to be subject to their husbands, so that no one will malign the Word of God.* How important that older believers not only be respected but also be given the opportunity to minister.

J. Vernon McGee: We overlook the wonderful widow in our own church who is lonely and seldom visited. If a church took care of its widows, its testimony would not go unnoticed by the world.[4]

What Others are Saying:

6 *The warning against love of money (I Timothy 6:3–10, 17–19).* We often hear it said, "money is the root of all evil." That's wrong. Paul wrote *for the love of money is a root of all kinds of evil* (I Timothy 6:10). The person who develops a passion for wealth is vulnerable to *foolish and harmful desires that plunge men into ruin and destruction* (I Timothy 6:9).

Having money can be a good thing—if the wealthy person is eager to be rich in good deeds, generous, and willing to share with others. But all too often the rich depend on their money rather than on God, and they become arrogant.

Paul's solution is for everyone to develop a passion for godliness, and to be content with whatever it takes to meet their basic needs. A good conscience and a good reputation are worth more than millions.

KEY POINT

The *love* of money is the root of all kinds of evil.

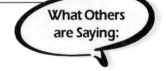

Warren Wiersbe: There is always more spiritual wealth to claim from the Lord as we walk with him. As we search the Word of God, we discover more and more of the riches we have in Christ.[5]

What Others are Saying:

II TIMOTHY

. . . *warning! warning! warning!*

Who	The Apostle Paul
What	wrote this letter to Timothy
Where	from prison in Rome
WHEN	about 67 A.D.,
WHY	to warn him about the danger of false teachers who were infiltrating the Church.

Just the FACTS

They Speak With Lies

The book of Acts ended with Paul under house arrest in Rome. He was there for two years. Tradition reports that after being realeased, Paul went on a missionary journey to Spain. However, within five years Paul was arrested again and imprisoned in Rome. This time Paul did not survive but was executed under the Roman Emperor Nero.

Most believe that this was the last letter Paul wrote before his execution. While the Christian community had begun to experience governmental persecution, the apostle was more concerned about those who were corrupting the Church by false teaching. In this letter Paul urges Timothy to serve as a good soldier of Jesus Christ, and remain committed to the truth revealed by God.

THE BIG PICTURE 🔍

> **II Timothy** This book is a call to remain faithful to Christ and to sound teaching. It was vitally important because of the threat posed by false teachers. Highlights of Paul's letter are 1) his statement about the confidence we can have in Scripture, and 2) his description of the attitude which should be adopted by people sharing God's truth with others.

Paul's letter follows this pattern:

Greetings .... II Timothy 1:1–2

1. Be faithful 1:3–2:13
   A. to the truth you learned as a child,   1:3–7
   B. as I have been faithful,   1:8–15
   C. as others have been faithful,   1:16–18
   D. as also are . . .   2:1–7
   E. soldiers,   2:4
   F. athletes,   2:5
   G. hard-working farmers,   2:6
   H. and as Christ is faithful to us.   2:8–13

2. Hold tightly to God's Word................................. 2:14–26
   A. Handle it correctly   2:8–19
   B. Prepare yourself to minister it   2:20–23

3. Present God's Word appropriately....................... 2:24–26

4. Be prepared for difficult times 3:1–4:8
   A. with unresponsive people   3:1–5
   B. led by false teachers.   3:6–9

Dig Deeper

5. Lead a godly life 3:10–13
    A. guided by the Scriptures, 3:14–17
    B. and keep on preaching, 4:1–5
    C. for I am about to depart. 4:6–8

Final remarks 4:9–18

Greetings 4:19–22

What's Special In II Timothy?

1 *Parents have a vital role in their children's faith (II Timothy 1:5).* The Apostle Paul traces Timothy's faith back to his mother and grandmother, who passed the flame of faith on to young Timothy when he was a child. God's plan for communicating faith from generation to generation has always focused on the family.

☞ Check It Out:

Deuteronomy 6:5–9

What Others are Saying:

Roy B. Zuck: God placed the responsibility of developing godly character in our children squarely on the shoulders of parents. The Bible views fathers and mothers as teachers—those who instruct their own in the ways of God.[6]

2 *The spiritual source of opposition to God's truth (II Timothy 2:24–26).* Paul describes the approach Timothy should take in addressing opposition. He warns against quarreling and prescribes an attitude of kindness which leads to gentle instruction. Why not rely on forceful argument and debate? Paul makes it clear that the real problem is spiritual, not intellectual. God alone can lead those who oppose the Gospel to a knowledge of the truth, for they have been *taken captive* by the devil *to do his will.*

What Others are Saying:

William Barclay: It is God who awakens the repentance; it is the Christian leader who opens the door to the **penitent** heart.[7]

penitent: feeling sorrow for sin

form: outward appearance

3 *Beware of churches having a **form** of godliness without its power (II Timothy 3:1–5).* Paul looks ahead to terrible times and describes people who are *lovers of money, boastful, proud, abusive, disobedient to their parents, ungrateful, unholy, without love, unforgiving, slanderous, without self-control, brutal, conceited,* etc. Yet he notes that they will have a *form of godliness.* They'll go to church, sing the hymns, and congratulate the preacher on his sermon. But true godliness is exhibited in lives that Jesus

Christ has transformed. Paul's admonition is good advice for the church where people go through the motions without exhibiting God's work in their hearts: *have nothing to do with them.*

4 *The importance of knowing and living Scripture (II Timothy 3:15–17).* Paul focuses our attention on the holy Scriptures *which are able to make you wise for salvation through faith in Christ Jesus.* What is it that makes Scripture so special?

The Bible is . . .

God breathed	As a breeze fills the sails of a ship, the Spirit filled the writers of Scripture and carried them along, so what they wrote was what God intended to say.
useful for teaching	It communicates God's truth.
useful for rebuking	It corrects false ideas about God.
useful for correcting	It directs us away from sin.
useful for training in righteousness	Its teachings, when followed, enable us to be men and women of God. . . . it is sufficient to thoroughly equip believers for good works!

Something to Ponder

Just the FACTS

Who's Who

If we expect God's Word to get into our lives, we must commit ourselves to get into God's Word—regularly!

TITUS

. . . living as God's people

WHO	The Apostle Paul
WHAT	wrote this letter
WHERE	to Titus, who was in Crete
When	about 65 A.D. or 66 A.D.
WHY	to correct problems in the church there and to motivate commitment to good works.

TITUS: Like Timothy, Titus was a young leader who carried the burden of instructing the churches once the apostles were gone. Titus successfully completed several missions for Paul, and the apostle had great confidence in his abilities.

Be Eager To Do Good

The inhabitants of the Mediterranean island of Crete (see Appendix A) had a questionable reputation. Paul quotes the poet Epimenides in Titus 1:12, who had written centuries earlier that "Cretans are always liars, evil beasts, lazy gluttons." Titus' mission to Crete was to motivate the Christians who had received the Gospel to be transformed by God's grace into a people who are eager to *devote themselves to doing what is good* (Titus 3:8).

When Paul wrote to Titus, he probably had less than two years to live. As Titus had been successful in other missions that Paul had assigned him, it seems likely that he was able to complete this mission too, and to lead members of this unruly church into a disciplined Christian life.

THE BIG PICTURE 🔍

> **Titus** Paul's advice to Titus is similar to that which Paul set out in his first letter to Timothy. Both were to see to the establishment of a strong local leadership for the church. Both were to concentrate on teaching sound doctrine, with a view toward producing godly persons whose lives would glorify God. Particularly significant is Paul's emphasis on the importance of good works, to be done by those who have experienced the grace of God.

In this brief letter Paul includes . . .

Greetings .... Titus 1:1–4

1. What to do on Crete: 1:5–16
   A. Appoint elders.   1:5–9
   B. Rebuke the rebellious.   1:10–16

2. What to teach on Crete: 2:1–15
   A. Positive Christian character and   2:1–10
   B. Rejection of ungodliness.   2:11–15

3. What to emphasize on Crete: 3:1–11
   A. True humility toward all men,   3:1–2
   B. Devotion to doing good, and   3:3–8
   C. Avoiding divisive persons   3:9–11

4. Final remarks 3:12–15

Dig Deeper

Church Leaders

elders

overseers

bishops

1 *Appointing elders in every town (Titus 1:5–9).* It was and is vital to the health of a local congregation to be led by a team of godly leaders. Paul charged Titus with *appointing* these leaders, which are called *elders, overseers,* or *bishops* interchangeably throughout the New Testament.

The word translated *appoint* here and in other passages that have to do with leaders means to *give official recognition to.* Members of the local congregation were expected to recognize mature Christians whose lives exhibited the Christian character Paul describes here and in I Timothy, and who had a firm grasp of the truth. The apostle or his representatives then met with these local congregations, and, after examining the persons recommended, confirmed them as elders.

☞ **Check It Out:**

Titus 1:5–9

I Timothy 3:1–13

2 *Teaching that is in accord with sound doctrine (Titus 2:1–15).* We most often think of *teaching* as communicating information. But in Titus 2 Paul portrays it as encouraging a lifestyle that fits with the truth contained in God's Word. Words for this kind of teaching include *train* (Titus 2:4), *encourage* (Titus 2:7), and *set an example* (Titus 2:8).

What kind of life is fitting for those who are committed to what the Bible says? Paul emphasizes temperance, self-control, reverence, integrity, and uprightness, while warning against slander, addiction to much wine, and anything that would give others anything bad to say about believers. When Christians show that they can be fully trusted, they *will make the teaching about God our Savior* attractive.

Teach

train

encourage

set an example

3 *Emphasizing the transforming moral power of grace (Titus 2:11–14).* These verses are among the most powerful in the New Testament.

> *For the grace of God that brings salvation has appeared to all men. It teaches us to say "No" to ungodliness and worldly passions, and to live self-controlled, upright and godly lives in this present age, while we wait for the blessed hope—the glorious appearing of our great God and Savior, Jesus Christ, who gave himself for us to redeem us from all wickedness and to purify for himself a people that are his very own, eager to do what is good.* (Titus 2:11–14)

William Barclay: There are few passages in the New Testament which so vividly set out the moral power of the **Incarnation** as this does. Its whole stress is on the miracle of moral change which Jesus Christ can work. Christ not only liberated us from the penalty of past sin; he can enable us to live the perfect life within this world of space and time; and he can so cleanse us that we become fit in the life to come to be the special possession of God.[8]

4 *Stressing rebirth and renewal by the Holy Spirit (Titus 3:3–8).* Paul reminds Titus that God has poured out his spirit on those who have been **justified** by faith in Christ. Paul urges Titus to stress this truth because the Spirit's presence is the basis for all Christian living, and those who recognize his presence are to be *careful to devote themselves to doing what is good.* Simply put, faith in Jesus changes human beings—and that change is to be expressed in our daily lives.

PHILEMON

. . . pleading for a runaway slave

WHO	The Apostle Paul
WHAT	wrote this letter to Philemon
WHERE	in Rome
WHEN	during his first imprisonment,
WHY	to plead the case of Onesimus, a runaway slave who had been converted and wanted to return to his Christian master.

PHILEMON: Philemon was a wealthy Christian who had been converted under Paul's ministry. Like other wealthy men in the Roman Empire, Philemon owned slaves.

ONESIMUS: Onesimus had been a slave of Philemon. Apparently, he stole from his master and ran away to Rome, where he met Paul and became a Christian. Tradition reports that Onesimus became the bishop of Ephesus in the second century.

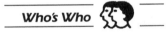
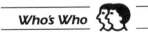

Forgive And Press On

Onesimus stole money from his master Philemon, one of Paul's converts, and ran away to Rome where he met Paul and became a Christian. Paul sent him back to his master with a letter.

In this letter Paul reminds Philemon of their close friendship, and urges him to welcome Onesimus back, not just as a slave but as a Christian brother. Paul offers to pay Philemon back for any loss due to Onesimus' past actions and delicately reminds Philemon that he owes his salvation to Paul's ministry.

THE BIG PICTURE 🔍

> **Philemon** This one-chapter letter is the briefest of the New Testament epistles. After a typical greeting and prayer, Paul pleads for his new *son* in the faith, Onesimus. Paul's letter of request has these features:

Greetings .... Pilemon 1–3

Prayer 4–7

1. Paul presents a request, not a command, ...8
   for a new Christian   9–10
   who formerly was worthless.   11

2. Paul is returning Onesimus   12–14
   as a slave but also as a brother in Christ.   15–16

3. Paul appeals to Philemon to welcome Onesimus
   as he would welcome Paul himself. 17–21

4. Paul hopes to visit soon. 22

Final greetings 23–25

Dig Deeper

Brothers In Christ

In the first century Roman Empires over 20 percent of the population were slaves, viewed as property by their owners. The institution was so deeply woven into the social fabric that it would have been impossible to eliminate without creating an economic disaster.

The New Testament launches no crusade against the evil of slavery. But Christianity introduced a new dynamic reflected in this letter and other epistles. Slaves and masters alike became believers, and each was urged to show love and concern for the other. In a household where both were believers, they were to view each other as brothers in Christ. Where the Gospel be-

☞ **Check It Out:**

Philemon; I Timothy
  6:1–2; Ephesians
  6:5–9; Colossians
  3:22–4:1

came entrenched, it was impossible to maintain the view that slaves were merely property, as Paul's letter to Philemon illustrates.

Study Question

1. Which three of Paul's four personal letters are called pastoral letters?
2. What are two essential characteristics of persons qualified to become church overseers or elders?
3. What ministry did the early Church have for widows?
4. How would you correct the quote, "Money is the root of all evil?"
5. What guarantees the usefulness of Scripture in equipping Christians for good works?
6. What is involved in Christian teaching besides communicating biblical truths?
7. The one who has been justified by faith will express that reality by devoting oneself to what?
8. What was the change in the relationship between Philemon and Onesimus that Paul relied on to move Philemon to welcome back his runaway slave?

CHAPTER WRAP-UP

- Paul wrote four personal letters to individuals rather than to churches.
- Paul's first letter to Timothy urged the younger man to be an example of the truths he taught.
- One of the most important tasks in strengthening a church was to see to it that the congregation had godly leaders.
- Paul's second letter to Timothy is probably the last of his epistles, written just before his execution.
- Paul warns Timothy against false teachers, and stresses the importance of teaching and living God's Word.
- Paul's letter to Titus emphasizes the importance of performing good works.
- Paul reminds Titus that God's grace brings personal rebirth and renewal. Good works are the product of saving grace.
- Paul's letter to Philemon illustrates how Christian faith bridged the gap between slave and slave owner in the Roman world.

22 THE SUPERIORITY OF CHRIST

Hebrews

CHAPTER HIGHLIGHTS

- New Covenant
- God's Son
- High Priest
- Perfect Sacrifice
- Faith and Discipline

Let's Get Started

Most of the New Testament epistles were written to predominantly gentile churches. But the letter called *Hebrews* was written specifically to converted Jews. They often felt a deep affection for the way of life they had known from birth, and sometimes wondered if they had been right in committing themselves to Christ. The writer of this powerful letter understands their feelings, and sets out to show them how faith in Christ promises a full experience of spiritual realities that Old Testament faith merely foreshadowed.

HEBREWS

. . . *the superiority of Christ*

WHO	An unnamed author
WHAT	compares Old and New Testament revelations
WHERE	to Hebrew Christians everywhere
WHEN	before 70 A.D.,
WHY	to demonstrate the superiority of Christ and Christianity as a fulfillment of Old Testament promises.

Just the FACTS

Jesus

fulfillment of all the Old Testament promised

New Covenant: the promise offered by Jesus, the perfect High Priest

Old Covenant: Mosaic Law

KEY Symbols:

**Old Covenant
(Old Testament)**

Moses

- divine revelation
- available to the Jews

**New Covenant
(New Testament)**

Jesus

- superior revelation
- available to all

**Dig
Deeper**

A New Covenant For All

In the beginning Christianity was a Jewish movement, centered in Jerusalem. The first Christians were Jews who, apart from their belief that Jesus was the Messiah, lived and worshiped like other Jews. But within a few decades the church became predominantly Gentile, and Jews who believed in Christ were cut off from the synagogue and the Temple. This seemed a tragedy to many Jewish Christians, who had a deep affection for the ways and worship of Judaism, and who were now isolated from friends and relatives who continued in the old ways. These and other pressures led some Jewish Christians to waver, wondering whether they should return to their roots.

The unknown writer of the book of Hebrews determined to resolve their doubts. He saw clearly that Jesus was the fulfillment of all that the Old Testament promised, and that the **New Covenant** Christ instituted on the cross is vastly superior to the **Old Covenant** Moses introduced at Mount Sinai. Enthusiastically the writer of Hebrews set out to show the superiority of Jesus, and the wonderful benefits of a personal relationship with the living Savior.

THE BIG PICTURE

> **Hebrews** Hebrews compares Old and New Testament revelations point by point. The Old Testament is divine revelation, which offered great benefits to Israel as God's special people. But the New Testament is a superior revelation, and its benefits are not only superior; they are available to all who believe in Jesus. The following outline reflects the major themes developed in Hebrews.

1. Jesus, the Living Word .... Hebrews 1:1–4:13
   A. As ultimate revelation   1:1–14
   B. (Warning against drifting)   2:1–4
   C. As source of salvation   2:5–18
   D. As superior to Moses   3:1–6
   E. The urgency of response   3:7–4:13
2. Jesus, our High Priest 4:14–8:13
   A. Jesus' priesthood   4:14–5:10
   B. Go on to maturity   5:11–6:20)
   C. Superiority of Jesus' priesthood   7:1–28
   D. Implications of Jesus' priesthood   8:1–13
3. Jesus, the perfect sacrifice 9:1–10:39

    A. His sacrifice cleanses 9:1–28
    B. His sacrifice removes sin   10:1–18
    C. (Warning against turning from God)   10:19–39

4. Jesus' continuing ministry 11:1–12:29
    A. Accessed by faith 11:1–40
    B. Experienced as discipline 12:1–13
    C. Missing God's grace 12:14–29)

5. Exhortations 13:1–21

Farewell 13:22–25

He's God's Son

THE BIG PICTURE 🔍

> **Living Word** In the past, God's revelation was transmitted in various ways, but now he has spoken through his Son. The Son, Jesus, is fully God and thus even greater than angels.

☞ **Check It Out:**

Hebrews 1:1–4:13

It would be disastrous to drift away from truth that is revealed by him. For the intended destiny of human beings depends on our link with Jesus, who became human to die for our sins, to free us from Satan's power, and to lift us with him far above the angels!

As for Moses, it is right to respect him, for he was a faithful servant in God's house. But Christ is the owner, architect, and builder of the house. He is worthy of far greater honor. It follows then that if anyone hears God's voice today, he must not be like the Israelites who followed Moses out of Egypt but disobeyed when God told them to enter Canaan.

What's Special In Hebrews 1–4?

1 *The identification of Jesus as God (1:1–3).* The writer begins by affirming Jesus' identity as God's Son, and by making clear just what this title means. As the *radiance of God's glory,* Jesus expresses God's very presence. As the *exact representation* of God's being, Jesus is identical with God, so that when we see Jesus we see exactly what God is like.

It is important to be completely clear about the identity of Jesus when examining Christianity. The fact that Jesus Christ is God incarnate is the central and foundational truth on which the New Testament rests.

KEY Symbols:

Jesus
God's Son
God's very presence
identical with God

2 *Jesus' superiority to angels (Hebrews 1:5–14).* The writer quotes seven Old Testament passages which establish the superiority of Jesus to angels. Jewish tradition held that angels served as mediators when God gave the Law to Moses. The active involvement of angels made the Law even more binding. But the new revelation was given personally by God's Son, who is superior to angels.

What Others are Saying:

KEY Symbols:

Jesus
  superior to angels
  source of man's
    salvation
  greater than Moses

atonement: *satisfying God's demand that sin be paid for*

Remember This . . .

F. F. Bruce: The authority of the Gospel which the readers of this epistle had embraced was the authority of Jesus, the Son of God, supremely exalted by his Father. As God had no greater messenger than his Son, he had no further message beyond the Gospel.[1]

3 *Warning against drifting (Hebrews 2:1–4).* The writer presents the image of a ship drifting away from its moorings to warn of the danger involved in drifting back into Judaism. His readers were familiar with the danger of disobeying God's Law. How much more dangerous to ignore a salvation announced by the Lord himself!

4 *Jesus as the source of man's salvation (Hebrews 2:5–18).* Jesus *shared our humanity* to save us in the only way possible—by making **atonement** for our sins. These verses compare the respective positions of Jesus and of human beings in relationship to angels before and after Jesus came.

> Jesus not only reveals God, but through his suffering
> he brings *many sons to glory* (Hebrews 2:10).

5 *Jesus is greater than Moses (Hebrews 3:1–6).* No one was more revered than Moses in Judaism. Demonstrating that Christ is greater than Moses was a powerful argument for the superiority of Christianity.

What Others are Saying:

☞ Check It Out:

Numbers 13:26–14:35

Leon Morris: Moses was no more than a member—even though a very distinguished member—of the household. He was essentially one with all the others. Christ has an innate superiority. He is the Son and as such is 'over' the household.[2]

6 *Warning against unbelief (Hebrews 3:7–4:13).* The writer returns to an incident recorded in Numbers. Through Moses, God told the Israelites to enter Canaan, but the people refused. As a result, the whole generation was doomed to wander in the wilderness for four decades until all its adult members had died. All because when God spoke to the people they hardened their hearts, refused to trust him, and so disobeyed.

Today, God has spoken by his own Son. What a terrible loss contemporary Jewish Christians would experience if they hardened their hearts, and refused to listen to and trust him.

7 *The promise of a "Sabbath rest" (Hebrews 4:1–13).* The writer draws an analogy between the Israelites' rest when in Moses' day they finally conquered Canaan and the rest that is available to them as Christians. In both cases the victory has been won. When a person fully trusts Jesus, he or she discovers that Christ has and in fact is the answer for all the needs of the heart.

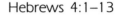 **Check It Out:**

Hebrews 4:1–13

F. F. Bruce: The moral must have been plain enough to the recipients of the epistle. For they too had experienced the redeeming power of God; they too had the promise of the homeland of the faithful to look forward to; but one thing could prevent them from realizing the promise, just as it had prevented the mass of the Israelites who left Egypt from entering Canaan—and that one thing was unbelief.[3]

What Others are Saying:

He's Our High Priest

THE BIG PICTURE

> **High Priest** The priests of the Old Testament era were **intermediaries** between God and man, offering the sacrifices which enabled worshipers to approach Israel's Holy God. But the High Priest alone had the privilege of making the annual sacrifice that atoned for all the people's sins. Jesus is presented as the ideal High Priest, who can sympathize with our weaknesses, and who was called by God to a priesthood far superior to that of Aaron and his descendants. After pausing to warn his readers again, the writer continues to explore the superiority of Jesus' priesthood. He explains why a change in the priesthood was essential. He further explains the benefits inherent in the fact that Jesus is not under an Old Law Covenant; he is under a New Covenant of transforming grace.

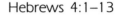 **Check It Out:**

Hebrews 4:14–8:13

intermediaries: go-betweens or mediators

Who's Who

KEY Symbols:

Jesus
HIGH PRIEST

☞ **Check It Out:**

Hebrews 5:1–10

perfected: not made him better, but equipped him

☞ **Check It Out:**

Hebrews 6:1–12

Remember This . . .

What's Special In Hebrews 4:14–8:43?

MELCHIZEDEK: He was both king of Jerusalem and a priest in the time of Abraham. Psalm 110:4 announced that God's Son would be a priest like Melchizedek. After Abraham's victory over some marauding kings (Genesis 14), Melchizedek blessed Abraham, and Abraham gave a tenth of what he had to this priest and king. To the writer of Hebrews, this indicated that the priesthood of Melchizedek was superior to that of Aaron, a descendant of Abraham.

1 *Seeing Jesus as a caring High Priest (Hebrews 4:14–5:10).* Jesus lived among us as a human being and so experienced the weaknesses that flesh and blood are heir to. Thus we can appeal to Jesus with complete confidence that he will hear us sympathetically. While Jesus was ordained to his priesthood by God, it was his obedient life as a human being that **perfected** him for his high priestly role.

2 *Warning—go on to maturity! (Hebrews 5:11–6:12).* The Hebrew Christians' failures to commit fully to Jesus had stunted their spiritual growth. Faith's foundation had been laid, and they were to build their lives on that foundation. A paraphrase of an often misunderstood passage (Hebrews 6:4–6) helps us grasp the writer's point. The writer challenges his readers, who want to go back to the old era, by asking them a hypothetical question:

> What would you want to do? View your failure as a falling away of God, so access is now lost? How then would you ever be restored—you who have been enlightened, tasted the heavenly gift, shared in the Holy Spirit, and known the flow of resurrection power? Do you want to crucify Jesus all over again, and through a new sacrifice be brought back to repentance? How impossible! What disgrace, this hint that Jesus' work for you was not enough!

The implicit warning is clear. Anyone who abandons hope in Christ abandons all hope! Jesus has been crucified for us, and this ultimate expression of God's love will never be repeated. Apart from Jesus their lives will be barren; with him their lives will be fruitful indeed.

3 *God's promises are an anchor for the soul (Hebrews 6:13–20).*
The writer reminds his readers that God has done everything possible *to make the unchanging nature of his purpose very clear.* Only now do we have God's promises and his oath, we have the resurrected Jesus in heaven itself, representing us as our High Priest. His presence there is an *anchor for the soul, firm and secure.* (Hebrews 6:19–20)

F. F. Bruce: Our hope, based on his promises, is our spiritual anchor. And our hope is fixed there because Jesus is there, seated, as we have already been told, at *the right hand of Majesty on high,* (Hebrews 1:3). Abraham rested his hope in the promise and oath of God; but we have more than that to rest our hope upon: we have the fulfillment of his promise in the exaltation of Christ. No wonder our hope is secure and stable.[4]

KEY POINT

Jesus is an anchor for the soul, firm and secure.

4 *The superiority of Jesus' priesthood (Hebrews 7:1–28).* Returning to the theme of Christ's priesthood, the writer contrasts Jesus as High Priest with the priests of the Old Testament (see GWDN, pages 261–262).

Jesus' Superiority Is Shown In . . .

- Melchizek's blessing of Abraham (Hebrews 7:1–10).
- Scripture's prediction of another priesthood (Hebrews 7:11–14).
- the fact that Christ's priesthood does not rest on lineage but on *the power of an indestructible life* (Hebrews 7:15–17).
- the inability of the old system to perfect, in contrast to the Christian's privilege of direct access to God (Hebrews 7:18–19).
- the fact that God himself ordained his priesthood to Jesus (Hebrews 7:20–22).
- the fact that the ever-living Jesus has a permanent priesthood which cannot be ended by death, and thus is able to save completely those who come to God through him (Hebrews 7:23–25).
- the fact that Christ offered only one sacrifice for sins, and then sat down, his saving work complete (Hebrews 7:26–28).

Something to Ponder

F. F. Bruce: Those who have Christ as their High Priest and mediator with God have in him a Savior whose saving power is available without end. The way to approach God through him is a way which is always open, because in the presence of God he represents people as a *priest forever*. And *he lives continuously to intercede for them (Hebrews 7:25).* [5]

KEY POINT

With the death and resurrection of Christ, the Old Covenant became obsolete.

5 *Implications of Jesus' priesthood (Hebrews 8:1–13).* Earlier the writer of Hebrews noted that *where there is a change of the priesthood there must also be a change of the Law* (Hebrews 7:12). His point was that each element of Old Testament religion—law, sacrifices, priesthood, worship, etc.—was linked to form a balanced whole.

The Old Testament itself contains the promise that God would one day replace the Old Mosaic Covenant with a New Covenant. With the death and resurrection of Christ, that Old Covenant became obsolete, and God began to work in a new way in the hearts of his own.

The writer of Hebrews quotes Jeremiah's words to make the difference clear:

> *I will put my laws in their minds*
> *and write them on their hearts.*
> *I will be their God,*
> *and they will be my people.*
> *No longer will a man teach his neighbor,*
> *or a man his brother, saying 'Know the Lord,'*
> *because they will all know me,*
> *from the least of them to the greatest.*
> *For I will forgive their wickedness*
> *and will remember their sins no more.*
> (Hebrews 8:10–12)

With Christ as our High Priest, the New Covenant is now operative. The Law that God wrote in stone is now being written on the living hearts of believers, each of whom has a personal relationship with the Living God, and each of whom has been forgiven all his or her sins.

Kay Arthur: Man can be right with God! Righteousness is more than goodness; it is right standing with God. Righteous means to be straight. It is to do what God says is right, to live according to his standards. But righteousness in man requires a new heart.

And man can have a new heart! *I will put my Law within them, and on their heart I will write it . . . for I will forgive their iniquity, and their sin I will remember no more* (Jeremiah 32:40).[6]

He's The Perfect Sacrifice

THE BIG PICTURE

> **Perfect Sacrifice** The Old Testament had its earthly sanctuary where priests offered sacrifices. While these sacrifices provided a superficial cleansing, they were not able to purify human beings within. The fact that they had to be repeated endlessly showed how ineffective they really were. But Jesus offered himself, not in an earthly temple but in heaven itself.
>
> By his one sacrifice Jesus has cleansed forever those who believe in him.

While the repeated sacrifices of the Old Covenant were annual reminders of the fact that human beings are sinners, the once-and-for-all sacrifice of Jesus is evidence that our sins truly have been forgiven. Because of Jesus there is no longer any sacrifice for sin.

Surely then, Hebrew Christians have all the more reason to persevere in their new faith.

What's Special In Hebrews 9:1–10:39?

1 *Significance of the earthly sanctuary (Hebrews 9:1–10).* The writer points out that every aspect of Old Testament religion had symbolic significance. For instance, the fact that the High Priest could only enter the inner room of the Tabernacle or Temple, the Holy of Holies (see GWRV, Illustration #5, page 153), once a year, and then only with a sacrifice, showed that people had no direct access to God under the old system. The sacrifices offered there were unable to *clear the conscience* of the worshiper.

Leon Morris: The reference to conscience is significant. The ordinances of the Old Covenant had been external. They had not been able to come to grips with the real problem, that of a troubled conscience.[7]

2 *The power of the blood of Christ (Hebrews 9:11–14).* Unlike Old Testament animal sacrifices, Christ's blood can *cleanse*

☞ **Check It Out:**

Hebrews 9:1–10:39

KEY Symbols:

Old Covenant
sacrifices are to be repeated over and over again

New Covenant
one permanent sacrifice
- Jesus

What Others are Saying:

☞ **Check It Out:**

Hebrews 9:11–28

our consciences from dead works, so that we may serve the living God (Hebrews 9:14). Christians are no longer held in the deadly grip of past sins; forgiveness sets the believer free to serve God.

prefigured: foreshadowed

3 The Old Testament sacrificial system **prefigured** Christ's death (Hebrews 9:15–28). The Old Covenant required that blood be shed if sins were to be forgiven and persons purified. But the blood of sacrificial animals was only for purifying material things, which themselves were merely copies of heavenly realities. All the Old Testament sacrifices pointed toward the one ultimate sacrifice Jesus would make on Calvary, shedding his blood to take away our sins.

KEY POINT

There is no longer any need for sacrifice—Christ's sacrifice is final.

4 The finality of Christ's sacrifice (Hebrews 10:1–18). The writer keeps the focus on the fact that Jesus, unlike the priests of the Old Testament, needed to offer only the one sacrifice, for *we have been made holy through the sacrifice of the body of Jesus Christ once for all* (Hebrews 10:10). The fact that Jesus offered only one sacrifice is proof that we have been forgiven: *where these have been forgiven, there is no longer any sacrifice for sin* (Hebrews 10:18).

5 A warning against turning away from God (Hebrews 10:19–39). The writer showed what a wonderful salvation God provided in Christ. The appropriate response to this is to accept him and *spur one another on toward love and good deeds* (Hebrews 10:24). To deliberately turn one's back on Jesus would be treating Christ's blood as an *unholy thing* and would be an insult to the Spirit of grace.

☞ **Check It Out:**

Hebrews 11:1–12:29

discipline: to train, not punish

THE BIG PICTURE 🔍

Faith By this point in the epistle, the readers understand why life under the New Covenant is superior to life under the Old; at every point the salvation Jesus provides is superior! The writer then goes on to show that New Covenant blessings are accessed by faith, and that God will continue to **discipline** his children that they might share his holiness. After warning his readers against refusing to respond to the Lord, the writer closes his letter with a series of exhortations.

What's Special In Hebrews 10–13?

1 *The importance of faith (Hebrews 11:1–40)*. The writer of Hebrews has clearly laid out the ways in which the Gospel message is better than the Old Testament revelation. It was **faith**—the conviction that God exists and that he rewards those who seek him—that enabled **Old Testament Saints** to accomplish the things for which we honor them.

F. F. Bruce: They lived and died in the prospect of a fulfillment which none of them experienced on earth; yet so real was that fulfillment to them that it gave them power to press upstream, against the current of the environment, and to live on earth as citizens of that commonwealth whose foundations are firmly laid in the unseen and eternal order.[8]

What can't we accomplish if we meet our challenges with their kind of faith?

2 *Jesus as the "author and perfecter of faith" (Hebrews 12:1–3)*. Jesus is not only the object of our faith, he is the supreme example of one who lived by faith, and thus is our inspiration.

F. F. Bruce: Christ has become his people's supreme inspirer of faith. When they become weary on the way, and grow faint at heart because there seems no end to the trials they have to endure, let them consider him. He suffered uncomplainingly the hostility and malevolence of sinful people; the recipients of this epistle had not been called upon to endure anything like the Master's suffering.[9]

3 *A new perspective on hardships (Hebrews 12:4–13)*. The writer encourages his readers—including us—to maintain a healthy perspective on our hardships. These are experiences provided by God himself as discipline. Rather than signaling our abandonment by God, they signal his great love for us. For every father who loves his children disciplines them to strengthen their character. And God disciplines us *that we may share in his holiness*. No lordship we experience is pleasant, but God will use it to produce a *harvest of righteousness and peace for those who have been trained by it*. (Hebrews 12:11)

☞ **Check It Out:**

Hebrews 11:1–31

faith: a trust in God that moves a person to respond to his Word

What Others are Saying:

Something to Ponder

What Others are Saying:

Old Testaments Saints: true believers in God who lived before the death of Christ

KEY POINT

Our hardships are experiences provided by God himself as training.

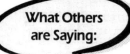
Leon Morris: It is important that suffering be accepted in the right spirit; otherwise it does not produce a right result.[10]

4 Warning—against missing God's grace (Hebrews 12:14–28). The writer contrasts Mount Sinai, representing the Old Covenant of Law, with Mount Zion, representing the Gospel of grace.

The sight at Mount Sinai was terrifying, for it spoke of judgment. The view at Mount Zion is one of blessing. If anyone refuses God's offer of grace to turn back to the Law, he will not escape the wrath of God?

5 Concluding exhortations (Hebrews 13:1–21). The book of Hebrews closes with a variety of brief encouragements to godly living, and with one of the most beautiful benedictions to be found in Scripture:

> May the God of peace, who through the blood of the eternal covenant brought back from the dead our Lord Jesus, that great Shepherd of the sheep, equip you with everything good for doing his will, and may he work in us what is pleasing to him through Jesus Christ, to whom be glory for ever and ever. Amen. (Hebrews 13:20)

KEY Symbols:

Old Covenant

MOUNT SINAI

- Law
- Judgment

New Covenant

MOUNT ZION

- Grace
- Blessing

Study Questions

1. To whom is Hebrews addressed?
2. Why did the author write this book?
3. What makes the fact that the New Testament revelation was delivered by Jesus so significant?
4. In what ways is Jesus a superior High Priest to the Old Testament's high priesthood?
5. What does the New Covenant do for believers that the Old Covenant could not do?
6. What is the significance of the fact that Jesus offered only one sacrifice for sins?
7. What does Hebrews 11 explore the significance of?
8. How are hardships evidence of the love of God?

- Jesus the Son of God brought humankind God's final and superior revelation.

- As God's Son, Jesus is superior to angels and to Moses, so the revelation he brought deserves our fullest attention.

- Jesus has been ordained by God as our High Priest: because he lives forever he can save *to the uttermost* all who come to God by him.

- Jesus offered his own blood to God as a sacrifice for sins.

- Jesus' one sacrifice cleanses believers and guarantees their forgiveness.

- Jesus' death initiated the promised New Covenant, not only promising forgiveness but also the inner transformation of believers.

- As with Old Testament Saints, it is faith that claims God's promises and enables believers to accomplish great things.

23 THE GENERAL EPISTLES

James
I, II Peter
I, II, III John
Jude

CHAPTER HIGHLIGHTS

- Practical Advice
- Suffering and Persecution
- False Teachers
- Importance of Love

Let's Get Started

In the past few chapters, we have learned about the epistles of Paul. However, others wrote letters to some of the first century churches, and these are usually called the "general epistles." They include writings of Peter and John, who were apostles, and Jesus' half-brothers James and Jude, who were leaders in the church. They also include the book of Hebrews

Each writer had a special reason for writing, and each letter makes a definite contribution to our understanding of Christian faith and life.

JAMES

. . . *faith at work*

WHO	James
WHAT	wrote this letter
WHERE	in Jerusalem, to Jewish Christians in the Middle East
WHEN	around 48 A.D.,
WHY	to encourage practical Christian living as an expression of true faith in Christ.

JAMES: James was a half-brother of Jesus, and became a leader of the church in Jerusalem. Tradition portrays him as a man of prayer, whose nickname was *the Just*.

☞ **Check It Out:**

Acts 15:13–21

Galatians 1:19

Just the FACTS

Who's Who

You Gotta Have Faith

☞ **Check It Out:**

James 2:14–26

James is probably the earliest of the New Testament epistles, written by a pastor who is deeply concerned that Christian faith find practical expression in daily life. In the early days of the Church, when James wrote, the debate of justification by faith alone, which Paul addresses, had not yet emerged. But James does distinguish between mere intellectual assent and a faith that involves both trust in and commitment to Jesus as Lord. James' concern is that the lives of those who claim Jesus as Savior honor him.

THE BIG PICTURE 🔍

> **James** This letter urges readers to pay attention to how faith is expressed in daily life. Writing within fifteen years or so of Christ's resurrection, James is rightly concerned that no one confuse **creeds** with vital Christianity. This brief letter makes even more mention of faith than Paul's letter to Galatians.

creed: *an accepted system of religious or other belief*

Greetings .... James 1:1

1. Practicing faith's lifestyle 1:2–2:13
   A. In our personal life   1:2–18
   B. In our interpersonal relationships 1:19–2:13

2. Principles underlying faith's lifestyle 2:14–26

3. Problems for faith's lifestyle 3:1–4:17
   A. Taming the tongue   3:1–12
   B. Subduing the self   3:13–4:10
   C. Judging   4:11, 12
   D. False pride   4:13–17

4. The prospects and promises of faith 5:1–19
   A. Future redress   5:1–6
   B. Patience rewarded   5:7–20

Dig Deeper

What's Special In The Book Of James?

The book of James is filled with special insights for Christians who want to honor the Lord by the way they live. Here are a few highlights:

KEY POINT

God never tempts anyone. The pull (temptation) we feel toward sin comes from within us—our old sin natures.

1 *Understanding temptation (James 1:13–15).* Let's not blame God for our reactions to situations in which we feel tempted. James says that God never tempts anyone. The pull we feel toward sin comes from within us, not from the situation. In fact, God only gives good gifts.

James' point is that <u>every situation</u> in which God places us is intended to bless us, not to trip us up. Harm will result only when we give into the inner pull toward sin. When we respond in a godly way, blessing will result, and this is what God intended all along.

2 *Faith that counts (James 2:14–26).* James does not argue that faith and deeds are necessary for salvation. Instead, he insists that a faith which does not produce right actions is a false, dead faith.

James does not teach that Abraham was pronounced righteous on the basis of his actions. James teaches that Scripture's announcement that Abraham was righteous is vindicated on the basis of Abraham's subsequent obedience. He did right because God had actually worked within him to make him righteous! James is speaking of two kinds of faith, only one of which is saving faith. He teaches that any claim of having saving faith will be vindicated by the actions that flow from that faith, and which in that sense complete it.

Leon Morris: The kind of faith [James] objects to is the kind of faith the devils have (James 2:19). They believe in God, but that does nothing more than produce a shudder. A faith that does not transform the believer so that his life is given over to doing good works is not faith as James understands it. That is dead faith.[1]

3 *Two problems with prayer (James 4:1–3).* James' practical approach to life is illustrated in two statements about prayer. He notes that some people go about getting what they want the wrong way. James writes *you do not have, because you do not ask God (James 4:2).* The Christian life is to be one of dependence on the Lord. But then James adds, *When you ask, you do not receive, because you ask with wrong motives, that you may spend what you get on your pleasures (James 4:3).* We're not to approach prayer as a magic lamp. The person who prays in Jesus' name should seek from God what Jesus sought—the Father's will, and the privilege of serving others.

C. S. Lewis: When the event you prayed for occurs your prayer has always contributed to it. When the opposite event occurs

GO TO:

Mark 10:27 (every situation)

KEY Symbols:

Two Kinds of Faith
dead faith
saving faith

What Others are Saying:

KEY Symbols:

Two Problems with Prayer
not asking
asking with the wrong motives

What Others are Saying:

your prayer has never been ignored; it has been considered and refused, for your ultimate good and the good of the whole universe.[2]

I PETER

. . . *following Jesus' example*

WHO	The Apostle Peter
WHAT	wrote this letter
WHERE	from Rome, to Christians everywhere
WHEN	about 64 A.D. or 65 A.D.,
WHY	urging Christians to follow Jesus' example and live holy lives

Just the FACTS

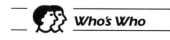

Who's Who

☞ **GO TO:**

Galatians 2:7 (believers)

PETER: The Apostle Peter had been Jesus' leading disciple from the beginning. After Jesus' resurrection, Peter preached the first gospel sermons and developed a special ministry to Jewish <u>believers</u>. He and Paul were both executed in Rome under the Emperor Nero.

And You Think You Have It Bad

Thirty years after the resurrection of Jesus, Christianity had been carried throughout the Roman Empire. By this time it was seen as distinct from Judaism, and as such was viewed by the Roman government as a foreign, illicit religion. The Emperor Claudius had been intent on restoring traditional Roman religion, and now a half-mad Nero ruled. Nero would torture and kill thousands of believers in the city of Rome, and the decades ahead would hold great suffering for those who identified themselves with Jesus and his people.

☞ **GO TO:**

I Peter 1:6 (danger)

Peter was well aware of the <u>dangers</u> that lie ahead and his letter, directed to all Christians scattered throughout the empire, was a call to holiness as well as an attempt to help his readers better understand the purpose of suffering in the believer's life.

THE BIG PICTURE 🔍

> **Peter** This letter of Peter provides Christians with the needed perspective on persecution, and reminds them that believers are called to both holiness and suffering. Peter wants his readers to see that suffering can be a gift of God, replete with benefits.

We can outline Peter's brief letter as follows:

Greetings ....I Peter 1:1, 2

1. A call to holiness............................... 1:3–2:12
   A. Our living hope   1:3–12
   B. Our holy calling   1:13–2:12

2. A call to submission 2:13–3:7

3. A call to suffering 3:8–4:10

4. Exhortations 5:1–11

Final greetings................................... 5:12, 13

Dig Deeper

What's Special In Peter's First Epistle?

1 *Joy in the midst of trials (I Peter 1:3–9)*. Peter writes of a joy that the believer experiences even while suffering *in all kinds of trials*. He likens our trials to the hot furnaces in which goldsmiths melt precious metal to rid it of impurities. *In praise, glory and honor when Jesus Christ is revealed* (I Peter 1:7). The fact that the salvation God provides is real enables us to feel joy despite the pain, and this is proof that God truly has saved us!

2 *Three characteristics of the Christian experience (I Peter 1:13–25)*. The image people have of Christians is that of sour and mean spoilsports. Peter reminds us that God has a very different idea of what Jesus' followers are to be like. This passage gives us three attractive characteristics:

- Christians are hope-filled and holy (I Peter 1:13–16).
- Christians have a deep respect for God (I Peter 1:17–21).
- Christians lead lives of love for one another (I Peter 1:22–25).

Something to Ponder

All this grows out of the fact that believers have been born again. They have been given a vital new life, which is God's own and which breaks through our hardness to find loving expression in our lives.

3 *The significance of Jesus' example (I Peter 3:8–18)*. What about situations where Christians suffer unfairly? What about those times when we do what is good, but bad things happen? Peter acknowledges that such things happen. He tells us that when they do, we should not be <u>terrified</u>, remember that Christ

☞ **GO TO:**

I Peter 3:14 (terrified)

is still Lord and remain positive. When people are amazed that we can remain positive despite being treated unfairly, we are to witness to the basis of our hope (I Peter 3:16). What enables us to remain positive? Peter points to Jesus, the prime example of one who suffered unfairly (I Peter 3:18):

> *For Christ died for sins once-and-for-all, the righteous for the unrighteous, to bring you to God.* (I Peter 3:18)

What appears to be history's greatest injustice was used by God to bring salvation to humankind!

Peter's point? If God could use such unfair treatment to bring about this wonderful good, he can use the unfair things that happen to us for good too!

Remember This . . .

What Others are Saying:

Leon Morris: Jesus' sufferings were thus an example to the readers who were also liable to suffer for no wrongdoing but simply for their Christian profession. It was a comfort to know their Savior had set them an example of how suffering should be borne.[3]

KEY POINT

Peter's point? If God could use such unfair treatment to bring about this wonderful good, he can use the unfair things that happen to us for good too!

4 *Suffering as a Christian (I Peter 4:12–19).* Peter reminds his readers that Christians should not be surprised at suffering. In a sense, suffering enables us to draw closer to Christ, who suffered before us. Peter's final word on the topic is good advice indeed.

> *So then, those who suffer according to God's will should commit themselves to their faithful Creator and continue to do good* (I Peter 4:19).

II PETER

. . . danger from false teachers

Just the FACTS

WHO	The Apostle Peter wrote this letter
WHAT	both warning and encouraging Christians
WHERE	while in Rome
WHEN	just before his death in 67 B.C. or 68 B.C.,
WHY	in view of emerging dangers from false teachers.

Evil From Within

Near the end of his life Peter became deeply concerned about the future of Christ's Church. In his first epistle, he wrote about dangers from outsiders who would persecute Christians. In his second epistle, Peter writes about dangers from the inside. Insiders who are pseudo-Christians were corrupting the faith by introducing false teaching. No foe from without could defeat Christ's Church, but the emerging dangers from within constituted a real threat. To overcome this menace, Christians would have to remain committed to the truth and to holy living.

This second epistle of Peter's is especially helpful in understanding **heresy**, and in showing how to deal with false teaching.

THE BIG PICTURE 🔍

> **II Peter** In this short letter Peter addresses two issues that most concerned him. He urges believers to concentrate on living productive lives, and he describes false teachers and their end. Here's how these themes are developed:

Greetings	II Peter 1:1–3
1. Confirming our calling	1:1–21

    B. By productive lives   1:1–11
    C. By God's sure Word   1:12–21

2. False teachers	2:1–22
3. The end of the world	3:1–18

What's Special In II Peter?

1 *God's part and our part in Christian experience (II Peter 1:3–9).* God has done all that's needed to equip us for life and godliness, by giving us promises that permit us to share in the divine nature itself. But we cannot be passive in our pursuit of godliness. Rather we are to focus on developing godly character.

Lawrence O. Richards: The qualities Peter exhorts are:

• faith	loyal commitment to Christian teaching
• goodness (virtue)	moral energy or excellence
• knowledge	understanding gained from revelation
• self-control	the ability to "hold yourself in"
• perseverance	continuing on in spite of opposition
• godliness	reverent conduct in view of God's presence
• brotherly kindness	affection for fellow believers
• love	commitment to act for the other's good.[4]

KEY Symbols:

I Peter
danger within

II Peter
danger without

heresy: *false teaching*

☞ **Check It Out:**

II Peter 1:3–9

Dig Deeper

What Others are Saying:

Dig Deeper

What Others are Saying:

KEY Symbols:

Preparing for the End
unbelievers scoff
- nothing will change

believers live holy and godly lives
- new heaven and new earth are coming

2 *Descriptions of false teachers and false teaching (II Peter 2:1–22).* Peter emphasizes the fact that God will deal with false teachers. In the meantime, this is one of three Bible passages that specifies the signs by which false teachers can be recognized.

Signs of a False Teacher	Jeremiah	II Peter	Jude
Doctrinal			
• introduce heresies, denying the Lord who bought them	23:13	2:11	
Personality			
• bold, arrogant	23:10	2:10	16
• despise authority		2:10	3
• follow desires of sin nature	23:14	2:10	4, 19
• love money		2:15	12
Ministry			
• appeal to "lustful desires"	23:14	2:17	16
• promise "freedom" to be depraved	23:16, 17		

3 *The coming end of the world motivates the godly (II Peter 3:1–14).* Peter describes two attitudes which people adopt in response to Christ's promise to come again.

The unbeliever scoffs, assuming that *everything goes on as it has since the beginning of creation.* They ignore Scripture's testimony to the Genesis Flood, which is evidence that God can and does step into history to judge sin.

The believer chooses to live a holy and godly life, in preparation for life in the new heaven and new earth that God will one day create.

William Law: If you attempt to talk with a dying man about sports or business, he is no longer interested. He now sees other things as more important. People who are dying recognize what we often forget, that we are standing on the brink of another world.[5]

I, II, III JOHN

. . . on leading lives of love and obedience

WHO	The Apostle John
WHAT	wrote these letters
WHERE	while living in Ephesus,
WHEN	near the end of the first century,
WHY	to encourage love for others and obedience to God as vital Christian qualities.

JOHN : The Apostle John was especially close to Jesus during Christ's life on earth. John outlived the other apostles of Jesus, and spent most of his life ministering in Asia Minor. These letters, and the book of Revelation, were written near the end of the first century when John was in his 90's.

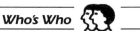
Who's Who

Light, Love, And Faith

With the crowning of the Emperor Domitian in 81 A.D., persecution of Christians became state policy. Even though John himself was later exiled, the apostle's letters ignore the external threat. John is most concerned with the inner life of God's people, and so focuses on the need to live in intimate fellowship with God and fellow believers.

Lawrence O. Richards: John's brief statements, made in simple words, feature contrast. He speaks of light against darkness, truth against error, God against Satan, life against death, love against hate. These few images, introduced and then returned to, blend in a powerful rhythm to impress on us the wonderful message of this short letter. We are invited by God to a unique experience of shared life with him. God calls us to fellowship, and we are eager to respond.[6]

What Others are Saying:

THE BIG PICTURE 🔍

> **John's Letters** Each of John's three letters is warmly relational, encouraging intimate fellowship with the Lord and with other Christians. In John's first letter, he introduces various themes and keeps returning to them, which makes his letter difficult to outline, but no less valuable. Perhaps the best way to approach this letter is to focus on three themes: John wants Christians to live in the light, to live lovingly, and to live by faith.

KEY Symbols:

John
live in the light
live lovingly
live by faith

Invitation ....I John 1:1–4
1. Living in the light 1:5–2:29
    A. Being honest with ourselves 1:5–2:2
    B. Being loving toward others 2:3–11
    C. Being separate from the world 2:12–17
    D. Being alert for antichrists 2:18–29
2. Living in love 3:1–4:19
    A. As God's children 3:1–10
    B. As concerned for others 3:11–20
    C. In fellowship with God 3:21–24

Dig Deeper

    D. In allegiance to God   4:1–6
    E. As moved by God's love   4:7–21
  3. Living by faith..5:1–21
    A. Assured of eternal life   5:1–12
    B. Assured that God hears us   5:13–15
    C. Freed from sin's control   5:16–21
II John   Holding fast to Truth
III John   Commendation for Loving

What's Special In I John?

1 *Walking in* **the light** *means being honest about sin (I John 1:8–10).* John calls on Christians to be honest with themselves and with God. In saying *God is light* with no darkness at all, he reminds us that God sees everything as it really is. The only way to get along with God is to be real, without deceiving ourselves or others.

This is particularly important when we sin, as all human beings do. John says *If we claim to be without sin, we deceive ourselves and the truth is not in us (I John 1:8).* What are we to do? We are to **confess** our sins—to acknowledge them to God and to ourselves. John reminds us that *he is faithful and just and will forgive us our sins and purify us from all unrighteousness! (I John 1:8–9)*

John Wesley: He says not, the blood of Christ will cleanse (at the hour of death or in the day of judgment) but it cleanses at the present time.[7]

F. F. Bruce: Those who deny their sin will feel no recourse to the cleansing power of Christ; those who, conscious of their sins, confess them have in Christ a Savior from whom forgiveness and cleansing from every sinful act may be freely received— not because he is indulgent and easy-going, but because his is *faithful and righteous.*[8]

2 *The warning against loving the* **world** *(I John 2:15–17).* What passions make human society corrupt? John identifies three:
- the cravings of sinful man (desires generated by the sin nature)
- the lust of his eyes (the desire for material things)
- the boasting of what he has (pride in possessions)

the light: in the books of John, in touch with reality

confess: to acknowledge, admit

What Others are Saying:

world: godless human society

Remember This . . .

The person who is *worldly* is in the grip of the same desires that motivate the lost—desires which are totally out of harmony with God's nature and of which he is not the source. Why is it foolish as well as wrong to adopt the values of human society? John says *The world and its desires pass away, but the man who does the will of God lives forever* (I John 2:17).

Francois Fenelon: You must violently resist the tides of the world. Violently give up all that holds you back from God. Violently turn your will over to God to do his will alone.[9]

3 *The warning against antichrists (I John 2:18–23).* John warns his readers against false teachers and others who would lead them astray. He calls such persons *antichrists.* How do we guard against **antichrists**? By being sensitive to the Holy Spirit within, who provides a built-in spiritual instinct that enables us to distinguish truth from falsehood by a simple objective test. Anyone who denies the deity of Jesus, who refuses to acknowledge *that Jesus Christ has come in the flesh,* is a false teacher.

4 *The call to love one another (I John 4:11–24).* John frequently reminds his readers of the importance of loving one another. God himself is love, so a failure to love fellow Christians is a sign that the believer is out of touch with God. Here is a sampling of what John says about loving our **brothers**.

I John 3:10—Whoever loves his brother lives in the light.
I John 3:11—Anyone who does not do what is right is not a child of God; neither is anyone who does not love his brother.
I John 3:14—We know we have passed from death to life, because we love our brothers.
I John 3:17—If anyone has material possessions and sees his brother in need but has no pity on him, how can the love of God be in him?
I John 3:23—And this is God's command: to believe in the name of his Son, Jesus Christ, and to love one another as he commanded us.
I John 4:7—Let us love one another, for love comes from God.
I John 4:8—Whoever does not love does not know God, for God is love.

What Others are Saying:

☞ **Check It Out:**

I John 3:18–27

I John 4:1–3

antichrists: all who oppose God and Jesus

☞ **Check It Out:**

John 13:34, 35

brother: any fellow believer

Something to Ponder

KEY POINT

A false teacher is anyone who denies that Jesus Christ has come in the flesh.

I John 4:11—Dear friends, since God so loved us, we also ought to love one another.

I John 4:12—If we love each other, God lives in us and his love is made complete in us.

I John 4:20—If anyone says, "I love God," yet hates his brother, he is a liar.

I John 4:21—And God has given us this command: whoever loves God must also love his brother.

What Others are Saying:

Leon Morris: We will never find out what love means if we start from the human end. Only because we have experienced the love we see in the cross do we love in the distinctively Christian way.[10]

JUDE

. . . contending for the faith

WHO	Jude, a half-brother of Jesus, wrote this brief epistle
WHAT	about false teachers who were infiltrating the Church,
WHERE	to Christians everywhere
WHEN	in the 80's A.D.,
WHY	to challenge believers to contend for the faith.

THE BIG PICTURE

Jude The writer had hoped to write about the glories of salvation, but found himself led instead to urge his readers to contend for the faith that had *once for all* been entrusted to God's saints. The bulk of Jude's letter is spent drawing analogies between false teachers threatening the Church and Old Testament enemies of God, emphasizing the fact that such persons are under the judgment of God.

Dig Deeper

Greetings .... Jude 1:1, 2

1. Descriptions of false teachers............................. 1:3–16

2. Encouragement and conclusion 1:17–25

Who's Who

JUDE: Early church fathers identify the author of this letter as the half-brother of Jesus and brother of James, named in Matthew 13:55 and Mark 6:3.

Sounds Just Like The Church Today

Like Paul, John and Peter, Jude recognized the danger false teachers posed to the Church. Both non-Christian, Jewish, and pagan teachers were active in the first century, busy reinterpreting Christian teachings to fit their philosophical presuppositions. Jude's letter, filled with allusions to the Old Testament, seems addressed primarily to Jewish Christians. Jude sums up the danger from false teachers by saying *they are godless men, who change the grace of our God into a license for immorality and deny Jesus Christ our only Sovereign and Lord* (Jude 1:4).

But Jude closes with a word of advice for true believers on how to defeat those who would divide them.

What's Special In Jude?

Jude's closing advice to his readers is on target for Christians today.

> *But you, dear friends, build yourselves up in your most holy faith and pray in the Holy Spirit. Keep yourselves in God's love as you wait for the mercy of our Lord Jesus Christ to bring you to eternal life* (Jude 1:20–21).

Something to Ponder

Study Questions

1. What are the seven general epistles discussed in this chapter?
2. What is the theme of the book of James?
3. What is the difference between a true faith in Christ and a dead or merely intellectual faith?
4. Why did Peter write about *all sorts of trials* that Christians were about to experience?
5. How does the example of Christ's suffering on the cross encourage Christians who suffer unjustly?
6. What are at least three characteristics of the false teachers against whom Peter warns in his second letter?
7. Why does John warn Christians against deceiving themselves after they sin?
8. What is one objective test that helps identify false teachers who infiltrate the Church?
9. Why does John believe loving our Christian brothers is so important?

- The general epistles in the New Testament include James, I & II Peter, I, II, III John, Jude, and also Hebrews.

- The epistle of James was the first of the New Testament books to be written.

- James gives practical advice on how faith in Jesus should work itself out in daily life.

- In his first letter Peter encourages believers about how to experience persecution, and helps them put suffering in Christian perspective.

- In Peter's second letter he warns against false teachers, and reminds Christians to live godly lives in view of the coming end of this world.

- The Apostle John wrote three letters which have found a place in our New Testament.

- In his first letter John emphasizes the importance of loving one another and obeying God.

- Jude, a half-brother of Jesus, adds an urgent warning against false teachers who reinterpret truths delivered by the apostles.

24 REVELATION

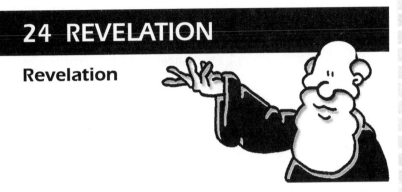

Revelation

Let's Get Started

The last book of the New Testament, **Revelation**, is a book of prophecy. While events in the first chapters of this mysterious book take place in the past, most of Revelation is about history's end and the eternity that lies beyond. The book of Revelation reminds us that God will one day act to judge sin, to purge evil from his universe, and to welcome those who have trusted Jesus as Savior to the new heavens and the new earth that he will create.

revelation: disclosure of what was previously unknown

KEY Symbols:

Revelation reminds Us God:

will one day judge sin

purge evil from the universe

welcome believers to a new heaven and a new earth

REVELATION

. . . *of things to come*

WHO   The Apostle John

WHAT   wrote this record of God-Given visions

WHERE   while exiled on the Island of Patmos

WHEN   about 90 A.D.,

WHY   to describe what God intends to accomplish at history's end.

Wow!

Much of the Old Testament is **predictive prophecy**, which describes events to take place at or near history's end. Jesus also spoke about the future, as did writers of the New Testament epistles. But these scattered references did little to fit future events together.

☞ **Check It Out:**

Isaiah 65:17–25

Matthew 24

II Peter 3

Then, near the end of the first century, the Apostle John was given a vision while he was on the Mediterranean Island of Patmos (see GWRV, page 18). He saw the resurrected Jesus in his glory, and in a vision observed history's culminating events. John's description of what he saw helps us to fit earlier prophecies together, and reassures us as well. God truly is in control, and history is moving toward his intended end. When that end comes, God will triumph, and those who have trusted in him will be welcomed to an eternity of blessing and joy.

THE BIG PICTURE

Revelation This book can be divided into three main parts. John is given a vision of the risen Christ, and is told to write letters to seven churches (see GWRV, pages 19–20) in Asia Minor. John is then caught up into heaven, and from this vantage point he observes terrible punishments that God hurls against the wicked on earth. The final section of Revelation pictures what will happen after Jesus physically returns to earth, and describes what eternity holds for both the **lost** and the **saved**.

We can outline the book of Revelation as follows:

The setting .... Revelation 1:1–3

1. Christ and the churches 1:4–3:21
2. Rapture to the Second Coming 4:1–19:21
   A. Events in heaven 4:1–5:14
   B. Seven seal judgments 6:1–7:17
   C. Seven trumpet judgments 8:1–11:19
   D. Satanic intervention 12:1–15:8
   E. Seven bowl judgments 16:1–21
   F. Destruction of man's religious and economic system 17:1–18:24
   G. The Second Coming of Jesus 19:1–2
2. Millennium and beyond 20:1–22:21
   A. Millennium and rebellion 20:1–10
   B. Final judgment 20:11–15
   C. Heaven ahead 21:1–2:6

Coming soon 22:7–21

Dig Deeper

Seven Examples

THE BIG PICTURE

> **Seven Churches** While on Patmos John was stunned by the sudden appearance of the risen Jesus. Christ dictated letters to seven churches in Asia Minor. Many believe the seven churches (see GWRV, pages 19–20) are representative either of the spiritual condition of churches from every era, or of the spiritual condition of Christians at different periods in history.

What's Special In Revelation 1–3

1 *The appearance of the risen Jesus (Revelation 1:12–16).* The vision uses <u>symbolic images</u> drawn from the Old Testament to emphasize the deity of Jesus. John had been close to Jesus while he was on earth. Yet when John saw Jesus in his glory, the apostle *fell at his feet as though dead* (Revelation 1:17). The Jesus of history is the eternal God.

2 *Past, present, and future (Revelation 1:19).*

> *Write, therefore, what you have seen, what is now and what will take place later.* (Revelation 1:19)

This verse gives us the key for understanding the book of Revelation. *What you have seen* (past tense) is the vision of Jesus in Chapter 1. *What is now* (present tense) refers to the seven churches to whom Jesus will dictate letters (Revelation 2, 3). And *what will take place later* (future tense) reveals what will happen after the **Church Age** (see GWRV, page 13) is over (Revelation 4–22).

3 *The letters to the seven churches (Revelation 2:1–3:22).* The seven churches to which the letters are addressed existed in Asia Minor at the time John wrote down what Christ dictated. But the description of the churches, with Christ's warnings and promises, surely apply to congregations today.

Alan F. Johnson: Even though the words of Christ refer initially to the first-century churches located in particular places, by the Spirit's continual relevance they transcend that time limitation and speak to all the churches in every generation.[1]

☞ GO TO:

Daniel 7:9 (images)

☞ Check It Out:

I Thessalonians 4:13–17

KEY Symbols:

Seven Churches

Ephesus

Smyrna

Pergamum

Thyatira

Sardis

Philadelphia

Laodicea

Church Age: *from the first century until Jesus takes Christians to heaven (the Rapture)*

What Others are Saying:

Trouble On The Way

> **Tribulation** John is taken to heaven, symbolizing the Rapture of the Church, where he witnesses preparations for terrible judgments about to strike the people left on earth. John struggles to describe what he sees as powerful angels pour out judgment after judgment on a rebellious earth.

☞ **Check It Out:**

Revelation 4–19

During this time of judgment, called the *Great Tribulation* or *the Day of the Lord* in the Old Testament, Satan marshals his forces to do battle with God. Satan energizes two individuals, the Beast (the Antichrist) and the **False Prophet** (see GWRV, pages 194–199), who unite mankind against God's Old Testament people, Israel. Continuous acts of divine judgment destroy the unified religious and political system that the Antichrist establishes, and the struggle is ended by Christ himself, who returns from heaven with an army of angels.

False Prophet: the second beast of Revelation, it seeks devotees for the Antichrist

apocalyptic: refers to writings from God that use symbolic language to tell of a divine intervention soon to come

What's Special In Revelation 4–19?

☞ **Check It Out:**

Revelation 6:12–14

1 *It's often difficult to know just what John is describing.* Some dismiss the language of Revelation as **apocalytic**, implying that the visions of John have no relation to reality. But in fact John describes actual events which will surely take place here on earth, just as portrayed. The difficulty with the language of Revelation is that John was forced to use the vocabulary available to him in the first century.

Imagine that a pilgrim who came to America on the Mayflower in the 1600's was suddenly given a vision of twenty-first century America. The pilgrim witnesses a landing on the moon shown on TV, watches as planes take off and land at a major airport, and observes traffic hurtling along Los Angeles highways. Imagine how that individual, with only a seventeenth century vocabulary, might try to describe what he saw to friends on the Mayflower, and you will have some insight into why it is so difficult to understand John's description of real events in Revelation.

KEY Symbols:

Tribulation Period

GREAT TRIBULATION

DAY OF THE LORD

time of judgment

KEY Symbols:

Satan

Antichrist (first beast)
False Prophet (second beast)

2 *The terrible judgments of history's end do not bring repentance* (Revelation 6:15–17). The nature of the judgments makes it unmistakably clear that God himself is their source. Even knowing the great day of God's wrath has arrived, the people of earth

refuse to repent. They continue in their sins, while trying to call on the mountains to hide them from *the face of him who sits on the throne and from the wrath of the Lamb* (Revelation 6:16)!

Don't wait to trust Christ until it's too late. Judgment is coming soon.

J. H. Melton: The Lord Jesus Christ will either be your Savior or your judge. Your sins will either be judged *in* Jesus Christ or they will be judged *by* Jesus Christ. Now he offers his mercy to save you. If you reject his mercy he will judge you in absolute justice and wrath.[2]

3 The 144,000 people **sealed** from the tribes of Israel (*Revelation 7:1–8*). The **cult** of Jehovah's Witnesses was launched with the conviction that *the 144,000* (see GWRV, page 108) represented all who would be saved, and that this group would be made up of their members only. But the text clearly states that these 144,000 people are Jews, who come from the twelve tribes of Israel. Who are they really, and what is their role during this period of terrible tribulation on earth? The simple answer is that they are Jews who will convert to Christ during this time, and will witness to him throughout the world.

Daymond R. Duck: Once God has sealed his 144,000, the whole world will hear his message. Multitudes will believe and be saved. The Antichrist and his False Prophet will be furious and try to stop the revival by forcing new believers to turn away from the faith. They will deny people food and medicine. Executions will be frequent and numerous.[3]

4 *Praise for God and Christ in heaven.* While terrible judgments cause terror for the peoples of earth, John portrays a very different reaction in heaven. There, angels and the saved join in praise of God. Both the judgments and the praise are appropriate, for at last God is acting to establish what is right. In the words of the elders and angels in heaven. . .

☞ **Check It Out:**

Revelation 9:20–21

Something to Ponder

What Others are Saying:

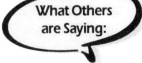

sealed: *a mark, sign, or symbol serving as visible evidence of something*

cult: *a religion or sect considered to be false, unorthodox, or extremist*

☞ **Check It Out:**

Revelation 14:1–5

What Others are Saying:

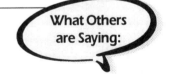

KEY Symbols:

144,000
Jews
  • from the twelve tribes of Israel

The time has come for judging the dead,
  and for rewarding your servants the prophets
and your saints and those who reverence your name,
  both small and great—
and for destroying those who destroy the earth.
(Revelation 11:18)

What Others are Saying:

Daymond R. Duck: The announcement that God and Jesus will be taking over will cause a tremendous reaction in heaven. They will thank him because he is alive and will be exercising his great power by starting his earthly reign.[4]

☞ **Check It Out:**

Revelation 18:9–24

5 *The end of the Antichrist's world-wide religious, economic and political empire (17:1–18:24).* These two chapters are among the most difficult to interpret in Revelation. However, it is clear that the dominant figure—*Mystery Babylon* (see GWRV, pages 245–278)—represents the unification of the Western world under the Antichrist. But the apparent success of this agent of Satan is to be short-lived. All that the Antichrist builds—a one-world religion and a totally materialistic society—soon comes tumbling down.

What Others are Saying:

Ed Hindson: The real tragedy in all this talk of global unity is the absence of any emphasis on the spiritual roots of democracy and freedom. The Gospel has been blunted in Western Europe for so long that there is little God-conscientiousness left in the European people. Without Christ, the Prince of Peace, there can be no hope for manmade orders of peace and prosperity. There will be no **Millennium** without the Messiah![5]

Millennium: *thousand-year reign of Christ on earth*

6 *The age ends with the return of Christ in triumph (Revelation 19:1–21).* The final scene on earth is that of the Antichrist and his forces gathered to do battle with Christ, who returns to earth at the head of the armies of heaven. The Antichrist and False Prophet are immediately thrown alive into the **Lake of Fire** (see GWRV, pages 253, 291), and their armies are destroyed.

Lake of Fire: *the final abode of Satan and his followers*

What Others are Saying:

Alan F. Johnson: John is showing us the ultimate and swift downfall of these evil powers by the King of kings and Lord of lords. They have met their master in this final and utterly real confrontation.[6]

Peace At Last

THE BIG PICTURE

> **The Millennium** At last Jesus rules on earth, fulfilling the predictions of the Old Testament prophets. The reign will last for a thousand years (a millennium), during which Satan will be bound. At the end of these thousand years Satan is released and again deceives human beings into rebelling against God. This time God responds by putting an end to the universe. Lost human beings are called before God's throne for final judgment, and all those who have not trusted Christ as Savior are consigned to the Lake of Fire. God then creates a new and perfect universe, to be populated by the saved for ever and ever.

☞ **Check It Out:**

Revelation 20–22

What's Special In Revelation 20–22?

1 *The Millennium (Revelation 20:1–6).* This is the only passage in the Bible which speaks specifically of a thousand-year period. Some have dismissed the idea of a millennial reign of Christ for this reason. However, the Old Testament prophets pictured just such a rule of the Messiah, and <u>Christ's reign on this earth</u> is mentioned dozens of times.

☞ **GO TO:**

Revelation 20:6 (reign)

Hal Lindsey: The heart of the Old Testament prophetic message is the coming of the Messiah to set up an earthly kingdom over which he would rule from the throne of David. The only important detail which Revelation adds concerning this promised Messianic kingdom is its duration—one thousand years.[7]

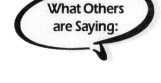

What Others are Saying:

2 *Satan's doom (Revelation 20:7–10).* Satan began his existence as a bright and powerful angel, who then rebelled against God and tricked Adam and Eve into joining his side. But from the very beginning Satan's doom has been fixed.

KEY Symbols:

God's Plan
Jesus on earth
Church Age
Rapture
Tribulation Period
Millennium
new heaven and new earth

> *And the devil, who deceived them, was thrown into the lake of burning sulfur, where the Beast [Antichrist] and the False Prophet had been thrown. They will be tormented day and night forever and ever. (Revelation 20:10)*

What Others
are Saying:

annihilated: utterly
destroyed

Something
to Ponder

3 *God's final judgment of the lost (Revelation 20:11–14).* John speaks of two *books* to be referred to at the final judgment. One book, the Book of Life, is a record of the deeds of every human being. The other book is called the *Lamb's* (or Christ's) *Book of Life* (see GWRV, pages 48, 302–303), where the names of those who have trusted Christ and whose sins have been paid for are written. Anyone judged on the basis of what he or she has done is condemned to the Lake of Fire. At that time all will know that hell is not a fiction, but is utterly and eternally real.

David Hocking: Those who are cast into hell are not **annihilated** as some religious groups teach. They experience torment forever and ever; it is an everlasting fire into which they are cast. Satan deserves it, and the justice of God demands it.[8]

4 *God's new heaven and new earth (Revelation 21:1–22:6).* We cannot know how wonderful eternity will be for those who have trusted God until we are welcomed into the new heaven and earth God will create. But these last chapters of the Bible tell us that it will be wonderful indeed.

What will Heaven be Like?

- God himself will be with us.
- God will wipe away every tear.
- There will be no more death, mourning, crying, or pain.
- The glory of the Lord will provide its light.
- Nothing impure will ever enter it.
- No longer will there be any curse.
- The throne of God will be in the city, and we will serve him.
- We will reign forever and ever.

5 *Jesus is coming soon (Revelation 22:12–21).* Revelation closes with a wonderful promise. Jesus says he is coming. He is coming *soon.* How eagerly all who are Christians can look forward to that wonderful day!

Study Questions

1. What is the subject of Revelation?
2. What is special about Jesus when John sees him?
3. How does Revelation 1:19 help us understand the book of Revelation?
4. What is the significance of the seven churches to which Jesus sends letters?
5. Will the terrible judgments predicted for history's end cause sinners to repent?
6. Who is the Antichrist and what does he do?
7. What is the Millennium?
8. What is the fate of those who fail to trust Christ in the final judgment?
9. What is the destiny of those who have trusted Christ and whose names have been written in the Lamb's Book of Life?

CHAPTER WRAP-UP

- The bulk of Revelation is "predictive prophecy."
- The prophecy in Revelation reveals what will happen at history's end.
- God will bring devastating supernatural judgments on those who continue to rebel against him.
- Satan will give supernatural powers to an Antichrist who will build a one-world political and economic empire.
- God will destroy the Antichrist and his forces when Jesus returns personally to set up a thousand-year reign on earth.
- Satan will lead a final rebellion at the end of Christ's reign, and will then be consigned to the Lake of Fire.
- This present universe will be dissolved, and all the dead will be revived to face God's judgment.
- Those who have failed to trust in God during their lives will be judged by their actions, and consigned to the Lake of Fire forever.
- Those who have trusted in God will be welcomed into a new heaven and earth which God will create, and will be with him eternally in glory.

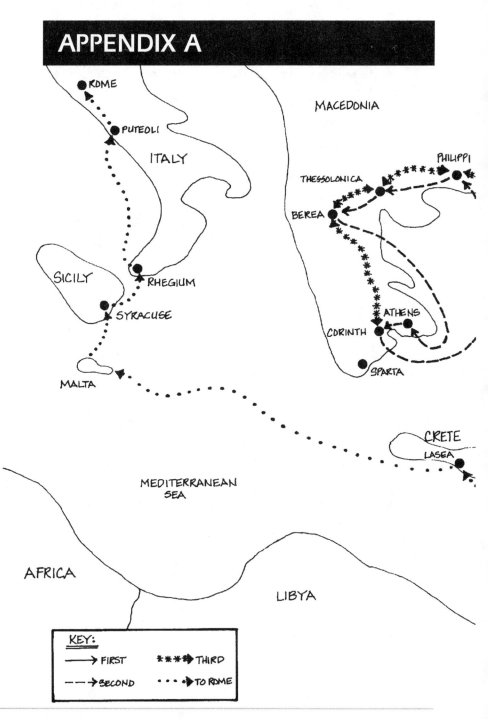

APPENDIX A

ROME

PUTEOLI

ITALY

MACEDONIA

PHILIPPI

THESSOLONICA

BEREA

RHEGIUM

SICILY

SYRACUSE

ATHENS

CORINTH

SPARTA

MALTA

CRETE

LASEA

MEDITERRANEAN
SEA

AFRICA

LIBYA

KEY:

→ FIRST

★★★★➤ THIRD

--➤ SECOND

•••➤ TO ROME

Paul's Missionary Journeys

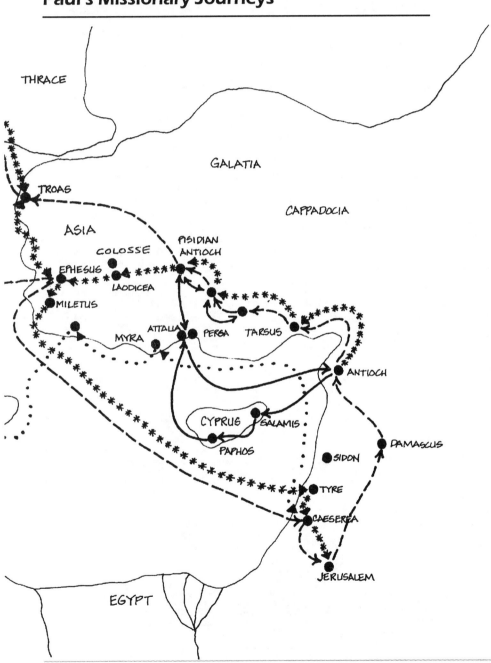

CHAPTER 1

1. If God did not create, then the universe "just happened;" life has no meaning or purpose, and death is the end.
2. Human beings are special because we were created in the image and likeness of God. (Genesis 1:26–27).
3. The evils in society and our own tendency to sin is a consequence of the Fall. (Genesis 4)
4. The Fall was the choice of Adam and Eve to disobey God. The Fall corrupted human nature and gave all human beings a sinful nature. (Ephesians 2:1–4)
5. The Flood tells us that God is a moral judge who will punish sin. (Genesis 6:5–7)

CHAPTER 2

1. Abraham was chosen by God to receive special promises, and Abraham responded to God with faith. (Genesis 15:6)
2. A covenant is a commitment, contract, oath, or treaty. The biblical covenants are commitments made by God. (Hebrews 6:13–20)
3. The Abrahamic Covenant is important because it spells out what God has committed himself to do through Abraham and his descendants. (Genesis 1–3)
4. The Abrahamic Covenant passed to Isaac, Jacob, and to the Jewish people who descended from them. (Genesis 21–50)
5. Faith is important because God will declare those who hold true faith to be righteous. (Romans 4: 18–25)

CHAPTER 3

1. Moses is important because God used him to deliver the Israelites from slavery in Egypt, to give Israel his law, and to write the first five books of the Old Testament. (Exodus 3–5)
2. A miracle is an event caused directly by God to accomplish a purpose of his own.
3. God struck Egypt with a series of devastating plagues which forced Pharaoh to release his Hebrew slaves. (Exodus 7:3)
4. A "promise covenant" states what God will most certainly do no matter what human beings do. A "contract covenant" states what God will do depending on what human beings choose to do. (compare Genesis 12:1–3 with Exodus 19:5)
5. The Ten Commandments reveal the moral character of God and define the behavior he expects from human beings. (Exodus 20 : 1–17)

CHAPTER 4

Answer to question on page 37:
1. Do not eat shrimp. — ritual law
2. Sacrifice after giving birth. — ritual law
3. Do not commit adultery. — moral law
4. Help your enemy if his cattle get loose. — moral law
5. Wash clothing after touching dead body. — ritual law

Answer to "Fear, Love, or Drive Out" table (on page 43):
Deuteronomy 6:1–3—*Fear*
Deuteronomy 6: 20–24 — *Love*
Deuteronomy 7:1–6 — *Drive Out*
Deuteronomy 7:7–10 — *Love*
Deuteronomy 10:12–22 — *Love*
Deuteronomy 11:16–17 — *Fear*

Answers to Study Questions
1. The theme of the book of Leviticus is holiness.
2. Important terms linked with the teaching of Leviticus on sacrifice include: guilt, forgiveness, blood, sacrifice, and atonement. These are im-portant because they lay the foundation for understanding the meaning of Jesus' death on the cross. (Leviticus 1–5, 16)
3. Ritual laws defined actions which made an Israelite ritually unclean. Moral laws defined acts which were sin. (compare Leviticus 11 with Leviticus 18)
4. Violation of a ritual law made an Israelite unclean. Normally ritual un-cleanness would be removed by washing with water after a specified period of time, or the offering of a sacrifice. (Leviticus 11:26–28; 12:1–8)
5. The Israelites refused to obey God when he commanded them to enter Canaan. (Numbers 14)
6. Love motivated the giving of the Law, as God revealed to Israel the way to experience his blessings. Love for God is the only motive which will produce true obedience to the Law God gave. (Deuteronomy 11)
7. A prophet is a person who delivers a message directly from God. True prophets could be recognized, for they had to be Israelites, who spoke in the name of the Lord, whose messages were in harmony with God's Word, and whose predictions came true. (Deuteronomy 18:14–22)

CHAPTER 5

Answer to Jephthah's Daughter puzzle (on page 54):

The Old Testament displays an absolute revulsion toward human sacrifice (Leviticus 18:21; 20:2–5; Deuteronomy 12:31; 18:10.). While some argue that Jephthah must have fulfilled his vow by killing and burning his daughter, this is not required by the text or Hebrew practices. Old Testament Law introduces a principle in Exodus 38:8 and illustrates it in I Samuel 1:28 and Luke 2:36,37. This principle is that a person or thing dedicated to God might fulfill the vow with a lifetime of service and the surrender of one's life.

Indicators that this is what happened in the case of Jephthah's daughter are (1) Jephthah had previously displayed knowledge of Old Testament history and law, as in his letter to the Ammonites (Judges 11:15–17); (2) every sacrifice to the Lord required that a priest officiate and no Hebrew priest would offer a human sacrifice; (3) the reaction of Jephthah's daughter, who went out with her friends to lament not over her immediate death but *because I will never marry* (Judges 11:37). All this leads us to the conclusion that Jephthah *did* fulfill his vow, by dedicating his daughter's life to the service of the Lord.

Answers to Study Questions
1. These books cover a period from about 1390 B.C. to 1150 B.C.
2. The major message of Joshua is that obedience brings victory, and dis-obedience brings defeat. (Joshua 6–8)
3. The major message of Judges is commitment to worshiping and obeying God is essential to maintain a just society. (Judges 3:6– 15)
4. The Judges of Israel were military, political, and religious leaders. They offered the Israelites someone to turn to for moral and spiritual leader-ship. (Judges 6:1–8)
5. The persons emphasized in the book of Judges are Deborah, Gideon, Jephthah, and Samson.
6. The major message of the book of Ruth is that godly people can live meaningful lives even in a corrupt society. (Ruth 3)

CHAPTER 6

1. The three key figures in the transition to monarchy are Samuel, Saul, and David.
2. When Samuel was born, Israel was a loose confederation of poverty-stricken tribes oppressed by foreign enemies. (I Samuel 2:12–4:27)
3. When David died, Israel was a wealthy, powerful nation whose territory had been expanded tenfold. (I Chronicles 18)
4. Both Saul and David had weaknesses, but David loved God and was

willing to take responsibility for and openly confess his sins. Saul was unwilling to repent, however, and God rejected his kingship. (compare I Samuel 15 with II Samuel 12)

5. David unified the Hebrew kingdom, organized it armies, defeated foreign enemies, established Jerusalem as the political and religious center of the nation, and organized Temple worship. (I Chronicles)

6. The Davidic Covenant established the fact that it would be a descendant of David who would fulfill the promises God had made to Abraham. (II Samuel 7)

7. A study of David's life teaches the importance of loving God, the vulnerability of the greatest saints to sin, and the willingness of God to forgive those who confess their sins to him. (Psalm 51)

CHAPTER 7

1. The two kings who ruled Israel during the golden age were David and Solomon. (I Chronicles – II Chronicles 10)

2. The golden age was marked by prosperity, military strength, and literary accomplishment. (I Kings 4:20–34)

3. Books of Bible poetry associated with the golden age are Proverbs, Psalms, Ecclesiastes, and the Song of Songs.

4. Hebrew poetry relied on symmetry of thought rather than on rhyme and rhythm. (Psalm 1)

5. The theme of these books is:
Job—faith's response to suffering. (Job 1,2)
Psalms—personal relationship with God, worship. (Psalm 9)
Proverbs—guidance in making wise and right choices. (Proverbs 1:1–6)
Ecclesiastes—the futility of seeking any meaning in life apart from a relationship with God. (Ecclesiastes 1:1–11)
Song of Songs—the delights of married love. (Song of Songs 4)

CHAPTER 8

1. Jeroboam established a counterfeit religious system. (I Kings 12:25–33)

2. All the kings of Israel were evil and maintained the counterfeit religious system instituted by Jeroboam I. (II Kings)

3. Elijah and Elisha are the two speaking prophets in the Bible's second age of miracles. (I Kings 18–II Kings 8)

4. Jonah, whose mission to Nineveh showed God's willingness to withhold punishment of those who would repent. Amos, whose preaching condemned Israel's false religion and social injustice. (Jonah 4; Amos 4)

5. The *Day of the Lord* is any period in which God acts directly to accomplish his purposes. (Amos 5:18–27)

6. The sins of Israel which called for judgment included institutionalized injustice and immorality. The newspaper headlines highlight similar sins in our own society. (Amos 2)

CHAPTER 9

1. II Kings and II Chronicles record the history of Judah after the division of Solomon's kingdom.

2. Godly kings stimulated religious revivals, which permitted God to act for his people. (II Chronicles 19:20)

3. Pagans turn to occult practices to seek supernatural guidance. God provided his people with prophets through whom the Lord himself gave guidance. (Deuteronomy 18:9–22)

4. The true prophet must be an Israelite who speaks in the name of the Lord, whose message is in harmony with Scripture, and whose predictions come true. (Deuteronomy 18:19–22)

5. Joel, plague of locusts (Joel 1); Obadiah, judgment on Edom (Obadiah 1); Micah, the Savior to be born in Bethlehem (Micah 5:2); Isaiah, God's sovereign rule (Isiah 44).

CHAPTER 10

1. Revival under Hezekiah saved Judah from destruction by Assyria. (II Chronicles 29–32)

2. The prophets of Judah pointed to idolatry and the worship of pagan deities. (Isaiah 1)

3. Nahum, Zephaniah, Habakkuk, and Jeremiah all preached in the surviving kingdom of Judah.

4. Ezekiel preached to the exiles in Babylon before the fall of Jerusalem. (Ezekiel 1:1)

CHAPTER 11

1. Lamentations expresses the despair of those Jews taken captive to Babylon.

2. The book of Daniel contains a specific prediction about the date of the entrance of the Messiah into Jerusalem. (Daniel 9:20–27)

3. The books of Ezra and Nehemiah tell of the return to Judah.

4. The book of Esther teaches that God is in control of every aspect of our lives.

5. Isaiah predicted that Cyrus would be the ruler who permitted the Jews to return to Jerusalem. (Isaiah 45:11–13)

6. Zechariah and Haggai encouraged the people to finish building God's Temple.

7. The last book of the Old Testament, Malachi, was written around 400 B.C.

CHAPTER 12

1. Jesus Christ is the central figure in the New Testament.

2. Psalm 2:7; 45:5,6; Isaiah 7:14; 9:6,7; Micah 5:2; and Malachi 3:1 all indicate that the Messiah will be God himself.

3. John 5:17,18; 8:58,59; Matthew 16:16,17; and Matthew 26:63,64 all report Jesus' claim to be God.

4. Philippians 2 says that *being in very nature God* Jesus was made *in human likeness.*

5. The resurrection proved that Jesus was truly God. (Romans 1:1–4)

CHAPTER 13

1. Matthew wrote the Gospel directed to the Jews. (Matthew 1:22)

2. Mark wrote the Gospel directed to the Romans.

3. The Gospel of John is not in chronological order.

4. The two genealogies of Jesus are different because one genealogy is Mary's and the other is from Jesus' stepfather, Joseph. (Matthew 1:1–17; Luke 4:21–38)

5. The appearances of angels marked Jesus' birth as unusual. (Matthew 1:15,24; Luke 1:11,26–38)

6. The message of John the Baptist was "Repent, because the Messiah is about to appear." (Matthew 3:2)

7. God spoke from heaven and the Holy Spirit descended as a dove. (Matthew 3:16–17)

8. To deliver us from our sins Jesus needed to be without sin. (Hebrews 4:14–16)

CHAPTER 14

1. The disciples were twelve men, specially chosen by Jesus, who followed Christ from the beginning of his ministry. (Mark 3:13–19)

2. The Pharisees and Sadducees were religious parties in Jesus' day.

3. Jesus performed miracles of healing, control of nature, control of demons, and power over death itself. (Mark 4,5)

4. The Beatitudes define what God values in human beings. (Matthew 5:1–10)

5. Jesus explained the Law and exposed its true meaning. (Matthew 5:17–47)

6. God's character as Father helps define the relationship he seeks with human beings. (Matthew 6)

7. The Pharisees started the rumor that Jesus' miracles were performed by Satan's rather than God's power. (Matthew 12:22–32)

CHAPTER 15

1. The Pharisees brought the false charges against Jesus. (John 8)

2. The fact that Jesus had not "studied" allowed the Pharisees to falsely charge that he was not qualified to teach. (Matthew 13:53–58)

3. God hears the prayers of the godly, not of wicked men. (John 9:13–21)

4. Jesus began to use parables after the crowds had refused to acknowledge him as the Messiah. (Matthew 13)

5. The subject of Jesus's parables was the kingdom of God. (Matthew 13)

6. The mark of a true disciple is the belief that Jesus is God the Son. (Matthew 16:13–20)

7. The key to greatness for a disciple of Jesus is willingness to serve others. (Matthew 20:20–28)

8. Jesus' "new commandment" was to love one another as he had loved them. (John 13:33–34)

CHAPTER 16

1. His triumphal entry into Jerusalem began Jesus' last week on earth. (Matthew 21)

2. He drove out the merchants. (Mark 11:12–19)

3. The Jews resented paying taxes to Rome and viewed it as a betrayal of their faith. Regardless of how Christ answered the Pharisees, he would be "guilty," of either commanding revolt against Caesar, or betraying the Jews. (see pages 213–214) (Luke 20:29–36)

4. Jesus called the Pharisees hypocrites. (Matthew 23)

5. By raising Jesus from the dead after his crucifixion, God answered Jesus' prayer. (Matthew 26:36–46)
6. In the Jewish courts, he was charged with blasphemy. Pilate charged him with being a king and rival of Caesar. (John 19)
7. The body was taken down from the cross and sealed in a tomb. (John 27:32–66)
8. By viewing it as a sacrifice for sins, made on our behalf. (Hebrews 10)
9. Jesus is alive to save and to guard us. (Hebrews 7:11–28)

CHAPTER 17

1. Acts is a historical narrative. (Acts 1:1–2)
2. The ascension of Christ begins Acts. (Acts 1)
3. The coming of the Holy Spirit provides the disciple with power to witness to Christ. (Acts 1:8; Acts 2:1–12)
4. Jesus is a historical person who was crucified, is risen again, and saves those who trust in him. (Acts 2:14–41)
5. Peter and Paul are the dominant figures in Acts.
6. Cornelius was the first gentile convert. (Acts 10)
7. Three of Paul's missionary journeys are reported in Acts. (Acts 13–19)
8. It determined that a person did not have to adopt Jewish practices to be a Christian. (Acts 15)
9. At the end of the book of Acts, Paul is imprisoned in Rome. (Acts 28)

CHAPTER 18

1. The epistles are letters of correspondence.
2. Tracing the argument of an epistle means to follow the writer's train of thought.
3. The theme of Paul's letter to the Romans is righteousness. (Romans 1:16–17)
4. Romans teaches us no human being is righteous, God requires us to be righteous, and God will declare those who trust in Jesus to be righteous. (Romans 3)
5. Our sinful nature. Ever since the Fall, humans have been inheritors of original sin. This means that humans are inherently flawed and in need of redemption. (Romans 5:12–20)
6. People have their own sense of right and wrong, and all have acted against their own standards. (Romans 2:12–16)
7. God's Law is meant to convince us that we are sinners and cannot help ourselves. (Romans 3:19–20)
8. The theme of Paul's letter to the Galatians is the inadequacy of the Law vs. the power of the Holy Spirit and grace.
9. The two contrary principles of a Christian's life are Law and grace. (Romans 7)
10. Relating to God through the Law involves dependence on our own on self-effort. Relating to God through the Spirit involves relying on God to do in us what we cannot do alone. (Romans 8)

CHAPTER 19

1. I,II Corinthians; I,II Thessalonians
2. Paul's solution was to expel the Christian who refuses to stop sinning. (I Corinthians 5)
3. They thought it indicated a special closeness to God. (I Corinthians 12:1–11)
4. God loves cheerful givers, we can meet the needs of others, and God is able to provide for all our needs. (II Corinthians 8–9)
5. God did not answer Paul's prayer for healing in order to keep him from becoming proud and to teach him to rely on God. (II Corinthians 12)
6. We should not grieve the death of loved ones because we will see them again when Jesus comes. (I Thessalonians 4:13–18)
7. God will punish those who persecute believers. (II Thessalonians 1:5–10)

CHAPTER 20

1. The theme of Ephesians is the Church of Jesus Christ as a living entity. (Ephesians 4)
2. Faith produces works. (Ephesians 2:8–10)
3. A husband's responsibility is to love his wife as Christ loved the Church. (Ephesians 5:25)
4. Joy and rejoice are the key words in the book of Philippians.
5. To gain freedom from anxiety, Christians can present requests to God with thanksgiving. (Philippians 4:8–9)
6. In the book of Colossians, Paul battles a heresy which argues that everything material is evil and only the immaterial can be spiritual, or good.
7. Colossians 1:15–17 shows that Jesus is God.

8. Fake Christians live by lists of do's and don'ts; real Christians show love, compassion, and forgiveness toward others. (Colossians 2:6–23)

CHAPTER 21

1. The three "pastoral" letters are I,II Timothy and Titus.
2. See list on page 440.
3. The widows' ministry was teaching younger women. (II Titus 2:3–5)
4. A love of money is a root of every evil. (I Timothy 6:3–10)
5. The fact that God inspired the Scriptures insures their usefulness. (II Timothy 3:16–17)
6. Also involved in Christian teaching is teaching to live in harmony with the truths. (II Timothy 2)
7. One justified by faith expresses that reality through good works. (James 2)
8. Philemon and Onesimus had become brothers in Christ. (Philemon 12–16)

CHAPTER 22

1. Hebrews is addressed to Jewish Christians.
2. Hebrews was intended to show that Christianity and Christ is better than Judaism.
3. The New Testament message was delivered by God the Son himself, rather than a messenger. (Hebrews 1:1–4)
4. Jesus brought a better revelation and offered a more effective (ultimate) sacrifice. (Hebrews 1)
5. It works an inner transformation by writing God's Law within our hearts. (Hebrews 8)
6. This shows that the sacrifice was efficacious and that we truly are forgiven. (Hebrews 10:1–18)
7. Hebrews 11 explores the significance of faith.
8. All loving fathers discipline (train) their children, and hardships are evidence of God's discipline in our lives. (Hebrews 12)

CHAPTER 23

1. The six epistles discussed in this chapter are James, I,II Peter, I,II,III John, and Jude.
2. The theme of the book of James is faith at work.
3. A true faith is transforming and will be expressed in the way we live. (James 2)
4. Christians need to understand how to relate to suffering. (I Peter)
5. God turned the injustice into good, and can do the same for us. (I Peter 3:13–18)
6. See the chart on page 489.
7. We need to confess our sins to remain in fellowship with God. (I John 1:9)
8. Are they willing to confess that Jesus is God come in the flesh. (I John 4:1–6)
9. Love is God's nature and he commands us to love our brothers. (I John 4:16–21)

Chapter 24

1. The subject of Revelation is the events to take place at history's end. (Revelation 2:19)
2. Jesus is seen in his essential nature, and he is so glorious that John is stunned. (Revelation 1:9–20)
3. Revelation 1:19 divides the content into "what was, what is now, and what is to come."
4. The churches are representative, and/or may symbolize periods in the Christian era.
5. Even in the face of the terrible judgments, the sinners will not repent. (Revelation 9)
6. The Antichrist will be a human being in league with Satan, who will claim the prerogatives of Christ and demand to be worshipped. (Revelation 13)
7. The Millennium will be the thousand year period during which Jesus will rule on earth, fulfilling Old Testament prophecy. (Revelation 20:1–6)
8. Those who fail to trust Christ are thrown into the Lake of Fire. (Revelation 20:11–15)
9. Those who have trusted Christ will spend eternity with God in the new heavens and earth God will create. (Revelation 21,22)

ENDNOTES

Introduction
1. Swindoll, Charles, *LIVING BEYOND THE DAILY GRIND*, p. 317.
2. Graham, Billy, *PEACE WITH GOD*, p. 15.
3. Graham, Billy, *BILLY GRAHAM ANSWERS YOUR QUESTIONS*, p. 171.

Chapter 1
1. Sproul, R. C., *REASON TO BELIEVE*, p. 113.
2. Graham, Billy, *BILLY GRAHAM ANSWERS YOUR QUESTIONS*, p. 165.
3. Steadman, Ray C., "*How to Worship*," sermon, http:\\www.pbo.org/dp/steadman/psalms/0389.html.
4. Youngblood, Ronald F., *THE BOOK OF GENESIS*, p. 23.
5. Ibid., p. 53.
6. Ibid., p. 99.

Chapter 2
1. Youngblood, Ronald F., *THE BOOK OF GENESIS*, p. 161.
2. Lucado, Max, *THE APPLAUSE OF HEAVEN*, p. 32.
3. Arthur, Kay, *LORD, WHERE ARE YOU*, p. 118.
4. Girard, Robert C., *MY WEAKNESS: HIS STRENGTH*, P. 77.
5. Mother Teresa, *A GIFT FROM GOD*, p. 37.

Chapter 3
1. Arthur, Kay, *LORD, I WANT TO KNOW YOU*, p. 63.
2. LaSor, William S., *OLD TESTAMENT SURVEY*, p. 136.
3. Lewis, C. S., *MIRACLES*, p. 60.
4. Geisler, Norman L., *MIRACLES AND MODERN THOUGHT*, p. 123.
5. Schuller, Robert, *THE BE (HAPPY) ATTITUDES*, p. 176.

Chapter 4
1. Toda, Joni Earickson, "*Spiritually Active*," in *THE WOMEN'S DEVOTIONAL BIBLE*, p. 123.
2. Goldberg, Lewis, quoted in *THE 365 DAY DEVOTIONAL COMMENTARY*, p. 163.

Chapter 5
1. Hendricks, Howard, *SAY IT WITH LOVE*, p. 79.
2. Luther, Martin, quoted in *THE 365 DAY DEVOTIONAL COMMENTARY*, p. 343.

Chapter 6
1. Richards, Larry, *THE NELSON ILLUSTRATED BIBLE HAND-BOOK*, p. 168.
2. Pascal, Blaise, quoted in *CHRISTIANITY TODAY*, March 2, 1998, p. 62.
3. St. Augustine, quoted in *THE 365 DAY DEVOTIONAL COMMENTARY*, p. 207.

Chapter 7
1. Swindoll, Charles, *GOD'S MASTERWORK, Volume 1*, p. 98.
2. Wiersbe, Warren, *WIERSBE'S EXPOSITORY OUTLINES*, p. 411.

3. Lucado, Max, *THE APPLAUSE OF HEAVEN*, p. 5.
4. Wiersbe, Warren, *WIERSBE'S EXPOSITORY OUTLINES*, p. 425.
5. Baylis, Albert H., *FROM CREATION TO THE CROSS*, p. 243.
6. Swindoll, Charles, *GOD'S MASTERWORK*, p. 52.
7. Ibid., p. 58.
8. Richards, Larry, *THE NELSON ILLUSTRATED BIBLE HAND-BOOK*, p. 270.
9. Graham, Billy, *BILLY GRAHAM ANSWERS YOUR QUESTIONS*, p. 17.
10. Wilkinson, Bruce, *GOD'S MASTERWORK*, p. 69.
11. Swindoll, Charles, *GOD'S MASTERWORK*, pp. 75–76.

Chapter 8
1. Swindoll, Charles, *GOD'S MASTERWORK, Volume 1*, p. 83.
2. Wiersbe, Warren, *WIERSBE'S EXPOSITORY OUTLINES*, p. 337.
3. Ibid., p. 601.
4. Graham, Billy, *PEACE WITH GOD*, p. 38.
5. Wiersbe, Warren, *WIERSBE'S EXPOSITORY OUTLINES*, p. 585.

Chapter 9
1. King Solomon, *PROVERBS* 14:34.
2. LaSor, William S., *OLD TESTAMENT SURVEY*, p. 459.
3. Alexander, John, quoted in *CHRISTIANITY TODAY*, February 9, 1998, p. 78.
4. Wiersbe, Warren, *WIERSBE'S EXPOSITORY OUTLINES*, p. 604.
5. Swindoll, Charles, *GOD'S MASTERWORK, Volume 1*, p. 96.

Chapter 10
1. Wiersbe, Warren, *WIERSBE'S EXPOSITORY OUTLINES*, p. 358.
2. Smith, Ralph L., *MICAH-MALACHI*, p. 83.
3. Geisler, Norman L., *MIRACLES AND MODERN THOUGHT*, p. 260.
4. Swindoll, Charles, *LIVING BEYOND THE DAILY GRIND*, p. 385.
5. L'Engle, Madeleine, quoted in *CHRISTIANITY TODAY*, February 9, p. 78.
6. Arthur, Kay, *LORD, HEAL MY HURTS*, p. 23.
7. Wiersbe, Warren, *WIERSBE'S EXPOSITORY OUTLINES*, p. 522 .

Chapter 11
1. Schultz, Samuel, *THE OLD TESTAMENT SPEAKS*, p. 343.
2. Richards, Lawrence O., *THE NELSON ILLUSTRATED BIBLE HANDBOOK*, p. 372.
3. Wiersbe, Warren, *WIERSBE'S EXPOSITORY OUTLINES*, p. 398.
4. LaSor, William S., *OLD TESTAMENT SURVEY*, p. 632.
5. Luther, Martin, quoted in *THE 365-DAY DEVOTIONAL COMMENTARY*, p. 1075.
6. Wiersbe, Warren, *WIERSBE'S EXPOSITORY OUTLINES*, p. 627.

Chapter 12
1. Smith, James, *THE PROMISED MESSIAH*, p. 180.
2. MacArthur, James, Jr., *GOD WITH US*, p. 46.
3. Young, Edward J., *THE BOOK OF ISAIAH*, p. 338.

4. Kiel, C. F., *COMMENTARY ON THE OLD TESTAMENT*, Volume 10, p.329.
5. Richards, Lawrence O., *THE BIBLE BACKGROUND COMMENTARY*, NT, p. 165.
6. Keener, Craig S., *THE IVP BIBLE BACKGROUND COMMENTARY*, p. 287.
7. Lewis, C. S., *CHRISTIAN REFLECTIONS*, p. 137.
8. Bruce, F. F., *THE EPISTLE TO THE HEBREWS*, p. 48.

Chapter 13
1. Scroggie, Graham, *A GUIDE TO THE GOSPELS*, p. 505.
2. Pentecost, J. Dwight, *THE WORDS AND WORKS OF JESUS CHRIST*, p. 38.
3. Edersheim, Alfred, *THE LIFE AND TIMES OF JESUS THE MESSIAH*, Volume 1, pp. 144–145.
4. Shepherd, J. W., *THE CHRIST OF THE GOSPELS*, p. 1.
5. Pentecost, J. Dwight, *THE CHRIST OF THE GOSPELS*, p. 66.
6. Edersheim, Alfred, *THE LIFE AND TIMES OF JESUS THE MESSIAH*, p. 221.
7. Pentecost, J. Dwight, *THE CHRIST OF THE GOSPELS*, p. 91.
8. Ibid., p. 95.
9. Ibid., p. 95.
10. Morgan, G. Campbell, *THE CRISES OF CHRIST*, p. 171.
11. Ibid., p. 183.
12. Pentecost, J. Dwight, *THE CHRIST OF THE GOSPELS*, p. 105.

Chapter 14
1. Ryrie, Charles C., *THE MIRACLES OF OUR LORD*, p. 11.
2. Pentecost, J. Dwight, *THE WORDS AND WORKS OF JESUS CHRIST*, p. 143.
3. Ibid., p. 146.
4. Ryrie, Charles C., *THE MIRACLES OF OUR LORD*, p. 37.
5. Pentecost, J. Dwight, *THE WORDS AND WORKS OF JESUS CHRIST*, p. 225.
6. Ibid., p. 159.
7. Ibid., p. 175.
8. Wiersbe, Warren, *WIERSBE'S EXPOSITORY COMMENTARY*, NT, p. 22.
9. Ibid., p. 25.
10. Wesley, John, *THE WORKS OF JOHN WESLEY*, 5:278.
11. Pentecost, J. Dwight, *THE WORDS AND WORKS OF JESUS CHRIST*, p. 185.
12. Wiersbe, Warren, *WIERSBE'S EXPOSITORY COMMENTARY*, p. 28.
13. Ibid., p. 26.

Chapter 15
1. Wiersbe, Warren, *WIERSBE'S EXPOSITORY COMMENTARY*, NT, p. 316.
2. Bruce, F. F., *THE GOSPEL OF JOHN*, p. 169.
3. Pentecost, J. Dwight, *THE WORDS AND WORKS OF JESUS CHRIST*, p. 283.
4. Bruce, F. F., *THE GOSPEL OF JOHN*, p. 219.
5. Wiersbe, Warren, *WIERSBE'S EXPOSITORY COMMENTARY*, p. 327.
6. Pentecost, J. Dwight, *THE WORDS AND WORKS OF JESUS CHRIST*, p. 213.
7. Ibid., p.276.
8. Wiersbe, Warren, *WIERSBE'S EXPOSITORY COMMENTARY*, p. 58.
9. Pentecost, J. Dwight, *THE WORDS AND WORKS OF JESUS CHRIST*, p. 311.
10. Wesley, John, quoted in *The 365-Day Devotional Commentary*, p. 671.

11. Wiersbe, Warren, *WIERSBE'S EXPOSITORY COMMENTARY*, p. 349.
12. a' Kempis, Thomas, *THE IMITATION OF CHRIST*, 6.1.
13. Bruce, F. F., *THE GOSPEL OF JOHN*, p. 301.
14. Pentecost, J. Dwight, *THE WORDS AND WORKS OF JESUS CHRIST*, p. 346.
15. Bruce, F. F., *THE SPREADING FLAME*, p.62.

Chapter 16
1. Pentecost, J. Dwight, *THE WORDS AND WORKS OF JESUS CHRIST*, p. 376.
2. Wiersbe, Warren, *WIERSBE'S EXPOSITORY COMMENTARY*, NT, p. 77.
3. Edersheim, Alfred, *THE LIFE AND TIMES OF JESUS THE MESSIAH*, Volume 2, p. 385.
4. Pentecost, J. Dwight, *THE WORDS AND WORKS OF JESUS CHRIST*, pp. 391–392.
5. Ibid., p. 455.
6. Stott, John, *COMMENTARY ON ROMANS*, p. 144.
7. Lucado, Max, *NO WONDER THEY CALL HIM THE SAVIOR*, p. 140.
8. Bruce, F. F., *THE GOSPEL OF JOHN*, p. 90.
9. Graham, Billy, *BILLY GRAHAM ANSWERS YOUR QUESTIONS*, p. 35.
10. Marshall, Peter, *THE FIRST EASTER*, p. 13.

Chapter 17
1. Richards, Lawrence O., *NELSON'S ILLUSTRATED BIBLE HANDBOOK*, p. 517.
2. Wiersbe, Warren, *WIERSBE'S EXPOSITORY COMMENTARY*, NT, p. 409.
3. Bruce, F. F., *NEW TESTAMENT HISTORY*, p. 215.
4. Wiersbe, Warren, *WIERSBE'S EXPOSITORY COMMENTARY*, p. 441.
5. Keener, Craig S., *THE IVP BIBLE BACKGROUND COMMENTARY*, p. 354.
6. Bruce, F. F., *NEW TESTAMENT HISTORY*, p. 290.
7. Wiersbe, Warren, *WIERSBE'S EXPOSITORY COMMENTARY*, p. 492.

Chapter 18
1. Richards, Lawrence O., *NELSON'S ILLUSTRATED BIBLE HANDBOOK*, p. 604.
2. Harrison, Everett F., "Romans" in *THE EXPOSITOR'S BIBLE COMMENTARY*, Volume 10, p. 7.
3. Wiersbe, Warren, *WIERSBE'S EXPOSITORY COMMENTARY*, NT, p. 519.
4. Harrison, Everett F., *THE EXPOSITOR'S BIBLE COMMENTARY*, p. 23.
5. Wiersbe, Warren, *WIERSBE'S EXPOSITORY COMMENTARY*, p. 519.
6. Lucado, Max, *IN THE GRIP OF GRACE*, p. 92.
7. Pannenberg, Wolfheart, "*Homosexuality and Revelation*," in *CHRISTIANITY TODAY*, November 11, 1996, p. 37.
8. Wiersbe, Warren, *WIERSBE'S EXPOSITORY COMMENTARY*, p. 519.
9. Harrison, Everett F., *THE EXPOSITOR'S BIBLE COMMENTARY*, p. 30.
10. Ibid., p. 31.
11. Wiersbe, Warren, *WIERSBE'S EXPOSITORY COMMENTARY*, p. 521.
12. Lucado, Max, *IN THE GRIP OF GRACE*, p. 92.
13. Wesley, John, *THE WORKS OF JOHN WESLEY*, 6:452.
14. Boice, James Montgomery, "*Galatians*," in *THE EXPOSITORS'*

BIBLE COMMENTARY, p. 409.

15. Ibid., p. 495.

16. Ibid., p. 496.

17. Wiersbe, Warren, WIERSBE'S EXPOSITORY COMMENTARY, p. 719.

Chapter 19

1. Graham, Billy, BILLY GRAHAM ANSWERS YOUR QUESTIONS, p. 86.

2. Wiersbe, Warren, WIERSBE'S EXPOSITORY COMMENTARY, NT., p. 678.

3. Moody, Dwight L., quoted in THE 365-DAY DEVOTIONAL COMMENTARY, p. 954.

4. Luther, Martin, THE BEST OF ALL HIS WORKS, p. 276.

5. Thomas, Robert L., "Thessalonians," THE EXPOSITOR'S BIBLE COMMENTARY, p. 233.

6. Lewis, C.S., quoted in THE 365-DAY DEVOTIONAL COMMEN-TARY, p. 1025.

Chapter 20

1. Wiersbe, Warren, BE RICH, p. 19.

2. Smedes, Lewis, quoted in CHRISTIANITY TODAY, November 13, 1995, p. 69.

3. Christianson, Larry, THE CHRISTIAN FAMILY, p. 270.

4. John Paul III (Pope), quoted in CHRISTIANITY TODAY, November 13, 1995, p. 69.

5. Clowney, Edmund P., quoted in CHRISTIANITY TODAY, April 27, 1998, p. 78.

6. Wiersbe, Warren, BE CONFIDENT, p. 18.

7. Ibid., p. 89.

Chapter 21

1. McGee, J. Vernon, THE EPISTLES OF 1,2 TIMOTHY, TITUS, & PHILEMON, p. 14.

2. Barclay, William, LETTERS TO TIMOTHY, TITUS, AND PHILEMON, p. 36.

3. McGee, J. Vernon, THE EPISTLES OF 1,2 TIMOTHY, TITUS, & PHILEMON, p. 66.

4. Ibid., p. 73.

5. Wiersbe, Warren, BE RICH, p. 26.

6. Zuck, Roy B., PRECIOUS IN HIS SIGHT, p. 114.

7. Barclay, William, LETTERS TO TIMOTHY, TITUS, AND PHILEMON, p. 181.

8. Ibid., p. 256.

Chapter 22

1. Bruce, F. F., EPISTLE TO THE HEBREWS, p. 65.

2. Morris, Leon, "Hebrews" in THE EXPOSITOR'S BIBLE COMMENTARY, p. 32.

3. Bruce, F. F., EPISTLE TO THE HEBREWS, p. 102.

4. Ibid., p. 155.

5. Ibid., p. 173.

6. Arthur, Kay, LORD, I WANT TO KNOW YOU, p. 157.

7. Morris, Leon, NEW TESTAMENT THEOLOGY, p. 306.

8. Bruce, F. F., EPISTLE TO THE HEBREWS, p. 330.

9. Ibid., p. 340.

10. Morris, Leon, NEW TESTAMENT THEOLOGY, p. 138.

Chapter 23

1. Morris, Leon, NEW TESTAMENT THEOLOGY, p. 313.

2. Lewis, C. S., MIRACLES, p. 181.

3. Morris, Leon, NEW TESTAMENT THEOLOGY, p. 318.

4. Richards, Lawrence O., NELSON'S ILLUSTRATED BIBLE HANDBOOK, p. 786.

5. Law, William, quoted in CHRISTIANITY TODAY, June 19, 1995, p. 33.

6. Richards, Lawrence O., NELSON'S ILLUSTRATED BIBLE HANDBOOK, p. 791.

7. Wesley, John, THE WORKS OF JOHN WESLEY, 6:15.

8. Bruce, F. F., THE EPISTLES OF JOHN, p. 45.

9. Fenelon, Franscois, quoted in CHRISTIANITY TODAY, November 13, 1995, p. 69.

10. Morris, Leon, NEW TESTAMENT THEOLOGY, p. 290.

Chapter 24

1. Johnson, Alan F., "Revelation" in THE EXPOSITOR'S BIBLE COMMENTARY, Volume 10, p. 432.

2. Melton, J. H., 52 LESSONS IN REVELATION, p. 93.

3. Duck, Daymond R., REVELATION FOR THE BIBLICALLY-INEPT, p. 109.

4. Ibid., p. 165.

5. Hindson, Ed., ed., FINAL SIGNS, p. 107.

6. Johnson, Alan F., "Revelation" in THE EXPOSITOR'S BIBLE COMMENTARY, p. 576.

7. Lindsey, Hal, THERE'S A NEW WORLD COMING, p. 252.

8. Hocking, David, THE COMING WORLD LEADER, p. 288.

The following excerpts are used by permission with all rights reserved:

Arthur, Kay, LORD, I WANT TO KNOW YOU; LORD, HEAL MY HURTS; LORD, WHERE ARE YOU?; Multnomah Publishers, Sisters, OR

Bruce, F.F., THE EPISTLE OF HEBREWS; Wm B. Eerdmans Publishing Co., Grand Rapids, MI

Duck, Daymond R., REVELATION—GOD'S WORD FOR THE BIBLICALLY-INEPT™; Starburst Publishers, Lancaster, PA

Lucado, Max, APPLAUSE OF HEAVEN; IN THE GRIP OF GRACE; NO WONDER THEY CALL HIM THE SAVIOR; Word Publishing, Nashville, TN

Pentecost, J. Dwight, THE WORDS AND WORKS OF JESUS CHRIST; Zondervan Publishing, Grand Rapids, MI

Swindoll, Charles, LIVING BEYOND THE DAILY GRIND; GOD'S MASTERWORK; Word Publishing, Nashville, TN

Wiersbe, Warren, WIERSBE'S EXPOSITORY OUTLINES; WIERSBE'S EXPOSITORY COMMENTARY; BE RICH; BE CONFIDENT; Chariot-Victor Publishing, Colorado Springs, CO

INDEX

Boldface numbers indicate specially defined (What?) terms and phrases as they appear both in the text *and* the sidebar.

Aaron:
  God chooses, 25
  golden calf idol made by, 31
  priesthood formed by sons of, 36
  (*See also* High Priest)
Abba, **205**
Abel, 8
Abhor, **39**
Abraham:
  faith of, 16–18
  God's covenant with, 15–16
  God's relationship with, 1, 15
  Hagar offered to, 19
  Jews descended from, 15
  righteousness of, 303
  weaknesses of, 18–19
  (*See also* Abrahamic Covenant)
Abrahamic Covenant:
  definition of, **17**
  Law Covenant different from, 30
Abyss, **172**
Acquitted, **224**
Acrostic, **130**
Acts, book of,
  early church described by, 217–219
  introduction to, 213
  Paul's journey in, 220
  Paul's trial in, 223–224
A.D., **1, 147**
Adam:
  creation of, 5
  disobedience of, 6
  (*See also* Man)
Adbon the Judge, 53
Advocate, **215**
Africa, 129
Agrippa, King (*see* Herod Agrippa II)
Ahab, King, 84, 86–87
Ahaz, King, 105
Ai, city of, 50
a'Kempis, Thomas, 196

Alexander, John, 104
Alienate, **230**
Allegory, **80**
Alms, **234**
Alms, **181**
America:
  before Abraham, 19
  while Israelites were in Egypt, 24
  while Israelites were in wilderness, 40
  at Jacob's time, 21
Amos, book of, 90–93
Amos, writing prophet:
  five visions of, 92
  Israel's judgment declared by, 90
Anarchy, **63**
Andrew the Apostle, 174
Angels:
  definition of, **166**
  at Passover, 28
  Peter freed from prison by, 220
  as Satan's servants, 6
Anna, prophetess, 168
Annihilated, **322**
Anoint, **57**
Antichrist:
  described by Paul, 255
  God destroys, 320
  Western world unites under, 320
Antichrists, **311**
Antioch, city of, 220
Aphek, city of, 59
Aphrodite, **244**
Apocalyptic, **318**
Apodictic law, **30**
Apostate, **84**
Apostles, **216**
Apostles' Creed, **150**
Archaeology, **19**
Archangel, **166**
Ark, Noah's:
  God's command concerning, 9
  illustration of, 10

Arthur, Kay:
  on faith, 18
  on God's mercy, 124
  on names of God, 26
  on righteousness, 294–295
Asa, King, 99
Ascetic, **246**
Asherah poles, **99**
Asia, 19
Asia Minor, **63**
Assyria:
  while Jews were captive, 129
  Nineveh capital city of, 89
  Northern Kingdom destroyed by, 91
Atone, **35**
Atonement, **290**
Augustine, Saint, 67
Authenticate, **86**

Baal, **86**
Babel, Tower of, 11
Babylon:
  before Abraham's time, 19
  definition of, **16**
  Jews settled in, 129
Balaam, 41
Baptism, **169**
Barclay, William:
  on Christian constraint, 275
  on incarnation, 283
  on repentance, 279
Barnabas, 218, 221
Bartholomew the Apostle, 174
Bathsheba, 66
Bayliss, Albert, 76
B.C., **1**
Beatitudes, book of, **179**
Beelzebub, **185**
Ben-Hadad, King, 87
Berea, city of, 221
Bethel, city of, 84
Bethlehem Ephrathah, town of, 106
Betrothed, **166**
Birthright, **20**
Blasphemy, **206**

Blessing, **20**
Bloodguilt, **66**
Body of Christ, **248**
Boice, James Montgomery:
  on Christian conflicts, 240
  on Galatians, 238
  on standards of conduct, 240
Book of life, 322
Booty, **50**
Born again, **305**
Bronze Age, **63**
Brothers, **44, 311**
Bruce, F. F.:
  on authority of Gospel, 290
  on Christ as High Priest, 294
  on Christ as inspiration, 297
  on confession of sins, 310
  on disciples' public witness, 217
  on God in Christ, 159
  on God's love, 210–211
  on hope, 293
  on Jesus' power, 190
  on Jesus' relationship to God, 189
  on love of the Father, 197
  on Old Testament Saints, 297
  on unbelief, 291
  on ways of life,
  on works of Jesus, 198

Caesar Augustus, **201**, 202
Caiaphas, **204**
Cain, 8
Calvary, **256**
Canaan:
  conquest of, 49
  definition of, 47
  forced labor pressed on, 52
  Jacob's move from, 2
  Israelites into, 39
  map of, 48

Moses defines borders of, 42

Caste, **63**

Casuistic law, **30**

Caught up, **254**

Census:
before conquering Moabites, 41
before entering Canaan, 40

Centurion, 208

Ceremonial law (*see* Ritual law)

Chafe, **102**

China:
in David's time, 63
in Jacob's time, 21
in Moses' time, 24
before Israelites enter Canaan, 40

Christ (*see* Jesus Christ)

Christiansen, Larry, 263

Chronicles, first book of, 62–67

Chronicles, second book of, 98–102, 111–114

Chruch, **217**

Church Age, **317**

Circumcision, **49, 221**

Clan, **51**

Cleanse, **37**

Clowney, Edmund P., 269

Colossians, book of, 267–270

Commandments, **7**

Concubine, **21**

Confederation, **63**

Confess, **310**

Conscience, 235–236

Contract covenant (*see* covenant)

Conversion, **219**

Corinth, city of, 221, 244

Corinthians, first book of:
argument of, 244–248
introduction to, 243
marriage explained in, 246
resurrection supported in, 248

Corinthians, second book of, 249–252

Cornelius:
conversion of, 220
introduction to, 218
Peter invited to house of, 219

Covenant, definition of, **16**
(*See also* Abrahamic Covenant; Law Covenant; Davidic Covenant)

Covenant, Ark of, **59**

Covet, **29**

Creation, 9

Creed, **150, 302**

Crucifixion:
definition of, 194
Jesus speaks of, 194

Cult, **319**

Cyrus the Persian, 137

Damascus, 92

Dan, city of, 84

Daniel, book of, 131–134

Daniel, prophet:
early life of, 132
influences of, 137
visions of, 133–134

Darius, King, 138

David, King:
failures of, 65–66
faith of, 60
Israel's second king, 57
Jesus descended from, 165
military victories of, 64–65
reforms of, 67
reign of, 62–65
story of, 60–61

Davidic Covenant, 65

Day of the Lord, **92**

Deacon, **216**

Dead in Christ, **254**

Deborah the Judge, 53

Dedicate, **31**

Deity, **4**

Demons, **176**

Depravity, **233**

Deuteronomy, book of, 42–45

Devil (*see* Satan)

Dirge, **130**

Disciple(s):
definition of, 174
Jesus teaches his, 194–195, 203–204

Discipline, **296**

Dispossess, **52**

Divination, **100**

Dominion, **4**

Duck, Daymond:
on God's final message, 319
on reaction in heaven, 320

Earth, 3

Ecclesiastes, book of, 78–80

Eden:
Adam in, 5
Garden of, 5
illustration of, 6
Satan's success in, 6

Edersham, Alfred:
on betrothal, 167
on Jesus in Nazareth, 168
on the Pharisees' trap, 202

Edom, 102

Ehud the Judge, 53

Egypt:
before Abraham's time, 19
during separation of Judah and Israel, 98
horses in army of, 24
in Jacob's time, 21
Israelites in, 23
Jacob moves to, 20
Jews flee to, 124
Joseph and Mary take Jesus to, 167
Joseph's preparations in, 23
plagues attack, 27–28

Elan the Judge, 53

Elijah the prophet:
sent to Israel, 86
stories of, 87

Elisha the prophet:
ministry of, 87
stories of, 88

Empowers, **215**

England, 19

Entrails, **100**

Ephesians, book of, 259–263

Ephesus, city of, 259

Epistles, **214**

Epitaph, **45**

Esau, 20

Esther, book of, 134–135

Eternity, **153**

Eunuch, **219**

Europe:
during the separation, 98
in Jacob's time, 21

Evangelistic, **168**

Eve:
creation of, 5
disobedience of, 6
temptation of, 7
(*See also* Woman)

Everlasting Father (*see* Jesus Christ)

Evil one (*see* Satan)

Exhort, **228**

Exodus, book of, 23–32

Exposition, **229**

Ezekiel, book of, 125–127

Ezekiel the prophet:
introduction to, 113
messages of, 125–127

Ezra, book of, 135–139

Faith, **16, 297**

Fall, The:
additional consequences of, 8
definition of, 7
Satan's role in, 6

Fall asleep, **254**

False prophet(s), **44**

False Prohpet, the, **318**

Fast, **38**

Fasting, **142**

Feast of Tabernacles, **187**

Felix, governor, 223–224

Fenlon, Francois, 311

Fertile Crescent, 18

Festus, governor, 223–224

Firstborn, 158

Flood, the, 9–11

Foolish, **59**

Form, **279**

Gabriel:
definition of, 166
messages delivered by, 166

Galatians, book of, 238–241

Galilee, 173, 215

Geisler, Norman L.
on Habakkuk, 119
on miracles, 28

Genealogy:
definition of, 8
differences in Jesus', 165
Usher's use of, 9

General Epistles, 227

Genesis, book of:
ancient ideas on origin contrasted with, 4
definition of, 3
story of, 4

Gentile(s):
Barnabas sent to church of, 220
Church accepts, 220
definition of, 219

Gethsemane, garden of, 205

Gibeon, 50

Gideon the Judge, 53

Gift of tongues, **248**

Girard, Robert C., 19

Glorify, **232**

Glory, **32**

God created, **3**

God's iron yoke, **121**

Godlessness, **231**

Goldberg, Lewis, 43

Gospel:
definition of, 161, 213
spreading the message of, 218
new Christians spread, 220

Grace, **168**

Graham, Billy:
on belief, 4
on Christ and Righteousness, 80
on forgiveness, 211
on love, 248
on man's selfishness, 92
on youth, 80

Great serpent (*see* Satan)

Great tribulation, **255**

Greece:
  during the separation, 98
  while Jews were captive,
    129

Habakkuk, book of, 117–119
Habakkuk the prophet, 118–
  119
Hades, **193**
Hagar, 21
Haggai, book of, 139–141
Hagggai the prophet:
  four messages of, 140
  Jews inspired by, 137
Haman, 134
Hananiah, false prophet, 101
Hannah, 58
Haran, 20
Harmony, **164**
Harrison, Everett F.:
  on God's place, 232
  on morals, 235
  on righteousness, 234
  on Romans, 229
Hazael, King, 87
Hebrew (*see* Israelites)
Hebrews, book of, 287–298
Hedonistic, **180**
Hell, **6**
Hendricks, Howard, 52
Heresies, **267**
Heresy, **307**
Herod Agrippa II, King, 223
Herod Antipas, governor, 220
Herodians, **201**
Herod the Great, 165
Hezekiah, King, 105
High places, **99**
High Priest:
  Aaron is first, 25
  privilege of, 291
  (*See also* Aaron; Priest)
Hindson, Ed, 320
Hocking, David, 322
Honed and buffeted, **121**
Holy, **33**
Holy Land, definition of, **161**
  (*See also* Promised Land)
Holy living, **33**
Holy Spirit:
  definition of, 150
  Jesus' followers empow-
    ered by, 216
Horn, **133**
Horoscope, **100**
Hosanna, **200**
Hosea, book of, 93–94
Hosea the prophet, 93–94
House, **65**
Hypocrite, **181**

Iconium, city of, 221
Idol:

golden calf as an, 31
  Jeroboam creates, 84
Idolatrous, **16**
Image and Likeness, **4**
Impediment, **252**
Incarnation, **283**
India:
  during Israel's formation,
    63
  during the separation, 98
Indictment, **105**
Infirmities, **209**
Indignation, **121**
Inheritance, 20
Iniquities, **209**
Inspired, **227**
Intermediaries, **291**
Interpreting, **248**
Iron age, **63**
Isaac:
  covenant inherited by, 19
  Esau and Jacob's father, 20
  God's relationship with, 1
Isaiah, book of, 107–109
Isaiah the prophet:
  introduction to, 107
  message of, 109
  prophecy of, 152
  story of, 108
Ish-bosheth, 63
Island of Patmos, **315–316**
Israel, Jacob's name changed
  to, 20
  (*See also* Jacob; Israelites)
Israel, kingdom of:
  Aramea threatens, 87
  first king of, 57
  God's complaints against,
    91
  judgment declared on, 90
  kings and prophets of, 85
  map of, 64
  pagans settle in, 137
  separation of, 83
Israelites:
  Aaron urged to build idol
    by, 31
  borders of Canaan defined
    to, 42
  definition of, **23**
  Egypt pursues, 23–26
  Moabites defeated by, 41
  preparations of, 49
  ritual laws affect, 37
Izban the Judge, 53

Jacob:
  covenant inherited by, 19
  family of, 21
  four wives of, 22–23
  God's relationship with, 1
James the Apostle, 174, 220
James, the book of, 301–304

James, the brother of Jesus:
  epistle of, 302–304
  introduction to, 301
  objections of, 302–303
James the less, 174
Jair the Judge, 53
Jehoram, King, 87
Jehoshaphat, King, 99
Jehovah:
  definition of, 26
  (*See also* Jesus Christ)
Jehovah's Witnesses, **319**
Jehu, King, 87
Jepthah the Judge, 53
Jeremiah, book of, 120–125
Jeremiah the prophet:
  introduction to, 101
  message of, 120
  New Covenant promised
    by, 122
  prophecies of, 121
Jericho, city of, 49
Jeroboam, King, 84
Jerusalem, city of:
  Council of, 221
  Jesus enters, 199–200
  riot in, 223
  Solomon's temple in, 70,
    84
Jesus Christ:
  allowances of, 157–159
  arrest of, 205–206
  baptism of, 169
  birth of, 165–167
  burial of, 211
  claims of, 154–155
  controversy over, 185–186
  crucifixion of, 208
  different impressions of,
    149–150
  disciples' instruction by,
    193–198
  genealogies of, 165
  identity of, 289
  John the Baptist precedes,
    169
  last day of, 204–208
  last week of, 199–207
  life of, 164–168
  miracles performed by,
    174–179
  Old Testament's lessons
    on, 150–153
  Pharisees question
    authority of, 188
  Pharisees reject authority
    of, 189
  portrayed in Colossians,
    268
  religious leaders exposed
    by, 201
  religious leaders plan to
    kill, 204

resurrection of, 211–212
  righteousness illustrated
    by, 181
  superiority of, 290, 293–
    294
  teachings of, 181–185
  temptation of, 170
  today's importance of, 149
  uncertainty about, 173
Jewish people:
  descendants of Abraham,
    15
  one hundred and forty-
    four thousand, 319
  origin of, 1
  (*See also* Israelites)
Jews, **154**
Jezebel, 86
Job, 72–73
Job, book of, 72–74
Joel, book of, 103–104
Joel, prophet, 103–104
Johannine writings, **196**
John the Apostle:
  book of, 163
  book of Revelation written
    by, 315
  Christ appears to, 317
  the gospel of, 164
  introduction to, 309
  three epistles of, 308
  visions of, 318–322
  the Word written by, 156–
    157
John the Baptist:
  Jesus baptized by, 169
  Messiah promised by, 168
  ministry of, 169
John, book of, 163–212
John, first, second, and third
  books of, 308–312
John Paul III (Pope), 265
Johnson, Alan F.:
  on the churches, 317
  on the defeat of evil, 320
Jonah, book of, 88–90
Jonah the prophet, 84, 89
Joseph, husband of Mary, 165
Joseph, son of Jacob, 21–22
Joseph of Arimathea, 208
Joshua:
  farewell of, 51
  introduction to, 47–48
  preparations of, 49
Joshua, book of, 47–51
Josiah, King:
  God's law discovered by,
    116
  spiritual revival under,
    111
Jotham, King, 105
Judah:
  Assyria defeats, 112

early kings and prophets of, 98
formation of, 83
later kings and prophets of, 113
locusts attack, 103
sins of, 122
spiritual and moral decline of, 111–112
violence and injustice in, 118
Judaizers, **238**
Judas Iscariot (the betrayer), 174
Jude, book of, 312–313
Jude, half-brother of Jesus, 312–313
Judea, 173
Judges:
   definition of, 52
   king anointed by, 57
   stories of, 53–54
Judges, book of, 52–54
Judgments, **26**
Justified, **209, 283**

Keener, Craig S.:
   on Gentiles, 220
   on Jesus' claim, 155
King of the Jews (*see* Jesus Christ)
Kings, first and second books of, 83–88, 97, 111–115
Kinsman Redeemer:
   definition of, **55**
   Boaz acts as, 55–56

Lake of Fire, **320**
Lamb of God (*see* Jesus Christ)
Lamech, 8
Lamentations, book of, 130–131
La Sor, William Sanford:
   on Ezra and Nehemiah, 139
   on God's existence, 26
   on injustice, 102
Law, **30**
Law Covenant:
   Abrahamic Covenant different from, 30
   consequences of, 44
   explanation of, 30
   Moses reviews, 33
   (*See also* Old Covenant)
Law and the Prophets, **180**
Law, William, 308
Leaven, **38**
Legalism, **270**
Legalistic, **43**
Legions, **206**
L'Engle, Madeleine, 124

Levites:
   cities of, 51
   explanation of, 34
   jobs assigned to, 40
Leviticus, book of, 34–39
Lewis, C. S.,
   on Christ's identity
   on God's role, 256
   on miracles, 27
   on prayer, 303–304
Light, the, **310**
Lindsey, Hal, 321
Literal, **133**
Lord, **16**
Lord's Supper, **247**
Lost, **316**
Lot(s), **51**
Lucado, Max:
   on the cost of our sins, 237
   on the crucifixion, 210
   on God's peace, 74
   on righteousness, 18
   on shameful lusts, 233
Lucifer (*see* Satan)
Luke the Apostle:
   Acts written by, 213
   gospel of, 163
Luke, book of, 163–212
Luther, Martin, **119**
   on faith, 140
   on God's gifts, 252
Lydia, 129
Lyric poem, **71**
Lystra and Derbe, cities of, 221

MacArthur, John F., 152
Macedonia, 250
Magi:
   definition of, 168
   introduction to, 167
Magistrate, **137**
Malachi, book of, 143–145
Malachi the prophet, 143–144
Man:
   creation of, 5
   nature of, 7
   (*See also* Adam)
Man of lawlessness, **255**
Manasseh, King, 116
Manifest, **159**
Manna:
   definition of, 27
   Israelites fed by, 40
Man of lawlessness, **255**
Mara (*see* Naomi)
Mark the Apostle, 162
Mark, book of, 162–212
Martyr, Justin, 224
Mary, mother of Jesus, 165
Marriage, 23
Marshall, Peter, 212

Matthew the Apostle:
   fulfillment of prophecy shown by, 167
   gospel of, 161–162
Matthew, book of, 161–212
Maxim, **190**
McGee, J. Vernon:
   on church leaders, 275
   on importance of age, 276
   on widows, 277
Mediate, **229**
Mediator, **275**
Mediums, **100**
Melchizedek, priest, 292–293
Melton, J. H., 319
Mesopotamia:
   definition of, 4
   ancient stories of, 9
   Israelites in wilderness, 40
Messiah, definition of, **107**
   (*See also* Jesus Christ)
Messianic prophecies, **106**
Metaphysical, **26**
Micah, book of, 105–107
Micah the prophet:
   message of, 105
   Messianic prophecies written by, 106
Mighty God (*see* Jesus Christ)
Miracle:
   definition of, 26
   during the exodus, 27–28
   three ages of, 86
Missionary, **221**
Mizpah, city of, 59
Moab, 41
Monarchy, **63**
Monogamous, **80**
Moody, Dwight L., 252
Moorings, **54**
Moral, **7**
Moral Judge, **10**
Mordecai, 134
Morgan, G. Campbell:
   on perfection, 171
   on trusting God, 171
Morris, Leon:
   on conscience, 295
   on dead faith, 303
   on Jesus' sufferings, 306
   on love, 312
   on Moses and Christ, 290
   on spirit of suffering, 298
Moses:
   borders of Canaan defined by, 42
   Christ compared to, 290
   early information of, 3
   God chooses, 25
   inspiration of, 4
   introduction of, 23
   Israelites reminded of God's law by, 42

Mother Teresa, 22
Mount Sinai:
   God displays power at, 27
   Moses given commandments at, 25
   Mount Zion compared to, 298
Mount Zion, 298
Muslim, 22
Mystery Babylon, 320

Nahum, book of, 115–116
Nahum, prophet, 115–116
Naomi, 55
Narrative, **21**
Nazareth, city of, **167**
Nebuchadnezzar, King:
   Daniel's friendship with, 132
   Jews taken to Babylon by, 129
   Judah's governor appointed by, 124
Nehemiah, book of, 136–139
Nero, Emperor:
   Paul executed by, 278
   Peter crucified by, 220
New Covenant, **288**
New Testament:
   Acts as prelude to, 213
   description of, 147–148
   Old Testament agrees with, 159
   Old Testament different than, 2
Nineveh, city of:
   definition of, 16
   Jonah's message to, 89–90
Noah:
   building the Ark, 10
   walking with God, 9–10
Northern Kingdom (*see* Israel)
Numbers, book of, 42

Obadiah, book of, 102
Obadiah the prophet, 102,
Occult, **100**
Occult practice, **44**
Offerings, **35**
Old Covenant, **288**
Old Testament:
   books of, 2
   crucifixion prophesied in, 209
   introduction to, 1
   New Testament agrees with, 159
   New Testament different than, 2
Old Testament Saints, **297**
Omen, **100**
Onesimus, 283–285

Oracle, **100, 120**
Orator, **251**
Origins, 4
Othniel the Judge, 53

Pagan, **52, 260**
Palestine, **173**
Parables:
  definition of, 191
  Jesus instructs using,
    191–192
Pascal, Blaise, 66
Passover, **28**
Patriarchal, **20**
Pannenberg, Wolfheart, 233
Paul the Apostle:
  acquittal of, 224
  Antichrist described by,
    255
  challenges of, 222
  Christ's death explained
    by, 209–210
  Churches established by,
    243
  Colossians written by, 267
  I Corinthians written by,
    243
  II Corinthians written by,
    249
  death of, 224
  Ephesians written by, 259
  Galatians written by, 239
  Jesus named Creator by,
    158
  journey of, 220–221
Philemon written by, 283
Philippians written by, 263
  reminders from, 157
  Romans written by, 228
  strategy of, 221
  I Thessalonians written by,
    252
  II Thessalonians written
    by, 255
  I Timothy written by, 273
  II Timothy written by, 277
  Titus given charges by,
    282–283
  Titus written by, 280
  trial of, 223
  (See also Saul)
Pauline Epistles, 227
Penitent, 279
Pentateuch, **2**
Pentecost, festival of, 216
Pentecost, J. Dwight:
  on baptism by fire, 169
  on the Beatitudes, 180
  on the branch and the
    vine, 197
  on Christ's authority, 179
  on Christ's baptism, 170
  on Christ's instruction of

leaders, 191
  on Christ's miracles, 176
  on Christ's prayer at
    Gethsemane, 205
  on Christ's presentation,
    170
  on Christ's teachings
    about sinners, 195
  on Christ's triumphal
    entry, 200
  on exorcism, 176
  on Jesus' rights of
    inheritance, 166
  on Jesus' trap for the
    Pharisees, 202–203
  on Lord's Prayer, 182
  on Pharisees' trap, 189
  on physical death, 178
  on third temptation, 172
  on witnesses, 168
Perfected, **292**
Persia, 129
Perversion, **233**
Peter the Apostle:
  first epistle written by,
    304–306
  gospels of, 217
  humanity's trials explained
    by, 305
  second epistle written by,
    306
  sermon of, 155–156
  vision of, 219
Peter, first book of, 304–306
Peter, second book of, 306–308
Pharaoh:
  definition of, **25**
  Joseph helped by, 21–22
  Moses confronts, 25
Pharisees:
  description of, 174
  Jesus' authority ques-
    tioned by, 188
  Jesus' followers oppressed
    by, 190
  Jesus opposed by, 187
  Jesus rejected by, 189
  Jesus' tomb secured by, 209
Philemon, 283–285
Philippians, book of, 263–267
Phillip, 218–219
Philistines
  definition of, **54**
  battles against, 59
Physical death, **7**
Piety, **181**
Pilate, Pontius, 206–209
Placated, **268**
Plague, 25
Poetry, 71–72
Polygamy, **21**
Praetorian Guard, **207**
Pragmatic, **162**

Preacher of righteousness, **11**
Predestined, **261**
Predictive prophecy, **315–316**
Preeminent, **270**
Prefigured, **296**
Premeditated, **51**
Preparation Day, **208**
Prerogative, **263**
Priest, definition of, **25**
  (See also Aaron; High
    Priest)
Prince of Peace (see Jesus
  Christ)
Procreate, **12**
Promise covenant
  (see Covenant,
    definition of)
Promised Land:
  definition of, 40
  invasion of, 103
Prophet(s):
  definition of, **25**
  distinguishing between
    false and true, 101
  God will provide, 44
  God warns Northern
    Kingdom through, 84
  Jesus revealed by, 150–153
  Moses as first, 25
Protestant Reformation, **119**
Proverbs, book of, 76–77
Providence, **135**
Provocation, **94**
Psalms, book of, 74–76
Pseudo, **251**
Psidian Antioch, city of, 221
Publican, **190**
Purify, **37**
Purview, **222**

Queen of Heaven, **124**

Rabbi, **174**
Rapture, **254**
Rebekah, 19–21
Reconciled, **270**
Redeem, **55**
Redemption, **261**
Refuge, cities of, 51
Rehab, 49
Remission, **217**
Remnant, **43**
Repentance, **89**
Rest, **53**
Resurrection:
  Apostles testify to Jesus',
    216
  definition of, 194
  Jesus prays for, 205
  Jesus speaks of, 194
  looking back on Jesus',
    211–212
Revelation, **3, 315**

Revelation, book of, 315–322
Reverend Fun:
  on Adam and Eve, 1
  on heaven, 147
Revival, **99**
Rhyme and meter, **71**
Richards, Larry:
  on David's monarchy, 63
  on Ecclesiastes, 79
Richards, Lawrence O.:
  on Daniel's prophecy, 133
  on the epistles, 228
  on Holy Spirit, 214
  on Jesus' claim, 154
  on John's message, 309
  on Peter's qualities, 307
Righteous, **17**
Righteous decree, **234**
Ritual, **36**
Ritual law, **36**
Roman Empire:
  Acts written in, 213
  definition of, 161
  map of, 214
Romans, book of, 228–238
Ruth, book of, 55–56
Ryrie, Charles C.:
  on Christ's miracles, 175
  on sickness, 177

Sabbath, **154**
Sabbath rest, 291
Sackcloth, **89**
Sacrifice:
  Baal fails to take, 87
  the cross as ultimate,
    210
  definition of, 35
  God forbids human, 100
  Jephthah's daughter
    offered as, 54
  Jews offer defective, 144
Sacrifice for sins, **8**
Sadducees, 174
Salvation, **18**
Samaria, 218
Samson the Judge, 53–54
Samuel, first book of, 58–62
Samuel, second book of, 62
Samuel the Judge, 53, 57–58
Sanhedrin, **155**
Sarah:
  Abraham's wife, 17
  Hagar offered by, 19
  mother of Isaac, 19
  womb of, 18
Satan:
  the Fall caused by, 6–8
  introduction to, 171
  Jesus tempted by, 170
Saul, King:
  David's sins compared to,
    66

Israel's first king, 57
weaknesses of, 59–60
Saul of Tarsus:
conversion of, 218
(*See also* Paul the Apostle)
Saved, **316**
Savior:
definition of, 107
(*See also* Messiah)
Schuller, Robert, 29
Schultz, Samuel, 130
Scourging, **208**
Scroggie, Graham, 166
Second death, **8**
Sejanus, 207
Sermon on the Mount, 179
Shamgar the Judge, 53
Sheperd, J.W., 167
Shulamite, 80
Silus, 221
Simeon, 168
Sin:
definition of, 1
origin of, 6
Sinai, Moses flees to desert of, 25
(*See also* Mount Sinai)
Sin nature, **8**
Smedes, Lewis, 262
Smith, Dr. James, 151
Smith, Ralph L., 116
Solomon, King:
death of, 83
Ecclesiastes written by, 78
epilogue of, 79
introduction of, 69
on righteousness, 99
Song of Songs written by, 80
weaknesses of, 71
wealth and wisdom of, 70
Son of David (*see* Jesus Christ)
Song of Songs:
definition of, 71
examples of, 81
voices of, 81
Song of Songs, book of, 80–81
Sorcery, **100**
Soul, **126**
Sound doctrine, **275**
Southern Hebrew Kingdom (*see* Judah)
Sovereign, **107**
Speaking prophets, 84
Spiritual death, **7–8**
Spiritual gift, **248**
Sproul, R.C., 4
Steadman, Ray C., 5
Steven, 218
Stott, John, 210
Submit, **262**
Subterfuge, **206**
Succoth, **38**

Sumer, **9**
Supernatural, **27**
Suppress, **231**
Swindoll, Charles:
on character, 121–122
on Christian marriage, 81
on common sense, 77
on Isaiah, 109
on prophets, 85
on Proverbs, 76
on Solomon, 71
Synagogue, **131**
Synoptic, **161**
Syria, 24

Tabernacle:
completion of, 32
dedication of, 40
definition of, 31
Feast of, 187
illustration of, 31
Tada, Joni Eareckson, 37
Temple:
restoration of, 127
Solomon erects, 69–70
Temptation:
definition of, **7**
Jesus challenged by, 170
Ten Commandments:
list of, 29
Moses chosen to give, 25
Moses restates, 43
Testament, definition of, **1**
(*See also* Old Testament; New Testament)
Testify, **197**
Thessalonians, first book of, 252–255
Thessalonians, second book of, 255–256
Thessalonica, 221, 253
Thomas, Robert L., 255
Tiberius, Emperor, 207
Timothy, 273–274
Timothy, first book of, 273–277
Timothy, second book of, 277–280
Titulus, **208**
Titus, book of, 280–283
Tola the Judge, 53
Transgressions, **209**
Transmigration, **63**
Tree of the Knowledge of Good and Evil, **7**
Trespassing, **262**
Tribulation Period, **92**
Tribunal, **206**
Trinity, **167**
Type, **56**

Uncleanness, **35**
Universe:
creation of, 3

definition of, **3**
different origins of, 5
Ur, city of, 15
Usher, Bishop, 9

Vaughn, Curtis, 268
Vizier, **21**

Wanton, **234**
Waxed, **168**
Week, **133**
Wesley, John, **119**
on blood of Christ, 310
on good deeds, 195
on spirit of the human mind, 237
Widows' corps, 276–277
Wiersbe, Warren:
on artificial righteousness, 181
on balance, 251
on book of Psalms, 75
on Christ's eminence, 270
on conversion, 219
on cost of sins, 114
on destiny, 261
on Elisha, 88
on foundation of the church, 193
on God's hand, 135
on God's ways, 74
on Hosea, 94
on human history, 231
on human sin, 236
on hypocrites, 182
on Jesus' authority, 188
on Jesus' excommunication, 190
on legalism, 270
on the lie, 232
on Matthew 6:30–33, 184
on the new commandment, 196
on Nineveh, 90
on Paul and Gentiles, 223
on Pentecost festival, 216
on point of no return, 125
on prayer, 184
on sins named by Paul, 233
on spiritual wealth, 277
on temple dealers, 200–201
on works and fruit, 241
on Zechariah, 143
Wilkinson, Bruce, 81
Witness, **215**
Women:
creation of, 5
purpose of, 5–6
nature of, 7
faith of, 22
(*See also* Eve)

Wonderful Counselor (*see* Jesus Christ)
Works, **262**
World, **310**
Worldly, **245**
Worship,
definition of, 31, 38
ritual laws affect, 36
Wrath, **231**
Wrest, **139**
Writing prophets, 84

Xerxes, King, 134

Young, Edward J., 153
Youngblood, Ronald F.:
on Abraham, 18
on creation, 5
on Noah, 11
on Satan's wiles, 7

Zechariah, book of, 141–143
Zechariah the prophet:
Jews inspired by, 137
visions of, 141–143
Zephaniah, book of, 116–117
Zephaniah the prophet, 117
Ziggurat, 11–12
Zion, 130
Zodiac, **100**
Zuck, Roy B., 279

Books by Starburst Publishers®

(Partial listing—full list available on request)

God's Word for the Biblically-Inept™ Series:

☞ **The Bible** *Daymond R. Duck*

☞ **Revelation** *Daymond R. Duck*

☞ **Daniel** *Larry Richards*

☞ **Health and Nutrition** *Kathleen O'Bannon Baldinger*

☞ **Women of the Bible** *Kathy Collard Miller*

(see pages iii and iv for ordering information)

On The Brink
Daymond R. Duck

Subtitled: Easy-to-Understand End-Time Bible Prophecy. Also by the author of *Revelation* and *Daniel—
God's Word for the Biblically-Inept*, *On The Brink* is
organized in Biblical sequence and written with simplicity so that any reader will easily understand end-
time prophecy. Ideal for use as a handy-reference book.
(trade paper)   ISBN 0914984586 $10.95

The World's Oldest Health Plan
Kathleen O'Bannon Baldinger

Subtitled: Health, Nutrition and Healing from the Bible.
Offers a complete health plan for body, mind and spirit,
just as Jesus did. It includes programs for diet, exercise and mental health. Contains foods and recipes to
lower cholesterol and blood pressure, improve the
immune system and other bodily functions, reduce
stress, reduce or cure constipation, eliminate insom-
nia, reduce forgetfulness, confusion and anger, increase
circulation and thinking ability, eliminate "yeast" problems, improve digestion, and much more."
(trade paper)   ISBN 0914984578 $14.95

God's Abundance
Edited by Kathy Collard Miller

Subtitled: 365 Days to a More Meaningful Life. This
day-by-day inspirational is a collection of thoughts by
leading Christian writers such as, Patsy Clairmont, Jill
Briscoe, Liz Curtis Higgs, and Naomi Rhode. *God's
Abundance* is based on God's Word for a simpler, yet
more abundant life. Most people think more about the
future while the present passes through their hands.
Learn to make all aspects of your life—personal, business, financial, relationships, even housework—a
"spiritual abundance of simplicity."
(hardcover)   ISBN 0914984977 $19.95

Promises of God's Abundance
Kathy Collard Miller

Subtitled: *For a More Meaningful Life*. The second ad-
dition to our best-selling *God's Abundance* series. This

perfect gift book filled with Scripture, questions for
growth and a Simple Thought for the Day will guide
you to an abundant and more meaningful life.
(trade paper)   ISBN 0914984098 $9.95

God's Unexpected Blessings
Edited by Kathy Collard Miller

Witness God at work and learn to see the *unexpected
blessings* in life through essays by such Christians writers as Billy Graham and Barbara Johnson.
(hardcover)   ISBN 0914984071 $18.95

Conversations with God the Father
Mark R. Littleton

Subtitled: *Encounters with the One True God*. Contemplate the nature of God with fictional answers to questions as God might answer them.
(hardcover)   ISBN 0914984195 $17.95

God's Vitamin "C" for the Spirit
Kathy Collard Miller & D. Larry Miller

Subtitled: "Tug-at-the-Heart" Stories to Fortify and Enrich
Your Life. Includes inspiring stories and anecdotes that em-
phasize Christian ideals and values by Barbara Johnson,
Billy Graham, Nancy L. Dorner, Dave Dravecky, Patsy
Clairmont, Charles Swindoll, and many other well-known
Christian speakers and writers. Topics include: Love, Fam-
ily Life, Faith and Trust, Prayer, and God's Guidance.
(trade paper)   ISBN 0914984837 $12.95

PURCHASING INFORMATION:

Books are available from your favorite bookstore, either from current stock or special order. To assist bookstore in locating your
selection be sure to give title, author, and ISBN #. If unable to
purchase from the bookstore you may order direct from
STARBURST PUBLISHERS® by mail, phone, fax, or through our
secure website at www.starburstpublishers.com.

When ordering enclose full payment plus $3.00 for shipping
and handling ($4.00 if Canada or Overseas). Payment in US Funds
only. Please allow two to three weeks minimum (longer overseas)
for delivery.

Make checks payable to and mail to:

STARBURST PUBLISHERS®
P.O. Box 4123
Lancaster, PA 17604

Credit card orders may also be placed by calling **1-800-441-1456**
(credit card orders only), Mon-Fri, 8:30 a.m.–5:30 p.m. Eastern
Standard Time. Prices subject to change without notice. Catalog
available for a 9 x 12 self-addressed envelope with 4 first-class
stamps.